Understanding Popular Music Culture

This extensively revised new edition of *Understanding Popular Music Culture* provides an accessible and comprehensive introduction to the production, distribution, consumption and meaning of popular music and the difficulties and debates that surround the analysis of popular culture and popular music.

Reflecting the continued expansion of popular music studies, the changing music industry and the impact of new technologies, Roy Shuker explores key subjects that shape our experience of music, including music production, musicians and stars, musical texts, music video and MTV, audiences and fans, scenes and subcultures and music as political activism and ideology.

This heavily revised and updated fourth edition includes:

- the role of social network sites, marketing and music retail
- the decline of the traditional model of the sound recording companies
- music genres, cover songs and the album canon
- case studies of artists such as Robert Johnson, the Sex Pistols, Shania Twain and Lady Gaga
- a comprehensive discography, based around musical metagenres, along with suggestions for further reading, listening and viewing.

The book now has an accompanying website, with focus questions and further study activities for each chapter, additional case studies and links to relevant websites.

Roy Shuker is Associate Professor in Media Studies at Victoria University of Wellington, New Zealand. His previous publications include *Understanding Popular Music Culture* (third edition, 2008) and *Popular Music: The Key Concepts* (third edition, 2012).

Understanding Popular Music Culture

Fourth edition

Roy Shuker

Routledge
Taylor & Francis Group

LONDON AND NEW YORK

Fourth edition published 2013
by Routledge
2 Park Square, Milton Park, Abingdon, Oxon OX14 4RN

Simultaneously published in the USA and Canada
by Routledge
711 Third Avenue, New York, NY 10017

Routledge is an imprint of the Taylor & Francis Group, an informa business

First edition published by Routledge 1994
Second edition published by Routledge 2001
Third edition published by Routledge 2008

British Library Cataloguing in Publication Data
A catalogue record for this book is available from the British Library

Library of Congress Cataloging in Publication Data
Shuker, Roy.
Understanding popular music culture / by Roy Shuker. – 4th ed.
p. cm.
Includes bibliographical references and index.
1. Popular music–History and criticism. 2. Popular culture–History–20th
century. I. Title.
ML3470.S54 2012
781.64–dc23
2012015366

ISBN: 978-0-415-51713-3 (hbk)
ISBN: 978-0-415-51717-1 (pbk)
ISBN: 978-0-203-09435-8 (ebk)

Typeset in Baskerville
by Taylor & Francis Books

Contents

Preface

This study is an extensively revised edition of *Understanding Popular Music Culture* (third edition, 2008). Reflecting the continuing proliferation of publications in popular music studies and significant shifts in the music industry, that earlier volume has been reorganized. A number of chapters have been recast and new examples provided of musical texts, genres and performers. I have paid greater attention to the role of the internet, whose influence has been felt across music production, dissemination and mediation and consumption. Each chapter ends with selected suggestions for further reading and, where appropriate, listening and viewing.

Popular music *culture* locates the musical recording in the wider social field. It refers to the ways of making, disseminating and consuming music; the economic and technological practices associated with these processes; and the sounds, images and discourse (thinking, debating and writing) created by these practices. The interrelationship of ritual, pleasure and economics in popular music continues to create audiences, to fuel individual fantasy and pleasure and to create musical icons and cultural myths. *Understanding Popular Music Culture* offers a contribution towards mapping this soundscape.

Acknowledgements

As in the earlier editions of this book, this heavily revised version has relied extensively on the work of many critics and 'colleagues at a distance', who have written extensively on cultural studies and popular music. Many of the 'best' ideas here are theirs; the errors of fact and argument – the bum notes – remain mine. To list them risks leaving out someone: a check of my text and references provides a roll call of sorts; my thanks to you all. I have benefitted enormously from my membership of IASPM – the International Association for the Study of Popular Music, through its conferences, publications, email discussions, and, above all, from the friendships and insights its members have provided me with.

A particular debt of gratitude is due to Mary Jane, for undertaking the bibliography and keeping me at the writing.

To the editorial staff at Routledge: Natalie Foster, for very helpful comments at various points in the early development of the book, and Eileen Srebernik, for helping get it through to production. And for exemplary copy-editing, Helen Baxter.

Permissions

Introduction: 'What's Going On'

Studying popular music culture

In July 2006 Bob Geldof visited New Zealand. The Live Aid founder and 'rock star', as the lead singer and main songwriter with Irish post-punk group the Boomtown Rats, then as a solo act, was widely reported when he described the country's foreign aid as 'shameful and pathetic'. Geldof's criticisms received prominent newspaper coverage, they were the subject of magazine cover stories and he appeared on leading television and radio current affairs shows. He used these opportunities to explain the goals and progress of his Make Poverty History campaign, which is also supported by Bono. The surrounding public debate saw the Minister of Foreign Affairs and the Prime Minister both anxious to defend New Zealand's aid record, while welfare groups and letter writers rallied to support Geldof. To the public, Geldof is the rock star forever linked to Live Aid, who used his musical celebrity as a platform for social activism.

This recent episode indicates how popular music is part of the wider culture. Currently, as I complete this book in March 2012, there were many further indications of such links:

- Considerable media coverage followed the sudden death of pop soul diva Whitney Houston, speculating on the cause and focusing on her long battle with drug addiction.
- Engelbert Humperdinck, now 75, is announced as the UK entry for the Eurovision Song Contest; *The Dominion Post* sarcastically sees the singer and the contest as ideally suited: 'The contest draws a TV audience of 100 million people, although no-one ever admits to watching it, while Englebert has sold 150 million albums [primarily in the 1960s], but it is impossible to find anyone who owns one.' (6 March 2012).
- Fender Musical Instruments announced an initial public offering of US$200 million, in a move to pay down a heavy debt load and create fresh working capital. The firm was strongly associated with the development of rock and roll, with their 'Strat' guitar a favourite of Jimi Hendrix and scores of other stars.
- Pink Floyd's *The Wall – Immersion Edition* goes on sale (for $190 New Zealand). It features the 'classic' studio album, first released in 1979, now digitally remastered and presented as a 'limited edition high quality boxed set'. This

includes rare and unreleased video material, a 44-page booklet designed by Storm Thorgerson, who created the original album cover, along with an exclusive photo book, exclusive merchandise and facsimile collectables.

- Teen idol Reece Mastin, winner of the Australian television music show *X Factor*, is mobbed by more than a thousand 'over excited girls' at an Auckland mall appearance prior to his concert there.
- Garth Brooks is inducted into the Country Music Hall of Fame. Now semi-retired, but talking about touring again, the singer was the top-selling artist in the United States during the 1990s, taking country music into stadiums and major metropolitan markets and leading the way in a major crossover of country music to the mainstream pop and rock market.
- Local music retail chain Marbecks announced that it was closing its remaining Wellington (New Zealand) store, as the company scaled down its retail operations to focus on digital and online sales.
- A new classic rock radio station – 97.3 FM The Sound of Wellington – is launched in the local market, with press advertisements featuring U2, Tom Petty, Freddy Mercury, the Police, Mick Jagger and Stevie Nicks.
- The semi-finals of the latest series of *American Idol* continue to be featured in prime time mainstream television coverage.
- It is announced that a 'lavishly illustrated' book, *The Rolling Stones: 50*, will be published on 12 July 2012, to mark the 50th anniversary of the rock group's first gig, at London's Marquee Club.

The daily press also included advertising and reviews for a variety of concerts and club gigs, newly released recordings and the usual proliferation of advertisements for music retail: instruments, sound systems, including iPods, music DVDs and recordings, along with a piece (in the business section) on the continued impact of digital delivery on the music industry.

This is part of the everyday discourse that surrounds popular music and which provides a context and focus for this study. Evident within these stories, reviews and advertising are notions of musical creativity and authorship, canonical texts, musical history, audiences and music as a blend of entertainment, art and commerce. Collectively, and alongside other such stories, they indicate the commercial and cultural significance of popular music. Its ubiquitous global presence is evident on a daily basis: through 'muzak' in shopping malls; on public transport and on the streets and parks as listeners create a personal private space though their use of iPods; on MTV and mainstream television music shows; in film soundtracks and narratives; on web and radio broadcasts; through the music press; and 'live' in a variety of settings, from street buskers to clubs, stadium concerts and music festivals. In cultural terms, popular music is of enormous importance in daily life and for some is central to their social identities. In economic terms, the products of the music industry make it a leading cultural industry, with income including not just the sales of recorded music, but also copyright revenue, tour profits, merchandizing, sales of the music press, musical instruments, sound systems and sheet music.

Popular music culture refers to the ways of making, disseminating and consuming music; the economic and technological practices associated with these processes; and the recordings, sounds, images and discourse (thinking, debating, writing) created by these practices. My approach to it is situated in the general field of cultural and media studies, recognizing that the analysis of institutions, texts, discourses, readings and audiences are best understood in their social, economic and political context. I use the term 'popular music culture' to indicate this and to signal my intention to integrate a range of topics into this introductory survey. While I refer to some basic aspects of musical analysis and have included the analysis of song lyrics in considering recordings as texts, this is not a musicological study; I do not analyze music scores.

Setting agendas

As Bruce Horner and Thomas Swiss (1999: 7) observe, the different meanings given to terms common to the vocabulary of popular music studies, including the very terms 'popular' and 'music', help shape the music and our experience of it. The meaning and utility of terms such as 'popular' and 'mass', especially in relation to 'culture' and 'media', are the subject of considerable discussion and debate. Similarly, 'popular music' and associated terms such as 'rock', 'rock 'n' roll' and 'pop' are used by musicians, fans and academic analysts in a confusing variety of ways. It needs to be remembered that it is difficult to define phenomena that are social practices as well as economic products and which are not static but constantly evolving. Indeed, precise definitions can be constraining; they should be regarded as frameworks for exploration and elaboration, rather than factual declarations to be defended. That aside, let me try to at least pin down the general nature of some of the concepts that are central to the analysis of popular music culture.

Popular

'Popular' is a contested term. For some it means simply appealing to the people, whereas for others it means something much more grounded in or 'of' the people. The former usage generally refers to commercially produced forms of popular culture, while the latter is usually reserved for forms of 'folk' popular culture, associated with local community-based production and individual craftspeople. In relation to popular music, for example, this is the distinction often made between folk music, especially when acoustically based, and chart-oriented recordings, such as dance pop. Such a clear-cut distinction, however, has become increasingly untenable.

In normal usage, 'popular' indicates that something – a person, a product, a practice or a belief – is commonly liked or approved of by a large audience or the general public. Applied to the media, this means that particular television programmes, films, recordings, books and magazines are widely consumed. Their popularity is indicated by ratings surveys, box office returns and sales figures. To a degree, this definition of 'popularity' reifics popular cultural texts, reducing them to the status of objects to be bought and sold in the marketplace and the social nature of their consumption must always be kept in mind.

With this in mind, this study equates the 'popular' with commercial, cultural forms of entertainment and I regard markets as an inescapable feature of popular culture. Popularity is central to popular culture, as its various products and creators (particularly stars, auteurs) attain general social acceptance and approval. Contemporary popular culture in the United States and Canada, the United Kingdom and New Zealand – to mention only the national settings I am primarily concerned with in this study – forms the majority of mass media content, while the majority of popular culture is transmitted through the mass media.

Obviously, my use of the term 'culture' rejects the argument that anything popular cannot, by definition, be cultural. Although a high–low culture distinction is still very strongly evident in general public perceptions of 'culture', the traditionally claimed distinction between 'high' and 'low culture' has become blurred. High art has been increasingly commodified and commercialized, as with classical music's star system of conductors and soloists, while some forms of popular culture have become more 'respectable', receiving state funding and broader critical acceptance. Yet clear distinctions and cultural hierarchies remain widely held, not least within particular cultural forms, by those involved in their production and consumption. My use of what is one of the most difficult words in the English language is in a sociological rather than an aesthetic sense of culture. In addition to an emphasis on the audiences and consumption aspects of popular culture, I am concerned with the relationship between the creation of cultural products and the economic context of that creation, a process which involves creating or targeting audiences and an active engagement between texts and their consumers. This is to recognize that neither texts nor their consumers exist in isolation.

In an influential and widely cited discussion, Raymond Williams argues that contemporary usage of 'culture' falls into three possibilities or some amalgam of these: 'a general process of intellectual, spiritual, and aesthetic development'; 'a particular way of life, whether of a people, period, or a group'; and 'the works and practices of intellectual and especially artistic activity' (Williams, 1983: 90). This can be seen as a useful, if overly expansive, definition. My interest here lies primarily between the second and third of these definitions; and in the relationship between them – the way in which particular social groups have used popular music within their lives. This is to shift the focus from the preoccupation, evident in much media/cultural studies, with the text in and of itself, to the audience. It is also to stress 'popular culture', rather than accept the reservation of the term culture for artistic pursuits associated with particular values and standards, sometimes referred to as elite or high culture – Williams' third definition. In short, the main concern of this study is with the interrelationship of context, texts and consumption, as demonstrated by the manufacture, distribution and consumption of popular music culture, primarily in its various recorded forms. But what, then, is 'popular music'?

Popular music

Popular music defies precise, straightforward definition. The terms 'rock' and 'pop' are frequently used to stand for 'popular music', when they are metagenres within a much wider body of musics (in Shuker, 2012, I identify and briefly introduce 12 metagenres). While some writers on popular music slide over the question of definition and take a 'common sense' understanding of the term for granted, various attempts to provide a definition can be identified:

1. Definitions that place an emphasis on 'popular'. Historically, the term popular was used in relation to 'the ordinary people'. It was first linked in a published title to a certain kind of music that conformed to that criterion in William Chapple's *Popular Music of the Olden Times*, published in instalments from 1855. Not until the 1930s and 1940s did the term start to gain wider currency. Richard Middleton observes that the question of 'what is popular music' is 'so riddled with complexities ... that one is tempted to follow the example of the legendary definition of folk song – all songs are folk songs, I never heard horses sing 'em – and suggest that all music is popular music: popular with someone' (1990: 3). However, the criteria for what counts as popular, and their application to specific musical styles and genres, are open to considerable debate. Classical music clearly has sufficient following to be considered popular, while some forms of popular music are quite exclusive (e.g. Norwegian black metal).
2. Definitions based on the commercial nature of popular music and embracing genres perceived as commercially oriented. Many commentators argue that it is commercialization that is the key to understanding popular music; an approach that is related to an emphasis on the popular, arguing that such appeal can be quantified through sales, charts, radio airplay and so forth. In such definitions, certain genres are identified as 'popular music', while others are excluded. However, this approach can suffer from the same problems as those stressing popularity, since many genres have only limited appeal or have had limited commercial exposure. Moreover, popularity varies from country to country and even from region to region within national markets. It needs to also be noted that this approach is largely concerned with *recorded* popular music, which is usually listened to in a fairly conscious and focused manner. Anahid Kassabian makes the useful point that what she terms 'ubiquitous musics' are frequently left out of such discussions: music in films, in stores, on the phone, in the office, on television and so on. 'These are the kinds of music that no one chooses for herself or himself but that nevertheless wash our everyday lives with sound' (Kassabian, 1999: 113).
3. Identification by general musical and non-musical characteristics. Philip Tagg (in Middleton, 2002; first published 1982), in an influential and much cited discussion, characterizes popular music according to (i) the nature of its distribution (usually mass); (ii) how it is stored and distributed, primarily as recorded sound rather than oral transmission or musical notation; (iii) the existence of its own musical theory and aesthetics; and (iv) the relative anonymity of its composers. The last of these is debatable and I would want to extend the notion of composers

and its associated view of the nature of musical creativity. However, musicologists have usefully extended the third aspect of Tagg's definition, while sociologists have concentrated on the first two dimensions.

In sum, only the most general definition can be offered under the general umbrella category of 'popular music'. Essentially, it consists of a hybrid of musical traditions, styles and influences, with the only common element being that the music is characterized by a strong rhythmical component and generally, but not exclusively, relies on electronic amplification. Indeed, a purely musical definition is insufficient, since a central characteristic of popular music is a socioeconomic one: its mass production for a mass, still predominantly youth-oriented market. At the same time, of course, it is an economic product that is invested with ideological significance by many of its consumers. At the heart of the majority of the various forms of popular music is a fundamental tension between the essential creativity of the process of making music and the commercial nature of the bulk of its production and dissemination.

As this discussion suggests, as with a term like 'popular culture', it is misguided to attempt to attach too precise a meaning to what is a shifting cultural phenomenon. For convenience, and despite its own associated difficulties, I use the term 'popular music' throughout this study as shorthand for the diverse range of popular music genres produced in commodity form, largely, but no longer exclusively for a youth market, primarily Anglo-American in origin (or imitative of its forms), since the early 1950s and now global in scope.

Histories

Studying the development of popular music culture requires an engagement with its history, to better situate and understand its contemporary status. How do we 'remember' the past, and what influences and informs our memories of 'what happened', and the relative significance of individual events, participants, and musical texts? This musical 'popular memory' is constructed through the interaction of a number of 'sites', which mediate and re-present popular music history. The main one is written accounts, books and journal articles, which have been drawn on throughout this book. I have also utilized film and television documentaries and biopics; the wider music press, especially music magazines and music biography; the recording industry's repackaging of it past, through reissues and boxed sets representative of particular styles and periods of music; and heritage sites, notably museums devoted to popular/rock music, which have become increasingly important. Combined, these various forms of history create public and individual popular memories about the musical past, establishing particular dominant narratives.

It is worth remembering that the history of popular music has been subject to internal critique and debate in a similar manner to other forms of historical writing. At issue are the boundaries of the field, including its tendency to privilege its Anglo-American developments; the treatment of various genres within it; and the emphases that should be accorded to the context within which popular music is produced. Indeed, it is more correct to talk of *histories*, rather than *history*, in order to stress the contested and contingent nature of historical explanation. As an aspect of popular music studies, these issues have recently enjoyed greater attention, with a dedicated journal (*Popular Music History*); a comprehensive reader (Brackett, 2009); new editions of various standard textbooks (for example Friedlander, 2006; Garofalo, 2011); and 'revisionist' studies of previously dominant narratives.

In a sense, all historical writing is 'revisionist', as each generation of historians take different perspectives on the past, informed by their contemporary location (see MacMillan, 2009). More specifically, however, revisionist history is characterized by asking different, sometimes awkward questions of orthodox 'standard' accounts; and the use of a wider range of primary sources, especially popular material, including oral history. In relation to popular music, in addition to these characteristics, revisionist accounts tend to focus on previously neglected periods, styles and performers, often drawing new connections between these. A recent example of such an approach, with a title indicating the revisionist intentions of its author, is Elijah Wald's *How The Beatles Destroyed Rock 'n' Roll An Alternative History of American Popular Music* (Wald, 2009). For Wald, rock 'n' roll is not so much a historical genre but rather a process, whereby black dance styles repeatedly transformed pop music and were remade by it in turn. (Shuker, 2010, considers this and similar accounts.)

Analysing popular music culture

The study of popular music culture is situated in the general field of cultural studies, which addresses the interaction between three dimensions of popular culture: lived cultures, the social being of those who consume popular cultures; the symbolic forms, or texts, that are consumed within the lived culture; and the economic institutions and technological processes that create the texts. My discussion of the interrelationship of these dimensions in relation to popular music draws primarily from critical media theory, contemporary political economy and cultural studies. I regard popular cultural texts as dynamic not static, mediated by patterns of economic and social organization and the relationship of individuals and social groups to these patterns. This puts politics in a position of central importance, as culture is viewed as a site of conflict and struggle, of negotiations that constantly confirm and redefine the existing conditions of domination and subordination in society. The construction of meaning in popular music can be seen as embracing a number of factors: the music industry and its associated technologies, those who create the music, the nature of musical texts, the constitution of audiences and their modes of consumption and attempts to influence and regulate all of these. It is, of course, not possible to deal with every aspect of popular music. Themes, topics and examples have been selected partly for their importance in exemplifying the diverse activities of the field of popular music, but primarily for their relevance to the general argument.

The organizational logic of the text is to begin with issues of the economic and technological context: the music industry, music and technology. I go from these to the process of making music and issues of authorship, the nature of musical texts (drawing on popular musicology) and the cultural practices of their production. This leads on to a consideration of consumption and identity, particularly the sites (scenes, social network sites), social groups (fans, collectors, subcultures) and practices involved. I then turn to the manner in which popular music is a form of cultural politics, involving the construction of social identities, and processes of regulation, restriction and empowerment. This is to see meaning in popular music as the product of a somewhat circular process, operating at a number of cultural levels in the personal and social and institutional domains.

The discussion here draws together material from several national contexts and places this within a historical dimension, both aspects at times absent from contemporary-oriented and nation-bound studies of popular music culture. A more historical and international perspective enables firmer conclusions to be made about the nature and impact of popular music, particularly given the continued growth of global multimedia conglomerates and the increasing evidence of the globalization of culture. That said, the geographical Anglo-American and English language-centric nature of the study must be conceded. There are numerous examples of popular music culture in other national and regional contexts, along with a considerable body of scholarship in languages such as Spanish, French, Swedish and German, that I have not been able to cover here. (References to some of this can be found through the website for IASPM: the International Association for the Study of Popular Music; see Further reading.)

More fully, the scope of the book is as follows: Chapter 1 considers the role of the music industry, in its drive to commodify performers and texts and to maximize profits, as central to the study of popular music culture. I look at the music industry as an example of the cultural industries, the operation of the record companies as part of these and the revolutionary impact of digital music on musical production and distribution. The traditional model of the music industry, and the dominance of the major record companies, has been undermined, but not replaced, in a new digital environment.

Chapter 2 examines the impact of technology on popular music and the closely related issue of copyright. Technological changes in recording pose both constraints and opportunities in terms of the organization of production, and innovation in musical instrumentation has facilitated the emergence of 'new' sounds. New recording formats and modes of transmission and dissemination, most recently digital, alter the nature of musical production and consumption, and raise questions about authorship, the legal status of music as property and the operation of copyright.

Chapters 3 through 6 examine musical authorship and the 'success continuum', texts and genres: Chapter 3 deals with the process of music making and sites of production; conceptions of the term 'musician' and a 'success continuum'; and the status accorded various categories of performer.

Chapter 4 provides a range of individual career profiles, both stars and auteurs, with brief examples of their work. These profiles illustrate the interaction of musical authorship with genres, audiences and history.

Chapter 5 considers the textual forms popular music takes, the application of musicology to popular song, and issues of lyric analysis, and the nature of song covers.

Chapter 6 looks at the nature and significance of genres, and the role of authenticity in their construction, and the concept of popular music metagenres, using rock and pop, heavy metal and world music as case studies of these. The identification of a rock album canon illustrates the debates around music and authenticity and the cultural and musical value of such forms and constructs.

Chapters 7 to 9 examine further institutional mediators of music, primarily the music media; along with the sound recording companies, considered earlier, these act as gatekeepers and disseminators. Linking them is marketing, the focus of Chapter 7, along with music retail and radio, with the charts providing a central link between these.

Chapter 8 considers the relationship between sound and pictures: popular music and film, television, music video and MTV and YouTube.

Chapter 9 is on the role of the music press, a term used here for the whole corpus of writing on popular music, ranging from the popular press to cultural journalism, in both physical publications and on the internet. Within this discussion, the focus is on music magazines and music critics as cultural gatekeepers, promotional adjuncts to the music industry and general purveyors of lifestyles.

Chapters 10 and 11 examine the consumption of music, in relation to the formation of social identities, at the level of the self and the group. Two factors are seen to underpin this: music as a form of cultural capital and music as a source of pleasure and empowerment. Chapter 10 shows the place of music in the lives of 'youth' as a general social category and as integral to fan culture. Dance and record collecting provide examples of music consumption as a social practice.

Chapter 11 considers music as a central component of the 'style' of youth subcultures and musical scenes and sounds, the musical geography of place.

Chapters 12 to 14 encompass aspects of music as cultural politics: Chapter 12 investigates popular music as a vehicle for political activism and social change, again in relation to the construction of social identities. Music as cultural politics returns us to the significance of the socioeconomic context in shaping cultural meaning in the music.

Chapter 13 uses historical case studies to show how attempts to regulate popular music, its fans and performers have constituted a form of 'moral panic'.

Chapter 14 is on state music policy. The validity of the 'cultural imperialism' thesis and the concept of globalization are discussed in relation to popular music in Canada and New Zealand. The response of each to the dominance of Anglo-American music provides possible models for wider emulation and insights into the question of what might constitute the 'national' in cultural forms.

A difficulty facing any introductory textbook is the balance between general discussion of relevant topics, key concepts and debates within these, and illustrative examples of each. Given the constraints of length, I have chosen breadth of coverage over depth. Each of the topics covered is substantial and clearly there is not scope to explore each one in detail; at times particular aspects can merely be introduced and further lines of enquiry suggested. At the end of each chapter, and of this introduction, we provide a selected range of key sources for further study, while there is further guidance and links to internet resources on the companion website for *Understanding Popular Music Culture*: www.routledge. com/shuker.

Further reading

The following is a selection of general overviews of the field, edited collections, and discussions of key terms and concepts:

Bennett, A., Shank, B. and Toynbee, J. (eds) (2006) *The Popular Music Studies Reader*, London, New York: Routledge.
Cateforis, T. (ed.) (2007) *The Rock History Reader*, New York, London: Routledge. (See also his insightful discussion of the process of producing the reader: Cateforis, T. [2009] 'Sources and Storytelling: Teaching the History of Rock through its Primary Documents', *Journal of Popular Music Studies*, 21, 1: 20–58.)
Clayton, M., Herbert, T. and Middleton, R. (eds) (2012) *The Cultural Study of Music. A Critical Introduction*, 2nd edn, New York, London: Routledge.
Frith, S. (2007) *Taking Popular Music Seriously. Selected Essays*, Aldershot: Ashgate.
Frith, S. and Goodwin, A. (eds) (1990) *On Record: Rock, Pop, and the Written Word*, New York: Pantheon Books. (The scope of this influential early study can be usefully set alongside and compared to later 'readers', to show the changing emphases in the field of study.)
Hesmondhalgh, D. and Negus, K. (eds) (2004) *Popular Music Studies*, London: Arnold.
Negus, K. (1996) *Popular Music in Theory*, Cambridge: Polity Press.
Shuker, R. (2012) *Popular Music: The Key Concepts*, 3nd edn, London: Routledge.

Leading journals include *Popular Music*; *Popular Music and Society*; *Perfect Beat*; *Popular Music Studies* (links to these, and further information on them, can be found on this book's website).

A still useful bibliography is:

Shepherd, J., Horn, D., Laing, D., Oliver, P., Wicke, P., Tagg, P. and Wilson, J. (eds) (1997) *Popular Music Studies: A Select International Bibliography*, London: Mansell.

It can be updated by referring to the International Association for the Study of Popular Music (IASPM) bibliography, on the Association's website. IASPM has international and regional conferences and also publishes a newsletter; see the website: www.iaspm.com

1 'Every 1's a Winner'

The music industry and the record companies

The music industry can best be defined as encompassing a range of economic activities or revenue streams. These are engaged in by various economic entities, primarily, but not exclusively, the sound recording companies, commonly referred to as the 'record labels'. These business institutions are characterized by accompanying social practices: the manner in which people operate within and in relation to them.

I regard an understanding of political economy and the associated notion of the cultural industries as central to the study of the music industry. Following an introduction to these related concepts, I focus on the heart of the industry, the record companies themselves. Historically, these have been engaged in a constant struggle to control an uncertain marketplace, primarily through concentration and consolidation (vertical integration), their operation as part of media conglomerates (enabling horizontal integration and facilitating marketing) and the regulation of copyright. The general view of the binary nature of the record companies, into 'majors' and 'independents', is problematic, but it does provide insights into their ideological underpinnings, their organization and operating practices. The music industry has used the extension and consolidation of copyright legislation, both domestically and internationally, in an attempt to maintain market control.

The late 1990s saw the beginning of a long decline of the sound recording companies and their market dominance, as the internet radically altered the production and marketing of music, with music increasingly going online and the digital environment posing a major challenge to the traditional operation of copyright. This shift is considered in the second half of the chapter, which looks at the arguments around this decline, the record labels' response to it and the present configuration of the industry.

The music industry

There is a tendency, especially in general discourse, to equate the 'music industry' with the sound recording companies, which develop and market artists and their 'records' in various formats, including digital. This sector has historically been at the heart of the music industry and it certainly remains a very significant part of it. In a broader sense, however, the music industry embraces a range of other institutions and associated markets, which can be considered 'income streams' (Hull *et al.*, 2011, provide an extensive overview). The most important of these are music publishing; music retail; the music press; music hardware, including musical instruments, sound recording and reproduction technology; tours and concerts, and associated merchandizing (posters, t-shirts, etc.); film, television and MTV, and royalties and rights and their collection/licensing agencies.

The following are a few indications of the nature and value of these activities:

- During 2011 Adele's album *21* sold 14.5 million copies globally, contributing to a 3 per cent increase in album sales in the US market alone.
- The concert business saw overall ticket sales in the US up by 5.3 per cent (15.9 to 16.7 million), boosted by U2's '360' tour.
- Music has been the top entertainment product driving the continued growth of mobile phone services, especially among the 18–35 age group.
- Prime TV music shows, notably *Idol*, *The Voice* and *Glee*, continued to play a significant promotional role, boosting record sales and panel participants' careers.
- With 114 million registered users, eBay has become a primary source for music buyers generally and record collectors in particular: in December 2011 a copy of the Beatles early 7" single, 'Please Please Me', signed by all four members of the group, sold for £8000.
- *Rolling Stone* magazine has partnered with online subscription service Spotify to offer playlists and reviews, along with free streaming music.

As the International Federation of the Phonographic Industries (IFPI) observed back in 2006:

> The recorded music industry is the engine helping to drive a much broader music sector, which is worth more than US$100 billion globally. This is over three times the value of the recorded music market, and shows music to have an economic importance that extends far beyond the scope of record sales.
>
> (IFPI, 2006)

I shall return to other aspects of 'the music industry' throughout this study, but concentrate here on the sound recording companies and their activities. The critical analysis of these has drawn heavily on political economy and a view of music as constituting a cultural industry.

Political economy

A political economy approach to the popular mass media has as its starting point the fact that the producers of mass media are industrial institutions essentially driven by the logic of capitalism: the pursuit of maximum profit. The fact that these institutions are owned and controlled by a relatively small number of people, and that many of the largest scale firms are based in the US, is a situation involving considerable economic and ideological power. A number of accounts have traced the pervasive and increasing inequality in access to information and cultural products due to the commercialization and privatization of broadcasting, libraries, higher education and other areas of public discourse. A small group of large industrial corporations have systematically acquired more public communications power than any private business has ever before possessed in world history, creating a new communications cartel. The music industry has been part of this process of consolidation. At issue is the consequent question of control of the media and in whose interests they operate and the relationship between diversity and innovation in the market.

The influence of political economy is evident in the argument of studies that emphasize the power of corporate capitalism to manipulate and even construct markets and audiences. The picture of a powerful corporate capitalist music industry, able to manipulate and even construct markets and audiences, stresses how the music business is now an integral part of a global network of leisure and entertainment corporations, typified by a quest for media synergy and profit maximization (Chapple and Garofalo, 1977; Goodman, 1997; Hesmondahlgh, 2007). An extension of this is the classic form of the cultural imperialism thesis, popularized in the 1970s, which implied that mass manufactured popular culture, primarily from the US, is swamping the integrity and vitality of local cultural forms (see Chapter 14).

Classical political economy tended to devalue the significance of culture, seeing it primarily as the reflection of the economic base of society, all too easily slipping into a form of economic determinism. A group of German intellectuals, active from the 1930s, the Frankfurt School theorists, criticized mass culture in general, arguing that under the capitalist system of production culture had become simply another object, the 'culture industry', devoid of critical thought and any oppositional political possibilities. Adorno applied this general view more specifically to popular music, especially in his attacks on Tin Pan Alley and jazz. Contemporary political economy theorists have become more sophisticated in their appreciation of the reciprocal relationships between base and superstructure, economics and social activity. As David Hesmondhalgh (2007) convincingly demonstrates, it is necessary to emphasize a view of the cultural industries as complex, ambivalent and contested. Media institutions have been examined by asking of media texts: Who produces the text? For what audience? In whose interests? What is excluded? Such an interrogation necessitates examining particular media in terms of their production practices, financial bases, technology, legislative frameworks and their construction of audiences. This new work has reasserted the importance of political economy, which has been prominent in the last decade in considering the nature of music as a cultural industry.

The cultural industries

A descriptive term first coined and developed by Adorno, who referred to them as the 'culture industries', the cultural industries are those economic institutions 'which employ the characteristic modes of production and organization of industrial corporations to produce and disseminate symbols in the form of cultural goods and services, generally, though not exclusively, as commodities' (Garnham, 1987: 25). In analyses situated in business economics, they are referred to as the entertainment industries. Such industries are characterized by a constant drive to expand their market share and to create new products, so that the cultural commodity resists homogenization. In the case of the record industry, while creating and promoting new product is usually expensive, actually reproducing it is not. Once the master copy of a recording is available, further copies are relatively cheap as economies of scale come into operation; similarly, a music video can be enormously expensive to make, but its capacity to be reproduced and played is then virtually limitless.

The increased concentration of the culture industries is a feature of late capitalism and the music industry was part of this process of consolidation. The move into Hollywood by Japanese corporate capital in the late 1980s was a clear indication of the emerging battle for global dominance of media markets. This battle reflected companies' attempts to control both hardware and software markets and distribute their efforts across a range of media products, a synergy that enables maximization of product tie-ins and marketing campaigns and, consequently, profits (see the examples of this in Chapter 7).

Such mergers reflected the economies of scale and global integration required to compete on the world media market. A small group of internationally based large corporations spread their interests across a variety of media, including sound recording, resulting in multimedia conglomerates such as Time-Warner. Two of the main corporate strategies used here are horizontal and vertical integration: horizontal integration describes the actions of a firm to buy out (or control, usually through marketing and distribution deals) competing companies at the same level, as with one music retail chain acquiring another music retail chain; vertical integration refers to a market in which a firm owns more than one aspect of the production chain from manufacture through distribution and marketing, as with a music distributor that owns a music retail chain. These linked economic concepts have been neatly explained in terms of a community fish tank: consuming, or controlling, other similar sized fish in the tank is an example of horizontal integration; vertical integration occurs when a large fish owns the tank, the water, the plants, the rocks and the food supply, which it distributes to the other fish (Bishop, 2005: 447).

German media giant Bertelsmann illustrates these processes at work. In 2008 Bertelsmann owned book publishing (Random House); magazines and newspapers (Grune+Jahr); printing and media services (Arvato Printing); direct marketing groups (book and CD clubs); online interests (CDnow); and, the heart of the company, Bertelsmann Music Group (BMG). In 2006 Bertelsmann had sold

BMG publishing, the world's third largest music publishing company, with 2005 revenue of €371 million, to Universal Music. Yet, indicating the huge scope of Bertelsmann's interests, that figure then only accounted for about two per cent of the company's total revenue.

The cultural industries are engaged in competition for limited pools of disposable income, which will fluctuate according to the economic times. With its historical association with youthful purchasers, the music industry is particularly vulnerable to shifts in the relative size of the younger age cohort, their loss of spending power in a period of high youth unemployment worldwide and their shifting modes of consumption in the era of the download. The cultural industries are also engaged in competition for advertising revenue, consumption time and skilled labour. Radio, television and music magazines are all heavily dependent on advertising revenue. Not only are consumers allocating their expenditure, they are also dividing their time among the varying cultural consumption opportunities available to them. With the expanded range of leisure opportunities in recent years, at least to those able to afford them, the competition among the cultural, recreational and entertainment industries for consumer attention has increased.

The record companies

The record companies are an important part of the culture industries. Since its initial development in the early 1900s, the sound recording industry has demonstrated four main characteristics (see Frith, 1988; Gebesmair, 2009):

- a high concentration of markets
- the vertical integration of firms
- their transnational and global operation
- a dependence on copyright regulations.

These remained evident in the subsequent evolution of the record companies, which into the 1990s continued to demonstrate the features identified as characteristic of the cultural industries (Vogel, 1994; he prefers the term 'entertainment industries'):

- Profits from a very few highly popular products are generally required to offset losses from many mediocrities; overproduction is a feature of recorded music, with only a small proportion of releases achieving chart listings and commercial success and a few mega-sellers propping up the music industry in otherwise lean periods (e.g. Michael Jackson's, *Thriller*, 1982, with sales of some 20 million copies throughout the 1980s).
- Marketing expenditures per unit are proportionally large; this applies in the music industry to releases from artists with a proven track record.
- Ancillary or secondary markets provide disproportionately large returns; in popular music through licensing and revenue from copyright (as with film

soundtracks). Capital costs are relatively high and oligopolistic tendencies are prevalent; in the music industry this is evident in the dominance of the majors, in part due to the greater development and promotional capital they have available.

• Ongoing technological development makes it ever easier and less expensive to manufacture, distribute and receive entertainment products and services.

• Entertainment products and services have universal appeal, as evidenced by the international appeal of many popular music genres and performers; this is enhanced by the general accessibility of music as a medium, no matter what language a song may be sung in.

A significant, albeit frequently debated, aspect of the record companies is their broad division into major and independent labels.

Calling the tune? The majors

The record industry has historically been dominated by a group of large international companies commonly referred to as the majors. The major labels are usually involved in all aspects of the management, production, distribution and sale of recorded music, attempting as far as possible to control these different aspects. They have similar organizational structures, with typical management hierarchies and various divisions: A&R; promotion; sales and marketing (for a detailed discussion, see Hull *et al.*, 2011; for an insightful analysis of the process in the 1980s, which remains relevant and provides an historical 'benchmark' for subsequent developments in the digital age, see Negus, 1992).

Historically, 'middle range' companies, such as Virgin, Motown and Island, have been absorbed by the majors, while the smaller independents are often closely linked to the majors through distribution deals. Each major commonly has branches throughout the Americas and Europe and, in most cases, in parts of Asia, Africa and Australasia and each includes a number of record labels.

By the late 1990s there were six majors, all part of large international media conglomerates: Thorn/EMI (UK based); Bertelsmann (Germany); Sony (Japan); Time/Warner (US); MCA (with a controlling interest purchased in 1995 by Canadian-owned company Seagrams); and Philips (Holland). By 2006 further consolidation and mergers had left four: Warner Music Group, part of AOL-Time-Warner; Universal Music Group, owned by Vivendi Universal SA of France; Sony-BMG, jointly owned by the Japanese Sony Corporation and Bertelsmann, which had merged in 2004; and EMI Ltd, a UK firm. In 2011 industry consolidation continued, as EMI, the smallest of the four remaining major labels, pending regulatory approval, was sold to Universal Music, with staff layoffs and roster cutbacks of performers likely to follow. This left Universal with a market share of around 40 per cent, overshadowing Sony and Warner, the other remaining majors.

The market share exercised by the majors varies from country to country, but in some cases is over 90 per cent. There is considerable debate over the economic and cultural implications of such market dominance, especially the strength of local music industries in relation to marked trends toward the globalization of the culture industries and governmental policy responses to this situation (see the examples of Canada and New Zealand, discussed in Chapter 14). Some commentators regard the natural corollary of such concentrations of ownership as an ability to essentially determine, or at the very least strongly influence, the nature of the demand for particular forms of popular culture. By the same token, more optimistic media analysts, with a preference for human agency, emphasize the individual consumer's freedom to choose, the ability to decide how and where cultural texts are to be used and the meanings and messages to be associated with them. The debate in this area is one of emphasis, since clearly both sets of influences or determinations are in operation.

At issue is the consequent question of control of the media and in whose interests they operate and the relationship between diversity and innovation in the market. Free market economists argue that innovation will occur more frequently under conditions of oligopoly (increased concentration, fewer producers), since larger firms are better able to finance innovation and pass the costs and benefits along to consumers. Conversely, other analysts argue that conditions of oligopoly mean a lack of incentive for firms to depart much from the tried and tested, resulting in a high level of product homogeneity.

Initial analyses of the relationship between concentration, innovation and diversity in popular music suggested a negative relationship between concentration and diversity in the recording industry, relating this to a cyclical pattern of market cycles in symbolic production. This suggests that original musical ideas and styles, generated organically, are taken up by the record industry, which then popularizes them and adheres to them as the standard form. Meanwhile, new creative trends emerge that have to break through the new orthodoxy. Thus develops a cycle of innovation and consolidation, which has been reflected in historical shifts in economic concentration and market control in the music industry.

The crucial question in this debate is how does such concentration affect the range of opportunities available to musicians and others involved in the production of popular music and the nature and range of products available to the consumers of popular music? In other words, what is the cultural significance of this situation and what role does it play in the creation of meaning in popular music?

The independents

While the 'majors' dominate the recorded music market, the 'independents', or 'indies', play an important role. These are generally small record labels that are independent of the majors (at least in terms of the artist acquisition, recording and promotion), although still reliant on a major for distribution and more extensive marketing (examples historically include Creation, 4AD, Sub Pop, Sugar Hill, Rough Trade and Stiff). These labels are frequently considered to be more flexible and innovative in their roster of artists and have frequently been associated with the emergence of new genres. The term 'indie' denotes not just a type of economic entity, but a musical *attitude*. Both senses of indie are linked to a set of dominant musical values, with authenticity at their core, with these values cast as diametrically opposed to a stereotyped mainstream and the majors. The crossover of indie bands from smaller labels into the mainstream music industry, as occurred with U2, REM and Nirvana, led to considerable debate among their fans.

Independents have a rich and often lauded role in the history of popular music. It has been argued that independent record companies in the 1950s did not have the corporate hierarchy of the majors and so had greater flexibility in picking up on and promoting new trends and talent and a greater ability to adjust record production. In companies such as Sun, the owner, record producer, sound technician and promoter often were the same person (as with Sam Philips at Sun). 'The 1950s decade was the golden era for small independents, which embraced blues, gospel, modern jazz, country, R&B, and rock 'n' roll', and from 1948 to 1954, about one thousand new record labels were formed' (Kennedy and McNutt, 1999: xvii).

To maintain their market control, the music majors adopted several strategies in relation to the independents: buying out their artists' contracts (RCA and Elvis from Sun) or persuading artists to move labels; entering into marketing and other business arrangements with them or simply by buying them out. Several independents acquired a significant market share, as did Motown in the 1960s; these became mid-range companies, situated between the majors and the independents, but were subject to absorption by their larger rivals. While there are a huge number of independent labels, and they produce two-thirds of the titles released, their market share remains small. The operation of the independents and the precise nature of their relationship with the majors continues to be debated and the interaction between them remains a dynamic process.

The independent sector has continued to be an important part of the music industry, made more viable by the opportunities (for marketing and distribution) facilitated by the internet, while often still acting as developers of talent for the majors. The examples of Creation and the career of Oasis and Rough Trade in the UK during the 1990s illustrated a definite blurring of the boundaries between the independents and the major companies. Accordingly, argues Dale, 'indie ceased to be an abbreviation of the word independent, and thus ceased to denote a significant distinction from the major labels' (Dale, 2008: 173). The contemporary music industry, where many indies are in fact part of larger networks of labels, requires a more flexible and qualified definition, with the indie record company 'characterized by some degree of separation from the business practices and creative control of the large corporations operating major labels' (Novara and Henry, 2009: 816).

Music in cyberspace: the industry goes online

The late 1990s saw the beginning of a long decline of the major recording companies and their market dominance, as the internet radically altered the production and marketing of music, with music increasingly being made available online; many indie labels also struggled to come to terms with the new digital environment. The old industry model no longer worked: 'The defining issue is that music users can access music they find satisfying *without buying it*, and this can only problematise historically embedded profit seeking production routines' (Jones, 2012: Chapter 8).

The internet is a computer-linked global communications technology, with dramatically increasing numbers of people accessing it since the late 1990s. Its impact is much debated: there is a utopian discourse of celebration at the democratic spaces and opportunities it has created, alongside of recognition of its colonization by traditional media institutions and power structures. The world wide web, a major part of the internet, includes sites for online music retail; for downloading music as digital files; for record companies, performers and fans; online music journals; online concerts and interviews; web radio and bulletin boards (Cantoni and Tardini, 2006). These represent new ways of interlinking the audience/consumers of popular music, the performers and the music industry. I shall return to these in later chapters; my emphasis here is on the impact of the web, and digital music, on the recording industry.

Early discussions of the significance of electronic commerce via the web emphasized the business and economic aspects: the benefits to firms and consumers; the barriers and difficulties associated with doing business via the net; the demographics of net users; and the opportunities for companies on the net. It was soon recognized that there were also significant cultural issues associated with popular music on the net, which linked up with ongoing debates in the political economy of popular music, notably the relative importance (power) of the music industry and the consumers of popular music (Jones, 2000). The net potentially created greater consumer sovereignty and choice by bypassing the traditional intermediaries operating in the music industry (primarily the record companies, but also physical music retail; see Chapter 7). The major record companies were initially slow to recognize its potential, but soon moved to create sites to showcase their activities and their artists.

In the early 2000s music continued to shift online, with legal downloading taking an increasing market share, made even more attractive by the development of the iPod and its competitors, portable music systems capable of storing huge numbers of songs in digital format. In 2006 a major IFPI report on digital music, a comprehensive review of the development of the digital music market internationally, presented some impressive statistical evidence. It showed the online shift had actually gained momentum, with two million songs now available online. The following summarizes the trends then evident:

- Digital music now accounts for about six per cent of record companies' revenues, up from practically zero two years ago.
- Sales of music via the internet and mobile phones proliferated and spread across the world in 2005, generating sales of US$1.1 billion for record

companies – up from US$380 million the previous year – and promising further significant growth in the coming year.

- Music fans downloaded 420 million single tracks from the internet last year – 20 times more than two years earlier – while the volume of music licensed by record companies doubled to over two million songs.
- The legitimate digital music business is steadily pushing back on digital piracy. In Europe's two biggest digital markets, UK and Germany, more music fans are legally downloading music than illegally file swapping.
- Mobile music now accounts for approximately 40 per cent of record company digital revenues. Record companies are seeing sharply increased sales of master ringtones (excerpts of original artist recordings).

IFPI Chairman and CEO John Kennedy, however, noted that this growth faced challenges from piracy and called for 'more cooperation from service providers and music distributors, to help protect intellectual property and contain piracy'. This view was challenged by observers not so comfortable with the shift to longer periods of copyright and greater industry regulation and prosecution of those breaking it. Central to these debates was the question of the operation of copyright in the new digital environment.

Copyright

In addition to industry concentration, copyright has been central to the recording industry's attempts to maintain market share and control of music. The basic principle of copyright law is the exclusive right to copy and publish one's own work. That is, the copyright owner has the right to duplicate or authorize the duplication of their property and to distribute it.

The Rome Convention and the Berne Convention are the major international agreements on copyright. The IFPI, the International Federation of the Phonographic Industries, globally regulates the application and enforcement of copyright. Rights income is collected by various local and regional agencies, such as AMCOS, the Australasian Mechanical Copyright Owners Society; and APRA, the Australasian Performing Rights Association, in New Zealand and Australia. In addition to deriving income from unit sales of records, record companies, performers, songwriters and music publishers derive income from the sale of rights. Ownership of rights is determined by copyright in the master tape, the original tape embodying the recorded performance from which subsequent records are manufactured. This rights income includes: (i) mechanical income: payable by the record company to the owner of the copyright, for permission to reproduce a song on record; this is a fixed percentage of the recommended retail price; (ii) performance income: a licence fee paid by venues, television and radio stations for the right to publicly perform or broadcast songs; and (iii) miscellaneous income: payment for the use of songs in films, adverts, etc. A fuller description of the nature of copyright is beyond my scope here (see Hull *et al.*, 2011: Chapters 3 and 4; for a fascinating history of challenges to the music industry's enforcement of copyright, see Kernfeld, 2011). Its significance lies in its changing application and associated cultural importance. The development of new technologies of sound recording and reproduction raise issues of intellectual property rights, copyright and the control of sounds.

As early case studies of the legal and moral arguments surrounding the sampling used in records by the JAMS, M/A/R/R/S, De La Soul and others showed (see Beadle, 1993), the issues involved in policing copyright were extremely complex. They focused on the questions of what is actually 'copyrightable' in music. Who has the right to control the use of a song, a record or a sound? What constitutes fair use and what needs copyright clearance and, possibly therefore, payment? What is the nature of the public domain? In the early 1990s Simon Frith could observe that the advent of new technologies of sound recording and reproduction had coincided with the globalization of culture and the desire for media/entertainment conglomerates to maximize their revenues from 'rights' as well as maintaining income from the actual sale of records. What counted as 'music' was changing from a fixed, authored 'thing' that existed as property, to something more difficult to identify (Frith, 1993). Governmental and industry organization attempts to ensure international uniformity in copyright laws initially met only with partial success; even within the European community conventions and practices varied considerably.

As remains the case, attitudes towards copyright diverge depending whose interests are involved. The 1990s saw an emerging hostility towards copyright among many music consumers and even some musicians, due to its regulatory use by international corporations to protect their interests. Contrariwise, the companies themselves began actively seeking to harmonize arrangements and curb what they saw as straightforward piracy, while the record industry associations, which are almost exclusively concerned with copyright issues, largely supported the industry.

The nature of intellectual property rights, and the regulation of these, was brought into even sharper focus with the electronic retrieval possibilities implicit in the net. Beginning around 1999/2000, the mainstream music industry showed increasing alarm at the impact on their market share of Napster *et al.* and practices such as the downloading of MP3s and P2P (person-to-person) file sharing.

Napster software was introduced in 1999, 'designed as a combination search engine, communication portal, and file-sharing software that facilitated the sharing process by granting users access to all other Napster users and the MP3 files they chose to share' (Garofalo, 2003: 31). Within a few months, transfers of music files using Napster reached millions per day and, at its peak, it was estimated that as many as 60 million people were using the service. The copyright violation, and consequent loss of revenue, led several artists (notably the band Metallica) and record labels to sue Napster for breach of copyright. The issues involved were complex and the litigation process was a lengthy and very public one. Napster was forced to close down, but was relaunched as a legitimate service in late 2003 (Napster 2.0). Newer technologies and providers moved things to another level:

> Whereas Napster required users first to log onto a central server to access other users' MP3 files, these newer networks allow direct user-to-user peer-to-peer connections involving multiple file types. These innovations expand the universe of file sharing activity and make it virtually impossible to track users or the files they choose to share.
>
> (Garofalo, 2003: 31)

MP3 challenged the recording company's control over distribution and, since the format had no built in way to prevent users from obtaining and distributing music illegally, could represent considerable lost revenue. The majors, through trade organizations such as the RIAA (Recording Industry Association of America), joined together to create the Secure Digital Music Initiative (see www. sdmi.org), in an attempt to reassert control over music distribution and also began legally targeting ISPs (internet service providers) and individual consumers who download and share music without permission/payment. National administrations introduced legislation attempting to modify copyright in regard to online music distribution, as with the 1998 US Digital Millennium Copyright Act (see Strasser, 2010: 54–5). An alternative industry strategy also emerged, when in 2000, record companies began establishing copyright deals with internet music producers. In 2003 the entry of Apple into the music marketplace, with its iTunes service, met with considerable success, encouraging the development of further such services, most notably eMusic, which only sells music from independent labels.

There is a basic tension between protecting the rights and income of the original artists and the restriction of musical output. Copyright was originally conceived as a mechanism to balance private and public interests by eliminating perpetual monopolies over creative works. To some commentators, the media conglomerates were now attempting to 'use their power and [intellectual] property to influence national and international laws in order to lock down culture and control creativity' (Bishop, 2005: abstract).

The battle over P2P file sharing has continued, with the music industry targeting new, post-Napster services and individual consumers whom they perceived as infringing copyright. National governments continue to be involved in such attempts at regulation. In New Zealand, for example, in May 2011 the government passed the Copyright (Infringing File Sharing) Amendment Act, giving more power to a copyright tribunal, enabling them to require ISPs to send warning notices if illegal downloading occurs. After three warning letters, a copyright holder can take a claim to the tribunal, which can then impose a maximum fine of (NZ) $15,000 to the current account holder. The act has already provoked considerable hostility and opposition, not least as unsuspecting parents whose children download would be targeted ('Internet law may catch parents unaware', *Dominion Post*, 15 April 2011: A4, was typical of news coverage); questions also remain around the cost of sending such letters (and who will fund them) and it remains to be seen if the legislation is workable. This local debate has mirrored the wider international discourse around downloading practices.

There are several core issues in these developments and debates. At an immediate level has been the question of the impact of downloading on 'legitimate' recording sales. From the industry point of view, and that of some observers, downloading was clearly hurting the industry. Others were not so convinced and there were some interesting comparisons with similar earlier episodes, notably tape copying. Second, market control was central to the debate around Napster and its successors: were artists and the recording companies being disempowered and consumers (end users) being empowered by the increasing availability of online music? (McLeod, 2005).

The recording industry fights back

In 2011 there were signs that the recording industry was making something of a comeback, after a decade of label mergers, staff layoffs and piracy lawsuits.

Digital music cloud services flourished: Spotify made its US debut; Apple released its iTunes Match cloud service; and Google and Amazon both launched their own cloud-based services. A major feature of this resurgence was the increased importance of live music. Concert ticket prices have risen well above inflation since 1996, at the same time there has been a decrease in revenue from recorded music. Consequently, live performance is now one of the primary income streams for performers and the music industry. Reunion concerts and tours by a number of previously long inactive bands or performers, who nevertheless retained the affection of their aging fan bases, have become a feature of the contemporary concert circuit (for example, the Eagles; 10cc; the Specials; Bob Seger). *Billboard* magazine regularly documents income generated by concert tours, showing how these are a major income stream for performers, including those who have not released 'new' music, or toured, for quite some time. In 2009, Coldplay's tour behind the release of the album 'Viva La Vida' earned (US) $24.7 million; the Jonas Brothers world tour netted them $31.4 million; and Leonard Cohen, playing his first US concerts in 15 years, earned $9.2 million in box office share.

The emergence of Live Nation as a major market force is indicative of the new prominence of live music as an industry income stream. In 1996 the American Robert Sillerman and his company SFX Entertainment began acquiring companies in the live music sector. In 2000 SFX was brought by the multinational corporation Clear Channel, which then combined its live entertainment assets into a separate company, Live Nation, in 2005. Live Nation now dominates concert promotion in both the United Kingdom and North America and is the second largest music company in the world (behind Universal). (Hull *et al.*, 2011: 166–8). Live Nation has struck deals with many of music's major performers. Madonna's long-term multi-rights Live Nation deal, valued at US$120 million, is based primarily on potential to generate touring income: her international Sticky and Sweet tour in 2009 was the highest grossing tour ever by a solo artist; in March 2012 Madonna began her second world tour with Live Nation. U2's similar 12-year multi-rights deal with Live Nation includes worldwide touring, merchandizing and the lucrative U2.com website, which digitally distributes all things U2.

Conclusion

The recording industry is now in a new post-industrial phase, characterized by the impact of digital music and the decentralizing of the means of recording, reproduction and distribution. At the same time, there is increasing consolidation of the music industry as a whole, as part of the global cultural industry. The international conglomerates not only compete with one another, but are increasingly interconnected in complex patterns of ownership and business practices. The majors remain dominant, but their market share continues to shrink. While the global music industry is still concentrated around the production and management of commodities, the management of rights is providing an increasingly important share of its revenues.

Through the 2000s, the impact of the internet and digital music has raised serious questions about the continued adequacy of the traditional business model adopted by the majors (for a helpful discussion of their various responses, see Furgason, 2008).

However, the frequently noted 'death of the music industry' has been overstated: 'While digital configurations may allow for new means of distributing text, audio and visual content, they do not – and, we argue, cannot – fundamentally alter the music industry, which ... follows its own imperatives' (Burkart and McCourt, 2006: 7).

Certainly, the sound recording industry has shown a steady and marked decline, underpinned by two factors: the ongoing consolidation of the majors; and a precipitous fall in sales revenue in the US, down from $14 billion in 1999 to $6 billion in 2009 (Jones 2012). At the same time, however, we are consuming more popular music culture than ever before. As Jones (2012) puts it: 'people and businesses go on paying for symbolic goods in music on a vast scale.'

Further reading

Burkart, P. and McCourt, T. (2006) *Digital Music Wars Ownership and Control of the Celestial Jukebox*, Lanham, MD: Bowman & Littlefield.
Frith, S. (2007) 'The Industrialization of Popular Music', *Taking Popular Music Seriously: Selected Essays*, Aldershot: Ashgate (first published 1986).
Furgason, A. (2008) 'Afraid of Technology? Major Label Response to Advancements in Digital Technology, *Popular Music History*, 3, 2: 149–70.
Gebesmair, A. (2009) 'The Transnational Music Industry', in D. Scott (ed.), *The Ashgate Research Companion to Popular Musicology*, Farnham: Ashgate.
Hesmondhalgh, D. (2007) *The Cultural Industries*, 2nd edn, London: Sage.

Hull, G., Hutchinson, T.W. and Glasser, R. (2011) *The Music Business and Recording Industry: Delivering Music in the 21st Century*, 3rd edn, New York: Routledge.

This is the most comprehensive overview available, based around the various income streams and with an emphasis on formal industry structures and practices; it includes extensive statistical documentation, informative case studies a useful glossary, and an associated website. It can be helpfully accompanied by looking at the account by Jones.

Jones, M.L. (2012) *The Music Industries. From Conception to Consumption*, Basingstoke: Palgrave Macmillan.

Jones focuses on the music industry as a process, rather than an institution; involving musicians, artist managers and music companies as 'they seek to convert original texts created by musicians into successful symbolic goods.'

Strachan, R. (2007). Micro-independent Record Labels in the UK: Discourse, DIY Cultural Production and the Music Industry, *European Journal of Cultural Studies*, 10, 2: 245–65.

The music press is essential to keeping up with current changes in the industry: *Billboard*, *Variety* and *Music Week*. Business magazine *Forbes* has included some useful material. Limited content can be accessed online, although fuller access is usually by subscription.

Websites

The British Phonographic Industry: www.bpi.co.uk
The International Federation of the Phonographic Industries: www.ifpi.org
The IFPI promotes the interests of the international recording industry world-wide. Its members include over 1400 major and independent companies in more than 70 countries; it also has affiliated industry national groups in 48 countries.
The Recording Industry Association of America: www.riaa.com
The various 'majors' labels, along with many 'independents', have web sites.
Live Nation: www.livenation.com

2 'Pump Up the Volume'
Music and technology

The history of music is, in part, one of a shift from oral performance to notation, then to music being recorded and stored and disseminated utilizing various media of sound (and, later, audiovisual) transmission. These are hardly discrete stages, but they do offer an organizing logic for the overview here. Any new medium of communication or technological form changes the way in which we experience music and this has implications for how we relate to and consume music. It is important to acknowledge that the impact of technology on music is not solely a twentieth-century phenomenon, associated with the advent of recorded sound. Prior to this, print was central to the transmission of music, with the circulation of hand-written songs and scores. The printing press facilitated the circulation of broadside ballads from the early sixteenth century, along with sheet music, which peaked at the end of the nineteenth century.

Technological changes in recording equipment pose both constraints and opportunities in terms of the organization of production, while developments in musical instrumentation allowed the emergence of 'new' sounds. New recording formats and modes of transmission and dissemination alter the process of musical production and consumption and raise questions about authorship and the legal status of music as property. It is not possible here to cover all aspects of these topics, which have been the subject of intensive study (see Further reading). Rather, I have attempted to signpost some of their cultural implications, with brief examples to illustrate the interaction of technological, musical and cultural change. As Paul Théberge observes, 'technology' is not to be thought of simply in terms of 'machines', but rather in terms of practice, the uses to which sound recording and playback devices, recording formats, and radio, computers and the internet are put: 'in a more general sense, the organization of production and consumption' (1999: 216–17). My discussion covers sound production, the influence of new instruments on music making, sound recording and sound formats, sound reproduction and sound dissemination.

Sound production

New technologies of sound production are democratizing, opening up performance opportunities to musicians and creating new social spaces for listening to music. However, these opportunities and spaces are selectively available and exploited by particular social groups. New instruments and modifications to instruments initiate debates around their legitimacy and place within musical culture. For instance: 'the arrival of the pianoforte into a musical culture that revered the harpsichord was for some an unwarranted intrusion by a mechanical device' (Pinch and Bijsterveld, 2003: 537). Further examples of this process are the impact of nineteenth-century brass band instruments; the microphone in the 1930s; the electric guitar in the early 1950s; the Moog synthesizer in the 1980s; and the MIDI (musical instrumental digital interface) since the late 1980s.

Victorian England saw an unprecedented expansion in participative music, with brass bands a major part of this. Trevor Herbert (1998) examines how and why brass bands developed, their distribution and adoption, and the nature and significance of their impact. In doing so, he illustrates the complex intersection of technology, urbanization and musical forms at work in shaping the brass band movement. The first half of the nineteenth century was the most important period in the history of brass bands. They emerged as a new form of leisure activity, with the development of new brass instruments made possible by the invention of the piston valve: 'Suddenly brass instruments possessed a new musical facility, and potentially a new social identity' (Herbert, 1998: 110). The advent of new instruments made possible new musical techniques and an expanded band repertoire.

The introduction of the microphone in the 1920s revolutionized the practice of popular singing, as vocalists could now address listeners with unprecedented intimacy. This led to new musical creativities and sites of authorship. Bruce Johnson traces the emergence of the microphone as a 'performance accessory' in Australia, showing how it was inscribed by gender politics. Masculine resistance to this 'artificial' aid left it primarily to women singers to exploit its possibilities in the 1930s. 'In particular, they experimented with projection, timbre and sensibility in a way that placed the intimate "grain of the voice" in the public arena, laying the foundations for the distinctive vocalisation of rock/pop' (Johnson, 2000: Chapter 4; see also Chanan, 1995: Chapter 7).

In a similar manner, the amplification of the guitar transformed popular musicianship: 'amplification allowed guitarists to play fluid and hornlike solos, while the country and jump blues genres popular in the late Forties encouraged them to elaborate a more percussive and riffing style' (Miller, 1999: 41). The Fender Esquire in 1950, the first mass-produced solid body electric guitar, changed the range and variety of people who could play, reducing the importance of controlling each string's resonance precisely, covering fingering mistakes. The electric guitar made it possible to play for much larger audiences, in bigger venues, creating new musical styles in the process. 'Chicago' or electric blues developed when black people from the south moved to urban centres such as Chicago, Memphis and New Orleans post-World War II, looking for work and better lifestyle opportunities. Performers such as Muddy Waters and John Lee Hooker 'plugged in' to entertain them (Waksman, 1996: Chapter 4).

The electronic synthesizer, developed in the late 1960s and early 1970s, became 'the most successful electronic instrument of the twentieth century' (Pinch and Bijsterveld, 2003: 546). Moog became the dominant manufacturer, in part because he made his machine available to as many musicians as possible and worked closely with them to constantly modify his design. His synthesizer became a keyboard device, providing an appealing feature of Moog advertising material: 'Whenever someone wanted to take a picture, for some reason or other it looks good if you're playing a keyboard. People understand then that you're making music' (Moog). The acceptance of a keyboard synthesizer reflected the influence of the wider culture and the historical status of the piano and organ.

Walter Carlos, a skilled studio engineer and composer of electronic music, formed a close relationship with Moog, exchanging advice for custom-built modules. In 1968, with Rachel Elkind, he produced *Switched On Bach*, an album of Bach's 'greatest hits' performed on the Moog synthesizer. The critical and commercial success of the album helped popularize the synthesizer. Psychedelic musicians, already fascinated with unusual instruments such as the sitar and theremin, took up the synthesizer. (For example, the Byrds on *The Notorious Byrd Brothers*, Columbia, 1968; and the Beatles on later albums such as *Revolver*, Parlophone, 1966). The production of the first portable keyboard, the cheaper and easier to use Minimoog, which became an essential part of progressive rock in the early 1970s, consolidated this popularity: 'It was the first synthesizer to have mass appeal and was sold in a new way, through retail music stores, thus laying the foundation for a retail market in synthesizers' (Pinch and Bijsterveld, 2003: 554). The Minimoog's portability, ease of use, reliability and hardwired sound, made it an important precursor to later digital instruments, notably the Yamaha DX7 (1983) with its wide array of presets.

The advent of MIDI (musical instrument digital interface) and digital electronics completely restructured music production from 1983 onwards, representing a paradigm shift in the history of popular music. The new generation of instruments and software created fresh sound possibilities, expanded style, techniques and concepts of production and raised the status of producers (see Chapter 3).

Sound recording

Sound recording is the process of transferring 'live' musical performance onto a physical product (the recording). The history of sound recording is one of technical advances leading to changes in the nature of the process and the shifts in tasks and status of those working with these technologies. Such changes are not narrowly technical, as different recording technologies and their associated working practices (e.g. multi-tracking, overdubbing, tape delay) enable and sustain different aesthetics (for a detailed history, see Cunningham, 1996; for a concise overview, see Millard, 2005: Chapter 14). In the recording studio, the work of the sound mixer, or sound engineer, was where music and modern technology met. Initially designated as 'technicians', sound mixers have converted a craft into an art, with consequent higher status and rewards. Zak refers to them as 'both craftsmen and shamans' (2001: 165), who are now responsible for much of what we hear on a recording, acting as a kind of translator for musicians and the other members of the recording team.

Particular recordings illustrate advances in sound recording, at times accompanied by greatly increased use of studio time. Approaching the history of popular music from this perspective creates quite a different picture of artistic high points and auteur figures, in comparison with the conventional chronologies. Compare, for example, the following recordings:

1   Les Paul and Mary Ford, 'How High is the Moon', which occupied the no. 1 position on the American chart for nine weeks in spring 1951, launched the concept of sound-on-sound recording, coupled with Paul's discovery of tape delay. The technique for recording Ford's voice was also innovative, as Paul recalls:

> 'The unwritten rules stated that a vocalist should be placed no closer than two feet from the microphone, but I wanted to capture every little breath and nuance in Mary's voice. So I had her stand right on the mic, just a couple of inches away. Then, what happened? Everybody started to record vocals that way!'
>
> (Cunningham, 1996: 25)

2   Elvis Presley, 'That's Alright Mama' (Sun, 1956), was recorded at the session in which producer Sam Philips introduced the slap-back delay sound, used on Presley's other Sun singles and the label's recordings by other rockabilly artists.
3   The Beach Boys, 'Good Vibrations' (Capitol, 1966), Brian Wilson's 'pocket symphony', utilized a huge range of instruments, including a theremin (a pre-synthesizer electronic gadget), made possible partly by his extensive use of overdubs.
4   Pink Floyd, *Dark Side of the Moon* (Capitol, 1973), set a new precedent in sound recording techniques; for example, in its use of noise gates, devices that allow audio signals to be heard once they rise above a predetermined volume threshold and an extensive use of synthesizers.
5   Danger Mouse, *The Grey Album* (2004), took an a cappella version of rapper Jay-Z's *The Black Album* and coupled it with samples from the Beatles' *The White Album*. The resultant 'mash-up' was widely distributed over the internet and was both popular and controversial (see the discussion of it in Chapter 5).

The profound changes wrought by samplers, MIDI and other new technological phenomena are credited with giving new life to a moribund music industry in the 1980s. Sampling can be viewed as part of music's historic tendency to constantly 'eat itself', while also exemplifying its postmodern tendencies:

> The willful acts of disintegration necessary in sampling are, like cubism, designed to find a way ahead by taking the whole business to pieces, reducing

it to its constituent components. It's also an attempt to look to a past tradition and to try and move forward by placing that tradition in a new context.

(Beadle, 1993: 24)

Through the 1990s and into the 2000s, new recording technologies have continued to open up creative possibilities and underpinned the emergence of new genres, notably the variants of techno and hip-hop. Most recently, technology has enabled the creation of 'mash-ups': recordings combining two existing recordings, usually illegally and from radically different musical styles and performers, to create a new text (as just seen with *The Grey Album*).

Digital sampling allows sounds to be recorded, manipulated and subsequently played back from a keyboard or other musical device. Introduced in the late 1970s and subsequently widely used, digital sampling illustrates the debates surrounding musical technologies. Its use is seen variously as restricting the employment of session musicians and as enabling the production of new sounds, e.g. the use of previously recorded music in the creation of rhythm tracks for use in rap and dance remixes. The increasing emphasis on new such technologies is significantly changing the process of producing popular music: 'As pop becomes more and more a producer's and programmer's medium, so it increasingly is a sphere of composition, as opposed to performance' (Goodwin, 1998: 130).

Sound formats

With the advent of sound recording, music became a 'thing', as recording technology in the late nineteenth century enabled its development in commodity form, independent of its 'live' performance aspects. Subsequent shifts in the popularity of various recording formats are important in explaining the historical evolution of popular music. Each new recording format offered fresh recording and marketing opportunities and affected the nature of consumption. Historically, these constitute a procession of formats, although some are never totally superseded and become the preserve of collectors: the wax cylinder; the shellac 78, the vinyl 45, the EP and the LP, cassette audio tape, the compact disk, digital audio tape, the erasable compact disc and MP3 downloads.

The shifting discourse surrounding formats reflects a search for realism, fidelity and portability, along with the ease of access and the associated cost. Changing formats usually appeal to consumers wanting better sound (although what constitutes 'better' is debated) or greater convenience and to those who possess a 'must have' consumerist orientation to such new technologies. New markets are created as older consumers upgrade both their hardware and their record collections. The balance sheet with regard to the declining status of the vinyl single and album, versus the ascendancy of the CD, is a mixed one. There were opportunities in this even for those still emotionally tied to vinyl, as the early 1990s saw a boom in the used record store business as CD converts sold off their record collections on their way to buying their first disk player. The current dematerialization of the sound recording, with MP3 down-loads, represents another revolutionary cultural shift. I shall have more to say on this later.

A short history of the single

A history of the vinyl single and its digital successor is an example of the relationship between music making, marketing and consumption in relation to a format. The introduction of the virtually unbreakable vinyl single (historically often referred to as a 45 – the rpm) in the early1950s was an important factor in the emergence of a proliferation of smaller independent record labels, which were significant in popularizing rock 'n' roll. The single was originally a 7" vinyl format, with an 'A' side, the recording considered most likely to receive radio airplay and chart 'action', and a 'B' side, usually seen as a recording of less appeal. Also important was the EP, an 'extended play' single, a vinyl 7", usually with four songs on it. In the UK, the EP represented an early form of 'greatest hits' package, with attractive record covers, and outsold albums until the early 1960s.

In the early 1950s the vinyl single overtook its shellac 78 counterpart as the dominant music industry marketing vehicle. Singles became the major selling format, the basis for radio and television programming and the most important chart listing, with these in an apparently symbiotic relationship. Singles appealed to young people with limited disposable income, wanting to keep up with the latest chart hits. For the record companies, singles were cheaper to produce than an album and acted as market 'testers'. While singles success was important for performers and the record companies, it was also important as a means of draw-ing attention to the accompanying, or subsequent album, with the release of both being closely related. With a few significant exceptions (for example Led Zeppelin), performers generally relied on the single to promote their album release. This approach became the 'traditional' construction of record marketing through the 1960s and 1970s. Album compilations of singles, either by one performer or from a genre or style of music, also became an important market. While some perfor-mers with high charting singles were 'one hit wonders', singles success frequently launched careers, leading to an album deal and moves from independent to major labels.

In the 1980s new single formats gained an increasingly significant market share. There was a massive increase in sales of cassette singles in America and Swedish band Roxette's 'Listen to Your Heart' (1990) became the first single to hit no. 1 in the US without being released as a vinyl 45. Twelve-inch singles, including remixes, became an important part of the dance music scene (see Straw, 2001), and, accompanying the general rise of the CD format, the CD single also began to emerge as a popular marketing form and consumer preference. Negus (1992: 65) documents the consequent decline of the vinyl single through the 1980s. In the US, sales of singles between 1979 and 1990 declined by 86 per cent, from 195.5 million to 27.6 million units, and despite the growth of new formats, total sales of singles declined by 41 per cent. In Britain, the single's decline was less dramatic, with total sales falling by 21 per cent, from 77.8 million in 1980 to 61.1 million in 1989. This reflected the continued industry practice in the UK of releasing one or two singles prior to the issue of an album. The relative decline of the single reflected the higher costs of the new formats and the pressure to produce a video to accompany a single, a practice that was regarded as necessary for supporting radio airplay and chart success (see Chapter 7).

Performers were affected by the shift to the CD format. Whatever the aesthetic status of the rock/pop single, its material significance lay in its availability to artists with limited resources. The 7" 45 and the 12" dance single, with their specialist market tied to the club scene, offered such performers only a partial substitute. Linked to this, is the point that many of the independent record companies could not initially afford to produce CDs, restricting the market options available to their artists.

In the 1990s the overall life of the single in the charts, due to radio airplay, remained important for drawing attention to the album. The single is now less important, with sales in all formats having continued to decline in the past decade. Nevertheless, it remains crucial to commodifying pop music for the teen market. The appeal of particular singles is primarily assessed by the placing achieved on the charts, as well as longevity there. (It should be noted that these are not quite the same; sustainability indicates a broader market appeal, following initial sales to a performer's niche market or cult support.) Making subsequent assessments of the commercial, and thereby presumed cultural, impact of a single on the basis of total sales and the length of time spent in the charts, a common practice.

The physical nature of the single, and its relation to promotion and the charts, underwent a radical change during 2005–2006 as the music market moved online. In the UK, by early 2006, digital singles made up some 80 per cent of the singles market as a whole, up from 23 per cent in 2004. Music megastores, such as Virgin on London's Oxford Street, moved their 'singles wall' to the rear of the shop and only featured the 'Top 20' singles; other record shops stopped stocking the format. This initially produced a strange situation in the weekly charts, with downloads only counting for one week before a CD single was released and two weeks after the CD is deleted. However, many singles were available to download several weeks before their CD release, often increasing in popularity as the recording's release date approached. Recognizing this situation, the Entertainment Retailers Association began to allow all digital sales to count, so that the singles chart would remain definitive of popularity. The availability of downloads transformed the way in which consumers obtained music, giving them greater direct input into the charts and at much less cost. A striking example of this occurred in the UK in late 2009, when a campaign on Facebook encouraged people to download Rage Against the Machine's single 'Killing in the Name' (originally released in 1992), to successfully get it to the prestigious no. 1 chart placing ahead of the *X Factor* winner.

Sound reproduction and dissemination

The historical development of the phonograph and various subsequent sound systems (hi-fi; home stereo; the transistor radio; audio tape players; the Walkman; the CD player; the iPod; the personal computer) is more than simply a succession of 'technical' triumphs. Reflecting changes in the technologies of sound recording and production, each new form of sound reproduction has been accompanied by significant changes in how, when and where we listen to music.

A talking machine

Edison invented the phonograph, a 'talking machine', in November 1877. The phonograph represented the true beginning of the reproduction of recorded sound, replacing 'the shared Victorian pleasures of bandstand and music hall with the solitary delight of a private world of sound' (Millard, 2005: 1). Edison's phonograph used cylinders and was able to record and reproduce sound. Other researchers developed the new technology further: Berliner's gramophone (1888), used a disc instead of a cylinder, while Edison considerably improved on his original in 1887.

Various commentators have identified a succession of phases in the technological history of the phonograph: an acoustic one from 1877 to the 1920s; the use of electrical/magnetic tape, from the 1920s; and the digital age, with the CD, from 1982. 'The industry built on the phonograph was driven forward by the constant disruption of innovation: new systems of recording, new kinds of machine, and newer types of recorded music' (Millard, 2005: 5–6; see also Steffen, 2005). The question is the cultural significance of such developments. For example, the domestic relocation of music consumption, facilitated by the phonograph, raised questions of the nature of the listening process:

> Anyone, living no matter where, has only to turn a knob or put on a record to hear what he likes. Indeed it is just in this incredible facility, this lack of necessity for any effort, that the evil of this so-called process lies. For one can listen without hearing, just as one can look without seeing. The absence of active effort and the liking acquired for this facility make for laziness. Listeners fall into a kind of torpor.
>
> (Stravinsky, in Eisenberg, 1988)

The phonograph was originally intended primarily as a business tool, but moved into entertainment initially through coin-operated phonographs (from 1889). With the development of prerecorded cylinders in the early 1900s, the phonographic industry took off. While in 1897 only about 500,000 records had been sold in the US, by 1899 this number had reached 2.8 million and it continued to rise. The impact of the talking machine was international. Gerry Farrell's discussion of the early days of the gramophone in India presents a fascinating story of the intersections between commerce and technological innovation and their impact on traditional Indian modes of music patronage and music making. Economics underpinned the move of GLT (Gramophone and Type-writer Ltd) into the Indian subcontinent. As John Watson Hawf, its agent in Calcutta, put it: 'The native music is to me worse than Turkish but as long as it suits them and sells well what do we care?' (Farrell, 1998: 59). For the first time Indian musicians entered the world of Western media, as photography and recorded sound turned 'native' music into a saleable commodity.

The gramophone arrived in India only a few years after its invention in the West and recorded sound brought many forms of classical Indian music out of the obscurity of performance settings such as the courtesans' quarter and onto the mass market. Recording these was a formidable exercise: the visits to various parts of India in the early 1900s were quite correctly termed 'expeditions', involving complex logistical problems. For the emergent Indian middle class, the gramophone was both a technological novelty and a status symbol. The images in the company catalogues, reproduced by Farrell, illustrate this, along with the use of traditional images of Hindu deities to add to the appeal of the new medium. The constraints and possibilities of the new technology affected the style and structure of the music recorded. While Farrell is cautious not to generalize from the one detailed example he presents, he suggests that one possible limitation of the brief duration of the early recordings 'was to lead artists to give greater weight to the composed or fixed parts of the performance than they would normally have done in live recitals' (Farrell, 1998: 78).

Stereo

Stereophonic sound was first developed for use in film theatres in the 1930s, with home stereo systems as scaled-down versions. In 1931 the first three-way speaker systems were introduced. The sound was divided into high, middle and low frequencies, with each band sent to three different transducers in the loud speaker, each designed to best facilitate that part of the sound spectrum: the large 'woofer' for the bass, a mid-range driver and the smaller 'tweeter' for the treble. Due to the Depression, and the difficulty of reaching agreement on a common stereo standard (compared with the battle over recording formats), this system was not turned into a commercial product until the late 1950s. In the 1950s tape was the format to first introduce stereo sound into the home. The increased sales of magnetic tape recorders and prerecorded tape forced the record companies to develop a competing stereo product, particularly for the classical music audiophile. By the 1960s, stereo sound was incorporated into the loudspeakers used in home stereos. December 1957 saw the first stereo records introduced to the market. These were not intended for the mass market and sales were initially not high, but home stereos became popularized during the 1960s.

Going mobile

Mobile forms of sound reproduction have been important for decentring the listening process and for being identified with particular lifestyles and social groups. Compact cassette audio tape and cassette tape players, developed in the mid-1960s, appealed because of their small size and associated portability. Initially a low-fidelity medium, a steady improvement of the sound, through modifications to magnetic tape and the introduction of the Dolby noise reduction system, enhanced the appeal of cassettes. The transistor radio (made possible by the invention of the transistor in 1948) and the audio cassette had become associated technologies by the 1970s, with widely popular cheap radio cassette players and the cassette player incorporated into high-fidelity home stereos.

An efficient format for the expansion into remote markets, tape cassettes became the main sound carriers in 'developing' countries and, by the end of the 1980s, cassettes were outselling other formats three to one. As a portable recording technology, the tape cassette was used in the production, duplication and dissemination of local music and the creation of new musical styles, most notably punk and rap, thus tending to decentralize control over production and consumption. Home taping is individual copying (to audio or video tape) from existing recordings or off-air; it was made possible by the development of cassette audio tape and the cassette tape player. The term 'cassette culture' has been applied to the 'do-it-yourself' ethic that underlies such practices and the network of musicians and listeners it embraces. Such practices were seen as a threat by the music industry, with their perceived violation of copyright, a stance echoed in the later controversy over digital downloads.

The development of powerful portable stereo players (boom boxes), associated with inner-city African-American youth, created a new form of social identification and a new level of noise nuisance. The Jamaican 'sound system', large, heavily amplified mobile discos and their surrounding reggae culture, had a similar impact. These first emerged in Jamaica, from the 1950s onwards, and were transplanted to Britain with the influx of Caribbean immigrants:

> The basic description of a sound system as a large mobile hi-fi or disco does little justice to the specificities of the form. The sound that they generate has its own characteristics, particularly an emphasis on the reproduction of bass frequencies, its own aesthetics and a unique mode of consumption.
>
> (Gilroy, 1987, in Gelder and Thornton, 1997: 342)

Another mobile form of sound system, the Walkman, had a major impact when it was introduced during the 1980s, enabling the listener to maintain an individual private experience in public settings (see Gay *et al.*, 1997). 'Walkman', although a Sony Corporation trademark, became a popular generic term for what Michael Bull terms 'personal stereos' (Bull, 2000). As he documents, personal stereos allow their users to reappropriate place and time, with listeners regaining control of their auditory environments by blocking out undesirable surrounding noise (and people!). They also rearrange user's experience of time, especially while waiting or during travel. Both these factors were part of the appeal of later personal stereos, but with added refinements enabled by the availability of digital music. MP3 players created practices that were not possible with earlier personal stereos, such as the Walkman and the Discman, which were tied to physical music formats. The first portable MP3 player released in the US was the Rio, from Diamond Multimedia in 1998. Since then many more have appeared on the market, but the most successful and ubiquitous is the Sony iPod from Apple Computer, launched in October 2001.

The iPod has become the sound carrier and fashion accessory of the day, a cross between the Walkman and a hard drive used to store files on a computer. The iPod does not play music from physical formats such as cassettes or CDs, but holds it internally as digital data. The iPod is not the only digital music player, but it is the most popular of the brands now on the market. In terms of use, the advantages of the iPod are presented by its marketers and supporters as threefold. First, it can store a huge quantity of music (how much depends on the capacity of the model) and all you need to carry with you is a small, self-contained device; second, 'you can listen to whatever you want, wherever you are'; and, third, it can be connected up to home stereos or car stereos: 'you can have your entire music collection instantly accessible at home, at friends' houses, when you're driving – even on holiday' (Buckley and Clarke, 2005: 4–5). In addition, using the associated iTunes, the iPod opens up access to a huge range of music:

> You can play tracks downloaded from the Internet without having the hassle of burning a CD. You can instantly compile playlists of selected songs or albums. Or have your player select your music for you, picking tracks randomly from across your whole collection or just from albums of a particular genre.
>
> (ibid.)

The extensive popular and academic discussion surrounding the iPod is reminiscent of that which accompanied the music video in the 1980s. The iPod raises questions of marketing and design, mobility and agency, consumerism and the continued validity of the album format and associated notions of a musical canon (see Chapter 6 on this last point). The control associated with the Walkman is refined by the iPod, as the ability to create customized playlists enables listeners to create their own soundtracks. These can be used to accompany routine activities, with the selections geared to the activity, in terms of both mood generation and required duration. In his quirky take on Descartes, *iPod Therefore I Am*, Dylan Jones (2005) celebrates the ability of his portable device to connect his past musical experiences and to thereby construct a personal musical history. Large parts of the book are made up of song lists and fictional constructions of meetings with pop and rock stars that influenced his formative tastes – along with those of many of his readers. There are now a number of books offering guides to the construction of song lists of artists, styles, lyrical themes, etc., and many music magazines feature lists of the latest 'essential downloads'.

The iPod has collapsed the musical text with its production and consumption. Along with digital music more generally, it has made the ownership of a huge and eclectic music collection commonplace.

Further into the digital realm

As indicated in Chapter 1, digital music and the internet have had a revolutionary impact on popular music culture. Several key new technologies contributed to this: the advent of the MP3; a steady improvement (primarily through increased broadband) in the speed of personal computers to download/stream music, and the improved quality of this; and, as already discussed, new portable sound carriers, most notably the iPod. Together, these have enabled new modes of disseminating and storing music, along with new sites for accessing it on: social network sites; cloud services; YouTube. Collectively, these have created new practices of consumption (I shall return to these in more detail in Chapter 10).

MP3

A digital encoding format which became an international standard in 1991, MP3 is the standard encoding for the transfer (P2P) and playback of music on computer hard drives and on portable digital audio players, such as the iPod. The MP3 was designed for ease of use, universal compatibility and freedom of movement: it is a 'container technology' for recorded sound, whose shape and function are, by design, oriented toward free circulation (Sterne, 2006). MP3 files are small enough to make it practical to transfer (download) high-quality music files over the internet and store them: CD-quality tracks downloadable in minutes, with audio quality dependent on the size of the file. Hardly surprisingly, MP3 rapidly became very popular as a way in which to distribute and access music. By the end of the 1990s, it was widely claimed that 'MP3' had become the word most searched for on web search engines.

For consumers, MP3 enabled access to a great variety of music and they can selectively compile their own collections of songs by combining various tracks without having to download entire albums. For artists, MP3 meant they could distribute their music to a global audience without the mediation of the established music industry. Yet MP3 also raised concerns about potential loss of income and led to heated debates around copyright and access (see Chapter 1).

Downloading and P2P (file sharing)

Matthew David (2010: 2) defines file sharing as 'the circulation of compressed digital computer files over the Internet using an array of location and exchange software'. In his comprehensive and nuanced study of the phenomenon, he provides a historical and contemporary account of the issues (in the fields of law, technology and culture), associated with the ongoing conflict over file sharing, emphasizing 'the contradictions and conflicts within established economic relation, and the possible alternatives that are prefigured in the present' (164). The last include the promise of sharing the world's culture, 'making mediated reproduction truly universal' (168). By encouraging a de-commodification of informational goods, peer-to-peer file sharing took network technology in a radical new direction.

Cloud music services

Cloud music services are split into two categories: 'digital lockers', such as iTunes Match, Google Music and Amazon Cloud, which allow users to store their digital collections online and stream them to any computer or mobile device; and subscription services, such as Spotify, which provide unlimited streaming for just about any song ever made (Knopper, 2011–12). In Europe, Spotify charges a monthly fee of £4.99 (Spotify Unlimited) or £9.99 (Spotify Premium) for unlimited access to its catalogue of 15 million songs, with charges depending on the sound quality and features members require. You can also listen to to Spotify for free for up to 10 hours per month, if you are prepared to listen to advertisements before each song. Spotify's royalty payments to artists are small and, as a result, some recordings are not available on the service, including those of the Beatles, Led Zeppelin and Bob Dylan. Other artists only release their albums to Spotify after they have been out for a certain period of time.

Conclusion

The discourse surrounding music and technology embrace divergent views about creativity and musicianship, artistic freedom and property rights (copyright). New technologies can be seen as democratizing music production and consumption or consolidating established music industry hierarchies; disruptive of traditional distribution processes or rationalizing them; challenging or confirming legal definitions of music as property; and enabling or inhibiting new forms of creativity and authorship. These transcend national boundaries, separating music from the time, place and social context of its production.

Further reading

Chanan, M. (1995) *Repeated Takes: A Short History of Recording and its Effects on Music*, London: Verso.

Cunningham, M. (1996) *Good Vibrations: A History of Record Production*, Chessington: Castle Communications.

David, M. (2010) *Peer to Peer and the Criminalization of Sharing*, Los Angeles, London: Sage.

Eisenberg, E. (1988) *The Recording Angel: Music, Records and Culture From Aristotle to Zappa*, London: Pan Books.

Millard, A.J. (2005) *America on Record: A History of Recorded Sound*, 2nd edn. Cambridge: Cambridge University Press.

Sterne, J. (2006) 'The MP3 as Cultural Artifact', *New Media & Society*, 8, 5: 825–42.

Waksman, S. (1996) *Instrument of Desire: The Electric Guitar and the Shaping of Musical Experience*, Cambridge, MA: Harvard University Press.

Major recording studios are historically identified with particular producers, house bands and sounds; see:

Cogan, J. and Clark, W. (2003) *Temples of Sound. Inside the Great Recording Studios*, San Francisco: Chronicle Books.

Documentary series: Howard Goodall, Big Bang; episode summaries and press reviews www/howardgoodall.co.uk/presenting/20centurygts.htm

3 'I'm Just a Singer'

Making music, the rock musician and the success continuum

In addressing the question of how meaning is produced in popular music, a central role must be accorded to those who actually make the music. But this is not to simply accept the 'creative artist' view of the production of cultural products, which sees 'art' as the product of the creative individual, largely unencumbered by politics and economics. Those involved in making music clearly exercise varying degrees of personal autonomy, but this is circumscribed by the available technologies and expertise, by economics and by the expectations of their audience. It is a question of the dynamic interrelationship of the production context, the texts and their creators and the audience for the music.

This chapter is concerned with the nature of music making and the roles and relative status of those who make music, primarily, but not exclusively musicians. While they are credited as the authors of their recordings, their ability to 'make music' is, to varying extents, dependent on the input of other industry personnel, including session musicians, song writers, record producers, sound engineers and mixers, along with those who regulate access to the infrastructure of the industry (such as venue owners, promoters).

For reasons of space, and reflecting their historical prominence, I am largely concerned with 'mainstream' rock and, to a lesser extent, pop, and the demarcations present within their musical production as sounds. I also focus on musicians seeking, at least ideally and in part, to make a living from their work. Other genres, notably disco and dance music, and 'musicians' such as the contemporary dance DJ, subvert many of the traditional assumptions of the 'rock formation' about the nature of musicianship (see Straw, 1999).

My discussion begins with the initial creation of a musical text. For performers 'starting out', this is through learning to first play one's instrument and reproduce existing songs, a form of musical apprenticeship. If the intention is to move beyond this, attention then turns to songwriting and the 'working up' of an original composition, for performance and (possibly) recording. The role of the producer is central to the preparation of the musical text as a material product – the sound recording. I then consider the role of live performance, with reference to the issue of authenticity and some of the situations live music occurs in. The final part of the chapter considers the differing roles and status of those who create music. I examine the distinctions frequently used by musicians themselves, as well as critics and fans, to label various performers. There is an obvious hierarchy of values at work here, both between and within various categories, and in the discourse around the application of terms such as creativity and authenticity.

Making music

As most biographies demonstrate, the career trajectory of popular musicians involves skill and hard work, not to mention a certain amount of luck. Our detailed knowledge of this process, of how performers actually create their music and attempt to create an audience for their efforts, was initially sparse. Writing in 1990, Sara Cohen's summary of the available literature observed that there had been a lack of ethnographic or participant observer study of the process of making music:

> What is particularly lacking in the literature (on rock) is ethnographic data and micro sociological detail. Two other important features have been omitted: the grassroots of the industry – the countless, as yet unknown bands struggling for success at a local level – and the actual process of music making by rock bands.
>
> (Cohen, 1991: 6)

In addition to Cohen's *Rock Culture in Liverpool*, there are now a handful of 'classic' accounts (including Finnegan, 1989; Shank, 1994), along with more contemporary studies of musicians involved in particular genres and local musical scenes (Fonarow, 2006; Stahl, 2011), and a large body of biographical profiles of varying usefulness (among the more informative are Cantin, 1997; Cross, 2005). To these we can add several compendiums of reflections from musicians (including Pollock, 2002; Shute, 2005); a number of producer autobiographies (for instance Boyd, 2006; Stock, 2004); in-depth studies of the making of particular recordings (such as Berkenstadt and Cross, 1998, on Nirvana's album *Nevermind*); and several insightful discussions of musical creativity (Negus and Pickering, 2005; Toynbee, 2000). I have drawn on these, and similar work, in the following discussion.

The 'musician'

To begin with, the term 'musician' is not as straightforward as it seems. Ruth Finnegan, in her study of music making in Milton Keynes, found it difficult to distinguish 'amateur' from 'professional' musicians:

> local bands sometimes contained many players in full-time (non-musical) jobs and others whose only regular occupation was their music; yet in giving performances, practising, sharing out the fees and identification with the group, the members were treated exactly alike (except for the inconvenience

of those in jobs that had to plead illness or take time off work if they travelled to distant bookings).

(Finnegan, 1989: 13)

Furthermore, the local musicians tended to use 'professional' in an evaluative rather than an economic sense, to refer to a player's standard of performance, musical knowledge and qualifications and regular appearances with musicians themselves regarded as professional. Later studies (Fonarow, 2006; Shank, 1994; Shute, 2005), and my own conversations with local musicians, also demonstrate this more expansive use of the term. Since the end of the 1950s, the demarcation between performer, songwriter and producer has gradually become blurred. Currently, while the three roles can be distinct, the term musician frequently embraces all three activities.

The realities of practice

There are still few formal study or apprenticeship programmes for aspiring popular musicians, in sharp contrast to the opportunities for classical and jazz instrumentalists. Learning the required musical skills takes time and perseverance as well as inclination and talent:

> The hardest thing to dawn on us was that if you practise a lot you get better a lot faster. I didn't realize that maybe there was a big distance between an hour and five hours of practice a day. We went through a transitional stage from being proud of being a garage band to really seeing the limitations and wanting to take it one step further.
>
> (Dan Zanes, guitarist, cited in Pollock, 2002: 30–31)

Even the proficiency of a 'genius' like Jimi Hendrix has its pragmatic foundation:

> Practising his guitar was the central activity of Jimi's life that year [1962]. He went to bed practising, he slept with the guitar on his chest, and the first thing he did upon rising was to start practising again. In an effort to find even more time to practise, he occasionally bought cheap amphetamines so he could stay up all night.
>
> (Cross, 2005: 98–9)

Stith Bennett's detailed early account of 'The Realities of Practice', showed that learning a song for most rock musicians was a process of 'copying a recording by playing along with it and using the technical ability to play parts of it over and over again' (Bennett, 1990: 224). The two Liverpool punk bands that Cohen studied demonstrated a complex process of musical composition, rehearsal and performance. Their creative process was typically incremental and participatory (Cohen, 1991). Later (auto-) biographical accounts of rock musicians, and various documentaries on the making of particular recordings, show a similar process at work. Reflecting the limitations of conventional notation when applied to rock music, little use is made of sheet music: 'It's so simple just to get things off the record, sheet music is just for people who can't hear' (piano player, cited in Bennett: 1990: 227). Composition and song copying initially takes place in private, with the next step the expansion of the song-getting experience to the group situation – transforming the song into a performable entity   and its extension to the creation of 'sets' of songs. These blocks of material, usually consisting of 10 to 15 songs to be played over a live set, are constructed for specific audiences and contexts (gigs) and, as such, usually represent a compromise between what bands want to play, what audiences want to hear and what is marketable.

Songwriting

With its romantic connotations of creativity and authenticity, composition is at the heart of discourses surrounding authorship in popular music. Examples of artistic and commercial success frequently accord song writing a key place:

> Kurt Cobain's ability to write songs with such strong hooks was the crucial ingredient in Nirvana's eventual world wide appeal. The melodies he wrote were so memorable, people found themselves singing along without even knowing or understanding the lyrics.
>
> (Berkenstadt and Cross, 1998: 63)

A canonical metalist of 'the top 30 albums' shows that, with one exception, all were composed by the musicians responsible for the recording (see Chapter 6). That exception was the Beach Boys *Pet Sounds*, for which Peter Asher contributed most of the lyrics.

While composing popular music can encompass several modes, such as the bricolage of electronic practices underpinning dance music, I am interested here in songwriting in mainstream, chart-oriented rock and pop music. In comparison with the writing or other roles in the music industry, and the nature of the creative process in popular music, the role of the songwriter initially received only limited attention. Published work has concentrated on song composition and the process of songwriting, and the contributions of leading songwriters (see Flanaghan, 1987; Thompson, G., 2008; Zollo, 1997) and there are numerous personal accounts of the process of songwriting. For example, Paul McCartney's recollections of his collaboration with John Lennon (Miles, 1997), Mike Stock's account of his work as part of the Stock Aitken Waterman production team (Stock, 2004); and Cantin's discussion of the collaboration between Alanis Morissette and Greg Ballard:

> she would sit on the floor. Ballard would perch on a chair. They'd both take acoustic guitars and fool around with melodies and lyrical ideas and see what

happened. When they really got rolling, Alanis would fall into a kind of trance-like state.

(Cantin, 1997: 126)

Keith Richards recollections of his composition of the well-known guitar riff for the Rolling Stones' 'Satisfaction', provides another example to illustrate the at times almost 'unworldly' nature of musical creativity:

> I wrote 'Satisfaction' in my sleep. I had no idea I'd written it, it's only thank God for the little Phillips cassette player. The miracle being that I looked at the cassette player next morning and I knew I'd put a brand-new tape in the previous night, and I saw it was at the end. Then I pushed rewind and there was 'Satisfaction'. It was just a rough idea. There was just the bare bones of the song.
>
> (Richards, 2010: 176)

Such accounts place songwriting in the realm of romantic views of creativity, but this must be tempered with an appreciation of the social conditions under which it takes place and the sheer graft involved:

> But it wasn't easy. The secret of our success lay in hard work, long hours and those magical 'eureka' moments. Our success rate didn't happen by accident. We knew exactly what we were doing on each record and, having discussed the artist and the song, we understood the audience we were trying to reach.
>
> (Stock, 2004: 100)

Songwriters have historically exercised considerable influence over artists/ styles. In the 1950s Leiber and Stoller got an unprecedented deal with Atlantic to write and produce their own songs; the resulting collaborations with performers such as the Drifters and Ben E. King produced sweet soul, a very self-conscious marriage of R&B and classical instruments, notably the violin. In the 1960s Holland, Dozier and Holland contributed to the development of the distinctive Motown sound. In the 1970s Chin and Chapman composed over 50 British top 10 hits in association with producers Mickie Most and Phil Wainman, 'using competent bar bands (Mud, Sweet) on to whom they could graft a style and image'(Hatch and Millward, 1987: 141), to produce highly commercial power pop, glitter rock and dance music. In the 1970s Stock, Aiken, Waterman wrote and produced successful dance pop for performers such as Kylie Minogue: 'Down at the Hit Factory, Matt and I were the band and the singers were the guest vocalists. The songs were doing the selling and the artists were an adjunct' (Stock, 2004: 100).

During the late 1950s and early 1960s a factory model of songwriting, combined with a strong aesthetic sense, was evident in the work of a group of songwriters (and music publishers) in New York's Brill Building. Incorporating

Tin Pan Alley's melodic and lyrical trademarks into R&B, the group included a number of successful songwriting teams: the more pop-oriented Goffin and King; Mann and Weil; and Barry and Greenwich; the R&B-oriented Pomus and Shuman; and Leiber and Stoller. Several also produced, most notably Phil Spector, Bert Berns, and Leiber and Stoller, who wrote and produced most of the Coasters hits. One factor that distinguished these songwriters was their youth: mainly in their late teens or early twenties, with several married couples working together, the Brill Building songwriters were well able to relate to and interpret teenage dreams and concerns, especially the search for identity and romance. These provided the themes for many of the songs they wrote, especially those performed by the teen idols and girl groups of the period. Pomus and Shuman, and Leiber and Stoller also wrote some of Elvis Presley's best material.

Collectively, the Brill Building songwriters were responsible for a large number of chart successes and had an enduring influence (Shaw, 1992). London in the 1960s had its own group of successful pop and rock songwriters (see Thompson, 2005: Chapter 5, for a detailed discussion of their work and influence). The role of such songwriters, however, was challenged by the emergence of a tradition of self-contained groups or performers writing their own songs (most notably the Beatles), which weakened the traditional professional songwriting market.

Professional songwriters are now more visible, often also producing, working with or for the proliferation of manufactured pop performers. Among the most successful examples of this process was 'Can't Get You Out of My Head' (2002). Written by Cathy Denis and Rob Davis for Kylie Minogue, the song topped the charts internationally, revived Minogue's career and the two songwriters won the British 2002 Ivor Novello Award.

Singer-songwriters

Some songwriters have been accorded auteur status, in several cases after initially writing for others and later recording their own material (e.g. Carole King: *Tapestry*, Ode, 1971; Neil Diamond; Jackson Browne; Joni Mitchell). The term 'singer-songwriter' has been given to artists who both write and perform their material and who are able to perform solo, usually on acoustic guitar or piano. An emphasis on lyrics has resulted in the work of such performers often being referred to as song poets, accorded auteur status and made the subject of intensive lyric analysis. The folk music revival in the 1960s saw several singer-songwriters come to prominence: Joan Baez, Donavon, Phil Ochs and, above all, Bob Dylan. Singer-songwriters were a strong 'movement' in the 1970s, including Neil Young, James Taylor, Joni Mitchell, Jackson Browne and Joan Armatrading; most are still performing and recording. In the 1980s the appellation singer-songwriter was applied to, among others, Bruce Springsteen and Elvis Costello; in the 1990s to Tori Amos, Suzanne Vega, Tracy Chapman and Toni Child; and more recently to performers such as Dido, David Gray, Lucinda Williams and Taylor Swift. The female predominance here led some observers to equate the 'form' with women performers, due to its emphasis on lyrics and performance rather than the indulgences associated with male-dominated styles of rock music. The application of the term to solo performers is awkward, in that most of those mentioned usually perform with 'backing' bands and at times regard themselves as an integral part of these. Nonetheless, the concept of singer-songwriter continues to have strong connotations of greater authenticity and 'true' authorship.

Once a song is composed, even if only in a limited form (partial lyrics, a melody or a riff to build on), it becomes 'worked up' for live performance and recording. Beyond creating a distinctive musical sound and original material, successful performers must also develop the different skills required of the live and studio recording settings. The way bands operate in the recording studio, or in home studios, until recently received limited attention in popular music studies, although is frequently the focus of accounts in the music press (and see the website for the Association for the Study of Sound Recording: see Further reading). It is a process that brings the role of the producer to the fore.

The producer

The occupation of producer emerged as a distinct job category and career path in the popular music industry during the 1950s, initially as someone who directed and supervised recording sessions and who also frequently doubled as sound engineer (e.g. Sam Phillips at Sun Records). Successful producers, such as song-writers Jerry Leiber and Mike Stoller at Atlantic, and George Martin at EMI, began exerting pressure on their recording companies to receive credits (on recordings) and royalties, rather than just a flat fee. By the mid-1960s, the studio producer had become an auteur figure, an artist employing multi-track technology and stereo sound to make their own mark on recordings, rather than simply documenting the musicians' performance. The most prominent examples of this new status were Jerry Wexler (primarily for his recordings of Aretha Franklin and Ray Charles), George Martin (primarily for his work with the Beatles), Leiber and Stoller and Phil Spector (see his profile in Chapter 4). In the UK, the work of Joe Meek acquired cult status (see Thompson, G., 2008: Chapter 2). During the 1970s and 1980s, the important role of producers as cultural intermediaries was consolidated with the development of new technology: synthesisers, samplers, and computer-based sequencing systems: 'Of course, technology helped. By the late 1980s we were using 48-track recording facilities and filling virtually every track ourselves' (Stock, 2004: 101). Producers became central figures in genres such as dub and techno and, above all, with disco and dance pop.

The way in which producers operate, their contribution to the session and the level of reward they are accorded vary widely, depending on the stature of the musicians they are working with and the type of music being recorded. Producers approaches to recording vary from the naturalistic, 'try it and see what happens', to a more calculated, entrepreneurial attitude. Production practices represent an amalgam of established techniques and the possibilities offered by the new technologies and a number of autobiographical accounts insightfully reveal the processes at work here (e.g. Boyd, 2006). Virgil Moorefield (2005) documents how recording has gone from being primarily a technical to an artistic matter, with the contemporary producer as auteur.

Live performance

Live music has been a central aspect of popular music, in its various forms operating to create audiences, to fuel individual fantasy and pleasure and to create popular music icons and cultural myths. Investigating the processes involved in how performance communicates musical meaning to its constituent audiences in different contexts has been a significant part of popular music scholarship, especially in relation to genres such as rock (Pattie, 2007), EDM and jazz. Elsewhere in this study, I have considered the significance of the live sector in terms of income (see Chapter 1) and state regulation of live music (Chapter 14). Here, I consider its role in giving – or not giving – musical credibility (or authenticity) to performers and genres; and to how it occurs in particular settings/venues: concerts, tours and festivals.

The equation of live performance with musical authenticity and 'paying your dues' as a performer remains a widely held ideology among fans, musicians and record company executives. Once a band or performer has 'learned' some music, assuming ambition and confidence, they will usually seek to perform live in public. Such performances take place in a range of informal and formal settings and social situations and are closely related to different valuations of authorship and authenticity (depending on the genre/performers involved). Live music is experienced in venues such as clubs, discos and pubs; and through concerts and music festivals.

'Pseudo-live' performances take place at one remove, as it were, from the original or actual performance and are usually experienced through intermediary technology: on film and television or in one of the various recorded formats via radio and sound reproduction systems, the internet or web broadcasts. The pseudo-live experience of music is not usually in the same time frame as the original performance, although this can be the case with radio and satellite TV linkups with 'live' events.

For both fans and musicians, there is a perceived hierarchy of such performances, with a marked tendency to equate an audiences' physical proximity to the actual 'performance' and intimacy with the performer(s) with a more authentic and satisfying musical experience.

Historically, prior to the advent of recorded sound, all music was live and was experienced as such. The term 'live' performance is now usually reserved for those situations in which the audience is in physical proximity to the performance and the experience of the music is contiguous with its actual performance.

This view was central to the ideology of 'rock' created during the 1960s. This emphasis on the 'live' as a key signifier of musical authenticity has since been undermined by performers who work primarily, and at times exclusively, in the studio setting. Some genres are now largely studio creations, especially recent styles of techno.

At times, performance events ('gigs', concerts, festivals) have had the capacity to encapsulate and represent key periods and turning points in popular music; examples include the first performance of the modernist composer Stravinsky's *Rite of Spring* (1919), the Beatles' first appearance on the *Ed Sullivan Show* (1964) and Bob Dylan 'going electric' at the Newport Folk Festival (1965). Their significance is indicated by their use in a cultural shorthand fashion among fans, musicians and writers; e.g. 'Woodstock', with an assumed set of connotations: the counterculture, music festivals, youth and 1960s' idealism. Such performances and their participants – promoters, musicians and audiences – are commonly celebrated in the musical press, documentaries and are the subject of several studies (Inglis, 2006).

Playing live is important to develop and trial new material and to popularize and promote recordings, especially on their initial release. It is also central to rock ideology, with its connotations of authorship and creativity, and the physical energy, emotional tension and release associated with live acts:

> That's what keeps you going. Those two hours on stage where everybody's in complete sync and it's like the universe is perfect. There's no flaw in the universe until the next morning. And then you can't find your breakfast and you gotta travel twelve hours in a day [to the next gig].
>
> (Joe Ely, in Pollock, 2002: 111)

Club gigs

Clubs and pubs remain the main venues for live music on a regular and continuing basis. Both serve as training grounds for aspiring performers operating at the local level, and provide a 'bread and butter' living for more established artists, often through being part of an organized 'circuit' of venues. Club appearances include 'showcase' evenings, similar to variety style concerts, with a number of performers featured; 'one-nighters', and extended engagements. All are important for gaining experience in live work, building an audience and making contacts in the music industry. Clubs also remain the main site for most music fans' engagement with live music, particularly in smaller towns not on the national concert itinerary of touring performers.

Clubs have historically assumed mythic importance for breaking new acts, as in the 1960s with the Who at the Marquee in London and the Doors at the Whisky in LA. They can also establish and popularize trends and musical genres, as in the 1970s with American punk at New York's Max's and CBGBs, Cleveland's Clockwork Orange and the Viking Saloon, English punk at London's 100 Club and the Roxy and Manchester's Electric Circus; and disco in the 1980s, DJ culture and techno and its various genres in the 1990s and indie rock.

Where there is not a strong club scene, pubs will sometimes take on the same role. In the process, they can legitimate a particular sound and performance ethos. In Australia, the strongly masculine 'Oz Rock' historically dominated the 1980s music scene and was defined by its association with the pub circuit there. A local network of clubs or pub venues can foster a local scene and arguably create a 'local' sound (see Chapter 11).

Tours and concerts

As with club and pub gigs, concerts, usually part of a tour, expose performers and their music to potential fans and purchasers, building an image and a following. Tours were important historically, for helping 'break' English bands in the US during the 1960s and remained a crucial part of the national and international music industry. During the 1990s purely promotional 'tours' became significant in building a fan base, for example Shania Twain's shopping mall stops in 1993–1994; and the importation of name DJs from the UK was a major factor in consolidating the international dance music scene in Australia and New Zealand in the past decade. As indicated in Chapter 1, tours currently represent a major income stream for musicians and the music industry.

The nature of tour concerts is an oddly ambivalent one. On the one hand, for the fan, it is a rare opportunity to see a performer, especially if you live in locations where the opportunity may be literally a once in a lifetime one. On the other hand, for the performer, each concert blurs into a series of 'one-night stands' and the challenge is to maintain freshness at each performance. Tour books, band biographies and music magazine profiles, and many classic rock songs document 'life on the road', with its attendant excesses and exhilaration at audience enthusiasm coupled with fatigue:

> It's funny; the road's like that. You never know what to expect. Especially when you're out of the country and you have all of these communication problems. You have transportation problems, and problems with the food and hotel reservations, and then you hit these places in the middle of nowhere and it turns into a memorable night.
>
> (Joe Ely, in Pollock, 2002: 112–13)

Concerts are complex cultural phenomena, involving a mix of music and economics, ritual and pleasure, for both performers and their audience. Different genres and performance styles create different forms of concert experience. Clearly, a slickly lit and choreographed boy or girl band pop concert is a different visual and aural experience from a drum and bass DJ's presentation in a club. At the heart of concerts is the sense of community that they engender, albeit a transient one. At their head, by way of contrast, lie economics and promotion.

The backstage area of the larger rock concerts is a highly complex work site, with a range of specialized workers. The number of personnel reflects the size of the tour and the economic importance of the performers, but can include technicians in charge of the instruments and equipment (amplifiers, etc.); stage-hands, often doubling as 'roadies', people to work the sound and lighting boards, security guards and the concert tour manager. The successful operation of the backstage area at concerts involves the integration of these workers into a stable and impersonal time schedule, where each person does their job as and when required. The scope of this task, at its most extreme, is shown in the documentary *Rock in Rio*, on the staging of the Rolling Stones free concert in Rio De Janeiro in 2006, with an estimated audience of almost two million.

There still exists a clear hierarchy of rock and pop tours and concerts. For a relatively unknown act, seeking to publicize a new or first release and create an audience, opportunities for live work will be few and venues will usually be small. The pub and university campus circuit remains essential for such performers. The scale of most 'national' tours is actually often localized, 'hitting' only a dozen or so urban centres. For established visiting bands and local acts, which have 'broken' into the charts and the marketplace, there are larger scale 'national' tours. These still largely play selected main centres, where venues and audiences are large enough to (hopefully) make the exercise economic. At the top end of the scale are the global tours of the top international acts, which are massive exercises in logistics and marketing – and also hugely profitable. The Rolling Stones' 2006 Tour, with more than 100 shows staged over half the world, involved effectively having three stage sets being shipped and flown at the same time and the band's entourage included 125 technical staff.

Tours remain central to creating consumer interest and sales and are about promotion as much as performance. Where artists once took part in radio and TV shows and made personal appearances at record stores, they are now more likely to appear on talk shows and via internet social network sites. Currently, the importance of revenue from the live sector has seen a proliferation of large-scale tours, undertaken by leading performers such as U2, Bruce Springsteen and Taylor Swift. As the music press indicates, a wide range of per-formers are on tour at any particular time, often coming together for the major festivals held during summer holiday seasons, especially in the UK, Western Europe and North America.

Festivals

There is an established historical tradition of popular music festivals, with regular events such as the Newport Folk and Jazz Festivals and the New Orleans Mardi Gras in the US and the UK's Cambridge Folk Festival. Festivals play a central role in popular music mythology. They keep traditions alive, maintaining and expanding their audience base, legitimating particular forms of that tradition and giving its performers and their fans a sense of shared, communal identity. This role has been maintained through historical retrospectives and anniversary cele-brations, as with the recent 40th anniversary of the 1969 Woodstock festival, which saw the (re-)release of a number of celebratory books, documentary films and recordings.

A number of festivals at the end of the 1960s and in the early 1970s helped create the notion of a youth-oriented rock counterculture, while confirming its commercial potential: Monterey, 1967; Woodstock, 1969; the Isle of Wight, 1970. The 1980s saw the reassertion of the music festival, with the success – both financially and as ideological touchstones – of the politically motivated 'conscience concerts': Live Aid, 1985 (see Chapter 12) and the various Amnesty International concerts. A summer festival season is now a feature of the UK, Europe and North America music calendars. The festivals usually include a range of performers, often spread across several days on multiple stages. In the face of an attractive range of choices facing fans, festivals often place an emphasis on a particular musical style, a grouping of artists aimed at attracting a particular fan constituency.

Since the early 1990s France has been the European leader in terms of the number and scale of festivals, including a variety of music, dance and theatre events. In 2006 French rock and pop music festivals had a combined audience of over 1.6 million people, including upwards of 650,000 at the Festival Interceltique de L'Orient, an 'ethnic' Celtic event launched in 2001 in Brittany. Barbara Lebrun identifies a tight regulatory system that codifies such festivals, 'whose structural and economic rigidity is somewhat at odds with the experience of them by audiences (and artists and critics) as places of instability' (Lebrun, 2009: 136). As her analysis demonstrates, popular music festivals are subject to a series of contradictions and inconsistencies, placing them at the intersection of commercial imperatives and 'alternative' authenticity.

The major festivals, such as Glastonbury and Knebworth (now Sonisphere) in the UK, are big business, while local communities are using (usually smaller-scale) music festivals as a form of cultural tourism. In addition to their economic importance, music festivals, as a form of extended concert, reinforce popular music personas, creating icons and myths in the process. The performers are made 'accessible' to those attending the festival and, increasingly with large-scale festivals via satellite television and documentary films, to a national and even a worldwide audience. At the same time as it forms a temporary community, joined in celebration and homage to the performers/the genre, the festival audience is being created as a commodity. If it attracts the projected audience, the festival is a major commercial enterprise, with on-site sales of food and souvenirs, the income from the associated television broadcasts via satellite to a global audience/ market and the subsequent 'live' recordings, for example from Knebworth and Rock in Rio. In sum, music festivals are sites at which commerce and popular ideology interact to produce historically significant musical meanings.

The different aspects of live music were fruitfully brought together in a three-year team research project in the UK (2008–2010): 'The Promotion of Live Music – A Historical, Cultural and Institutional Analysis'. This included a wide range of musical events, venues and genres, exploring live music 'both as a social event and aesthetic experience, and as something produced in the context of legal and state regulations and economic and marketing strategies' (Frith, 2011).

I turn now to the discourse surrounding various perceived categories of musician, primarily 'rock' musicians, and the hierarchy of value frequently attached to these. Popular music is, for the majority of its participants, an essentially 'amateur' or 'quasi-professional' activity that may become a career option. Indeed, the great majority of people who make their living playing music live near the poverty line. In the late 1990s there were said to be 10,000 functional bands in the greater Los Angeles area alone, 'all slugging it out night after night in a never-ending cacophony of competition, strategic repositioning, and reconfiguration' (Kirschner, 1998: 250).

Writing in 1988, Simon Frith identified a traditional model of the rock music career, which he termed the 'Rock', involving a career process that was established in the 1960s. Musicians started at the base of this pyramid model, working the local scene through clubs and pubs, building up a following. They then might move up through several tiers, first, to regional live work, recording for small, indie labels and gaining success and recognition at the regional level. Beyond this were a major recording contract, with national exposure and hits and touring. At the highest level, there are international hits, tours, media exposure and 'superstar' status. He regarded this model as underpinned by a dynamic and ideology emphasizing 'a Horatio Alger-type account of success being *earned* by hard work, determination, and skills *honed* in practice' (Frith, 1988: 112). However, Frith was concerned that while there were still careers (e.g. U2) that followed this model, the 1980s' corporatization of the music business and the key role of video in selling new pop groups had seen the rise of an alternative success story:

> The Talent Pool: The dynamic here comes from the centre. There are no longer gatekeepers regulating the flow of stardom, but multi nationals 'fishing' for material, pulling ideas, sounds, styles, performers from the talent pool and dressing them up for world wide consumption.
>
> (ibid.: 113)

MTV, which began in 1981, played a major part in this (see Chapter 8).

As Frith acknowledged, the two models are ideal types. During the 1990s, there was both a reassertion of the significance of the traditional model and a merging of the two career paths. While video exposure remained important, it no longer had the status it enjoyed in the mid-1980s. Genre is a factor here, with clear differences between the success routes for 1990s' dance pop bands, such as the Spice Girls and S Club 7, and alternative and grunge performers in the early 1990s and beyond. For the latter, as the Seattle scene indicated, success at the local and regional level, or nationally on a smaller scale, with a niche or cult audience, on 'independent' labels and via college radio and the club scene, was necessary to attract the attention of the major record companies. Over the past 15 years, the proliferation of pop and rock reality TV shows have provided fresh example of Frith's talent pool at work. At the same time, the 'Rock' model of hard work, self-belief perseverance and live performance remains applicable to genres such as indie rock and some styles of electronic dance music and is also evident in the careers of performers such as Lady Gaga.

Creating and working-up new musical material for performance, studio and home recording and touring, and once again back to creating and recording to keep the momentum going, is the musicians' work cycle. Furthermore, musical skills are not all that is involved. While the original basis of most groups is in peer friendships, this will change once things get 'more serious', with problems created by the differing levels of ability and commitment of group members and commitment to a practice schedule and the need for group cohesion and leadership:

> Being successful definitely put a whole lot of pressure because the band was so communally oriented. People joined the band just 'cause of the vibe of the music. What happened once the money and the fame got involved was that everybody wanted their own manager, so everyone got management, everyone got lawyers, and everything got very complicated.
>
> (Speech from Arrested Development, in Pollock, 2002: 96)

Then there are the well-documented physical and emotional strains of 'the rock/pop lifestyle', amply illustrated in many popular memoirs of drugs, sex and music (e.g. Kiedis, 2004; Richards, 2010), and its growing list of casualties (most recently Whitney Houston, Amy Winehouse and Michael Jackson).

One reason, and probably the dominant one, behind the willingness of so many musicians to enter the Darwinian struggle for commercial success is the ultimate possibility of stardom, with its allure of a lifestyle of glamour and affluence. This is not to ignore the appeal of gaining the approval of fans and critics, but it is clear that the majority of performers aspire to that *and* 'the money'. As Tony Kirschner (1998: 252) observes, 'Success should be seen as a central trope in popular music, informing and motivating the entire domain of rock culture' and creating what he terms the 'continuum of success'. Talent aside, success is governed by access to the differing resources and opportunities available for making music. Accordingly, our interest now moves to the 'pecking order' of popular music.

The success continuum

There exists a status hierarchy among performers, especially evident in rock music, a hierarchy endorsed by critics and fans, as well as by musicians themselves. This hierarchy ranges from those starting out, largely reliant on 'covers', to session musicians, to performers who attempt, with varying levels of critical and commercial success, to make a living from music. This last group has its own differentiations, with tribute bands, house bands and notions of 'journeymen' players. There are hierarchies of 'artists' and stars, often likened to some sort of sports league table: a minor or major league band; first and second division performers; stars and 'megastars'; and supergroups. The bases for such evaluations are vague and the status of particular performers frequently varies among critics and over time. Taste and subjectivity necessarily feature, as much as any elaborated artistic and musical criteria.

Cover bands

At the base of this hierarchy are cover bands, which are often accorded little critical artistic weight. A common view is that reliance on someone else's material concedes that you have nothing of your own to say. However, playing covers fulfills aesthetic, educational and economic roles. Some covers, as I shall show in Chapter 5, take the original recording as a starting point and modify, reinvent or subvert it in a creative manner. Bands starting out rely on cover versions for a large part of their repertoire out of necessity, mastering them as part of a learning process. Even 'original' performers will usually play a few covers. The distinction between 'cover' and 'original' is important, since upward career mobility is directly tied to notions of originality (Kirschner, 1998: 265). Learning such songs is part of the apprenticeship process in acquiring musicianship through engaging with a musical tradition. An example is the development of 'rock' in England in the 1960s through local bands covering imported copies of American rhythm and blues hits, as with the Rolling Stones' versions of Arthur Alexander's 'You Better Move On' (1966) and Solomon Burke's 'Everybody Need Somebody To Love' (1965). Cover songs are literally music to the ears of the managers of smaller venues like clubs and pubs, as they are tapping into a proven product that the audience can identify with. For each new generation of listeners, a 'good' song is a good song, regardless of any historical memory.

Tribute bands

The extreme example of cover bands are those performers who not only directly model themselves on established bands, but actually copy them, presenting themselves as simulacra of the originals. Such tribute bands, as the industry prefers to call them, rate few plaudits artistically, but they have become big business, with several enjoying lengthy and successful careers (Homan, 2006). Australian band Björn Again, primarily performing the music of Swedish band, Abba, had played over 1500 shows in some 40 countries worldwide by 2000, and undertook a highly successful 10th anniversary world tour in 1999.

There are hundreds of tribute bands internationally, imitating almost everyone from defunct groups such as CCR, the Beatles and the Ramones, to bands that are still performing, such as Metallica. On the positive side, the imitators are bringing the music to a new, younger audience, a generation who never saw the original performers, encouraging them to seek out the earlier material. Other views are less complimentary, pointing to the difficulties in policing copyright and the fact that the original artists are frequently having to share audiences with their imitators. The main objection made to the nostalgia and cover bands, however, is that they generally do not create new music. Ironically, the same charge has not been levelled at the industry's tendency since the 1990s to produce a steady stream of 'tribute' albums, in which various artists pay homage by covering the work of artists as varied as the Clash, Gram Parsons and Jimi Hendrix.

Session musicians and house bands

Generally anonymous, session musicians are the pieceworkers of the music industry, yet their role is more important than is usually recognized. The label is a generic one, referring 'to a range of practices, all of which involve the participation of a musician in a recording session featuring an artist or band with which the session musician does not regularly perform' (Bowman, 2003: 104). The emergence of session musicians as musical labour was historically tied to greater professionalism and spiralling costs of recording sessions. During the 1960s music centres such as Nashville, New York and London, developed highly competitive session musician scenes, with a select group of players able to make a lucrative living playing sessions. The role could be a demanding one:

> To be a session musician, one was generally expected to be able to sight-read musical notation quickly and accurately, to be able to transpose a part from one key to another instantly, to be able to play in a wide range of styles and emulate the licks, techniques and stylistic nuances of other notable instrumentalists, and, in some genres, to be able to continuously develop appropriate and catchy grooves, riffs and lines for recording after recording.
>
> (Bowman, 2003: 105)

Some session musicians attain critical recognition for their contributions. Reggae performers Sly Dunbar and Robbie Shakespeare established themselves as 'the' rhythm section and keyboard player Billy Preston is credited, along with the Beatles (the only time they shared authorship), for their single *Get Back*. The efforts of a few session musicians attain near legendary status, as with Jeff Beck and Jimmy Page's guitar solos on a variety of records in the 1960s, but usually only when they later become successful in their own right, creating interest in this aspect of their back catalogue. Session musicians continue to be widely used, with their contribution to recordings now usually indicated by their inclusion on the album credits.

House bands are the backing musicians used by particular record labels at a majority of their recording sessions, usually drawn from leading session musicians in an area. Their emergence was also linked to increased musical specialization and studio costs, as well as studio recording convenience. The practice began with jazz in Chicago in the 1920s and was revived by rock music in the 1960s. Several house bands, such as Booker T and the MGs, at Stax in Memphis, received considerable credit for their creative input. Others, equally talented, tended to remain more in the background, as with the Funk Brothers at Motown in Detroit.

Current trends

There are several types of group that have become more prominent recently: revival, or reunion bands; supergroups; and virtual bands. Each would be worth further investigation but can only briefly be referred to here.

Revival/'reunion' bands

These are performers who have reformed to tour and, at times, to record. At times their credibility and authenticity have been questioned, as their line-up no longer includes key members. For example, still touring Creedence Clearwater Revisited include the bassist and drummer from the original 1960s' band (Creedence Clearwater Revival), but are minus its central figure, singer-guitarist-songwriter John Fogerty. The trend is not confined to 'classic rock' bands, as in the 2000s, a number of alternative bands have already reformed to exploit the nostalgia market and the current prominence of live music, among them Suede, the Pixies and Soundgarden. Once prominent pop acts such as the Spice Girls and Take That have also briefly re-formed and toured.

There are obvious opportunities offered by the name recognition the members of such groups bring to the marketplace. Longevity can be considered a factor here. Surviving performers have aged along with their earlier fan base, for whom seeing them/buying their new recordings functions as a form of homage and a celebration: 'I'm still standing and so are they', as I heard one fan observe at a Leonard Cohen concert, when Cohen, aged 76, undertook a global tour in 2010–11.

Supergroups

Consisting of well-known musicians from several established, at times no longer active, bands, coming together to record and perform, a 'supergroup' as a notion is hardly new and dates back at least to the 1960s with Cream, which brought together Eric Clapton, formerly with the Yardbirds and John Mayall's Blues-breakers, on lead guitar; Jack Bruce, from Manfred Mann, on bass and Ginger Baker from Graham Bond's Organisation, on drums. The blues rock power trio enjoyed a short-lived but very successful career. Later similar collaborations included the Traveling Wilburys (1988–90), whose members included Bob Dylan, George Harrison, Roy Orbison and Tom Petty. Current 'supergroups' include SUPERHEAVY (Mick Jagger, Dave Stewart, Joss Stone, Damian 'Jr Gong' Marley, A.R. Rahman); the Good, the Bad, and the Queen; the Dead Weather; and Chickenfoot. At times, such collaborations have produced critically well-received live performances and recordings, as with SUPERHEAVY's 2011 album (SUPERHEAVY, A&M Records, 2011). As with reunion bands, name recognition is a factor with the marketing of these groups, although there is the added weight of expectation on these performers to produce 'new music', rather than simply replicate former glories.

Virtual bands

The term 'virtual band', sometimes called a cartoon band, refers to groups whose members are animated characters rather than 'real' musicians, although their recordings are made by human musicians and producers. Media related to the virtual band, including stage performance visuals, videos and album artwork, will feature the animated line-up. The best known historical example is the Archies, whose bubblegum pop was a feature of the late 1960s. The most notable contemporary example is Gorillaz, formed by Damon Albarn, formerly in Blur, in 2001, and still active. The appeal of such bands would repay further investigation, but would appear to be linked to the multimedia environment, with their use of fantasy characters and worlds, sometimes drawing from graphic novels and comics; and their extensive use of sampling, remix and music video technology.

Conclusion

I have outlined the nature of music making and the roles and relative status of those who make music, primarily, but not exclusively musicians. Beyond the bands at the base of Frith's performance pyramid of the 'Rock' are those who are working at the middling levels of the industry. These performers are sometimes described as 'journeymen': they may enjoy a fair measure of commercial success, but they are not seen as particularly innovative, even though they may have a distinctive style and themes. But this label is unnecessarily pejorative, resting as it does on contestable (in part because they are rarely fully articulated) aesthetic distinctions. It makes more sense to talk of 'mid-level' status performers, who enjoy a mix of commercial and critical recognition. These are performers whose names are recognizable to the majority of popular music fans, even when they may not necessarily buy their records or attend their performances. Beyond this are performers who are considered stars and auteurs, the subject of the next chapter.

Further reading

Cohen, S. (1991) *Rock Culture in Liverpool: Popular Music in the Making*, Oxford: Clarendon Press.

Fonarow, W. (2006) *Empire of Dirt. The Aesthetics and Rituals of British Indie Music*, Middletown, CT: Wesleyan University Press.

Lebrun, B. (2009) *Protest Music in France. Production, Identity and Audiences*, Farnham, Burlington, VT: Ashgate.

Leiber, J. and Stoller, M., with David Ritz (2009) *Hound Dog: The Leiber and Stoller Autobiography*, New York, London: Simon & Schuster.

Moorefield, V. (2005) *The Producer as Composer. Shaping the Sounds of Popular Music*, Cambridge, MA: MIT Press.

Straw, W. (1999) 'Authorship', in B. Horner and T. Swiss (eds), *Key Terms in Popular Music and Culture*, Malden, MA; Oxford: Blackwell, pp. 199–208.

Thompson, G. (2008) *Please Please Me Sixties British Pop, Inside Out*, Oxford: Oxford University Press.

Toynbee, J. (2000) *Making Popular Music: Musicians, Creativity and Institutions*, London: Arnold.

DVD documentaries

Dig!, Australia: Palm Pictures, 2003.

I Am Trying To Break Your Heart, Wilco, 2002.

Metallica: Some Kind of Monster, Metallica, 2004.

Standing in the Shadows of Motown, the Funk Brothers, 2002.

Also the series: *Classic Albums*, on the making of particular 'iconic' or classic albums.

Websites

Association for the Study of Sound Recording: www.artofrecordproduction.com

Björn Again: www.bjornagain.com

4 'So You Want To Be a Rock 'N' Roll Star'

Auteurs and stars

At the pinnacle of the success continuum discussed in Chapter 3 are stars and auteurs.

Following an introduction to these two concepts, I provide a number of case studies of such figures in popular music, with reference to examples of their work: 1930s' bluesman Robert Johnson; producer Phil Spector and his 'wall of sound' in the early 1960s; the Spice Girls and manufactured pop; country crossover star Shania Twain; and Lady Gaga, a pop star born in and of the internet age. In each profile, with brief reference to their career, I want to situate these performers in terms of their influence and status and in relation to issues of creativity and commerce, genre and authorship

An important starting question here is how do you 'justify' a particular figure and their music as worthy of attention? The majority of the artists included in this chapter were selected for their innovative break with, or reworking of, established traditions and conventions. They generally exemplify two central aspects of a popular music aesthetic: first, extending the traditional form; and, second, working within the form itself, breaking it up and subverting its conventions. While this is arguably not the case with either the Spice Girls or Lady Gaga, I have included them as they established new approaches to the production and marketing of pop and are examples of debates around authorship, authenticity and celebrity.

While attention is given to the musical qualities of each performer, they are also situated in terms of genre, the music industry, the personal stance of the musicians and their place in popular music history and the audience reception of the work. The musical examples included show that we must go beyond simple musical aesthetics to explain why particular songs 'work' in terms of creating an audience and establishing an artist's profile.

Authorship and stardom

Auteur theory attributes meaning in cultural texts to the intentions of an individual creative source. The auteur concept is historically linked to writing and literary studies, where it has been applied to 'significant' works deemed to have value, which accordingly are considered part of high culture. An ideological construct, it is underpinned by notions of creativity and aesthetic value. The concept of auteur has been especially important in relation to film, emerging as a core part of fresh critical studies in the 1950s, with the auteur usually regarded as the director (see Hayward, 2000). The concept has since been applied to other forms of popular culture and their texts, in part in an attempt to legitimate their study vis-à-vis 'literature' and 'art'.

Applying auteurship to popular music means distinguishing it from mass or popular culture, with their connotations of mass taste and escapist entertainment and instead relating the field to notions of individual sensibility and enrichment. The concept underpins critical analyses of popular music which emphasize the intentions of the creator of the music (usually musicians) and attempts to provide authoritative meanings of texts and has largely been reserved for the figures seen as outstanding creative talents. It is central to the work of some musicologists, who identify popular music auteurs as producers of 'art', extending the cultural form and, in the process, challenging their listeners. Auteurship has been attributed primarily to individual performers, particularly singer-songwriters, but has also been attributed to producers, music video directors, songwriters and DJs. Indeed, in some cases, as Phil Spector demonstrates, these figures, rather than the musicians, may provide the dominant input. It can also be argued that, as with contemporary filmmaking, the creative process in rock is a 'team game' with various contributions melding together, even if a particular musician is providing the overall vision. Despite this multiple authorship, however, as Will Straw acutely observes, 'typically we evaluate a musical recording or concert as the output of a single individual or group'(1999: 200).

In the late 1960s popular music criticism began to discuss musicians in auteurist terms. John Cawelti, for example, claimed that 'one can see the differences between pop groups which simply perform without creating that personal statement which marks the auteur, and highly creative groups like the Beatles who make of their performance a complex work of art' (Cawelti, 1971: 267). American critic Jon Landau argued that the criterion of art in rock is the 'capacity of the musician to create a personal, almost private, universe and to express it fully' (cited in Frith, 1983: 53). By the early 1970s:

> self-consciousness became the measure of a record's artistic status; frankness, musical wit, the use of irony and paradox were musicians' artistic insigna – it was such self commentary that revealed the auteur within the machine. The skilled listener was the one who could recognize the artist despite the commercial trappings.
>
> (Frith, 1983: 53)

The discourse surrounding 1960s rock established a paradigm aesthetic that has, until recently, dominated the application of the concept of authorship in popular music.

At a common-sense level, auteurship would appear to be applicable to popular music, since while they are working within an industrial system, many individual performers are primarily responsible for their recorded product. There are also 'artists' – the term itself is culturally loaded – who, while working within the commercial medium and institutions of popular music, are seen to utilize the medium to express their own unique visions. Such figures are frequently accorded auteur status and, on the basis of their public celebrity and visibility, will frequently be stars as well. The concept of auteur stands at the pinnacle of a pantheon of performers and their work, a hierarchical approach used by fans, critics and musicians to organize their view of the historical development of popular music and the contemporary status of its performers. Auteurs enjoy respect for their professional performance, especially their ability to transcend the traditional aesthetic forms in which they work.

Particular popular music metagenres (see Chapter 6) have their own commonly recognized auteurs. In rock and pop, for example, musicians often accorded the status of auteur include the Beatles, the Rolling Stones, Bob Dylan, Aretha Franklin, James Brown, Jimi Hendrix, David Bowie, Prince, Michael Jackson, Bruce Springsteen and Radiohead, all of whom have achieved commercial as well as critical recognition. (Note the general absence of women from this list and, further, its domination by 1960s performers.) The status of several has waned, with their later work largely being found wanting when placed against earlier rerecordings, as with Bob Dylan and the Rolling Stones. However, such figures retain auteur status on the basis of their historical contribution, as do auteur figures whose careers were cut short, for example Jimi Hendrix, Janis Joplin and Kurt Cobain. There are also performers whose work has had only limited commercial impact but who are regarded as having a distinctive style and ouevre that has taken popular music in new and innovative directions, such as Frank Zappa, Brian Eno and Captain Beefheart.

Since all music texts are social products, performers working within popular genres are under constant pressure to provide their audience with more of the music that attracted that same audience in the first place. This explains why shifts in musical direction often lose a performers' established audiences, while hopefully creating new adherents. This is to emphasize the contradiction between being an 'artist' and responding to the pressures of the market, and to claim particular performers as auteurs despite their location within a profit-driven commercial industry (a similar process to that applied in film studies in the 1950s to Hollywood cinema's studio system). This leads to pantheons of musical value that are problematic, since all musical texts 'arrive on the turntable as the result of the same commercial processes' (Frith, 1983: 54). Furthermore, as in any area of 'creative' endeavour, there is a constant process of reworking the 'common stock' or traditions of generic popular forms, as continuity is self-consciously combined with change.

Stars and stardom

Stars are individuals who, as a consequence of their public performances or appearances in the mass media, become widely recognized and acquire symbolic status. Stars are seen as possessing a unique, distinctive talent in the cultural forms within which they work. Initially associated with the Hollywood film star system, stardom is now widely evident in sports, television and popular music. While there is a large body of theoretically oriented work on film stars (see Hayward, 2000, for a helpful overview), the study of stardom in popular music is largely limited to personal biographies of widely varying analytical value.

The important question is not so much 'what is a star?' but how stars function within the music industry, within textual narratives, and, in particular, at the level of individual fantasy and desire. What needs to be explained is the nature of emotional investment in pleasurable images. Stars are invested with cultural value and are popular because they resonate with particular lifestyles and cultures, while also representing a form of escapism from everyday life and the mundane.

Stardom in popular music, as in other forms of popular culture, is as much about illusion and appeal to the fantasies of the audience, as it is about talent and creativity. Stars function as mythic constructs, playing a key role in their fans ability to construct meaning out of everyday life (see the essays in Kelly and McDonnell, 1999). Such stars must also be seen as economic entities, used to mobilize audiences and promote the products of the music industry. They represent a unique commodity form, which is both a labour process and a product. Audience identification with particular stars is a significant marketing device. Several popular music stars have continued to generate enormous income after their death, which freezes their appeal in time while enabling their continued marketing through both the back catalogue and previously unreleased material. Elvis Presley, Jimi Hendrix, Bob Marley, Kurt Cobain (Nirvana) and Michael Jackson are examples of what has been termed 'posthumous celebrity'.

Madonna must be viewed as much as an economic entity as she is a cultural phenomenon, as over the course of her contract with Time-Warner she generated more than $US500 million in worldwide music sales. Madonna represents a bankable image, carefully constructed in an era of media globalization, an image that made her attractive to Live Nation, to which she moved in October 2007. Similarly, pop star Britney Spears, whose wealth was estimated at US$123 million by *Forbes* magazine in 2004, had by then sold more than 76 million records worldwide for her label Zomba. While Spears did not release any new recordings in 2005–2006, the media attention devoted to her marital split in late 2006 demonstrated her continued celebrity status. In 2011 country singer-songwriter Taylor Swift sold more than 1.8 million copies of her albums in the US and had a highly lucrative world tour. Such success helped establish her as a brand, with her own management company, lucrative contracts with companies such as Covergirl and the launch of her own line of perfume, Wonderstruck. All of these combined to place Swift at the top of *Billboard* magazine's list of the biggest music industry money makers for the year.

Yet the enormous fascination with stars' personal lives suggests a phenomenon that cannot be simply explained in terms of political economy. Fans both create and maintain the star through a ritual of adoration, transcending their own lives in the process. Stars appeal because they embody and refine the values invested in specific social types; e.g. Kylie Minogue in the1980s as 'the girl next door'; Bruce Springsteen, whose work and image is founded on associations with urban working-class authenticity. Contemporary 'established' stars are frequently at pains to exercise considerable control over their artistic lives, perhaps because this has often been hard won; all have an ability to retain an audience across time, either through reinventing their persona and image or through exploring new avenues in their music. Many have produced a substantial body of work, often multimedia in form; while seeking, to varying degrees, new ways of reinterpreting or reaffirming popular music styles and traditions. In these respects, such stars are frequently considered to be auteurs.

The construction of a popular music star's persona and image may change across time, at times in a calculated attempt to redefine a performers audience and appeal. A number of commentators have observed how Madonna has been able constantly to reinvent her persona and retain a high degree of creative control over her work. Her audience appeal and commercial success lies primarily in performance, through both concerts and music video, and her ability to keep herself in the public eye and the creation and maintenance of image is central to her success. The career of Lady Gaga follows a similar pattern.

The two most extensively considered popular music stars are Elvis Presley and the Beatles. The Beatles are routinely considered to be auteurs: they dramatically altered the status of popular music in the 1960s and their commercial and critical success made them iconic public figures. Elvis was certainly a star and, as the appeal of Graceland shows, continues to be one. In *Dead Elvis*, Greil Marcus (1991) offers a fascinating account of the ongoing cultural preoccupation with 'the King' since his death in 1977. However, Presley is rarely accorded auteur status, although he has a claim to this based largely on his early career at Sun Records. Springsteen and Madonna are the popular music stars and auteurs of the past 30 years who have generated the greatest amount of academic and popular analysis and discussion, with considerable attention being paid more recently to U2, Radiohead and Lady Gaga. In sum, the discourse surrounding these performers shows how authorship and stardom have become linked constructs with a number of dimensions: the economic, the cultural and the aesthetic. This is also the case, to varying degrees, with the following examples.

Robert Johnson: 'Hellhound on my Trail'

Robert Johnson was an auteur who posthumously became a star. He is regarded as the 'key transitional figure working within the Mississippi Delta's blues culture. He bridged the gap between the music's rural beginnings and its modern urban manifestations' (Barlow, 1989: 45).

Born in 1911, Johnson was raised by his mother, who routinely moved from place to place in the mid-south. His own adulthood was similarly restless and provided a recurring message in his work. Fellow bluesman and travelling companion, Johnny Shines, said of Johnson: 'People might consider him wild because he didn't think nothing of just taking off from wherever he was, just pack up and go. He had that about traveling.' Johnson had only limited commercial success during his short life. His few recording sessions were held in San Antonio late in 1936 and in Dallas in early 1937, when he recorded a total of just 29 blues tracks. This small output was to have an influence out of all proportion to its size, not only on the blues, but also on the development of 'rock' in the 1960s, as British bands such as the Rolling Stones and Cream covered songs by Johnson (see Weisman, 2005). The singer was murdered in Greenwood, Mississippi, in 1938, poisoned by a jealous lover, aged only 27.

While Johnson started out in the blues as a harmonica player, he soon switched to guitar. He was strongly influenced by Son House's bottleneck slide technique, which formed the core of his own playing style, and by other contemporary Delta bluesmen such as Charley Patton and Willie Brown. But Johnson assimilated a range of other influences, incorporating them into his own distinctive style: 'His guitar work was also influenced by the recordings of Kokomo Arnold, Scrapper Blackwell, Willie Newbern, and Lonnie Johnson, who also influenced many of his vocal inflections, along with Leroy Carr, Peetie Wheatstraw, and Skip James' (Barlow, 1989: 45–6). Contemporaries commented on the breadth of Johnson's musical tastes, and marvelled at his ability to 'pick a song right out of the air. He'd hear it being played on the radio and play it right back note for note. He could do it with blues, spirituals, hillbilly music, popular stuff. You name it he could play it' (Robert Lockwood, Jr.).

> He'd be sitting there listening to the radio – and you wouldn't even know he was paying any attention to it – and later that evening maybe, he'd walk out on the streets and play the same songs that were played over the radio, four or five songs he'd liked out of the whole session over the radio and he'd play them all evening, and he'd continue to play them.
>
> (Johnny Shines, cited in Barlow, 1989: 46)

Johnson was influential in three areas. First, through his guitar playing:

> As a guitarist he almost completely turned the blues around. His tightening of the rhythmic line was the basis for the instrumental blues scene that followed him in Chicago – letting the upper strings play a free melodic part, but using the thumb for a hard rhythm in the lower strings that was also a drum part.
>
> (Samuel Charters, cited in Barlow, 1989: 47)

Robert Palmer notes how Johnson made his guitar:

> sound uncannily like a full band, furnishing a heavy beat with his feet, chording innovative shuffle rhythms and picking out high treble-string lead with his slider, all at the same time. Fellow guitarists would watch him with

unabashed, open mouth wonder. They were watching the Delta's first
modern bluesman at work.

(ibid.)

Second, Johnson recorded a number of strikingly original songs, which cap-
tured a timeless feeling of desperation and intensity. In songs like 'Rambling on
My Mind,' 'Dust My Broom' and 'Sweet Home Chicago' Johnson celebrated
mobility and personal freedom; double entendres and sexual metaphors abound
in 'Steady Rolling Man', 'Terraplane Blues' and 'Traveling Riverside Blues';
and in 'Crossroad Blues' and 'Hellhound on My Trail' Johnson encouraged the
legend that he had flirted with the devil:

> I've got to keep moving, I've got to keep moving
> Blues falling down like hail, Blues falling down like hail
> And the days keeps on 'minding me
> There's a hellhound on my trail

Third, Johnson's voice is particularly effective at conveying a fatalistic sense of the
social and spiritual forces he saw arrayed against him. His vocal intonation is
especially compelling in his poignant 'Love in Vain', with its themes of painful
departure and separation:

> I followed her to the station with her suitcase in my hand
> And I followed her to the station with her suitcase in my hand
> Well it's hard to tell, its hard to tell when all your love's in vain
> All my love's in vain.
>
> (On *King of the Delta Blues Singers*, Vol. 2, CBS Records UK, 1970;
also available on the boxed set *Robert Johnson.*
The Complete Recordings, Columbia, 1990)

An analysis based on the song lyrics would not convey the emotional impact of
Johnson's voice and its interplay with guitar in the recorded version of the song.
In performance, the song is stripped down to its bare essentials, making it almost
minimalist in contemporary terms. Obviously, if judged by the standards of traditional, classical musicology, it would be found wanting. The vocal is weak and
wavering and the singer does not project well. Yet Johnson's voice has an edge of
desperation and hints at depths of experience. This is abetted by the use of
repetition and the interplay between the amplified acoustic guitar and the voice.
The piece also exemplifies the role of improvization and performance in styles
such as rock and blues. Although its contemporary impact is limited by the
primitive recording technology of its day, this also contributes to the song's
authenticity.

Johnson has a claim to being an auteur on the basis of his recordings and their
influence, but his now iconic star status owes much to other factors. The singer
was widely thought to have sold his soul to the devil in return for the ability to be

an outstanding blues singer and guitarist, since he disappeared for a short period and returned amazingly proficient. This, along with his early death and the lack of details about his life, created Johnson as a mythic figure in the history of popular music. The force of this myth, and public and scholarly fascination with it, has led to a spate of books and documentaries on Johnson (for an excellent review of these, and the creation of 'the Johnson myth', see Pearson and McCulloch, 2003). When one of only two known photos of him was used on a US commemorative stamp, the fact that it had been altered to remove the cigarette from Johnson's mouth created a good deal of controversy.

There is continued interest in his recordings and his performing style and Johnson retains the ability to affect listeners today. My own students regard his recording as somewhat maudlin, yet remain conscious of its force. They also find Johnson's original of 'Love in Vain' an interesting comparison with the Rolling Stones' 'cover' version (on the album *Let It Bleed*) that they are more familiar with. Certainly they concede that their 'appreciation' of the song is greatly enhanced by locating it as a key text in the development of post-1950s' 'rock'. This is to emphasize the point that knowledge of the performer and their influence on the 'popular music canon' adds dimensions beyond simple listening to the piece purely on its own terms.

Phil Spector: behind the wall of sound

In the 1960s, producer and songwriter and occasional performer Phil Spector was an auteur and a star. Later musicians and popular music history were to recognize his achievements despite his subsequent relative commercial decline.

Spector started by writing songs and achieved intitial success with 'To Know Him Is To Love Him', sung by the Teddy Bears, a group he created. In 1960 Atlantic Records permitted him, at the age of 19, to produce some sessions. He created hits for Ray Peterson and Curtis Lee, wrote 'Spanish Harlem' for Ben E. King and then founded his own label, Philles. Three years of whirlwind success followed, during which he produced a series of songs which became teen anthems: 'Then He Kissed Me', 'Be My Baby', 'You've Lost That Lovin' Feeling', 'Da Doo Ron Ron' and 'He's a Rebel'. Although these featured some great female vocalists, the performers were virtually interchangeable; the star was Spector. As a producer, he celebrated the girl group phenomenon of the 1960s, while transcending it, using quality songs, first-class arrangements and leading session musicians. The noise he created, the so-called 'wall of sound', was overwhelming in its intensity:

> Through multitracking, he made his rhythm sections seem like armies, and turned the beat into a murderous mass cannonade. No question; his records were the loudest, fiercest, most magnificent explosions that rock had yet produced, or dreamed of. And Spector stood in the center, swamped by this mayhem, twiddling the knobs, controlling everything.
>
> (Cohn, 1980: 153)

At one level, the wall of sound was simply putting a lot of instrumentalists in the studio and have them all play at once. For example, on 'River Deep, Mountain High', recorded with Ike and Tina Turner in 1966, the recording sessions included:

Four guitars
Four basses
Three keyboards
Two percussionists
Two drummers
Two obbligato vocalists
Six horns
And a full string section

(Ribowtsky, 1989: 221)

According to Billy Preston, one of the keyboardists, Spector 'had every machine going all at once; it was a circus and he was the ringleader' (ibid.: 155). His approach to production also incorporated extensive use of echo chamber and tape echo effects.

There is a tendency to see Spector as a pure innovator, a perception encouraged by essays such as Tom Wolfe's 1963 essay 'The Tycoon of Teen' (reproduced in the boxed set, *Back To Mono*: see Further reading):

He does the whole thing. Spector writes the words and the music, scouts and signs up the talent. He takes them out to a recording studio and runs the session himself. He puts them through hours and days to get the two or three minutes he want. Two or three minutes out of the whole struggle. He handles the control dials like an electronic maestro.

Spector was certainly the dominant figure, but he was influenced by earlier producers, notably Leiber and Stoller, with whom he worked, and by Sam Phillips' use of echo at Sun Records in the 1950s. Also, as did most producers of the period, Spector worked with a group of regulars, including arranger Jack Nitzsche and engineer Larry Levine. And his songwriting credits were shared, or reluctantly conceded where Spector's input to them was minimal, with Brill Building teams such as Gerry Goffin and Carole King.

A millionaire at 21, Spector was hailed by the industry as a genius, but the impetus slackened in the mid-1960s. In 1966 he made his finest record, 'River Deep, Mountain High', with Ike and Tina Turner. When it failed commercially, Spector announced his retirement. A subsequent return from several years of self-imposed exile saw a few successes. He produced 'Imagine' with John Lennon and 'My Sweet Lord' with George Harrison and albums for both the former Beatles. But the dizzy earlier heights were not to be scaled again, in part because he no longer had total control, but was working as a hired hand. His presence alone was now insufficient to virtually guarantee a record's success. Writing his profile at the end of the 1970s, Nic Cohn painted a picture of a reclusive figure whose myth had swamped his present reality.

Spector's success can be attributed to a combination of two factors. First, he established the concept of business independence, seeking to control every aspect of his own enterprise: production, publicity and distribution. Second, Spector was one of the first self-conscious pop artists, 'the first to rationalize, the first to comprehend precisely what he was up to. With him, there was immediately a totally new level of sophistication, complexity, musical range' (Cohn, 1980: 154). Paradoxically, Spector managed to raid every musical source he could and still be completely original; to be strictly commercial while concerned with the records as art. He combined the two great rock 'n' roll romances – rebellion and teen dream – into one.

Spector's achievement remains impressive and the positive response to the 1991 reprise of his work, the CD set *Back To Mono (1950–1969)*, was indicative of the continued interest in his work. On this, Spector remastered 60 of his singles (plus his attempt to create an album as a total entity, *Christmas Gift to You*), retaining their original mono sound. Spector's claim to auteur status rests on a combination of initial musical innovation and the aura of mystery and controversy created by his 'star' lifestyle; a mix of eccentricity (episodes with guns in the studio), a messy divorce in the 1970s and his increasing social isolation. His arrest on suspicion of murder in 2003, and subsequent lengthy trial, added to this mystique, yet, ironically, prompted fresh interest in his work. As Virgil Moorefield concludes: 'By taking total artistic control of a recording, Spector in fact redefined what it meant to produce a record. He changed forever the way the producer's role would be viewed' (Moorefield, 2005: 12).

The Spice Girls

As with Madonna, the Spice Girls' success story raises issues of the status of musical genres, image and representation, the commodification of popular music and the nature and operation of celebrity in pop culture more generally.

The Spice Girls were originally put together by the management team of Bob Herbert and his son Chris. Chris drew up a flyer, which he distributed in London and the southeast of England: 'R.U. 18–23 with the ability to sing/ dance. R.U. streetwise, outgoing, ambitious, and dedicated?' Four hundred showed up for the auditions at Danceworks Studios, just off London's Oxford Street. The original five Spice Girls (including Michelle Stephenson, who dropped out and was replaced by Emma Bunton) met for the first time in March 1994. Victoria Adams, Melanie Brown, Emma Bunton, Melanie Chisholm and Geri Halliwell came from varying backgrounds and the combination of personalities to make up the group was chosen quite deliberately. The press, and their fans, later referred to them as Posh (Victoria), Sporty (Mel C), Baby (Emma), Scary (Mel B) and Ginger (Geri); labels which became pervasive public signifiers and helped consolidate the Spice Girls' image.

Chris Herbert used Trinity, a dance/rehearsal/recording studio in Woking, Surrey, as a base for the group, who spent almost a year there, working on their singing, developing embryonic songwriting skills and beginning the process of selling themselves to the music industry. The Herberts had no official contract with the girls and were a relatively small company and the band, now increasingly confident in their abilities, looked around for a deal that offered greater support to their increasing ambitions. In April 1995 they left manager Chris Herbert and signed with Simon Fuller's 19 Management. In 1996 they signed to Virgin Records for a reported £2 million advance.

Fuller commissioned three teams of songwriters, all of whom had considerable music industry experience, credits and success, to work with/for the group, to develop their song ideas. Their input is shown on the group's debut album. Stannard and Rowe, who had previously written material/hits for East 17 and Take That, came up with three of the Spice Girls' four number 1 singles, 'Wannabe', '2 Become 1' and 'Mama', and also wrote 'If U Can't Dance'. Absolute (Paul Wilson and Andy Watkins) provided 'Who Do You Think You Are', 'Something Kinda Funny', 'Naked' and 'Last Time Lover'. The remaining two songs on the first album, 'Say You'll Be There' and 'Love Thing' were written by Eliot Kennedy (one with Cary Bayliss). The Spice Girls get songwriting credit on all the songs on the *Spice* album, but Davis (1997) claims that they actually only got about one-twentieth of the composer's royalties apiece.

The debut single 'Wannabe' was released in July 1996. It went to number 1 in the UK within a few weeks and stayed there for two months – a record for a debut single by a UK girl group. Subsequently it reached the number 1 chart position in 31 countries, including the US, selling four million copies worldwide. The Spice Girls next three singles also topped the UK charts, making them the only group to have had four UK no. 1s with their four first singles and already the most successful British girl group ever. The appeal of the group was enhanced by their videos and energetic dance routines and performances on leading music television show *Top of the Pops*. The *Spice* LP went triple platinum in the UK within three weeks of its release and by mid-1997 had sold over 10 million copies worldwide. The Girls' personal lives, notably earlier modelling efforts and personal relationships, came under intense scrutiny by, first, the British and then the international press, especially the tabloids. The group's slogan, 'Girl Power', 'a hybrid of 90s' good-feel optimism and cheery fun-pub feminism which alienates no one' (Davis 1997: 35), attracted considerable debate (see Lemish, 2003).

During 1996 and into 1997, the Spice Girls solidified their success in Britain and then tackled America. A carefully orchestrated marketing campaign was undertaken by Virgin in the US, partly to offset initial critical reception of the records. For example, the *Rolling Stone*'s negative March 1997 review of *Spice*, which labelled the music a watered down mix of hip-hop and pop and accorded it only one and a half stars (on a five-star scale). 'Despite their pro-woman posing', wrote reviewer Christina Kelly, 'the Girls don't get bogged down by anything deeper than mugging for promo shots and giving out tips on getting boys into bed' (cited in Dickerson, 1998: 205). Virgin marketed the band with heavy emphasis on their videos and the Girls visual appeal, largely avoiding the more potentially awkward print media. This meant 'high profiles for MTV, short interviews for television, and staged events where cameras could only get passing glimpses of the Spice Girls in controlled situations'. MTV was crucial, 'showing the Girls' nipple-friendly video (for "Wannabe") at every opportunity' (Dickerson, 1998: 205). In July 1997, *Spice* topped the *Billboard* album charts and *Rolling Stone* ran a cover story headlined 'Spice Girls Conquer the World', a nine-page article, which told readers everything they could possibly want to know about the Spice Girls (10 July 1997 issue). All this without playing a concert or playing live, except on the television show *Late Night with David Letterman*.

The Spice Girls filled a market niche. As Chris Herbert observed:

> The whole teen-band scene at that time was saturated by boy bands. I felt that if you could appeal to the boys as well, you'd be laughing. If you could put together a girl band which was both sassy, for the girls, and with obvious sex appeal, to attract the boys, you'd double your audience.
>
> (Davis, 1997: 35)

The Spice Girls also provided an antidote to the 'laddish' culture of UK Brit Pop in the early 1990s, associated with performers such as the Gallagher brothers (Oasis). The Spice Girls were the subject of considerable hostility from many 'rock' critics/fans, who saw them as a media artifact, a view underpinned by the historical denigration of dance pop as a genre.

Their success was made possible by a combination of their music, their marketing and their personalities. The Spice Girls' music is 'a mixture of dance, hip-hop, R&B, and smooth-as-silk pop ballads. Technically solid. Middle of the road. Nothing extreme' (Dickerson, 1998: 203). This is to overlook the appeal of the clever and catchy lyrics of songs such as 'Wannabe', with its catchphrase 'Zig-a-zig-ah' for sex and the highlighting of ongoing friendship and a streetwise attitude toward relationships:

> Yo, I'll tell you what I want, what I really really want,
> So tell me what you want, what you really really want,
> I'll tell you what I want, what I really really want,
> So tell me what you want, what you really really want,
> I wanna, I wanna, I wanna, I wanna,
> I wanna really
> really really wanna zig-a-zig-ah
> If you want my future forget my past,
> If you wanna get with me better make it fast,
> Now don't go wasting my precious time,
> Get your act together we could be just fine.
> If you wanna be my lover, you gotta get with my friends,
> Make it last forever friendship never ends,
> If you wanna be my lover, you have got to give,
> Taking is too easy, but that's the way it is.

What do you think about that now you know how I feel,
Say you can handle my love are you for real,
I won't be hasty, I'll give you a try
If you really bug me then I'll say goodbye.

> (The Spice Girls, 'Wannabe', Virgin, 1996)

However, this well-crafted pop is not the foundation for their mega-success, which was due mainly to the band's public image, which they partly created for themselves through force of personality and an irreverent attitude to the music industry and the media. They were seen as five 'sassy' individuals who combined girl-next-door appeal with considerable sex appeal. 'They introduced the language of independence to a willing audience of pre-teen and teenage girls – girl power' (Whiteley, 2000: 215). In a discourse reminiscent of Madonna's early career, critics pointed to a contradiction between the Spice Girls' self-expression and their subversion of standard 'feminine' images and their incorporation into a male-dominated industry. The group members themselves, and their defenders, claimed in response that this was of their own choosing and on their own terms.

The franchizing (through product endorsements) of a huge range of Spice Girl products added to the Girls' ubiquitous presence through 1997 and 1998. In December 1997 *Q* magazine rated the Spice Girls the 'biggest rock band in the world', based on the amount of airplay they had received, total income from record sales, concert tickets etc. and the number of appearances on national magazine covers (both music and 'general' titles). In 1998 the Spice Girls released their second album, *Spice World*, again topping the charts internationally, and a movie of the same name. In August 1998 'Viva Forever' became their seventh UK number 1 single and they sold out a 40-concert 'world' tour. During 1999 and into 2000 the group's momentum eased: Geri departed and was not replaced; the remaining members devoted themselves to individual projects (e.g. Mel C's *Northern Star*); and Victoria and Mel B became mothers. A third Spice Girls' album was released in November 2000; its limited success contributed to the effective breakup of the band.

Shania Twain: on her way

Country emerged in the US as a major market force in popular music in the 1990s (see Sernoe, 1998) and classic stereotypes associated with the genre (especially its maudlin themes and limited appeal) no longer hold up. *Billboard* placed Garth Brooks as 'Top Country Album Artist' and 'Top Pop Album Artist' for the years 1990, 1991 and 1993. In 1993 all six of his albums were included among the 100 most popular albums of the year, with two – *No Fences* and *Ropin' the Wind* – having sold about 10 million copies each. His crossover success opened the way on the pop charts for other country artists, often referred to as 'new country', with Billy Ray Cyrus, Dwight Yoakum, Mary Chapin Carpenter and Reba McEntire among the best-selling artists of the early to mid-1990s. At the same time, country radio became the second most listened to music format in the US, second only to adult contemporary, and video channel CMT (Country Music Television) achieved a significant market share. The success of Shania Twain during the late 1990s was in part made possible by this aggressive resurgence of country music and the receptive context that it created. Her crossover to the commercial mainstream and massive success, however, lifted the 'country' tag from her and by 1998 she was an international pop star.

Shania Twain was born in Canada. Her life story has, slightly cynically, been compared to a fairytale:

> A country girl from Timmins, Ontario, is raised dirt poor, starts performing in bars as a child, loses her parents at age 22 when their car collides with a logging truck, sings to support her three teenage siblings, then finds her prince – reclusive rock producer Robert John (Mutt) Lange – who gives her a studio kiss of stardom.
>
> (Brian Johnson, 'Shania Revealed', cover story in *Maclean's*, Canada's leading magazine, 23 March 1998; Hager, 1998, provides a detailed and balanced biography).

Her success is based on a combination of her songwriting, her striking and attractive looks, her music videos and, as Johnson suggests, the role of Mutt Lange in her recordings. The weighting variously accorded to these factors, illustrates the controversy that has surrounded her status as a star and a popular music 'auteur'.

Twain moved to Nashville in 1991 after signing a deal with Mercury Nashville, changing her name from Eileen to Shania, which means 'I'm on my way' in Ojibwa (the language of her foster father). Her self-titled debut album (1993) featured only one of her own compositions, her producers opting instead for songs from established songwriters, a common practice in Nashville. The debut was respectable, without making a major impact: it sold around a hundred thousand copies, two singles from it got to no. 55 on the *Billboard* Hot Country Singles Chart and Shania made *Billboard*'s 1993 list of promising new artists. The accompanying music video for 'What Made You Say That', her own composition, broke with country tradition, celebrating her 'wholesome' sexuality, as she frolicked on a tropical beach with a male 'hunk'. It featured her bared navel, which became a 'trademark' on later videos and magazine covers. Screened on CMT Europe, the video also brought Shania to the attention of leading English producer John 'Mutt' Lange. The two started collaborating on songwriting, became close friends and were married in December 1993.

Shania's second album, *The Woman in Me* (1995), was produced by her husband, who also partially financed it. Featuring a number of the songs turned down for the first album, *The Woman in Me* took a year and a half and more than half a million dollars to complete, a recording effort which stunned Nashville, where budgets of one-tenth of that amount were standard (Hager, 1998: 54). It sold 12 million copies by the end of 1998. Of the 12 songs, 10 were co-written by Shania and Lange and there was a solo contribution from each. As Hager describes it, this was a creative collaboration, with each contributing from their strengths and complementing the other. In producing *The Woman in Me*, Lange drew on the 'rock' style that he had used for very successful records with Def Leppard, AC/DC and Bryan Adams. The album was a combination of 'irresistible songs, sassy lyrics, all backed by Lange's onion-skin production, which reveals more of each song with each play' (*Q* review, November 1999). Her third album, *Come on Over* (1998) sold 4.2 million during its first five months of release. The first single from it, 'You're Still the One', topped the *Billboard* country chart in May 1998 and went on to reach no. 1 on the pop chart. Both the album, and the several singles from it, topped charts internationally.

This success was achieved, her critics observed, without Twain performing 'live'. This claim conveniently overlooked the fact that she had been performing in public from the age of three, but really referred to the singer's not initially undertaking a concert tour to promote her albums. Instead, Shania did a series of promotional appearances, in shopping centres, on talk shows and at industry showcases. This led to claims that her songs were largely the product of the recording studio and raised questions about her ability to present them in performance. Twain was also frequently accused of being a 'packaged' artist, created by her high-powered management (Jon Landau, who also represents Bruce Springsteen). The success of her extensive touring in 1998 and into 1999, and the quality of her stage performance, erased these doubts. The tour also enabled the production of a best-selling concert video.

Cover stories (for example, *Rolling Stone*, 3 September 1998; *Q*, November 1999) accentuated Shania's 'natural' physical appeal, particularly her bare midriff, a feature of several of her early videos. In her songs and videos, Twain combines a flirtatious glamour and self-empowerment: 'a country singer who looks like a supermodel' who 'on camera projects a playful allure that is part come-on, part come-off-it' (Johnson, *Maclean's*, 23 March 1998: 50). This is feminism very much in the mould of the Spice Girls.

Her songs, mainly co-written with Lange, reinvigorate tired county formats. They range from ballads of domestic bliss ('You're Still the One') and feisty reassurance ('Don't Be Stupid. You Know I Love You'), to clever assertions of women's rights ('Honey I'm Home' is a neat role reversal). Within its pop ballad format and catchy tune, 'Black Eyes, Blue Tears' alerted listeners to domestic violence.

Come On Over established Shania Twain as a successful crossover artist. Remixed versions of singles from the album placed less emphasis on country style instrumentation, creating greater airplay on non-country radio. Her next album, after a two-year 'time out' suffering from exhaustion, continued this marketing strategy. *Up!* (2002), a double album, featured 29 songs in a country mix on one disc and the same songs in pop mixes on the other. The album, and several singles from it, topped the charts. *A Greatest Hits* album, in 2004, maintained Twain's commercial success. Over the next few years, the singer took 'time out' to become a mother, divorced from Lange and published her autobiography. In December 2012 she will start a two-year residency in Las Vegas, with a show 'Shania: Still the One' and is planning to record again. Shania Twain is a popular music auteur whose work and marketable image made her a star, although her success illustrates the frequent contribution of others to musical authorship.

Lady Gaga

Stefani Germanotta, better known by her stage name Lady Gaga, is a pop star born in and of the internet age. She has exploited the reach of the web and social media, constantly communicating with her dedicated and extensive fans (the 'little monsters') through Facebook and Twitter; she debuts her videos on YouTube and is the most downloaded artist in history. As leading business magazine *Forbes* observed in November 2009: 'Lady Gaga isn't the music industry's new Madonna. She's its new business model' (cited Callahan, 2010: 12).

While some accounts see Gaga as moving in 18 months (2009–2010) from being an 'unknown' performer to being 'the biggest star in the world' (Callahan, 2010: 1), hers was not an overnight success story. Gaga, who began learning piano at age four, had been song writing and performing since high school and in New York clubs since 2005. Early performance clips on YouTube, demonstrate her already evident talent in musicianship, vocal ability and commanding stage presence. Biographical accounts and interviews (Grigoriadis, 2010; Hiatt, 2009), emphasize her drive and determination from an early age to succeed in the music business. Indeed, in many ways, Gaga personifies the traditional route to success, based on hard work and live performance, sketched earlier (Chapter 3).

Gaga created a performance persona and spectacle, which creatively pulled together a bricolage of hundreds of pop art threads. Maureen Callahan, attending a sold-out Lady Gaga concert at the Manchester Evening News Arena, the largest in the UK, holding 21,000, observed that among the people and things Gaga referenced, overtly and covertly, on the night were:

> The Wizard of Oz; the late designer Alexander McQueen's 2006 fashion show, in which Kate Moss appeared as a ghostly 3-D floating hologram; a famous image of McQueen binding a model – face painted white, streaks of red paint streaming from the eyes, mouth gagged with black ribbon – in swathes of white; the Broadway musical *Rent*; the archly art-directed interstitial clips MTV pioneered on its award shows; Elton John and Billy Joel; Rob Reiner's classic 1984 rock spoof, *This is Spinal Tap*; Cirque du Soleil; Japanese horror films of the 1950s; shock artists Tracey Emin and Damien Hurst; David Bowie and Freddie Mercury; the entire gay subculture of the past three decades; the stark black-and-white aesthetic of the great rock photographer Anto Corbijn. And, of course, Madonna.
>
> (Callahan, 2010: 6)

Lady Gaga's debut single 'Just Dance' was released on 8 April 2008; it preceded her first album by four months, to set up the album release and create a demand for it. *The Fame* (or *Fame*, in some markets) was released on 8 October

2008. By this time, 'Just Dance' had done well internationally, especially in the European dance music market and the single now spent the North American summer on the *Billboard* Hot Dance Music – Club Party Chart, peaking at no. 1 in January 2009. It was followed by the release of a further single from the album, 'Poker Face', which was an international no. 1 hit. The market trajectory of the album reflected the success of the singles and the impact of Gaga's subsequent success at major music awards, along with several high-profile media appearances. A career 'tipping point' was her performance of 'Paparazzi' at the 2009 MTV Video Music Awards (13 September), when she won Best New Artist. Gaga was then *Billboard's* Artist of the Year for 2010 and *Time* magazine named her one of the most influential people in the world.

The Fame peaked at no. 2 on *Billboard* and by mid-2011 had sold 4.2 million copies in the US alone. The success of her next release, the eight-track EP, *The Fame Monster*, which reached no. 5 on *Billboard* and sold 1.5 million copies, enabled Lady Gaga to embark on the 18-month long Monster Ball Tour, which became one of the highest grossing concert tours of all time. Her 2011 album, *Born This Way*, also topped charts internationally, selling 1.1 million copies in the first week of its release in the US market, boosted by online retailer Amazon's controversially selling the album for 99c, to promote its new cloud service.

Lady Gaga is not only a highly successful contemporary recording and touring artists, she is a celebrity within the wider pop culture. She continues to be featured in numerous music and fashion magazine cover stories and appears on leading talk shows and at music and fashion awards. In October 2010, eight wax models of the singer were unveiled by Madame Tussauds' waxwork museums around the world, at a cost of US$2.4 million, with each dressed differently in celebration of the singer's provocative fashion sense. Gaga is actively and publically involved with humanitarian causes. Her stage show statements and tweets following the Japanese tsunami disaster (in February 2011) brought the rebuilding effort to the attention of her 20 million followers on Twitter. In 2012, at Harvard University, she launched her 'Born This Way Foundation' aimed at empowering young people through addressing issues such as self-confidence, well-being and stamping out bullying.

Conclusion

The auteurs and stars I have considered here share a number of characteristics. At a fairly self-evident level, in their musical careers they all exercise considerable control over their artistic lives, perhaps because this has often been hard won. All have an ability to retain an audience across time, either through reinventing their persona/image or through exploring new avenues in their music. They all have produced a substantial body of work, often multimedia in form; and they have all been, to varying degrees, seeking new ways of reinterpreting or reaffirming popular music styles. These characteristics apply to both auteurs and stars, but the latter go beyond them, to function as mythic constructs, related to their audiences collective and individual relationship to the music and performer (Marshall,

1997: 163). Popular music stars and auteurs also represent economic entities, a unique commodity form which is both a labour process and product. The continuity of their careers contributes to stability in the marketplace, thereby enhancing the cultural and potential commercial value of their musical 'texts'.

Further reading

Stardom and celebrity

Hayward, S. (2000) *Key Concepts in Cinema Studies*, London, New York: Routledge.
Kelly, K. and McDonnell, E. (1999) *Stars Don't Stand Still in the Sky*, London: Routledge.
Marshall, P.D. (1997) *Celebrity and Power; Fame in Contemporary Culture*, Minneapolis, MN: University of Minnesota Press.

Biographical material, often situated around interviews and new releases, is a staple part of the music press. The brief career profiles included here can be supplemented by the extensive entries on each in Wikipedia, and official artist websites.

Robert Johnson and the blues

Robert Johnson. The Complete Recordings, Columbia, 1990 (boxed set).

The two known photos of Johnson can be seen at: www.deltahaze.com
Pearson, B. and McCulloch, B. (2003), *Robert Johnson: Lost and Found*, Urbana, IL: University of Illinois Press (especially Chapter 13).

Documentaries:
The Search for Robert Johnson, Sony, 1992 (DVD).
Can't You Hear The Wind Howl? The Life and Music of Robert Johnson, Shout, 1997 (DVD).

Phil Spector

Back To Mono (1958–1969), Spector/Abko, 1991 (boxed set).

Moorefield, V. (2005) *The Producer as Composer. Shaping the Sounds of Popular Music*, Cambridge, MA: MIT Press. (Includes a case study of the Ronettes, 'Be My Baby'.)
Ribowtsky, M. (1989) *He's A Rebel*, New York: E.P. Dutton.
Thompson, D. (2005) *Wall of Pain. The Biography of Phil Spector*, Bodmin: Sanctuary Publishing.

The Spice Girls

Spice, Virgin, 1996.
Spice World, Virgin, 1997.
Forever, Virgin, 2000.

Golden, A.L. (1997) *The Spice Girls*, New York: Ballantine Books.
Lemish, D. (2003) 'Spice World: Constructing Femininity the Popular Way', *Popular Music and Society*, 26, 1: 17–29.

Movie: *Spice World*, Virgin, 1997.

Shania Twain and country

Come On Over, Mercury Records, 1998.
Greatest Hits, Mercury, 2004.

Hager, B. (1998) *On Her Way. The Life and Music of Shania Twain*, New York: Berkeley Boulevard.
Twain, S. (2011) *From this Moment On*, New York: Atria Books.
Official web site: www.shaniatwain.com

Lady Gaga

Born This Way, Interscope Records 2011.
The Fame, Interscope Records, 2008.
The Fame Monster, Interscope Records, 2009.
Official web site: www.ladygaga.com

Callahan, M. (2010) *Poker Face. The Rise and Rise of Lady Gaga*, New York: Hyperion.
Grigoriadis, V. (2011) 'Growing Up Gaga', in A. Rossand D. Carr (eds), *Best Music Writing 2011*, Philadelphia, PA: Perseus Books/ Da Capo Press.
Hiatt, B. (2009) 'New York Doll', *Rolling Stone*, August, cover story: 'The Rise of Lady Gaga'.

5   'Message Understood?'

Textual analysis and popular musicology

The term 'text' has traditionally been used to refer to an author's original words, or a prose work – especially one recommended for student reading. More recently, as a cultural studies term, text refers to any media form that is self-contained and conveys cultural meaning, including television programmes, recordings, films and books. Popular music texts are quite diverse, embracing both sound and visual examples, with these at times combined. The most prominent are aural texts: sound recordings, in various formats, the focus of this chapter. In addition, there are graphic texts, most notably album covers, and audiovisual texts, primarily music videos. Other forms of popular music text include music magazines, posters, t-shirts, tour brochures and fan club merchandise. Musical performances, especially concerts, and DJ discourse have also been analyzed as forms of musical text. These various forms are frequently interconnected and mutually reinforcing.

Following a brief consideration of the nature of textual analysis, I turn to musical texts with particular reference to issues around musicology, the analysis of song lyrics, and the nature and status of 'covers'. Chapter 6 considers texts as 'collectivities', through discussions of genre and the album canon. Due to its close association with MTV and YouTube, music video, the main example of an audiovisual music text, is discussed in Chapter 8.

It is obviously difficult to express through language qualities that are often visual and aural, rather then linguistic. Accordingly, the book's associated website provides links to websites where album cover art, song lyrics and recordings can be accessed.

Textual analysis

Textual analysis is concerned with identifying and analyzing the formal qualities of texts, their underpinning structures and constituent characteristic. As such, it has become closely associated with various approaches to content and discourse analysis, including semiotic analysis. Studies of album covers, for example, show how they convey meaning through the semiotic resources they draw on and display, via language, typography, images and layout (Machin, 2010). They make an artistic statement in relation to the style of music though their association with particular iconography, for example the use of apocalyptic imagery in heavy metal and the fantasy imagery of progressive rock (see the examples in Ochs, 1996). Album covers also consolidate and sustain the representation of artists as iconic figures. For example, Island's marketing of Bob Marley and the Wailers, with covers constructing Marley as a star figure and the band as politically authentic style rebels, was important to their commercial success and the main-streaming of reggae in the 1970s (see the discussion of this in Chapter 7). The album covers of the Beatles recordings were especially notable: 'groundbreaking in their visual and aesthetic properties (and) their innovative and imaginative designs' (Inglis, 2001: 83), they forged a link with the expanding British graphic design industry and the art world, while making explicit the connections between art and pop in the 1960s.

A major form of textual analysis is the examination of the musical components of songs, including their lyrics, in their various recorded formats. Musicology is central to this, although its traditional approach has been modified in relation to popular music. While recordings are usually analyzed independently, they can also be considered collectively, as with content analysis of chart share in terms of genres, record labels (especially majors compared to independents), performers and country of origin. A similar approach has been applied to radio and MTV airplay, especially in relation to relative shares of local content and imported repertoire (see Chapter 14).

Intertextuality is important here: the idea that a text communicates its meaning only when it is situated in relation to other texts; it is often characterized as meaning that 'arises' between texts (Gracyk, 2001: 56). An example of this process is the musical dialogue that occurs between cover versions of songs, their ante-cedents and the performers of both (see later). Intertextuality is also evident in the discourse around preferred styles and performers and implicit in the repackaging of the back catalogue of recordings as generic compilations and boxed sets. Theodore Gracyk (2001: Chapter 3) provides a number of interesting musical examples, making the point that such 'influences, connections, and allusions create nuances of meaning that cannot be grasped simply through a general intertextuality' (59).

A point of debate around popular culture is its ideological role in reinforcing and reproducing dominant values through their representation in popular texts. Critics who concentrate on the text itself, often using concepts from semiotic and psychoanalytic analysis, argue that there frequently exists in the text a pre-ferred reading, that is, a dominant message set within the cultural code of estab-lished conventions and practices of the producers/transmitters of the text. However, while many consumers may, at least implicitly or subconsciously, accept such preferred readings, it must be kept in mind that it is not necessarily true that all listeners do so. In particular, subordinate groups may reinterpret such textual messages, making 'sense' of them in a different way. The Strawbs 'Part of the Union', intended as a direct attack on trade unionism, achieved the opposite effect when sung by striking Coventry car workers. The study of pop fans simi-larly suggests that cultural meanings are ultimately made by consumers, even if this process is under conditions and opportunities not of their own choosing (see Chapter 10). This opens up the idea of popular resistance to, and subversion of, dominant cultures, a view that has informed analysis of the nature and reception of popular song lyrics and music videos.

Musicology and popular song

Clearly, the central textual form in popular music is the song, primarily reproduced as individual sound recordings: the single. The analysis of these has been dominated in popular discourse by fans, the music press and music critics and in academic work by musicology. To illustrate the issues, the discussion here concentrates on rock and pop, the dominant metagenres in popular music.

Musicology developed with Western art music and historically privileged the text by placing the emphasis firmly on its formal properties. Musicologists have investigated genres such as the blues, jazz and, more recently, pop and rock, as music, using conventional concepts derived from the study of more traditional/ classical forms of music: harmony, melody, beat and rhythm, along with vocal style and the lyrics. A major early debate in popular music studies was around the value of such an approach to pop and rock musical texts. Indeed, there was an argument as to whether popular music, especially rock and pop genres, even merited such a 'serious' analysis. This was clearly evident in the 1980s, in the bemused reaction of the mainstream British press to the emergence of 'popular music studies', reflecting conservative notions of high culture set against the mass society critiques of popular music.

Academic musicologists at first largely ignored rock and pop music, although a notable early exception was Wilfred Mellers' sympathetic study of the Beatles, *Twilight of the Gods* (1974); his example was followed by the pioneering work of, among others, John Shepherd, Philip Tagg, Robert Walser and Susan McLary. Most musicologists, however, were reluctant to engage with a form of music accorded low cultural value in comparison with 'serious' music. At the same time, many sociologists writing on popular music were wary of musicology. Simon Frith, in one of the first extended academic treatments of pop and rock music, noted how both rock musicians and rock commentators generally lacked 'the vocabulary and techniques of musical analysis, and even the descriptive words that critics and fans do use – harmony, melody, riff, beat – are only loosely understood and applied' (Frith, 1983: 13).

Frith saw rock critics as essentially preoccupied with sociology rather than sound and identified what has been too ready a willingness to dismiss musicology as having little relevance to the study of popular styles. The arguments here were well rehearsed through the 1980s: traditional musicology neglected the social context, emphasized the transcription of music (the score) and elevated harmonic and rhythmic structure to pride of place as an evaluative criterion. Popular music, by way of contrast, was seen to emphasize interpretation through performance and as received primarily in terms of the body and emotions rather than as pure text. Many rock musicians observed that classical music operated according to a different set of musical criteria, which had little validity for their own efforts.

Certainly, attempts to apply traditional musicological criteria could all too easily appear pretentious, as shown by Frith's comparison of two explanations of the Animals' 1964 hit 'I'm Crying'. Richard Middleton, a musicologist, in his explanation emphasized the formal musical qualities of the composition, including the point that:

> The cross relations in the ostinato (which is melodic and harmonic) are the equivalents of blue notes, arising from a similar conflict between melodic and tonal implications. The modal melodic movement of the ostinato, with its minor thirds, clashes with the tonal need for major triads imposed by the 12-bar blues structure.
>
> (cited in Frith, 1983: 13)

Compare this with Alan Price's description: 'I wrote the music and Eric (Burdon) did the words and we just threw it together in rehearsal in Blackpool. We just stuck it together and recorded it and by chance it was successful' (Frith, 1983: 13). Middleton's analysis, while accurate, places considerable demands on the reader, while Price's casual explanation reflects a romantic rock ideology, with its ideal of spontaneous and inspired creativity.

In the early 1990s, there were signs that the largely negative attitude toward applying musicology to popular music was changing. Several musicologists engaged with popular music genres and texts (for example: McLary and Walser, 1990; Moore, 1993; Tagg and Clarida, 2003), while popular music scholars generally began to accord musicology more weight in their analyses. This work varied in the degree to which such analysis simply took as a given the concepts and tools of traditional (e.g. more classical music oriented) musicology or modified these in relation to popular music.

Much of this work recognized that the traditional conception of musicology, especially as present in the study of western art/classical music, was inadequate when applied to popular music in any straightforward manner (equating the two forms). For example, a concentration on technical textual aspects alone – the score – fails to deal with how the effects listeners celebrate are constructed, what Susan McLary and Robert Walser (1990: 287) term 'the dimensions of music that are most compelling and yet most threatening to rationality'. This takes into consideration the role of pleasure, the relationship of the body, feelings and emotions, and sexuality in constructing responses to genres such as dance, rock and the blues.

The past decade has produced a substantial body of what came to be termed 'popular musicology' (Hawkins, 2002), with several substantive edited volumes containing extensive discussion and examples (Middleton, 2000; Moore, 2003; Scott, 2009). This work has engaged further with the more affective domains of the relationship between the text and its listeners and into the generic and historical locations of texts and performers. A prominent part of such an approach is the question of 'listening'.

Listening: why do songs have words?

Listening is a physical process situated in social contexts and mediated by technology. Listening to music is an activity that takes place with varying levels of intensity, influenced by the consumption context and the style of the performer: 'the "distracted" environment of many club settings and the hushed concentration typical of singer-songwriter concerts might represent two extremes' (Middleton, 1990: 95). More melodious and 'non-abrasive' styles of music form the staple of radio 'easy listening', and the loose genre of 'lounge music', while louder genres (heavy metal, hard rock) have been seen as dangerous to listeners' hearing. The development of headphones and portable stereos, such as the Walkman, as well as the iPod, enabled different styles of listening, while reconfiguring the social locations and contexts within which it occurred.

Listening to particular musical styles requires distinct cultural capital, including, but not limited to, knowledge of the sonic codes and conventions of the genre and the previous work of the performer and similar artists. Unfamiliar music requires 'work', musical labour to situate the piece in relation to other, already familiar music. Antoine Hennion (2003) has been prominent in developing what he calls a sociology of mediation, and a related history of listening. Undertaking fascinating empirical research into how people listen, he argues that listening technologies have transformed, and in a sense created, the act of listening (see also Tagg and Clarida, 2003).

This is to utilize a more extended definition of 'musical', where what is crucial is the link between musical structures and people's use of them. As Stan Hawkins observes, 'the task of interpreting pop is an interdisciplinary task that deals with the relationship between music and social mediation. It is one that includes taking into account the consideration of the sounds in their relationship to us as individuals' (2002: 3).

Even when there has been a concern to address popular genres such as 'rock' as music, this has largely concentrated on its lyrical component, an approach I have cautiously followed here. In his insightful historical discussion, 'Why Do Songs Have Words?', Simon Frith showed how through the 1950s and 1960s the sociology of popular music was dominated by the analysis of the words of the songs. This was largely because such an approach was grounded in a familiar research methodology–content analysis. It did make a certain amount of sense given the dominance of popular music by the well-crafted but generally bland songs of Tin Pan Alley, but assumed, however, 'that it was possible to read back from lyrics to the social forces that produced them' (Frith, 1988:106). I want to consider two instructive examples of such difficulties.

Stand by your lyric

'Stand By Your Man', co-written (with Billy Sherrill) and sung by Tammy Wynette, was a no. 1 hit on its release in 1968 and the song remains one of the best-selling records by a woman in the history of country music. Wynette adopted it as her theme song, performing it in all her concerts and using it as the title for both her autobiography and the television movie about her life. The song even sparked a no. 1 hit response: Ronnie Milsap's Grammy-winning '(I'm A) Stand By My Woman Man' (1976). The popularity of 'Stand By Your Man' was matched by the controversy and critical response it created. This focused on the song's apparently sexist message:

> Stand by your man
> Give him two arms to cling to
> And something warm to come to
> On nights he's cold and lonely
> Stand by your man
> And tell the world you love him
> Keep giving all the love you can
> Stand by your man.

This chorus was generally interpreted as a simple clarion call for women to subserviently support their male partners, reducing the woman's role essentially to a physical one, providing 'arms' and 'something warm'. *Newsweek* headlined a 1971 article on Wynette's music: 'Songs of Non-Liberation', while other reviewers labelled her work 'pre-feminist' and equated it with traditional views of women's 'allegiance to the stronger sex'. But while the dynamics of the song emphasize the chorus, the lyrics to its only verse make its interpretation more problematic:

> Sometimes it's hard to be a woman
> Giving all your love to just one man
> You'll have bad times
> And he'll have good times
> Doin' things you don't understand
> But if you love him
> You'll forgive him
> Even though he's hard to understand
> And if you love him
> Be proud of him
> 'Cause after all he's just a man.

The verse is presenting the hardships women face in their relationships with men, with the last line a neatly condescending assertion of women's superior gender status. A literal reading of the lyrics (especially in print, as here) is misleading. The slightly maudlin and world-weary tone of Wynette's recorded vocal suggests an ironic stance. Another dimension that reinforces this emphasis was Tammy Wynette's personal life. Then a twice-divorced mother of three, several of her previous hits had asserted the views of a wronged and righteous single woman, especially her song 'D-I-V-O-R-C-E'. Furthermore, her subsequent tortured personal life (she died in 1998), including three additional marriages and further songs elaborating the earlier pro-woman themes, suggested Wynette was using 'Stand By Your Man' to make an ironic statement about the contradictory dimensions of women's experience of relationships. The verse and chorus of the song represent the dilemma women face of meeting their gender obligations, while anticipating their ideal achievement, and must be understood as a totality.

The Sherrill–Wynette songwriting partnership was mirrored in the song, with the male-mandated chorus providing the main theme, which is countered by the female-authored verse. It is also significant that Wynette distanced herself from the interpretations of the song as sexist, observing in her autobiography:

> I never did understand all the commotion over the lyrics of that song. I don't see anything in that song that implies that a woman is supposed to sit home and raise babies while a man goes out and raises hell.
>
> (Wynette, 1980: 193)

To validate this interpretation of 'Stand By Your Man' as ironic, it would be necessary to ask women (and men?) how they respond to and interpret the song, given that listeners respond in a variety of ways to the same musical text. This simple but essential point is also illustrated by the song 'Born in the USA'.

Patriotism and irony in the US

Songs create identification through their emotional appeal, but this does not necessarily mean that they can be reduced to a simple slogan or message, although some listeners may do just that. Bruce Springsteen was a dominant figure in 1980s' rock music and his song 'Born in the USA' (1984) represents one of his most powerful political statements. It reflecting the self-consciously political stance evident in his work, then and now, and his view that 'I don't think people are being taught to think hard enough about things in general, whether its about their own lives, politics, the situation in Nicaragua, or whatever' (1987 interview, cited in Pratt, 1990). 'Born in the USA' is a bitter narrative of life in the American underclass. The first person singer–narrator, Springsteen, joins the army to avoid 'a little hometown jam', fights in Vietnam, where his brother is killed and returns to unemployment, seemingly with no hope or future.

> Born down in a dead man's town,
> The first kick I took was when I hit the ground
> You end up like a dog that's been beat too much
> Til you spend half your life just covering up.

The music has a militaristic flavour, especially in the upbeat chorus sections, with the anthemic refrain:

> BORN IN THE USA
> I was BORN IN THE USA

I was BORN IN THE USA
BORN IN THE USA

It is an open question to what extent Springsteen's listeners appreciate the song as a resigned and ironic comment on the US. Springsteen himself was highly conscious of this:

> I opened the paper one day and saw where they had quizzed kids on what different songs meant to them and they asked them what 'Born in the USA' meant. 'Well, it's about my country', they answered. Well, that is what it's about – that's certainly one of the things it's about – but if that's as far in as you go, you're going to miss it, you know?
>
> (1987 interview, cited in Pratt, 1990)

Casually listening to the song, many of my own students regard it simply as a straightforward homage to America, picking up on the celebratory anthem-like chorus, rather than the verse narrative. This perspective is adjusted when a provocative comparison with the original recorded version of the song is provided by Springsteen's live acoustic version, which appears on *Tracks*, 1999. Here, due to Springsteen's vocal and guitar being fairly constant throughout, the verses 'compete' on an equal footing with the chorus and listeners are more conscious of the song's ironic celebration of the US.

'Stand By Your Man' and 'Born in the USA' both demonstrate that listeners use songs for their own purposes and the popularity of particular performers is only in part derived from the substantive musical content of their work. As the earlier discussion of stardom showed, performers can function as 'texts' in a broader sense, with particular cultural meanings attached to them. This involves considering how particular stylistic and musical techniques serve to encourage certain responses from their listeners and the role of genre in determining musical meaning. The following examples illustrate such an approach.

The Who: 'Talkin' 'bout My Generation'

Always very self-reflexive in his attitude towards rock in the early years of the Who, their lead guitarist and main songwriter Pete Townshend was concerned to promote rock as an art form, capable of inspiring and promoting social change. Townshend wrote a string of hits dealing with the frustrations of youth, most notably the anthem 'My Generation', a no. 2 chart success in the UK in 1965. (In the US, where the Who had yet to perform, and receiving limited promotion, it only reached no. 74 on the *Billboard* chart). The record established the band as one of the most innovative of the new British rock groups in the wake of the Beatles; it became the end piece of their concerts and provided the title song on their first album (on Brunswick in the UK): 'Suddenly the Who went from being one, albeit the most promising, of a mass of beat groups to spokesmen, stuttering on behalf of an entire generation' (Perry, 1998: 30). While the song had a very spontaneous sound to it, 'My Generation' had actually been laboriously developed by Townshend, through a number of intermediate stages.

As a band, the Who and 'My Generation' were linked to the mod subculture, which began in London around 1963. In a deliberate marketing move by the group's managers, the Who were originally called the High Numbers, whose first single, 'I'm the Face/Zoot Suit' (1964) drew on mod slang and dress. A youth subculture, mod was basically a working-class movement with a highly stylized form of dress, the fashions of which changed frequently and an interest in American R&B music. Living for weekend partying, the mods took pep pills, particularly 'purple hearts' (amphetamines). Several class-based strains of mod appeared, each with distinctive styles: an art school, high-camp version; mainstream mods; scooter boys; and the hard mods, some of whom developed into skinheads. The mod lifestyle parodied and subverted the respectable conventions of their class backgrounds and the relatively unskilled office jobs many of them held.

'My Generation', claims Gary Herman, 'epitomises everything that Mod meant to the mods themselves and to a whole generation of kids for whom mod was the only adequate expression of their feelings' (Herman, 1971: 62). The song presents a picture of a confused and inarticulate adolescent, with lead singer Roger Daltrey singing the vocal in a stuttering fashion that mimics the speed-induced verbal stoppages associated with mod methedrine use.

> People try to put us down
> (Talkin 'bout my generation)
> Just because we get around
> (Talkin 'bout my generation)
> Things they do look awful cold
> (Talkin 'bout my generation)
> Hope I die before I get old
> (Talkin 'bout my generation).

The song itself employs what Townshend called 'the Who brag form', with its self-assertive aggressiveness concealing a basic insecurity. Its pace is fast and frantic. It is a combination of bravado and inarticulateness; the stuttering conveys a mix of rage and frustration – as if the singer can't get the words out.

'My Generation' was a logical progression from the earlier Who singles 'Can't Explain' and 'Anyway, Anyhow, Anywhere'. Like them, it opened with a series of power chords and rustling drums, which Keith Moon subsequently develops into a slashing attack on his drum kit and John Entwistle's rumbling bass ('perhaps the most prominently recorded electric bass in rock up to that time': Marsh, 1983: 186). This style, which had developed because the Who had no rhythm guitarist, accordingly meant Townshend's lead guitar is strongly rhythmic, emphasizing chord structures rather than melodic lines. A series of simple chord changes keep the momentum going. The song builds in intensity, with a crescendo of feedback, climaxing with sounds reminiscent of the demolishing of lead guitar and drum kit which formed part of the Who's auto-destructive stage act. But what was most revolutionary about the song was its use of feedback. Rather than being used 'as a gimmick separate from the basic flow of the music', 'My Generation' uses feedback 'for the first time as an integral part of a rock composition – without it, the song would be incomplete' (Marsh, 1983: 187).

This indicates Townshend's reputation as a lead guitarist, in addition to his standing as the writer of some of the most memorable lyrics in rock. The Who toured exhaustively through the 1960s, particularly in the US where explosive stage appearances at the Monterey Pop Festival (1967) and Woodstock (1969) consolidated their standing as one of rock's premiere live acts. Townshend's guitar work earned him recognition among his peers and fans and he consistently placed well in performers' polls in the music press. What made his playing distinctive was his incorporation of it into the group's stage act, with his trademark propeller-arm playing style earning him the nickname the Birdman. Townshend's destruction of his guitar at the end of many of the Who's early concerts became a performance trademark, as did his experimentation with feedback.

The reputation of the Who, and Townshend, rests largely on their early hits: 'musical acid bombs, uniquely summing up that Sixties teenage attitude which compounded swaggering confidence with spluttering frustration', and which 'are still touched by a magic that has rarely been duplicated in English rock' (Sinclair, 1992: 381–82; see also Perry, 1998). 'My Generation' is regularly included in volumes presenting a canon of rock records and today's youth still finds it of interest. It has clear links with the later 'three-chord thrash' of late 1970s' punk and the recent revival of 'garage rock', which many students listen to. This, and the mod association, acts as a nostalgic prompt to further investigation of the song and the Who.

The Sex Pistols, 'Anarchy in the UK', and punk rock, further illustrates how songs are situated in terms of a combination of their formal musical properties, genre and social context, along with listeners' responses to them.

Sex Pistols: 'Anarchy in the UK'

Punk rock was a musical style with a closely associated youth subculture. The historical roots and antecedents of punk have been much debated, as have its subsequent influence (see Sabin, 1999). Punk emerged in response to a specific social and political context, in the UK in 1976 and 1977, affirming a politics of dissatisfaction with contemporary social and economic upheaval, which included sharp rises in youth unemployment, racism and industrial unrest.

Evaluation then and since gives 'Anarchy in the UK' (Virgin, 1976) and the Sex Pistols debut album *Never Mind the Bollocks* (Virgin,1977), which for many listeners was their first exposure to the song, a key place in the advent of punk rock in 1977–1978 in the UK and accords it a lasting influence. For Dave Marsh, it illustrates the musical fracture presented by punk in the late 1970s:

> somebody had figured out how to make artistically and commercially viable
> pop music based on a rhythmic process outside R&B, a feat unequalled since

the advent of Elvis Presley; consequently, things were fundamentally different thereafter. It was a true historic disjuncture.

(Marsh, 1989: 72)

For Jon Savage (1991), it was 'an index of their increasing ambition ... a call to arms, delivered in language that was as explosive as the group's name'. For Greil Marcus (1992: 594), it was part of the Sex Pistols' rupturing of rock 'n' roll, as they 'broke the story of rock & roll in half', turning it back on itself, and recasting key questions as to its cultural weight (see also the reviews collected in Heylin, 1998: 137ff.).

Savage traces the genesis and impact of 'Anarchy', giving it a definite political intent and accusing John Lydon (Johny Rotten) of 'deliberately using inflamma-tory imagery' particularly the terms 'antichrist' and 'anarchist', both conveying images of apocalypse, the second coming and social chaos: 'there seems little doubt that Lydon was fed material by Vivienne Westwood (McLaren's designer partner) and Jamie Reid (the Pistol's graphic artist), which he then converted to his own lyric' (Savage, 1991: 204).

The raw sound of the song is hardly accidental, as it went through a number of versions and recording sessions. 'Anarchy in the UK' was one of seven songs recorded by the group in July 1976 and it was these tapes that their manager Malcom McLaren took to the recording companies. With a stagnant music industry largely reacting to trends rather than initiating them, the Pistols' material at first created little interest:

> When production values were complex and smooth, the Goodman (produ-cer, Dave Goodman) tapes capture the group's live sound 'of broken glass and rusty razor blades'. In 1976, they must have sounded to the uninitiated like a rougher, more inept version of the new wave of Pub Rock bands, none of whom had reached the attention of the industry.
>
> (Savage, 1991: 206; see also Heylin, 1998)

Two days after they signed for EMI, the Sex Pistols again recorded 'Anarchy in the UK', which was to be their first single. The first attempts 'to get the spirit of live performance' (bass player Glen Matlock) proved unsatisfactory and it was eventually re-recorded with a different producer, Chris Thomas replacing Dave Goodman. On 26 November 1976 the single was finally released: 'A much clea-ner, more mainstream version, it was by that stage so loaded with expectation that it was difficult to listen objectively' (Savage, 1991: 255). Following the infa-mous Grundy interview of the group on Thames Television on 2 December and the subsequent controversy and distribution problems, the single climbed to no. 43 on the *NME* British chart and eventually reached no. 27 in late December; it never charted in the US, however.

The ingredients of 'Anarchy in the UK' typify punk rock (the following dis-cussion is based largely on Laing, 1988). First, punk bands relied on live shows to establish an identity and build a reputation, consequently 'techniques of recording and of arrangement were adopted which were intended to signify the "live" commitment of the disc' (Laing, 1988: 74). In short, punk records generally sound 'live', as if the studio had not come between the intentions of the musicians and their listening audience. Second, the use of the voice is in an identifiably punk mode, blurring the lyric with the singer's aggressive vocal, which lies between ordinary speech and singing. This makes the sound of the recording (voice plus instruments) more important than the actual identifiable lyric. Thus, for Laing 'any hope for the pure message, vocals as reflector of meaning, is doomed', which makes it 'possible (if difficult) to find pleasure in this celebrated punk rock song without the necessity of agreeing with the message' (Laing, 1988: 75–6; 78). This is rather at odds with Savage's view of 'Anarchy' as a political text, but is the dominant impression of the song retained by most casual listeners. Indeed, how 'seriously' are we to take punk lyrics like 'Anarchy'? The ideology of sincerity was central to punk and, in interviews, 'the stated beliefs of musicians, and their congruence with the perceived messages of their lyrics, became routine topics' (ibid.: 90). But, as various analyses demonstrate, in many cases punk lyrics are like collages, a series of often fractured images, with no necessarily correct reading.

Third, there is punk's mode of address. Compared with much popular music, the confidential stance is rare in punk rock and 'Anarchy' is strongly in a sardonic declamatory mode. As with other punk songs, there is also an emphasis on addressing individuals other than 'lovers' and a 'plural specific' address. Fourth, the tempo of punk is usually described as 'basic' and 'primitive'. As a musically minimalist genre, punk rock eschewed the growing use of electronic instruments associated with 'progressive' rock, and featured a strict guitar and drums instrumental line-up: 'this was a sound best suited to expressing anger and frustration, focusing chaos, dramatizing the last days as daily life and ramming all emotions into the narrow gap between a blank stare and a sardonic grin' (Marcus, 1992: 595). What also set punk apart from other rock styles was its rhythmic patterns, the main reason for the 'un-danceability' of much punk rock. This 'provided a feeling of unbroken rhythmic flow, enhanced by the breakneck eight to the bar rhythm of much punk rock' (Laing, 1988: 85), adding to the urgency that the voice and aggressive vocals evoked. The lack of emphasis on instrumental virtuosity reflected punk's frequent association of skill with glibness. The frequently alleged musical incompetence of punk bands, however, was largely a myth, often fuelled by the bands themselves. (On this point, see McNeil and McCain, 1996; and Marcus Gray's study of the Clash, *Last Gang in Town*, 1995, which takes issue with much of the received wisdom regarding punk's supposed values.)

As even this abbreviated discussion indicates, 'Anarchy' demonstrates the congruence between punk as music and the social location and values of the associated punk subculture. Music here exists very much within a broader set of social relations. My last example takes us into a different sort of musical politics from punk, with new technologies for producing music combining with the internet to create another field of debate around musical texts and their creators.

Danger Mouse: **The Grey Album** *(2004)*

The Grey Album is a mash-up created and released in limited quantities on the internet by then underground hip-hop artist Danger Mouse (Brian Burton) in 2004. The album combines (mashes) an a cappella version of rapper Jay-Z's *The Black Album* with instrumentals created from numerous unauthorized samples from the Beatles self-titled LP, better known as *The White Album*.

Although mash-ups came to public prominence with the release of *The Grey Album* and the controversy that followed, such a 'cut-and-paste' approach had its origins in sample-based music from the late 1970s onward, including early forms of hip-hop and disco medleys in which a mixer would segue from one song to another (on the evolution of the mash-up, see McLeod, 2005b; Sinnreich, 2010: Chapter 3). Mash-ups were made possible by the advent of simple computer programs that allowed home-based amateur composers to juxtapose two or more songs and the digital distribution facilitated by the internet and file-sharing networks that emerged through the early 2000s (Napster, Limewire).

Danger Mouse pressed only 3000 copies of his album, but it spread rapidly on file-sharing networks (see Chapter 2), boosted by favourable coverage in music magazines (*Rolling Stone*) and the mainstream press, including *The New York Times*. It was estimated that more than 100,000 downloads of the album initially occurred, enough for it to achieve 'Gold' status in the United States (Howard-Spink, 2004: 5).

Mash-ups are created exclusively from prerecorded sources and as such challenged traditional conceptions of copyright and 'fair use'. Although Jay-Z's work was copyrighted, he had actually released it to encourage remixes and mash-ups and praised the creativity he saw in *The Grey Album*. Paul McCartney also acknowledged that he was comfortable with Danger Mouse's project, but EMI, the Beatles' label, attempted to prevent the distribution of *The Grey Album*. Music activists responded by coordinating a major online protest, 'Grey Tuesday', with at least 170 websites risking a lawsuit by hosting the album (Howard-Spink, 2004; McLeod, 2005b).

In his extensive analysis of new 'configurable' technologies, Aram Sinnreich sees such mash-ups as further examples of the social and economic ramifications posed by these technologies, which are undermining the traditional consumer/producer dichotomy of musical production. Along with remixes, mash-ups problematize the distinction between the 'original' and the 'copy', in the process raising questions of authorship and the musical division of labour: 'Who is the author of a mash-up, and who is its audience? Are DJs composers or performers? Is a digital music file source material or finished product?' (Sinnreich, 2010: 8).

Finally, I want to consider a particular form of song text, cover versions, which again demonstrate debates around commerce, creativity and authenticity.

Cover versions

Cover versions are performances and recordings by musicians not responsible for the original recording. Historically, these were often 'standards' and were the staples of singers' repertoire for most of the 1940s and 1950s. Reflecting industry competition and as part of marketing strategy, record companies would release their artists' cover versions of hits from their competitors. In the 1950s, white singers covered the original rock 'n' roll recordings by black artists, often sanitizing them in the process (e.g. Pat Boone's cover of Little Richard's 'Tutti Frutti'), in an effort by record companies to capitalize on the ethnic divide in American radio. Criticism of this frequently exploitative practice led to covers being equated with a lack of originality and regarded as not as creative, or authentic, as the original recording. This view was reinforced by the aesthetics and ideology of 1960s' rock culture, valuing individual creativity and the use of one's own compositions (Keightley, 2003). More recently, it has been recognized that many song covers have been creative in their own right (The Wire, 2005; Solis, 2010; and see the examples that follow).

There is an economic dimension to covers, since they are a proven product that an audience can often identify with. Accordingly, many covers, especially when played by cover and tribute bands, seek to replicate the original recorded version as closely as possible. Covers have also featured strongly in the charts, especially since the late 1980s. There is a fresh generation of listeners and a new market for a recycled song, as reissues, compilation albums and film soundtracks continue to demonstrate. Such marketing practices and career choices can undermine the status of covers, but the negative image of the cover song is undeserved. Interpretation of the original recording aside, covers have provided a training ground for musicians and have often served as a form of homage to the original artists. Playing and recording covers is a way for artists to authenticate themselves with their audience, through identification with respected original artists. Elvis Presley's Sun performances of 'That's Alright Mama' (Sun, 1955), originally recorded by R&B singer Arthur 'Big Boy' Crudup, and his version of the bluegrass classic 'Blue Moon of Kentucky', rehearsed the singer's influences and contributed to the formation of rockabilly and rock 'n' roll in the 1950s. Later in their careers, established bands and performers will sometimes record entire albums of covers, in a 'tip of the hat' to their influences (for example, Metallica, Matthew Sweet and Susanna Hoffs).

In the UK, in the late 1950s and early 1960s, a number of musicians became intensely interested in black American performers, including those whose work provided the antecedents of rock 'n' roll. Groups such as the Rolling Stones, the Yardbirds, and the Animals began playing covers or reworked versions of American R&B and blues, gradually transforming the music into what became known as 'rock'. A significant audience emerged for this music, stimulated by tours of England by several leading American bluesmen, including Howlin' Wolf and Muddy Waters. Guitarist Eric Clapton was prominent among those reaching back beyond 1950s' rock 'n' roll to country and electric blues for inspiration and musical texts. In 1966, with two other key figures in the British rhythm and blues movement, Ginger Baker (drums) and Jack Bruce (bass), Clapton formed Cream. The trio came together in a conscious attempt to push the boundaries of rock through developing the potential of blues-based music and performed and recorded versions of blues' classics, notably Willie Dixon's 'Spoonful', itself based on Charlie Patton's 'A Spoonful of Blues' (1929). Headlam (1997) instructively traces these back to their original sources in Chicago and Delta blues.

To illustrate how artists 'seek to define themselves in relation to traditions and genres other than their own', Butler examines two covers by the Pet Shop Boys: 'Where the Streets Have No Name', originally by rock band U2 (1987) and 'Go West', originally by the disco/dance group the Village People (1979). The musical sound, performance style and lyrical themes of each pair of songs, and the discourse surrounding their production and reception, show how these covers provide an intertextual commentary on the original works. He argues that the Pet Shop Boys subvert the U2 song, 'poking fun at certain common ways of exposing authenticity in 1980s rock' and their cover of 'Go West', as a 'stomping disco record', repositions disco as a form of roots music for the gay community of the 1990s (Butler, 2003: 1).

Covers are a significant part of the repertoire of many other performers, with the ability to 'mine' and revise the musical past, regarded as a virtue. Joan Jett, who played rhythm guitar in the teenage female hard rock band the Runaways, initiated a solo career with 'I Love Rock 'n' Roll' (Boardwalk, 1982). A remake of an obscure B side by British band the Arrows, Joan Jett and the Blackhearts' version was one of the biggest hits of the 1980s, spending seven weeks at no. 1 on the US *Billboard* chart. The song provided the title track for a successful album, which also included 'Crimson and Clover', originally a no. 1 hit for Tommy James and the Shondells in 1967. Released as a single, Jett's cover of this reached no. 7. She had further chart success with a cover of Gary Glitter's 'Do You Wanna Touch Me (Oh Yeah)' and subsequently released an album of covers, *The Hit List* (Epic, 1990), featuring songs she had frequently played in concert. As a quirky footnote to this, the Arrows' version of 'I Love Rock 'n' Roll' was itself an oblique form of cover, being written in response to the rather cynical and world-weary tone of the Rolling Stones' single, 'It's Only Rock 'n' Roll'.

At the beginning of her music career, punk poet Patti Smith appropriated and adapted songs associated with masculinity and the romantic rebel tradition in rock, inflecting them with a radical feminism. In her first single, a cover of 'Hey Joe', Smith replaced the original wife-murderer in the song with female terrorist and media celebrity Patti Hurst. On her critically acclaimed debut album *Horses* (Arista, 1975), Smith covered Van Morrison's 'Gloria' (originally recorded by Them, in 1966). Them had recorded 'Gloria' in a proto-punk, garage rock style, with a basic beat, Van Morrison's growled vocals and a ragged chanted chorus: 'G-L-O-R-I-A: Gloria'. The song's lyrics emphasize the appeal of Gloria – 'she'll make you feel alright' – and cater to the male fantasy of seduction by a female temptress. Them's 'Gloria' can be considered an example of male-coded rock 'n' roll, sometimes referred to as 'cock rock'. This became an alternative term for hard rock, highlighting the genre's often explicit and aggressive expression of male sexuality, its misogynist lyrics and its phallic imagery. Cock rock performers were regarded as aggressive, dominating and boastful, a stance, it was argued, evident in their live shows.

Against this tradition, Patti Smith reworks the song from a female point of view, exposing Morrison's macho stance with an exaggerated leering 'male' vocal performance and using gender ambiguities to parody the 'maleness' of Van Morrison's song. At various points in the song, Smith slips into gendered 'characters', undermining the dominant male rock vocal of the original, along with its numerous cover versions by male rock bands (Daley, 1997: 237). On stage and in her personal style, Smith emulated the toughness of male rebellion, but regarded her band's music as 'feminine music'. In her striking photograph (by Robert Mapplethorpe) on the cover of *Horses* (Arista, 1975), Smith is dressed in jeans and a white shirt, with a tie draped around her neck, conveying an air of self-assurance and sexual ambiguity. Along with her music, this stance enabled Smith to challenge patriarchal control and attempt to bridge rock's gender gap, as have later performers such as Björk, P.J. Harvey and Tori Amos.

Recent analyses of covers have extended the earlier considerations of issues of gender and sexuality and ethnicity, to show how 'cover versions can supply case studies for the textual illustration and mounting of discussion around questions of identity and political power' (Griffiths, 2002; see also Solis, 2010).

Conclusion

I have argued that musicology has much to offer as an approach to the analysis of musical texts, provided that we also recognize that songs exist very much within a broader set of social relations. As the musicologist Nicholas Cook puts it, there is a need for 'the reconciliation of today's broadened agenda with the traditional discipline's practices of close textual reading. In other words, we need to find ways of talking about music and its social or ideological meaning at the same time' (Cook, n.d.). Obviously, my discussion of the songs included here has been limited, especially in relation to the way in which the music 'works' with the lyrics to create an aural text: the recording. To engage with them further, it is necessary to listen to the recordings (through iTunes) and view them as performances (through YouTube). At the same time, it is necessary to go beyond musical texts as individual entities, and their qualities as music, to consider how they create particular listening experiences and an audience for their performers. This includes considering texts as 'collectivities' and the role of genre.

Further reading

Popular musicology

[See also Appendix 2: Musical analysis.]

Beard, D. and Gloag, D. (2005) *Musicology: The Key Concepts*, Abingdon, New York: Routledge.

Cook, N. 'What is musicology?', www.rma.ac.uk/articles

Frith, S. (2007) 'Why Do Songs Have Words?' in *Taking Popular Music Seriously. Selected Essays* Aldershot: Ashgate (first published 1988).

Hennion, A. (2003) 'Music and Mediation: Towards a New Sociology of Music', in H. Clayton, T. Herbert and R. Middleton (eds), *The Cultural Study of Music: A Critical Introduction*, New York, London: Routledge, pp. 80–91.

Middleton, R. (ed.) (2000) *Reading Pop: Approaches to Textual Analysis in Popular Music*, Oxford, New York: Oxford University Press.

Moore, A.F. (ed.) (2003) *Analyzing Popular Music*, Cambridge, New York: Cambridge University Press.

Scott, D. (ed.) (2009) *The Ashgate Research Companion to Popular Musicology*, Farnham, Burlington, VT: Ashgate.

Tagg, P. and Clarida, B. (2003) *Ten Little Title Tunes: Towards a Musicology of the Mass Media*, New York, Montreal: Mass Media Musicologists' Press.

Mash-ups

Howard-Spink, S. (2004) 'Grey Tuesday: online cultural activism and the mash-up of music and politics', *First Monday*, 9, 10.

McLeod, K. (2005) 'Confessions of an Intellectual (Property): Danger Mouse, Mickey Mouse, Sonny Bono, and My Long and Winding Path as a Copyright Activist–Academic', *Popular Music and Society*, 28, 1: 79–94.

Sinnreich, A. (2010) *Mashed Up. Music, Technology and the Rise of Configurable Culture*, Amherst, Boston, MA: University of Massachusetts Press.

Covers

Griffiths, D. (2002) 'Cover Versions and the Sound of Identity in Motion', in D. Hesmondhalgh and K. Negus (eds), *Popular Music Studies*, London: Arnold.

Keightley, K. (2003) 'Covers', in J. Shepherd, D. Horn, D. Laing, P. Oliver and P. Wicke (eds) *The Encyclopedia of Popular Music of the World, Volume 1*, London: Cassell.

Plasketes, G. (guest ed.) (2005) *Popular Music and Society*, 28, 2, 'Special issue: Like a Version – Cover Songs in Popular Music'.

Solis G. (ed.) (2010) *Play it Again: Cover Songs in Popular Music*, Aldershot: Ashgate.

6 'It's Still Rock 'n' Roll to Me'

Genre, authenticity and the canon

Genre, its nature and significance, are a central aspect of popular music studies. I begin with a preliminary discussion of the concept and its study, including the concept of metagenres and then examine a number of examples of these. Rock and pop, often situated as in opposition to each other, illustrate the importance of authenticity in framing distinctions between genres, their associated musicians and audiences; heavy metal shows a common pattern of genre differentiation, with a range of subgenres developing during the history of the form; world music shows the importance of marketing to genre formation, and illustrates debates around cultural appropriation; and hip-hop demonstrates the shift to the commercial mainstream of once marginal musical styles. Finally, the influential notion of a 'rock canon' further illustrates debates around the authenticity and cultural value of different popular music texts.

Genre

Genre can be basically defined as a category or type. A key component of textual analysis, genre is widely used to analyze popular culture texts, most notably in their filmic and popular literary forms (e.g. thrillers, science fiction, romance and horror).

Identifiable genres of popular music are understood as such by musicians, the music industry and by consumers. At the same time, there is considerable argument about the historical location and development of particular genres, their characteristics and the boundaries between them. Genres are constantly debated and contested; while they may share formal musicological characteristics and histories, they are situated in a commercial and cultural nexus. As Fabian Holt (2007: Chapter 1) claims, the complex cultural work associated with genre, and the multiplicity of sites in which it is active, mean that genre is not a simple concept amenable to easy definition. That said, there have been a number of substantive attempts to develop a broadly applicable definition of music genre (Fabbri, 1999; Frith, 1996; Negus, 1999; some accounts, wanting to ground the discussion more in musicology, prefer the term style to genre, for instance Charlton, 1994) and studies of particular genres have been forced to grapple with the issue.

Genre is central to the wider popular music culture. Genre categories are evident in the A&R and marketing practices of sound recording companies; the data collected by recording industry organizations (for example, the RIAA's consumer profile statistics); industry publications such as *Billboard*, especially its chart listings; the formats of radio stations and MTV channels; music retail; and the music press. Fans will frequently identify themselves with particular genres, often demonstrating considerable knowledge of the complexities of their preferences (subgenres). The various popular music encyclopedias, the standard histories, journalistic and academic analyses, all use genre as a central organizing concept.

Jennifer Lena and Richard Peterson (2008) provide a useful survey of what they see as two dominant approaches to the study of musical genre: those grounded in musicology, which identify genre as music sharing distinctive musical characteristics, and accounts that place genre study more firmly in a social context, which they see as having greater explanatory power. Following the 'social context' approach, they define music genres as 'systems of orientations, expectations, and conventions that bind together an industry, performers, critics, and fans in making what they identify as a distinctive sort of music' (2008: 698). This situates genre is a process: as Frith has observed, for musicians genre categories constitute an effective shorthand for discussing and making music; for listeners, genre helps organize the listening process; and for the industry, genre combines musical style (the sound) and the marketing of it (Frith, 1996: 79–95).

In part, critical analysis has concentrated on the tension between an emphasis on 'standardized codes that allow no margin for distraction' (Fabbri, 1999), and the fluidity of genres as these codes are elaborated on and challenged and displaced by new codes. While musical genres continue to function as marketing categories and reference points for musicians, critics and fans, particular examples clearly demonstrate that genre divisions must be regarded as highly fluid. No style is totally independent of those that have preceded it and musicians borrow elements from existing styles and incorporate them into new forms. Charles Kronengold (2008) provides an insightful example of this, in his discussion of the links between three late 1970s' genres – disco, new wave and album-oriented rock – normally viewed as distinct, but that 'overlap in varying degrees with respect to their historical moment, modes of dissemination, institutional frames (like record labels), musical materials, personnel, and audiences' (43). He observes that:

> When you study these genres you can't entirely abandon the notion of genre as a set of rules and constitutive features; but these and other genres of the seventies can often be better referenced to their internal variety and proliferation of subgenres, their modes of revision and transformation, and their movement towards other genres.
>
> (43)

Drawing on this literature, several distinguishing characteristics of genres can be identified and applied to their study. First, there are the stylistic traits present in the music: their musical characteristics, which produce an identifiable sound, according to conventions of composition, instrumentation and performance. These may vary in terms of their coherence and sustainability, particularly within metagenres. Along with other aspects of genre, particular musical characteristics can be situated within the general historical evolution of popular music. Second, there are other, essentially non-musical, stylistic attributes, most notably image and its associated visual style. This includes standard iconography and record cover format; the locale and structure of performances, especially in concert, and the dress, makeup and hair styles adopted by both the performers and their listeners and fans. Musical and visual stylistic aspects combine in terms of how they operate to produce particular ideological effects, a set of associations that situate the genre within the broader musical constituency. Third, there is the primary audience for particular styles. The relationship between fans (and subcultures) and their genre preferences is a form of transaction, mediated by the forms of delivery, creating specific cultural forms with sets of expectations. Genres are accorded specific places in a musical hierarchy by both critics and fans and by many performers. This hierarchy is loosely based around the notions of authenticity, sincerity and commercialism. The critical denigration of certain genres, including disco, dance pop and the elevation of others, such as alt. country, reflects this and mirrors the broader, still widely accepted, high/low culture split. Fourth, there are the institutional frames and practices, especially within the recording companies (see Negus, 1999), which help shape genres.

Elsewhere (Shuker, 2012), I have identified and provided brief introductions to 12 popular music metagenres: blues (including R&B and gospel), country, EDM: electronic dance music, folk, heavy metal, jazz, pop, hip-hop, reggae, rock, soul and world music. Obviously, especially given the fluidity of genres I mentioned earlier, these designations are open to debate. For example, should R&B and gospel be 'lumped in' with blues or is the latter more appropriately placed with soul? These metagenre divisions are, in part, necessary heuristic devices, 'umbrella' terms to give some structure to a cultural field. Each is characterized by having a specific geographical, social and cultural and historical point of origin; a broad musicological identity; and a subsequent history of stylistic and international diffusion, with emergent associated major genres and subgenres. As an example of the framing of metagenres, let me consider the two most commonly referred to: rock and pop.

Rock, pop and authenticity

The terms 'pop' and 'rock' are often used as shorthand for 'popular music', at the same time as there is a tendency to contrast and polarize the two styles. They are best regarded as broadly constituted metagenres and as commercially produced music for consumption by a mass market. Similarities of production aside, there are important ideological assumptions behind the distinctions between pop and rock, largely based around the concept of authenticity.

Authenticity

A central concept in the discourses surrounding popular music, authenticity is imbued with considerable symbolic value. As commonly used, the term authenticity assumes that the producers of music texts undertook the 'creative' work themselves; that there is an element of originality or creativity present, along with connotations of seriousness, sincerity and uniqueness; and that while the input of others is recognized, it is the musicians' role that is regarded as pivotal. Important in identifying and situating authenticity are the commercial setting in which a recording is produced, with a tendency to dichotomize the music industry into independent labels (more authentic, less commercial) and the majors (more commercial, less authentic). Perceptions of authenticity (or non-authenticity) are also present in the degree to which performers and records are assimilated and legitimized by particular subcultures or communities. As I outlined in Chapter 3, authenticity is traditionally associated with live performance, a view undermined by the rise of disco and later dance cultures. The use of authenticity as a central evaluative criterion is commonly seen in the discussions of the relative nature and merits of particular genres and performers within popular music culture, e.g. vernacular community-based styles of folk, country blues and roots music are frequently perceived as more authentic than their commercialized forms.

Alan Moore usefully moves the discussion of the concept beyond simple polarities (authentic versus unauthentic), by postulating a tripartite typology dependent on asking who, rather then what, is being authenticated. As he suggests, authenticity is most usefully conceived of as 'a construction made in the act of listening' (Moore, 2002: 210). Accordingly, we should be asking not if particular stylistic characteristics can be considered 'authentic', or non-authentic, but rather how authenticity is constructed in particular music genres and performers and the strategies involved. This process is evident in relation to pop and rock.

Pop: 'Silly Love Songs' (Paul McCartney)

As Philip Ennis (1992) documents, pop music was evident in three of the defining 'streams' that eventually overlap and fuse in the evolution of American popular music:

1 'Pop' as the commercial music of the nation, associated with Tin Pan Alley, musical theatre, the motion picture and the rise of radio.
2 'Black pop', the popular music of black Americans, commercially domesticated around 1900 and from 1920 to 1948 known as 'race music'.
3 'Country pop', the popular music of the American white south and southwest.

Alongside these were three smaller streams: jazz, folk and gospel.

Collectively, these six streams were the basis for the emergence in the 1950s of what Ennis, in common with many other commentators, terms 'rock 'n' roll', his seventh stream. Following its Tin Pan Alley antecedents, pop was seen as a somewhat watered-down, blander version of rock 'n' roll, associated with a more rhythmic style and smoother vocal harmony, characteristic of the period of teen idols in the late 1950s and early 1960s.

Musically, pop became defined by its general accessibility, its commercial orientation, an emphasis on memorable hooks, or choruses and a lyrical pre-occupation with romantic love as a theme. The musical aesthetics of pop are essentially conservative: 'It is about providing popular tunes and cliches in which to express commonplace feelings – love, loss, and jealousy' (Frith, 2001: 96). Along with songwriters, producers are often regarded as the main creative force behind pop artists. Accordingly, as a genre in the marketplace, pop's defining feature is that 'It is music produced commercially for profit, as a matter of enterprise not art' (Frith, 2001: 94). Over the past half century it has frequently been collapsed into and equated with 'popular' and includes a range of styles under labels such as 'chart pop' and 'teen pop'. Much of pop is regarded as disposable, for-the-moment dance music; the best of it survives as 'golden oldies' and 'classic hits'.

While pop has a long musical history, predating the 1950s, it became used in a generic sense as the umbrella name for a special kind of musical product aimed at a teenage market, especially in the UK. Reflecting the dominance of teen pop in the late 1950s, pop became used in an oppositional, even antagonistic sense, to rock music (see later). 'Pop' became used to characterize chart- and teenage audience-oriented music, particularly the genres of dance pop, bubblegum, power pop, and the new romantics, and performers such as the girl groups of the 1960s, their 1990s' equivalents, and the ubiquitous boy bands of the modern era. Pop is also currently prominent in reality television shows such as *Pop Idol* (see Chapter 8). The most significant of these styles has been chart-oriented, dance pop. As with pop generally, dance pop is often maligned, in part because of its perceived commercial orientation and its main audience of adolescent girls – 'teenyboppers'. Commercially highly successful exponents include Kylie Minogue, Paula Abdul and Bananarama in the 1980s; the Spice Girls and Britney Spears in the 1990s; and, currently, Katy Perry, Justin Bieber and Lady Gaga.

The debate around the Spice Girls, who had enormous international success in the late 1990s, exemplified the discourse around dance pop, especially regarding its commodification and authenticity. The Spice Girls slogan, 'Girl Power', stressed female bonding, a sense of sisterhood, friendship and self-control, evident through their personas, press interviews and the lyrics to their songs. However, critics pointed to the contradictions between the Spice Girls professed self-expression and their subversion to standard sexualized 'feminine' images and their incorporation into a male-dominated music industry, thereby sustaining dominant gender ideologies (see their career profile in Chapter 4).

The success of these pop performers was frequently attributed to the Svengali-like influence of producers and professional songwriters (e.g. Stock Aiken Waterman and British 'new pop' in the 1980s) and exposure through MTV and energetic video performances (e.g. Britney Spears), as much as or more than musical talent. Today, pop is increasingly identified with the wider culture of celebrity. Some pop performers capitalize on their prior public visibility in film and television, fashion and society, using this to (they hope) launch a recording career (Paris Hilton, Hillary Duff). Conversely, others use pop success and celebrity as a launch pad to commodify themselves more widely, as with Kylie Minogue, Madonna and Beyoncé.

'Rock On' (Gary Glitter)

'Rock' became the broad label for the huge range of styles that have evolved out of rock 'n' roll since the mid-1960s; these include hard rock, blues rock, progressive rock, punk rock, psychedelic or acid rock, heavy metal, country rock, glitter rock, new wave, indie rock and alternative rock (Shuker, 2012). A semantic shift was confirmed in March 1967, when the influential *Crawdaddy* magazine changed its subtitle from 'The magazine of rock 'n' roll' to 'The magazine of rock'.

Rock is often considered to carry more 'weight' than pop, with connotations of greater integrity, sincerity and authenticity. Dave Hill, writing of the 1980s, observed:

> Pop implies a very different set of values to rock. Pop makes no bones about being mainstream. It accepts and embraces the requirement to be instantly pleasing and to make a pretty picture of itself. Rock on the other hand, has liked to think it was somehow more profound, non-conformist, self-directed and intelligent.
>
> (Hill, 1986: 8)

Similarly, for Martin Strong:

> Rock music is written by the artist(s) for him or herself, not with the initial intention of making money, but to make music – and, possibly, to stretch its limits and boundaries a little further. This is music that may last forever, becoming 'classic' in the process. On the other hand, POP music is written with the sole intention (normally) of making a quick buck, either for the artists(s) or (more than likely) their record label.
>
> (Strong, 2006: Preface)

Such distinctions attempt to keep commerce and artistic integrity apart on a central yardstick to identify particular artists with either pop or rock 'n' roll. This reflected a tendency in the 1980s (and still evident) to view popular music in terms of a series of dichotomies: mass v. community/local; commerce v. creativity; manufactured v. authentic; major record companies v. independents. This is a legacy of the mythology of 'rock', which was a product of the 1960s, when leading American critics – Jon Landau, Dave Marsh and Robert Christgau – elaborated a view of rock as correlated with authenticity, creativity and the romantic cultural tradition and a particular political moment: the 1960s' protest movement and the counterculture. Closely associated with this leftist political ideology of rock was *Rolling Stone* magazine, founded in 1967 (see Chapter 9).

This demarcation between rock and pop has continued to be evident in the music industry, the music press and among fans and musicians. The distinction is difficult to maintain, given the commercial production and marketing of both metagenres. Historically, the frequent refusal of rock musicians and fans to admit to commodity status, and attempt to position themselves as somehow above the manufacturing process, have all too easily have become marketing ploys – 'the Revolution is on CBS' slogan of the late 1960s being perhaps the best example. Nevertheless, using authenticity to distinguish between rock and pop continues to serve an important ideological function, helping differentiate particular forms of musical cultural capital. Such distinctions also occur *within* the two metagenres, as with indie rock setting itself apart from mainstream rock music.

Heavy metal

Heavy metal, now often referred to simply as metal, can also be considered a metagenre. It has a substantial history, distinctive fans and now encompasses a wide range of subgenres. The musical parameters of heavy metal (HM) as a genre cannot be comfortably reduced to formulaic terms. It is usually louder, 'harder' and faster paced than conventional rock music and remains predominantly guitar oriented. The main instruments are electric guitars (lead and bass) drums and electronic keyboards, but there are numerous variants within this basic framework (see Berelian, 2005). Some forms of the genre have enjoyed enormous commercial success and have a large fan base; other extreme subgenres have a cult following. As a subject of academic inquiry, 'metal studies' can now be regarded as a subfield in its own right, with a substantial body of recent scholarship (see Brown, 2011; also Cope, 2010; Waksman, 2009).

Some critics see heavy metal as beginning in the late 1960s, its origins variously being traced to several key recordings: Blue Cheer's 1968 reworking of Eddie Cochran's 1950s hit 'Summertime Blues', which turned Cochran's great acoustic guitar riff into distorted metallic-sounding electric guitar chords, accompanied by a thumping percussion, and Steppenwolf's 'Born To Be Wild' (1967) with its reference to 'heavy metal thunder' (from the William Burroughs' novel, *Naked Lunch*) in the song's second verse. HM was a logical progression from the power trios of 1960s groups such as the Jimi Hendrix Experience and Cream, who played blues-based rock with heavily amplified guitar and bass reinforcing one another.

However, histories of the genre generally see the release of Black Sabbath's eponymous debut album (1970), which reached no. 8 in the UK album chart and spent three months on the US album chart, and their follow-up album *Paranoid* (1970) as establishing the early parameters of heavy metal. The band's origins in industrial Birmingham were reflected in their music, characterized by Tony Iommi's style of guitar playing (born of necessity following an industrial accident; see his interview in *Seven Ages of Rock*, episode 4), singer Ozzy Osbourne's vocal wail and lyrics drawing on black magic and the occult (see Hoskyns, 2004;

see also Christe, 2004). Also important contributors to shaping the new genre were albums from Deep Purple (*Deep Purple in Rock*) and Uriah Heap (*Very 'eavy, Very 'umble* in the UK, self-titled in the US), both also released in 1970. Christe (2004), writing from the viewpoint of a sympathetic critic, sees metal's early success as based on its devoted fans: an audience linked by tape trading and established by heavy touring and a strong commitment to the live concert event by bands such as Sabbath.

The commercial success of the British bands Black Sabbath, Deep Purple and, above all, Led Zeppelin, along with Grand Funk and Mountain in the US – despite the general critical 'thumbs down' for their efforts – consolidated heavy metal as a market force in the early 1970s and established a heavy metal youth subculture. Even this short list of performers demonstrates the difficulties of bounding the genre and there are notable differences in their treatment in the various histories and commentaries on metal. Led Zeppelin performed more traditional blues-based material and combined acoustic outings with electric guitars, yet are considered HM in influential early studies of the genre (Walser, 1993; Weinstein, 2000). Although Deep Purple and their American counterparts are often considered as HM bands, they have also been classified as 'hard' or 'heavy' rock. In the 1980s there was a clear distinction possible between the more overtly commercially oriented MTV-friendly HM bands, such as Bon Jovi and Poison with their glam rock images, and mainstream HM bands, whose styles merge into hard rock, such as Guns 'n' Roses, and Aerosmith.

Drawing on the work of Franco Fabbri (1999), Andrew Cope provides an insightful re-evaluation of HM as a musical genre and its distinction from heavy rock, with an extensive discussion of 'the actual musical sounds, timbres and structures that uniquely combine to generate the identifiable fingerprint that listeners recognize as the heavy metal sound' (Cope, 2010: 1). Of particular interest is his examination of the differences between Black Sabbath and Led Zeppelin, identifying a 'clear musical and aesthetic dichotomy between the two bands'. Cope develops a convincing argument that 'Black Sabbath, through radical transgressions of their origins, initiated the evolution of heavy metal whilst Led Zeppelin, through a reworking of blues conventions significantly contributed to the evolution of hard rock' (2010: 4, 5, Chapter 3).

Until the publication of Deena Weinstein's comprehensive sociological studies (1991, 2000), Robert Walser's more musically grounded treatment (1993) and Jeffrey Arnett's study of its fans (1996), there were few attempts to seriously discuss the genre. Yet, as these studies showed, heavy metal displayed a musical cogency and enjoyed a mass appeal, existing within a set of social relations. During the mid-1970s, there developed a heavy metal subculture, predominantly working class, white, young and male, identifying with the phallic imagery of guitars and the general muscularity and oppositional orientation of the form. The symbols associated with heavy metal, which include Nazi insignia and Egyptian and Biblical symbols, provided a signature of identification with the genre, being widely adopted by metal's youth cult following (see Arnett, 1996). The audience for HM later moved beyond this traditional male, white working-class constituency, with glam metal playing an important role in the 'feminization' of metal.

Once established, heavy metal demonstrated the common pattern of genre fragmentation and hybridization. There are a number of identifiable heavy metal subgenres or closely related styles, notably:

- NWOBHM (new wave of British heavy metal)
- glam metal (also referred to as lite, hair or pop metal)
- thrash/speed metal
- rap metal
- extreme metal (including death, black and doom metal; grindcore).

Although historically specific, each of these has continued to be represented in the wide variety of contemporary metal performers (see the entries on each in Shuker, 2012). Metal has also been part of several hybrid styles, notably prog metal, and been drawn on by performers who are largely situated in mainstream commercial rock, such as the 'funk metal' of the early Red Hot Chili Peppers (*Blood Sugar Sex Magic*, WB, 1991). In addition, metal has interacted with related genres, notably punk (see Waksman, 2009) and grunge (Weinstein, 2000: Chapter 8).

Extreme metal demonstrates the process of intensification that occurs with the ongoing maturation of popular music genres. Keith Kahn-Harris observes that on the edge of metal culture, forms of metal that are much more obscure and that attract far less attention than contemporary mainstream heavy metal are thriving: 'These forms of metal represent the most diverse, the most artistically vibrant, the most dynamic and also the most problematic aspects of metal culture. Collectively they are known as extreme metal' (2007: 20). Although extreme metal 'frequently teeters on the edge of formless noise', it has been influential in providing 'a crucial motor of innovation within metal' (5, 6). The following discussion and page references are drawn from Kahn-Harris.

Black metal was arguably the first form of extreme metal to appear, popularized by the British band Venom, whose 1982 album *Black Metal* gave the style a label and inspired a new generation of metal bands. Venom presented 'more extreme occult imagery than other metal bands' and 'a speeded up and stripped-down version of the genre', which helped shape thrash metal. In the mid-1980s, death metal developed out of thrash, with bands such as Cannibal Corpse and Morbid Angel featuring fast, growled vocals, lyrics that dealt with themes such as war, violence and the occult, and complicated guitar work (albeit with few solos). Grindcore represented a 'punk-influenced radicalisation of death metal' (3), utilizing extreme speed and featuring short songs. Doom metal also emerged in the 1980s, as 'an extremely slow form of metal with long epic song structures and melancholic lyrics' (4). Nationally based variants of these styles developed, as with Norwegian black metal in the early 1990s. These genres 'share a musical radicalism that marks them out as different from other forms of heavy metal' (5) and are disseminated through small-scale but global 'underground' networks, rather than mainstream commercial modes of distribution.

Heavy metal has maintained a high market profile, despite frequent critical derision and a negative public image. The success of Metallica and newer bands such as Godsmacked and Disturbed has consolidated metal as part of mainstream commercial popular music, with its own dedicated festivals (e.g. Donnington's Monsters of Rock and, more recently, Donnington's Download), magazines (e.g. *Metal Hammer* and *Kerrang!*), web fan sites and record labels. At the same time, the intensification of the genre has created substyles on the margins of metal itself. Heavy metal fans are attracted by its sheer volume, the 'power' of the music; the genre's problem oriented lyrics, at both the global and personal levels; and by its performers general lack of a commercialized image. This is a form of authenticity, with metal fans seeking greater 'substance' than available through mainstream chart-oriented music.

World music

While it can be considered a metagenre, world music is really more of a marketing category. World music became prominent in the late 1980s, as a label applied to popular music originating outside the Anglo-American nexus. The term was launched in 1987 as a new category of popular music by 11 independent British, European and American record labels specializing in music from developing countries, who were seeking to better market their catalogues. In the US, the term world beat was sometimes initially used, along with roots music for American forms. It is useful to distinguish between world music primarily situated within the western music industry and styles of 'world music', which are the subject of ethnomusicology.

World music was encouraged by the interest in, enthusiasm for and borrowings from non-western national musical styles by western artists such as David Byrne, Peter Gabriel and Paul Simon, although Simon's use of African forms, notably in *Graceland* (1986), has proved contentious. The category has been defined in essentially two related ways. First, world music is seen in a very heterogeneous manner as 'the other': music in opposition to the mainstream, Anglo-American and European genres. Second, in an extended form of the first definition, world music includes music from Europe, America and Australia and New Zealand geographically, but this is largely music from diasporic, oppressed or marginalized minorities (such as Aboriginal music in Australia). Both definitions recognize world music as the result of processes of globalization and the hybridization (and, in some cases, appropriation) of regional and nationally based music (for a helpful discussions of the definition of world music, see Guilbault, 2001).

The resultant breadth of world music is seen in the steadily expanding *Rough Guides* to the metagenre: the first was published as a single (albeit large) volume in 1994; this was subsequently expanded to two regionally based volumes; and recently these have been revised and published in three large reference guides. The series constructs the category around national identity, even though that is clearly tenuous, given the diversity of styles within particular countries. As such, discussions of world music will embrace, among others, rai music from Algeria, Nigerian juju, Caribbean zouk and Brazilian bossa nova. Hybrid forms like the Anglo-Indian bhangra and Franco-American Cajun and zydeco, along with the globalized 'Celtic' are also included under the broad rubric.

A further aspect is the manner in which world music has becoming self-defined by virtue of musical festival programming (especially the success of WOMAD: World of Music Arts, and Dance, established by Peter Gabriel in 1982); the role of the music industry in constructed it as a 'genre market' (Laing, 2008; Negus, 1999), primarily through record labels specializing in the metagenre, notably Real World; and through several music magazines (*fRoots*; *Songlines*), along with regular coverage of performers and recordings in more general 'rock' magazines, such as *UNCUT*.

Perhaps more so than other forms of popular music, world music is open to processes of hybridization and musical acculturation, factors, which, in part, account for the considerable attention given to it in recent academic literature. An important aspect here is the role of race/ethnicity in categorizations of 'world music' (Haynes, 2010), which in popular perceptions and in the music press is often equated with 'non-white' or 'black' music. The discourse around world music tends to be polarized between celebration and condemnation (Frith, 2000). But as Jocelyne Guilbault argues:

> world music should not be seen as simply oppositional or emancipator. Neither, however, should world music be viewed as merely the result of cultural imperialism or economic domination. To understand world music fully, we must look at its place within the complex and constantly changing dynamics of a world which is historically, socially and spatially interconnected.
>
> (Guilbault, 2001: 176)

Hip-hop: from the margin to the mainstream

Genres can develop as oppositional, but then become part of the musical 'mainstream', usually through 'crossing over' into the pop and rock mainstream and charts. During the 1990s, this occurred with grunge, beginning with the huge success of Nirvana's album *Nevermind* (Geffin, 1991) and in country, with Garth Brooks and Shania Twain (see Chapter 4). Crossover has commonly occurred with black music in the US, with debate over whether this has compromised the authenticity of the music or can be seen more positively as part of the integration and upward social mobility of the black community (George, 1989). An example of crossover at its most successful is rap, which shifted from its origins in New York in the late 1970s, with a local following, to large-scale commercial success internationally in the late 1990s.

Initially a part of a dance style that began in the late 1970s among black and Hispanic teenagers in New York's outer boroughs, rap became the musical centre of the broader cultural phenomenon of hip-hop: the broad term that encompassed the social, fashion, music and dance subculture of America's urban, black and Latino youth of the 1980s and 1990s (see Potter, 1995). The antecedents of rap lie in the various storytelling forms of popular music: talking blues, spoken passages and call-and-response in gospel. Its more direct formative influences were in the late 1960s, with reggae's DJ toasters and stripped-down styles of funk music, notably James Brown's use of stream-of-consciousness raps over elemental funk backup. Rappers made their own mixes, borrowing from a range of musical sources – sampling – and talking over the music – rapping – in a form of improvized street poetry. This absorption and recontextualizing of elements of popular culture marked out rap/hip-hop as a form of pop art or postmodern culture. The style was economically significant as black youth were 'doing their own thing', largely bypassing traditional music retail outlets. Many of the early rappers recorded on independent labels, initially on 12" singles, most prominently Sugar Hill Records in New York. The label's 1982 release, Grandmaster Flash and the Furious Five, 'The Message', was one of the first rap records to have mainstream chart success and led to greater interest in the musical style. Run DMC, *Raising Hell* (London, 1986) was the first rap album to cross over to the pop charts and brought rap into wider public consciousness. As with other maturing musical metagenres, a number of identifiable genres emerged within rap (see the entries in Shuker, 2012; see also Chang, 2005; Krims, 2000). The genre was soon taken up by white youth, white artists (Eminem) and the major record labels, in a familiar process of the appropriation of black musical styles.

By the late 1990s, rap and hip-hop had become bracketed together as part of mainstream American culture. A *Time* magazine cover story, featuring Lauryn Hill, proclaimed the arrival of the 'Hip Hop Nation', referring to the music revolution that has changed America (*Time*, 8 February 1999: 40–57). The Fugees, *The Score*, Sony/Columbia, 1996, was a huge international success, with sales of 7 million by early 1997. In adding elements of R&B, soul and ragga rock to the genre, it foreshadowed the contemporary orientation of rap. By 1998, rap was the top-selling music format in the US market and its influence pervaded fashion, language and street style. The *Time* story noted that the two terms, rap and hip-hop, were now 'nearly, but not completely, interchangeable' (ibid.).

This conflation was cemented through the next few years. The record sales, product endorsements, associated fashion merchandising and public celebrity of artists such as Beyoncé (and her former group Destiny's Child), Kanye West and Eminem made rap and hip-hop, in effect, the mainstream. The broad genre also became globalized, with distinctive national variants of rap developing (Basu and Lemelle, 2006). In a major edited study, *Global Noise*, Tony Mitchell argued that 'Hip-hop and rap cannot be viewed simply as the expression of African-American culture; it has become a vehicle for global youth affiliations and a tool for reworking local identity all over the world' (2001: Introduction).

The rock canon

Art forms are frequently discussed in terms of a canon, where works are 'typically presented as peaks of the aesthetic power of the art form in question, as ultimate manifestations of aesthetic perfection, complexity of form and depth of expression which humans are capable of reaching through this art form' (Regev, 2006: 1). The canon embraces value, exemplification, authority and a sense of temporal continuity (timelessness). Critics of the concept point to the general social relativism and value judgments embedded in it, and the often associated privileging of western, white, male and middle-class cultural work. The gendered nature of the musical canon and its dominance by Anglo-American performers and recording has been strongly critiqued. Marcia Citron (1993) poses the question: 'Why is music composed by women so marginal to the standard "classical" repertoire?' Her study looks at the practices and attitudes that have led to the exclusion of women composers from the received 'canon' of performed musical works, important elements of canon formation: creativity, professionalism, music as gendered discourse and reception. The historical absence or marginalization of women in popular music histories has also been noted in popular music studies, along with the privileging of male performers and male-dominated or oriented musical styles/genres in discussions of authorship and the consequent domination of popular music canons by male performers.

Notions of canon are frequently present in popular music discourse, implicitly in everyday conversations among fans and more directly in critical discourse. As Motti Regev puts it: 'Canonisation in popular music has gone hand in hand with its very recognition as a legitimate art form' (ibid.). Music critics and the music press are major contributors to the construction of a musical canon, with the use of ratings systems for reviews, annual 'best of' listings, and various 'guidebooks' to key recordings. The canon also underpins accounts of the history of popular music.

A number of academic studies have focused on the historical construction of particular genre canons, including the western classical tradition (Tagg and Clarida, 2003: Chapter 1), jazz (Gabbard, 1995) and blues. An example of this process at work is provided by John Dougan in his insightful discussion of canonization and blues record collectors in the US. He describes these collectors as 'musical archaeologists, culture brokers, creators, keepers, and, through their entrepreneurial efforts (influenced by the release of Harry Smith's 1952 compilation *Anthology of American Folk Music*, on Folkways Records) disseminators of a blues canon'. He sees this role as playing a vital part in the taxonomy of the genre:

> At its core, canon formation among blues record collectors involves organizing and defending a set of selections made from several possible sets of selections. The resulting 'canon' represents the essence of the tradition, and the connection between the texts and the canon reveals the veiled logic and internal rationale of that tradition.
>
> (Dougan, 2006: 42, 45)

General coverage of historical figures, musical trends and recordings are standard content in rock music magazines, especially those aimed at an older readership, for example *MOJO* and *UNCUT*. In addition, many of these titles have begun publishing special issues and series. Given that many of these are rapidly sold out, this is a lucrative market, tapping into and reinforcing popular memory. Examples here include the *NME Originals*, the *UNCUT Legends* and the *Rolling Stone* special issues, such as *The 50th Anniversary of Rock: IMMORTALS. The 100 Greatest Artists of All Time* (Issue 642, August 2005). In addition to their economic motivation, these publications are playing an important ideological role. They contribute to the identification and legitimating of a canon of performers, in the same way as lists of 'greatest albums', with which, of course, they are closely aligned. The selection process at work here is an interesting one, indicative of particular views of creativity and authorship. The title *IMMORTALS. The 100 Greatest Artists of All Time* displays no lack of ambition and confidence, but the choices of artists from the 1950s excludes Bill Haley, presumably as his image does not conform to a notion of 'rock' authenticity.

The nature of the canon and the difficulties surrounding it are evident in the recurring presentation of a canon of rock and pop recordings in 'best of/greatest albums of all time' lists. Ralf Von Appen and Andre Doehring (2006) provide a meta-analysis of such lists, drawing on 38 rankings made between 1985 and 1989 and 2000–2004 (see Appendix 3). This 'top 30' is dominated by rock albums of the 1960s and 1970s, notably the Beatles and there is an absence of both women and black artists. The list represents the staple musical repertoire for 'classic rock' radio, which both reflects and reinforces the visibility and value accorded to such performers and albums. They suggest that two criteria underpin this pattern: aesthetic and sociological. The aesthetic places a premium on artistic authenticity and there is at times a limited relationship between such rankings and sales and chart success. The exclusion of compilation and greatest hits albums from most of the lists included reflected the view that the album must represent a showcase of the work of an artist at a particular point in time.

Von Appen and Doehring's discussion of the sociological factors at work here shows the role of the music press and industry discourse in shaping taste and the cultural capital and social identities of those who voted on the lists. The following chapters engage with some aspects of these.

Further reading

Genre: general

Borthwick, S. and Moy, R. (2004) *Popular Music Genres: An Introduction*, Edinburgh: Edinburgh University Press.
Fabbri, F. (1999) 'Browsing Musical Spaces: Categories and the Musical Mind', conference paper, produced online by permission of the author: www.tagg.org

Lena, J. and Peterson, R. (2008) 'Classification as Culture: Types and Trajectories of Music Genres', *American Sociological Review*, 73, 5: 697–718.

Shuker, R. (2012) *Popular Music Culture: The Key Concepts*, 3rd edn, London, New York: Routledge.

Authenticity

Barker, H. and Taylor, Y. (2007) *Faking It: The Quest for Authenticity in Popular Music*, New York, London: Norton.

Moore, A. (2002) 'Authenticity as Authentication', *Popular Music*, 21, 2: 225–36.

Pop

Ennis, P.H. (1992) *The Seventh Stream: The Emergence of Rock 'n' Roll in American Popular Music*, Hanover, NH; London: Wesleyan University Press.

Frith, S. (2001) 'Pop Music', in S. Frith, W. Straw and J. Street (eds), *The Cambridge Companion to Pop and Rock*, Cambridge: Cambridge University Press.

Rock

Dettmar, K. (2006) *Is Rock Dead?*, New York, London: Routledge.

Keightley, K. (2001) 'Reconsidering Rock', in S. Frith, W. Straw and J. Street (eds), *The Cambridge Companion to Pop and Rock*, Cambridge: Cambridge University Press.

Heavy metal

Brown, A. (2011) 'Heavy Genealogy: Mapping the Currents, Contraflows and conflicts of the Emergent Field of Metal Studies', *Journal for Cultural Research*, 15, 3: 1213–42.

Cope, A. (2010) *Black Sabbath and the Rise of Heavy Metal Music*, Basingstoke: Ashgate.

Harris, K. (2007) *Extreme Metal: Music and Culture on the Edge*, Oxford, New York: Berg.

Walser, R. (1993) *Running With the Devil: Power, Gender and Madness in Heavy Metal Music*, Middletown, CT: Wesleyan University Press.

Weinstein, D. (1991, 2000) *Heavy Metal: The Music and Its Culture*, rev. edn, Boulder, CO: Da Capo Press. (The 2000 edition adds a chapter on the 1990s.)

Documentary:

Metal. A Headbanger's Journey, directed and produced by Sam Dunn, Scot McFadyen, Jessica Wise, Canada, 2006.

World music

Guilbault, J. (2001) 'World Music', in S. Frith, W. Straw and J. Street, (eds), *The Cambridge Companion to Pop and Rock*, Cambridge: Cambridge University Press, pp.176–92.

Laing, D. (2008) 'World Music and the Global Music Industry: Flows, Corporations and Networks', *Popular Music History*, 3, 3: 213–31.

Rap and hip-hop

Chang, J. (2005) *Can't Stop Won't Stop. A History of the Hip-Hop Generation*, New York: Ebury Press/Random House.
Forman, M. and Neal, M. (eds) (2004) *That's The Joint! The Hip-Hop Studies Reader*, New York, London: Routledge.

Canons

Dougan, J. (2006) 'Objects of Desire: Canon Formation and Blues Record Collecting', *Journal of Popular Music*, 18, 1: 40–65.
Regev, M. (2006) Introduction to theme (canon) issue of *Popular Music*, 25, 1.
Von Appen, R. and Doehring, A. (2006) 'Nevermind The Beatles, Here's Exile 61' and Nico: 'The Top 100 Records of all Time' – A Canon of Pop and Rock Albums from a Sociological and an Aesthetic Perspective', *Popular Music*, 25, 1: 21–40.

7 'Shop Around'
Marketing and mediation

Marketing has come to play a crucial role in the circulation of cultural commodities. It is a complex practice, involving several related activities: research, product planning and design, packaging, publicity and promotion, pricing policy and sales and distribution; it is also closely tied to merchandizing and retailing. Central to the process is product positioning and imbuing cultural products with social significance to make them attractive to consumers. In popular music, this has been concentrated on the marketing of genre styles and stars, which have come to function in a similar manner to brand names, serving to order demand and stabilize sales patterns. I begin this chapter with an examination of the marketing of Bob Marley and the Wailers to illustrate this.

The marketing process illustrates the manner in which the music industry includes a range of people and institutions that 'stand between' consumers and the musical text, once it has been produced as a commodity. I use the phrase 'stand between' as shorthand for what are complex processes of marketing and consumption at work. The concepts of 'gatekeepers' and 'cultural intermediaries' have been used to analyse the way in which workers in the cultural industries select, reject and reformulate material for production, broadcast and publication. Based on a filter-flow model of information flow, gatekeepers 'open the gate' for some texts and information and close it for others. The gatekeeper concept became critiqued for being too mechanistic and oversimplified and, following the work of Bourdieu (1984) was largely superceded by the more flexible concept of 'cultural intermediaries'.

The sound recording companies have a number of such personnel making the initial decision about who to record and promote and filtering material at each step of the process involving the recording and marketing of a song. Beyond the record companies are a number of institutions and related practices mediating music, including retail, film, radio, television, the music press, MTV and the internet. These form something of a historical succession; the second part of the chapter takes up the first of them: retail and radio and the manner in which they are linked by the charts.

Marketing and commodification

It is noteworthy that by the 1990s the cant term for music within the industry was 'product'. Although this process was hardly new, it referred to popular music being an increasingly commodified product: merchandise to be packaged and sold in the market. There are aspects of popular music as a commodity form that distinguish it from other cultural texts, notably its reproducibility, its ubiquity of formats and its multiple modes of dissemination.

Recorded music can be reproduced in various formats – vinyl, audio tape, CD, video, digital files – and variations within these: the dance mix, the cassette single, the limited collector's edition, the live performance and so on. These can then be disseminated in a variety of ways – through radio airplay, discos and dance clubs, television music video shows and MTV-style channels, live concert performances and on the internet. Then there is the exposure of music and musicians through the use of popular music within film soundtracks and as part of television advertising for consumer goods (Klein, 2010). In addition, there is the assorted paraphernalia and memorabilia available to the fan, especially the posters and the t-shirts. Complimenting all of these may be reviews of the musical text and interviews with the performer(s) in various print publications or online.

In sum, these reinforce one another within the wider music culture and society more generally.

This enables a multimedia approach to be taken to the marketing of the music and a maximization of sales potential, as exposure in each of the various forms strengthens the appeal of the others. Marketing includes the use of genre labels as signifiers, radio formatting practices and standardized production pro- cesses (e.g. Stock Aitken Waterman and dance pop in the 1980s). Above all, it involves utilizing star images, linking stars and their music with the needs, demands, emotions and desires of audiences. The case of Bob Marley and the Wailers is instructive here.

Marketing Marley

Island Records was started by Chris Blackwell, the Jamaican-born son of an English plantation owner, in 1962 to supply Jamaican music to West Indian cus- tomers in Britain. The company had its first major success when Millie Small's ska tune 'My Boy Lollipop' reached no. 2 in the English pop charts later that year. The company diversified to black music in general, setting up Sue Records in 1963 as a subsidiary to market American soul, blues, ska, and rhythm and blues tracks under licence. In the later 1970s Island hooked into the commercial end of the British counterculture, releasing records by Traffic, Fairport Convention and Free. In 1972 Blackwell signed the Wailers, with Bob Marley (see Barfe, 2004: 259–62).

Conventional histories see this move as inevitably successful, riding the bur- geoning western interest in reggae. But in fact the marketing of reggae and the Wailers is illustrative of record company attempts to maximize their investment at their most successful moment. Island shaped and marketed Marley and the

Wailers as ethnic rebellion for album buyers, both black and white (Barrow and Dalton, 1997; Jones, S., 1988; White, 1989). The strategies used included recording *Catch a Fire* (Island, 1972), the Wailers' first album, in stereo; doubling the pay rates for the session musicians involved, enabling them to record for longer; employing the latest technical facilities of the recording process to 'clean up' the music; and remixing and editing the backing tracks in London, after they had been recorded in Jamaica. Blackwell, a very hands-on label boss, also accelerated the speed of the Wailers' basic rhythm tracks by one beat, thinking that a quicker tempo might enhance the appeal of reggae to rock fans. The result was a more 'produced sound', with keyboards and guitars, moving away from reggae's traditional emphasis on drums and bass. (*Catch a Fire: Deluxe Edition* of Island/ UME, includes the UK remixed and overdubbed album [2001], along with the original, previously unreleased version recorded in Jamaica.)

Catch a Fire had an elaborated pop art record cover, designed as a large cigarette lighter, while the Wailers' second album, *Burnin'* (Island, 1973) pictured rastas in various 'dread' poses, and printed the song lyrics. 'These ploys seemed to confirm Island's intention to sell the Wailers as "rebels" by stressing the uncompromising and overtly political aspects of their music' (Jones, 1988: 65). At the same time, however, this stance was watered down for white consumption. The group's third album had its title changed from *Knotty Dread*, with its connotations of rasta militancy and race consciousness symbolized by dreadlocks, to *Natty Dread*, with its white connotations of fashionable style.

Island carefully promoted the Wailers concert tour of Britain in 1973 to include appearances on national radio and television. This level of exposure was new for reggae, previously constrained by the genre's limited financial support. Later marketing of the band, following only fair success for their first two albums, included pushing Bob Marley to the fore as the group's frontman and 'star'. This strategy proved particularly successful during the 1975 tour of Britain, as the band – now 'Bob Marley and the Wailers' – commercially broke through to a mass white audience. Original founding members Peter Tosh and Bunny Wailer left towards the end of 1974, both feeling that too much attention was now being given to Bob. In another strategic marketing move, instead of simply replacing them with similar characteristically Jamaican male harmonies, the more gospel-inflected female backup vocals of the I-Threes were brought in to supply a sound more familiar to rock audiences at that time (Barrow and Dalton, 1997: 131). A string of record hits and successful tours followed in the late 1970s, due at least in part to the music becoming more accessible and pop oriented. In 1981, Bob Marley and the Wailers worldwide album sales were estimated to be in excess of $US190 million.

The success of Island with the Wailers helped usher in a period of the international commercialization of reggae. For the multinational record companies, 'reggae was a rich grazing-ground requiring low levels of investment but yielding substantial profits' (Jones, 1988: 72). Jamaican artists could be bought cheaply compared to the advances demanded by their western rock counterparts. Yet while reggae spurred the success of dub and the ska revival of the early 1980s, and was a crucial influence on commercially successful bands like the Police, Bob Marley remained the only major star to emerge from reggae. His international success arguably owed as much to Blackwell and Island as to his personal charisma and the power of the music.

Marley's death in 1981 did little to diminish his commercial worth, as Island successfully marketed a greatest hits package, *Legend* (1984), which was no. 1 in the UK for several months. Indeed, the continued appeal of Marley was indicated by the album's remarkable longevity: by 1997 it had sold 12 million copies worldwide (Barrow and Dalton, 1997: 135), and has remained the top-selling (back) 'catalogue' album in *Billboard* since that chart's creation in 1991. By 1984 Dave Robinson was running Island, and his market research indicated that:

> You should keep the word 'reggae' out of it. A lot of what people didn't like about Bob Marley was the threatening aspect of him, the revolutionary side. So the (album cover) picture chosen was one of the softest pictures of Bob. It was a very well conceived and thought-out package. And a very well put-together record.
>
> (Blackwell, cited in Stephens, 1998: 145)

This approach set the trend for the subsequent marketing of the reggae star, as his image was subtly remoulded, moving from the Rastafarian outlaw of the 1970s to the natural family man of the 1980s to the 'natural mystic' in the 1990s. This process reflected not only the incorporation of his music but also the incorporation of his image and message. A new CD compilation, *The Natural Mystic* (1995) and a four-CD boxed set *Songs of Freedom* (1992), both reflected how 'The Marley of the 1970s, rude boy, revolutionary, Rastafarian, needed to be exorcised for the singer to appeal to a more mainstream white audience' (Stephens, 1998: 142). The cover of *Natural Mystic*, a profile head shot of a gently smiling Marley with his hand at his chin, was similar to that used on the Legend cover and indeed came from the same photo session in 1977. The booklet accompanying the 1992 boxed set tells the story of Marley's origins as a rude boy in Trenchtown, Jamaica, the turn to Rastafari in the late 1960s and his rise to international stardom in the 1970s. The accompany CDs parallel this history. The booklet and its images, and in the choice of songs for inclusion in the package, emphasize Marley's growing commitment to spiritual and social issues, playing down his increased political consciousness and desire to connect with a black audience as illness looked likely to end his career.

Prince and the bat

A further instructive example of marketing, illustrating newer synergies within the music industry was Prince's soundtrack for the film *Batman* (1989). This was part of a carefully orchestrated marketing campaign to create interest in the film, the first in what became a franchise, and to break Prince to a wider audience, primarily through exposure on MTV. Warner Communications Inc. (WCI) invested US$30 million in the *Batman* film, seeing it not simply as a one-off film, but as a package of ongoing projects: a series of films, albums, sheet music, comics and novelizations. The soundtrack for *Batman* was actually put out in two forms: an album by Prince, which featured songs for the film soundtrack and music inspired by the film, which achieved double platinum sales; and an orchestral album by composer Danny Elfman, with respectable sales of around 150,000 copies. WCI had recently acquired Chapple, making the corporation the largest song publisher in the world and the two albums generated further income for the company through their sales of sheet music. Both album jackets featured the bat logo, an icon that reinforced publicity for the film and its associated products. Unusually, Prince's video of the album's lead song, 'Batdance', featured no footage from the film, but used the actor's lines as a lead-in to the rap/funk style number. The video received heavy airplay on the MTV channel, watched primarily by white middle-class youth and adults. WCI had established Prince's main audience as white females in their late twenties to early thirties, so the MTV exposure helped broaden his appeal, while also bringing the *Batman* film to the attention of non-comic book fans and white women.

The marketing of popular music has become increasingly sophisticated since the efforts of Island with Bob Marley and the Wailers and WCI with Prince. The expansion of the music press, the sophistication of retail, the continued formatting of radio, the popularization of MTV and music video and the emergence of the internet have all contributed to the ability of the industry to coordinate marketing internationally across a range of media. The star as a form of commodity has been exemplified in the careers of, among others, Kylie Minogue, Beyoncé and Taylor Swift.

Mediation and cultural intermediaries

These case studies of marketing indicate the role of other cultural intermediaries, primarily various music media in disseminating and popularizing music. There is a historical progression of these media, which provides a logic and structure for the discussion that follows. Based in the established sector of sheet music sales, retail shops were where sound recordings could first be listened to and purchased. Later, film and radio provided cultural spaces in which music could be experienced, informing and shaping consumption. The music press, established in the 1920s, played a similar role, especially in the emergence of 'rock culture' in the 1960s. The introduction of television in the 1950s, followed by MTV in the 1980s, provided new sites of mediation. Most recently (as indicated in Chapters 1 and 2), the internet has dramatically altered the relationship between the sound recording industry and the manufacture, distribution and consumption of music. The opportunities offered by the new digital environment, with practices and institutions such as web radio, blogs and YouTube, have both inflected and, in some cases superseded, the older historically dominant forms of mediation. In the remainder of this chapter, I consider the role of retail and radio in mediating popular music, with subsequent chapters looking at the place of later media in such processes.

Music retail

Marketing includes the sites at which music is sold, including street markets (Laing, 2012), the physical 'record shop', music megastores and online retail. Their inventory can encompass sheet music, musical instruments, music-related merchandise, concert tickets, music DVDS, music magazines and books. Primarily, however, the term 'music retail' refers to the sale of sound recordings to the public. Information on this topic is sparse and there is a history of music retail yet to be written, but a quick sketch is possible.

Sound recordings were first available through shops selling sheet music and musical instruments. In the early 1900s, chains of department stores began supplying hit songs, along with sheet music. Later, smaller, independent and sole proprietor shops (the 'mom and pop' stores in the US) emerged. By the 1950s, and the advent of rock 'n' roll, record retailers included independent shops, often specializing in particular genres; chain stores; and mail order record clubs. The subsequent relative importance and market share of each of these has reflected the broader consolidation of the music industry, along with shifts in recording formats and distribution technologies. Retailers have had to adapt to changes as mundane as the need for different shelf space to accommodate new formats. The advent of electronic bar coding in the 1990s enabled retail, distribution, and production 'to be arranged as an interconnected logistic package'. This allowed 'music retailers to delineate, construct and monitor the consumer of recorded music more intricately than ever before' (du Gay and Negus, 1994: 396). A similar process now occurs with the tracking of the preferences of browsers and purchasers in online music retail sites, such as Amazon.

Retail chains have, at times, also assumed a direct gatekeeping role, by censoring or not stocking particular artists, genres and recordings (for example Wal-mart in the US). Record company sales and distribution practices can be directly tied to music retail. Several leading mail order record clubs in the 1950s were adjuncts of labels, receiving discounts on stock, a situation successfully challenged legally by their competitors (Barfe, 2004). Linked independent record stores have been part of labels, such as Rough Trade and Beggars Banquet in the UK, although the importance of such arrangements declined in the 1990s.

As with the culture industries generally, increased concentration of ownership has been a feature of the music retail industry since the mid-1990s, as CD sales peaked and then declined. In 2006 Matt Brennan documented how the increased concentration of music retail in Britain constrained the availability of releases from indie and specialist genre labels. In addition to central buying, the five major chain stores have introduced the use of 'retail packs', with only a limited number of sales spaces available:

> At HMV there's 24 non-pop retail packs up for grabs every month. And that's for folk, world music, classical *and* jazz. If you don't get one of them, you're not going to sell even 1000 records.
>
> (Tom Bancroft, owner of jazz label Caber Music, cited in Brennan, 2006b: 224)

As he observed, this 'can mean almost guaranteed commercial failure for independent artists not offered a pack' (ibid.). Further, the central buyer's decision to offer a pack will be based on an artist and labels 'track record': a combination of favourable press coverage; radio airplay; band tours and promotional activities; and previous retail history. Obviously, there is a process of validating existing advantages likely to occur here: to those who have, shall be given.

Smaller local music chains have been forced to retrench by consolidating shops and 'downsizing' staff or have kept operating through niche marketing and their increased use of the internet. In New Zealand, local music retail chain Marbecks announced in March 2012 that it was closing its remaining Wellington store, after 17 years of trading at the site, as the company scaled down its retail operations to focus on digital and online sales. 'It's really just a change in our industry', said Roger Harper, the co-owner and major shareholder. This was the latest in a succession of music retail stores to close in Wellington, New Zealand's capital.

An increasing proportion of recordings are now sold through general retailers (e.g. Woolworths, Wal-mart) and the surviving music megastores. This concentration influences the range of music available to consumers and the continued economic viability of smaller retail outlets. The general retailers frequently use music as a loss leader: reducing their music CD and DVD prices to attract shoppers whom they hope will also purchase other store products with higher profit margins. This situates music as only one component of the general selling of lifestyle consumer goods. In New Zealand, for example, this marketing strategy is central to the Warehouse national chain, now the country's largest music retailer. The Warehouse has used its bulk purchasing power, along with heavy advertising of discounts through blanket media coverage (the press, flyers to home mail boxes, TV, radio advertising) to secure market dominance. What this means for consumers, however, is a relatively restricted range of music on offer, with a heavy emphasis on the discounted chart-oriented recordings, which are available only on CD.

Historically, indie or specialist and second-hand record shops occupied a distinct space within the music market. In many cases, they contributed significantly to local music scenes by promoting shows, supporting local artists, and selling tickets, t-shirts, fanzines and other merchandise not handled by major retailers. Part of the appeal of such shops is the shoppers' relationship with the staff, which frequently involves trusting their musical knowledge and recommendations, along with a reciprocal recognition, often hard won, of the buyers' own expertise. The 1980s was something of a high point for the specialist and used record store. As Hayes notes of the US:

> While many small (largely regional) labels continued to release music on 7" and 12" records throughout the '90s, locating their products was often a difficult task since mainstream retail outlets such as Tower Records and HMV shelved few if any LP releases after deleting previous stock.
>
> (Hayes, 2006: 56)

This limited vinyl enthusiast to two main sites of acquisition: a small number of independent retailers who continued to stock vinyl releases, usually limited pressings by small labels; and used record stores.

Emma Pettit (2008) has documented how independent (and second-hand) record shops continue to form a minor but still culturally significant part of record retail. However, they have increasingly struggled, with the impact of the internet and its auction websites, increases in rent for traditional central city areas, especially as these become 'gentrified'/renewed and the ongoing concentration of music retail generally. They have managed to survive and, in some cases, even flourish, by using the internet, by catering to specialist interests and continuing to stock vinyl. The shift online of music retail continues, and has resulted in changes in the nature of music consumption (see Chapter 10).

Radio

Radio developed in the 1920s and 1930s as a domestic medium aimed primarily at women in the home, but also playing an important role as general family entertainment, particularly in the evening. Radio in North America was significant for disseminating music in concert form and helped bring regionally based forms such as western swing and jazz to a wider audience (Ennis, 1992). Historically the enemy of the record industry during the disputes of the 1930s and 1940s around payment for record airplay, radio subsequently became its most vital promoter. Until the advent of MTV in the late 1980s, radio was indisputably the most important broadcast medium for determining the form and content of popular music.

The state has played a significant, yet often overlooked, role in radio. First, it has shaped the commercial environment for radio, primarily through licensing systems, but also by establishing broadcasting codes of practice – a form of censorship. This state practice has at times been challenged, most notably by pirate radio (see later). Second, the state has at times attempted to encourage 'minority' cultures and local music, with the two frequently connected, through quota and other regulatory legislation. Examples of this are attempts to include more French-language music on Canadian radio (Grenier, 1993), a case illustrating the difficulties of conflating 'the national' in multicultural/bilingual settings; and the New Zealand government's recent introduction of local content quotas for radio (see Chapter 14).

The organization of radio broadcasting and its music formatting practices have been crucial in shaping the nature of what constitutes the main 'public face' of much popular music, particularly rock and pop and their associated subgenres. Radio has also played a central role at particular historical moments in popularizing or marginalizing music genres. Two examples of this follow: the popularizing of rock 'n' roll in the 1950s and the impact of British pirate radio in the 1960s.

Radio meets rock 'n' roll: payola and the cult of the DJ

The reshaping of radio in the 1950s was a key influence in the advent of rock 'n' roll. Radio airplay became central to commercial success, especially through the popular new chart shows. Hit radio was 'one of America's great cultural inventions', revitalizing a medium threatened by television (Barnes, 1988: 9). The DJ (disc jockey) emerged as a star figure, led by figures such as Bob 'Wolfman Jack' Smith and Alan Freed.

The place of radio in the music industry was brought to the fore by the debate around payola, a term used for the offering of financial, sexual or other inducements in return for promotion. In 1955 the US House of Representatives Legislative Oversight Committee, which had been investigating the rigging of quiz shows, began looking at pay-to-play practices in rock music radio. Payola, as the practice was then known, had long been commonplace, but was not illegal. 'Song plugging', as the practice was originally termed, had been central to music industry marketing since the heyday of Tin Pan Alley in the 1920s. By the 1950s DJs and radio station programmers frequently supplemented their incomes with 'consultant fees' and musical credits on records, enabling them to receive a share of songwriting royalties. During the committee hearings, Dick Clark admitted to having a personal interest in around a quarter of the records he promoted on his influential show *American Bandstand*. He divested himself of his music business holdings and was eventually cleared by the committee. A clean-cut figure, Clark survived the scandal because he represented the acceptable face of rock 'n' roll. Pioneer DJ Alan Freed was not so fortunate; persecuted and eventually charged with commercial bribery in 1960, his health and career were ruined.

Payola did not target all music radio, but was part of a conservative battle to return to 'good music', a campaign underpinned by economic self-interest. The American Society of Composers, Authors and Publishers (ASCAP) supported the attack on payola by criticizing rivals BMI (Broadcast Music, Inc.), whose writers were responsible for most rock 'n' roll. The major record labels participated in the campaign as part of a belated attempt to halt the expansion of the independents. Hill goes so far as to conclude that one way to see the payola hearings was as an attempt – ultimately successful – 'to force a greater degree of organization and hierarchical responsibility onto the record industry so that the flow of music product could be more easily regulated' (Hill, 1992: 39). The involvement of conservative government officials, and a number of established music figures (including Frank Sinatra), was largely based on an intense dislike of rock 'n' roll, a prejudice with only loosely concealed racist overtones, given the prominence of black performers associated with the genre.

Payola did not disappear, merely becoming less visible and concealed under 'promotion' budgets. In the US in 2005, echoing the earlier controversy, New York Attorney-General Eliot Spitzer initiated a sweeping payola investigation, implicating all four major record labels in pay-for-play practices.

Pirate radio and the BBC

Pirate radio broadcasts are those made by unlicensed broadcasters as an alternative to licensed, commercial radio programming. However, the pirate stations usually rely on the same popular music that is programmed on commercial radio, rarely programming music other than the main pop and rock styles. A major exception was in the 1960s, when the British pirates challenged the BBC's lack of attention to pop/rock music. British pirate radio in its heyday, 1964–1968, was an historical moment encapsulating the intersection of rock as cultural politics and personal memory with market economics and government intervention. Twenty-one different pirates operated during this period, representing a wide range of radio stations in terms of scale, motives and operating practices.

The myth of the pirates is that they were about providing pop music to their disenfranchised and previously ignored youthful listeners, representing a somewhat anarchic challenge to radio convention and commerce; indeed, this is the narrative of the recent celebratory feature film *The Boat that Rocked* (2010). However, as Robert Chapman argues, the reality was rather more commercial. Given that the BBC's popular music policy was woefully inadequate in the early 1960s, the pirates did cater for a largely disenfranchised audience; they also pioneered some innovative programmes and boosted the careers of leading DJs of the time Kenny Everett and John Peel. But, as their programming indicated, they were never predominantly about popular music and were heavily oriented toward advertising. All the pirates were commercial operations: 'though work-place and legal judicial circumstances were not typical, in all other respects these were entrepreneurial small businesses aspiring to become entrepreneurial big businesses' (Chapman, 1992: 167). This was particularly evident in the case of Radio London, set up with an estimated investment of £1.5 million, whose 'overriding institutional goals were to maximize profit and bring legal commercial radio to Great Britain' (Chapman, 1992: 80). In this respect, the station succeeded, with the BBC's Radio 1, established in 1967 as the pirates were being closed down, borrowing heavily from the practices of pirate radio and even hiring pirate DJs.

From FM to web radio

FM radio was developed in the early 1930s, using a frequency modulation (hence FM) system of broadcasting. It did not have the range of AM and was primarily used by non-commercial and college radio until the late 1960s, when demand for its clearer sound quality and stereo capabilities saw the FM stations become central players in the commercial market. They contributed to what became a dominant style of music radio in the 1970s and 1980s (radio friendly; high production values; relatively 'easy listening': 'classic rock', exemplified by the Eagles and Fleetwood Mac). The appeal of FM witnessed a consolidation of the historically established role of radio in chart success. Independent programme directors became the newest powerbrokers within the industry, replacing the independent record distributors of the early sixties (Eliot, 1989). Most radio stations now followed formats shaped by consultants, with a decline in the role of programme directors at individual stations, a situation that persisted into the 1990s and continues today.

Terrestrial radio's audience dropped steeply in the early 2000s. In response to this dwindling market share and its serious impact on advertising revenue, eight of the top radio companies in the North American market formed the HD Digital Radio Alliance in 2005 and began launching digital radio stations in key markets. These new stations offered listeners near CD-quality sound and up to three additional channels per frequency, along with alternate versions to their primary format (*Rolling Stone*, 23 February 2006: 18. 'Radio's Next Generation').

Web radio and new broadcasting technologies have continued to foster an explosion of radio stations, even although many have a localized signal. In the commercial sector, digital technologies have produced new production aesthetics and reshaped the radio industry. The last decade has seen a renaissance of radio, exploiting the new platforms of cable, satellite, digital transmission and the internet. 'Though often widely scattered, the audiences for internet stations are not necessarily large but they gain the potential for interactivity: they can download music and other material' (Starkey, 2010: 169). In the United Kingdom, thanks to the Broadcasting Act of 1990, there has been a remarkable expansion of the 'independent' or commercial sector along with the many stations available through Sky and Freeview television services. Radio continues to expand at local, regional and national levels, 'with a greater choice of programming today than ever before' (Starkey, 2010: 165).

Stations and formats

Radio stations are distinguishable by the type of music they play, the style of their DJs and their mix of news, contests, commercials and other programme features. We can see radio broadcasts as a flow, with these elements merging. The main types of radio station include college, student, pirate and youth radio (e.g. the US college stations; New Zealand's campus radio; Australia's Triple J network); state national broadcasters, such as the BBC; community radio; and, the dominant group in terms of market share, the commercial radio stations. There is a long-standing contradiction between the interests of record companies, which are targeting radio listeners who buy records, especially those in their teens and early twenties, and private radio's concern to reach the older, more affluent audience desired by advertisers. To some extent, this contradiction has been resolved by niche marketing of contemporary music radio.

Station and programme directors act as gatekeepers, being responsible for ensuring a prescribed and identifiable sound or format, based on what the management of the station believes will generate the largest audience – and ratings – and consequent advertising revenue (the classic study here is Rothenbuhler, 2006).

The station's music director and the programme director – at smaller stations the same person fills both roles – will regularly sift through new releases, selecting three or four to add to the playlist. The criteria underpinning this process will normally be a combination of the reputation of the artist; a record's previous performance, if already released overseas; whether the song fits the station's format; and, at times, the gut intuition of those making the decision. Publicity material from the label/artist/distributor plays an important role here, jogging memories of earlier records or sparking interest in a previously unknown artist. Chart performance in either the US or UK is especially significant where the record is being subsequently released in a 'foreign' market. In choosing whether or not to play particular genres of popular radio functions as a gatekeeper, significantly influencing the nature of the music itself (Neill and Shanahan, 2005; the situation they outline in relation to New Zealand's commercial networks remains evident).

Historically, radio formats were fairly straightforward, and included 'top 40', 'soul', and 'easy listening'. Subsequently, formats became more complex and by the 1980s included 'adult-oriented rock', classic hits (or 'golden oldies), contemporary hit radio and urban contemporary (Barnes, 1988). Urban contemporary once meant black radio, but now included artists working within black music genres. In the US, black listeners constitute the main audience for urban contemporary formats, but the music also appeals to white listeners, particularly in the 12–34 age group. Today, radio in most national contexts includes a range of formats: the dominant ones, reflecting historical developments in addition to current demographics, are rock, contemporary chart pop, adult contemporary and classic hits.

As channel switching is common in radio, the aim of programmers is to keep the audience from switching stations. Common strategies include playing fewer commercials and running contests that require listeners to be alert for a song or phrase to be broadcast later, but the most effective approach is to ensure that the station does not play a record the listener does not like. While this is obviously strictly impossible, there are ways to maximize the retention of the listening audience. Since established artists have a bigger following than new artists, it makes commercial sense to emphasize their records and avoid playing releases from new artists on high rotation (i.e. many times per day) until they have become hits, an obvious catch-22 situation.

Classic rock radio

The most extreme example of this approach is classic rock radio, which has its origins in progressive rock radio in the mid-1960s. DJs began playing tracks from albums such as the Beatles *Sergeant Pepper's Lonely Hearts Club Band* (1967) which had not had any singles released from them. A subsequent variant of this practice was album-oriented rock (AOR), which emerged in the mid-1970s and which evolved into 'classic rock' on many of the new FM radio stations, a format that included singles along with album tracks (Barnes, 1988). The first station to call itself 'classic rock' was WYSP in Philadelphia, in January 1981 and the format became firmly established over the next few years. Some radio stations used the related term 'classic hits', mixing the classic rock playlist with hits from pop and R&B and drawing on both historical and contemporary material. Classic rock radio became prominent in part because of the consumer power of the aging post-war 'baby boomers' and the appeal of this group to radio advertisers. The format continues to concentrate on playing 'tried and proven' past chart hits that will have high listener recognition and identification. Its playlists are largely drawn from the Beatles to the end of the 1970s and emphasize white male rock performers (see Thompson, D., 2008).

Ideologically, 'classic rock' serves to confirm the dominant status of a particular period of music history – the emergence of rock in the mid-1960s – with its associated values and set of practices: live performance, self-expression and authenticity; the group as the creative unit, with the charismatic lead singer playing a key role and the lead guitar as the primary instrument. This was a version of romanticism, with its origins in art and aesthetics. It incorporated particular notions of authenticity, valorized by first generation rock critics such as Robert Christgau, Dave Marsh and Lester Bangs (see Chapter 9).

Classic rock radio depends heavily on British hard rock and progressive rock bands; notably the Rolling Stones, the Who, Pink Floyd, Led Zeppelin and Cream. American artists who are staples of classic rock include Jimi Hendrix, the Doors, Creedence Clearwater Revival, Lynyrd Skynrd and Fleetwood Mac. However, these artists represent only a selection of the music of the 1960s and 70s. Some commercially successful rock acts, such as Kiss and Grand Funk Railroad, receive only limited airplay on classic rock radio and there are also examples of commercially successful styles that coexisted with rock during the period, such as soul, funk, and Motown and performers such as Sly and the Family Stone and James Brown are noticeably absent. The reasons for such absences warrant further investigation.

The concern to retain a loyal audience assumes fairly focused radio listening. Paradoxically, while the radio is frequently 'on', it is rarely 'listened' to, instead largely functioning as aural wallpaper, a background to other activities. Yet high rotation radio airplay remains vital in exposing artists and building a following for their work, while radio exposure is also necessary to underpin activities such as touring, helping to promote concerts and the accompanying sales of records. The very ubiquity of radio is a factor here. In its terrestrial formats, it can be listened to in a variety of situations and with widely varying levels of engagement, from the Walkman to background accompaniment to activities such as study, doing domestic chores and reading. However, the internet radio experience is very different from mainstream listening, given it is much less portable and flexible.

The charts

Historically, the charts provided a crucial link between music retail and radio, one that remains prominent despite the shift of music online. The popular music chart is a numerical ranking of current releases based on sales and airplay, usually over a week; the top ranked album/single is no.1 and the rest are ranked correspondingly. The charts were a feature of the music press from early on its development. The first UK chart appeared in 1928 (the *Melody Maker* 'Honours List'); in the US, leading trade paper *Billboard* began a 'Network Song Census' in 1934. Such charts quickly became the basis for radio 'Hit Parade' programmes, most notably the 'top 40' shows.

The popular music charts represent a level of industry and consumer obsession with sales figures almost unique to the record industry. The charts are part of the various trade magazines (e.g. *Billboard, Variety, Music Week*), providing a key reference point for those working in sales and promotion. The record charts also play a major role in constructing taste: 'to the fan of popular music, the charts are not merely quantifications of commodities but rather a major reference point around which their music displays itself in distinction and in relation to other forms' (Parker, 1991: 205). This role remains evident, although arguably less influential, in the digital age.

The precise nature of how contemporary charts are compiled, and their basis, varies between competing trade magazines and national approaches differ. In the US, singles charts are based on airplay, while the album charts are based on sales. Current releases are generally defined for the singles charts as up to 26 weeks after the release date. In the UK, the charts are produced by market research organizations sponsored by various branches of the media. In both countries, data collection is now substantially computerized and based on comprehensive sample data. Airplay information is compiled from selected radio stations, with sales information from online retail and wholesalers, assisted by bar coding.

This represents a form of circular logic, in that the charts are based on a combination of radio play and sales, but airplay influences sales and retail promotion and sales impacts on radio exposure. Historically, there has been frequent controversy over attempts to influence the charts and debate still occurs over perceived attempts to manipulate them. The charts continue to provide the music industry with valuable feedback and promotion and help set the agenda for consumer choice.

Changes in the presentation of the charts can have important repercussions for the relative profile of particular genres/performers. The charts are broken down into genre categories; these can change over time, acting as a barometer of taste, as with the change in *Billboard* from 'race' records to R&B in 1949. The decline of the single has influenced the way in which the charts are constructed. In the UK, in 1989 the music industry reduced the number of sales required to qualify for a platinum award (from one million to 600,000) to assist the promotional system and ensure charts continued to fuel excitement and sales. In 2006 greater chart recognition of online sales of singles reflected their increasing market share (see Chapter 2). More recently, the proliferation of formats has complicated the tracking of sales and undermined the place and influence of the charts. When Robbie Williams' *Intensive Care* album was released in 2005 there were 164 elements and configurations of material you could buy. As David

Jennings observes: 'It's increasingly difficult for chart rules to keep up with this kind of proliferation and provide a credible measure of the overall market impact of an album packaged in the age of digital convergence' (Jennings, 2007: 67).

The following chapter picks up the theme of mediation and marketing in an examination of the relationship of various audio visual media to the production and consumption of popular music culture.

Further reading

Retail

Barfe, L. (2004) *Where Have all the Good Times Gone? The Rise and Fall of the Record Industry*, London: Atlantic Books.
Pettit, E. (2008) *Old Rare New: The Independent Record Shop*, London: Black Dog.
Straw, W. (1997) 'Organized Disorder: The Changing Space of the Record Shop', in S. Redhead (ed.) *The Club Cultures Reader*, Oxford: Blackwell, pp. 57–65.

Music industry websites include considerable accessible information on marketing and sales.

Radio

Barnes, K. (1988) 'Top 40 Radio: A Fragment of the Imagination', in S. Frith (ed.), *Facing the Music*, New York: Pantheon Books.
Crissell, A. (ed.) (2004) *More Than a Music Box: Radio Cultures and Communities in a Multi-Media World*, Oxford: Berghahn.
Ennis, P. (1992) *The Seventh Stream*, Hanover, London: Wesleyan University Press (especially Chapter 5: 'The DJ Takes Over, 1946–56').
Rothenbuhler, E. (2006) 'Commercial Radio as Communication', in A. Bennett, B. Shank and J. Toynbee (eds), *The Popular Music Studies Reader*, London, New York: Routledge (first published 1985).
Starkey, G. (2010) 'Radio' in D. Albertazzi P. and Cobley, *The Media: An Introduction*, 3rd edn, Harlow: Pearson Education Limited (Chapter 11).

8 'U Got the Look'

From film to video games: music and pictures

This chapter continues the theme of mediation, examining the relationship of popular music production, dissemination and consumption to an historical succession of audiovisual media: film and television, music video and MTV, video games. With film, my focus is on commercial feature film and popular music, primarily the popular/rock musicals that followed in the footsteps of classic Hollywood musicals. With television, I am interested in the impact of the new medium on the impact of rock 'n' roll and the subsequent role of mainstream television music shows, including those that are a form of reality television (*S Club 7*; *Idol*). Both film and television have screened popular music documentaries, biopics, validating and mythologizing particular performers, styles and historical moments. Music video and MTV illustrate, once again, the global reach of the music industry and the synergy between music, marketing and audiences. Video gaming represents an increasingly important contemporary site for the production and consumption of popular music. Currently, YouTube has enabled access to a wide range of music in all its previous audiovisual forms.

Film

Film has an important historical relationship to popular music. Early silent films often had a live musical accompaniment (usually piano); and with the arrival of the 'talkies' musicals became a major film genre in the 1930s and continued to be important into the 1960s. Composers and musicians, primarily stars, provided a source of material for these films, as did Broadway musicals. The various genres of popular music, its fans and performers have acted as a rich vein of colourful, tragic and salutary stories for filmmakers. A new form of musical, the 'rock musical', played an important part in rock 'n' roll in the mid-1950s. Allied with such musicals were youth movies, with a range of subgenres. Over the past 40 years or so, considerable synergy has been created between the music and film industries; film soundtracks and video games represent another avenue of revenue for recordings, including the back catalogue and help promote contemporary releases.

The classic Hollywood musical was a hybrid film genre, descended from European operatta and American vaudeville and the music hall. While *The Jazz*

Singer (Alan Crosland, 1927) was the first feature film with sound, the first 'all-talking, all-singing, all dancing' musical was *The Broadway Melody* (Harry Beaumont, 1929), which was important also for establishing the tradition of the backstage musical. The musical soon became regarded as a quintessentially American or Hollywood genre, associated primarily with the Warner and MGM studios and RKO's pairing of Fred Astaire and Ginger Rogers. Mainly perceived as vehicles for song and dance, the routines and performance of these became increasingly complex, culminating in the highly stylized films of Busby Berkeley. *The Wizard of Oz* (Victor Fleming, 1939) introduced a new musical formula, combining youth and music. Other new forms of the musical were introduced during the 1940s, including composer biographies and biographical musicals of 'showbiz' stars. The vitality and audience appeal of the musical continued into the 1950s, with contemporary urban musicals such as *An American in Paris* (Vincent Minnelli, 1951), which portrayed a dynamic Paris music scene, with a cast including musical stars Frank Sinatra and Bing Crosby. Although the 1960s did see several blockbuster musicals, notably *The Sound of Music* (Robert Wise, 1965), the heyday of the classic musical had passed, with fewer Broadway hits now making it to the screen. The 1960s saw a move towards greater realism in the musical, exemplified by *West Side Story* (Robert Wise, Jerome Robbins, 1961), an updated version of *Romeo and Juliet*. The classic musical established a link between music and the screen, featuring stars from both media and creating a market synergy between them, a relationship that rock 'n' roll was able to build on in the 1950s.

Popular and rock musicals

The classical musical's place was taken by a plethora of new forms associated with the popular musical genres spawned by the advent of rock 'n' roll. These films are frequently treated as a generic group – 'popular musicals' – but this term could apply equally to their historical predecessors, or as 'rock films', although their subject matter goes beyond rock as a genre. There are a substantial number of such films, including a number of identifiable subgenres, and there is a considerable literature on them.

During the 1950s, the decline of the Hollywood studio system and a dwindling cinema audience led to the need to more systematically target particular audience demographics. Hollywood linked up with the record industry to target youth, with a spate of teenage musicals. Many of these starred Elvis Presley, with his song and dance routines in films such as *Jail House Rock* (Richard Thorpe, 1957). Most early popular musicals had basic plots involving the career of a young rock performer: *Rock Around the Clock* (Fred Sears, 1955), *Don't Knock the Rock* (Fred Sears, 1956), and *The Girl Can't Help It* (Frank Tashlin, 1957). These were frequently combined with the other stock form, films serving purely as contrived vehicles for their real-life stars. Most of Elvis Presley's movies, from *Love Me Tender* (Robert Webb, 1956) onward, were of this order, while British examples include Cliff Richard in *The Young Ones*

(Sydney Furie, 1961) and Tommy Steele in *The Tommy Steele Story* (Gerard Bryant, 1957).

Any interest such films retain is largely due to their participant's music rather than their acting talents, although they did function as star vehicles for figures like Presley. In helping establish an identity for rock 'n' roll, the teenage musicals placed youth in opposition to adult authority and for conservatives confirmed the 'folk devil' image of fans of the new genre, associating them with juvenile delinquency, a major concern internationally through the 1950s. Thematically, however, the popular musicals actually stressed reconciliation between generations and classes, with this acting as a point of narrative closure at the film's ending.

Such musicals also helped create an audience and a market for the new musical form, particularly in countries distant from the initial developments (see Chapter 13). These related roles continued to be in evidence in the subsequent development of the popular rock musical. The single 'Rock Around the Clock', by Bill Hailey and the Comets, provides an example of the market power of cinema in the popularization of rock 'n' roll. Originally released in May 1954, the song barely dented the US *Billboard* chart, peaking at no. 23, where it stayed for only one week. Greater success came when the song was prominently used on the soundtrack for *Blackboard Jungle* (Richard Brooks, 1954). One of the most successful and controversial films of the period, it used the new genre of rock 'n' roll to symbolize adolescent rebellion against the authority of the school. Re-released in May 1955, 'Rock Around the Clock' went to no. 1 in the UK and the US. By the end of 1955 it had become the most popular recording in the US since 'The Tennessee Waltz', selling 6 million copies and having an international impact.

British beat and the 'British Invasion' of the early 1960s were served up in a number of films. Gerry and the Pacemakers brought a taste of the moment to a broader audience with *Ferry Across the Mersey* (J. Summers, 1964). This stuck to what had already become a standard formula – struggling young band makes good after initial setbacks – which was only shaken when the Beatles enlisted director Richard Lester to produce the innovative and pseudo-biographical *A Hard Day's Night* (1964). Along with Lester's *Help* (1965), this consolidated the group's market dominance and extended the rock film genre into new and more interesting anarchic forms. In the mid- to late 1960s, with the emergence of the counterculture, popular music was a necessary backdrop and a cachet of cultural authenticity for films such as *Easy Rider* (Dennis Hopper, 1969) and *The Graduate* (Mike Nichols, 1967). Both fused contemporary rock soundtracks with thematic youth preoccupations of the day: the search for a personal and cultural identity in contemporary America.

During the 1970s and 1980s there was a profusion of popular musicals: the realist Jamaican film *The Harder They Come* (Perry Henzel, 1972); the flower power and religious fantasy of *Godspell* (David Greene, 1973) and *Hair* (Milos Forman, 1979); the disco dance musical *Grease* (Radnal Kleister, 1978); and the dance fantasies of *Flashdance* (Adrian Lyne, 1983) and *Dirty Dancing* (Emile Ardolino,

1987). The 'rock lifestyle' was the focus of *That'll Be The Day* (1973) and Ken Russell's version of *Tommy* (1975). Nostalgia was at the core of *Amercian Graffiti* (George Lucas, 1973), *The Blues Brothers* (John Landis, 1978), *The Buddy Holly Story* (Steve Rash, 1978) and *Quadrophenia* (Franc Rodham, 1979). The success of these popular musicals helped prepared the ground for the success of MTV, launched in 1981, by reshaping the political economy of popular music, shifting the emphasis from sound to sound *and* images.

Since the 1980s popular musical films have continued to mine a range of themes: youth subcultures (*River's Edge*, Tim Hunter, 1987); adolescent and young adult sexuality and gender relations (*Singles*, Cameron Crowe, 1992); class and generational conflict; nostalgia; stardom and the rock lifestyle (*Purple Rain*, Albert Magnoli, 1984; *Backbeat*, Iain Softley, 1995; *Rock Star*, Stephen Herek, 2001); dance fantasies such as *Strictly Ballroom* (Baz Luhrman, 1992) and *Take the Lead* (Liz Friedlander, 2006); and fandom and the joy of making music, as in *High Fidelity* (Stephen Frears, 2000), *School of Rock* (Richard Linklater, 2004) and *Scott Pilgrim vs The World* (Edgar White, 2010). *The Rocky Horror Picture Show* (Jim Sharman, 1975) created a new subgenre: the cult musical, with the audience becoming an integral part of the cinematic experience, an indulgence in fantasy and catharsis. The film went on to become the king of the 'midnight movies' – cult films shown at midnight for week after week, usually on Friday and Saturday nights.

The storylines of such musicals involve popular music to varying extents, ranging from its centrality to the narrative theme, to its use as soundtrack. These films articulate with the hopes and dreams, and fantasy lives, which popular music brings to people. When an actual artist is drawn on, or featured, such films help the process of mythologizing them, as with Elvis Presley, the Beatles and Jim Morrison. Dominant themes include youth and adolescence as a rite of passage, frequently characterized by storm and stress, and using subcultural versus 'mainstream' affiliations to explore this; reconciliation, between generations, competing subcultures and genders, frequently expressed through the emergence of couples; and the search for independence and an established sense of identity. Given such themes are ones identified in the literature as central adolescent 'tasks' and preoccupations, they clearly appeal to youthful cinema audiences and to filmmakers looking for box office success.

A particular form of popular music film is the biopic: a biography presented as a film or television feature, but differing from a documentary in that it is aimed at a popular audience and will balance reliability and accuracy against commercial considerations and the need to entertain. A popular music biopic is 'a film which purports to tell, in part or in full, the biography of a musical performer (living or dead), and which contains a significant part of his or her music' (Inglis, 2007: 77; he was referring to rock/pop biopics, but his definition can stand for the genre). The subjects for music biopics can be found in a range of genres, including blues, rap, jazz, soul, country, and pop and rock. Examples include *Sid and Nancy* (Alex Cox,1986), on Sid Vicious of the Sex Pistols; *Bird* (Clint Eastwood, 1988), about Charlie Parker; *The Doors* (Oliver Stone,1990); *Ray* (Taylor Hackford, 2004), about Ray Charles; *Walk The Line* (James Mangold, 2005), about Johnny Cash;

Nowhere Boy (Sam Taylor-Wood, 2009), on the early life of John Lennon; and *The Runaways* (Floria Sigismondi, 2011), on the influential teen girl rock band of the late 1970s.

As Spencer Leigh (2009: 348) observes, reviewing *Nowhere Boy*, to some degree makers of such films are, of necessity, 'playing fast and loose with the truth', as they are constrained by the limited time to tell a story that covers several years and may include considerable musical experimentation. The original source material, where there are widely varying popular biographies/memoirs and so forth of a figure like Lennon, can also be problematic.

Soundtracks

As mentioned earlier, *Rock Around the Clock* (1956) and many of the films featuring Elvis Presley demonstrated the market appeal of popular musical soundtracks, as had many Hollywood musicals before them. Mainstream narrative cinema has increasingly used popular music soundtracks to great effect, with accompanying commercial success for both film and record. A key film to initially demonstrate the advantages of such synergy to the music industry was *Saturday Night Fever* (John Badham, 1977). As shown in Chapter 7, Prince's soundtrack for the film *Batman* (1989) was part of a carefully orchestrated marketing campaign, which successfully created interest in the film and helped break Prince to a wider audience, primarily through exposure (of the promotional video clip) on MTV. The soundtrack to *The Commitments* (Alan Parker, 1991), featuring some impressive covers of soul classics and the powerful voice of Andrew Strong (who plays the part of the lead singer Deco), charted internationally, reaching no. 1 in several countries.

Such soundtracks feature popular music composed specifically for the film, or previously recorded work which is thematically or temporally related to the film, as with *American Graffiti* (1973), *The Big Chill* (1983), *Boyz N The Hood* (1991) and *High School Musical* (2006). This enables multimedia marketing, with accompanying commercial success for both film and record. Several musicians better known for their band recordings have followed Ry Cooder's example and moved into composing music for such films, for example Trent Reznor (Nine Inch Nails) for *Natural Born Killers* (1994) and *The Social Network* (2010) and Kirk Hammet (Metallica) and Orbital for *Spawn* (1999). Television series have also provided a vehicle for music soundtracks. *Northern Exposure* (1990–95) set the pattern for later shows, using a local radio station and the local bar's jukebox to get artists from Nat King Cole to Lynyrd Skynyrd into each episode.

Television

Television has been an important mode of distribution and promotion for the music industry. It is now commonplace for successful television series to include popular songs, situating them historically and lending themselves to narrative themes. When carefully selected, these add to the effectiveness of the programme, while also providing an income stream and publicity for musicians and their labels; for example, for its series *Case Histories* (2011) the BBC provides web links on its website to the music used and its performers. Popular music plot themes, music segments and signature tunes are an important part of many television genres, including those aimed at children (e.g. *Sesame Street*) and adolescents (*The Simpsons*, *The X Files*), but also 'adult' dramas such as *The Sopranos* and *Grey's Anatomy*, with the accompanying release of soundtrack albums from these series.

I now want to consider the role of free-to-air, broadcast television and the popular music programmes that form part of its schedules: light entertainment series based around musical performers, music documentaries and the presentation of musical acts as part of television variety and chat/interview shows (MTV and similar cable channels are dealt with later). A contradictory relationship initially existed between television and popular music. Television is traditionally a medium of family entertainment, collapsing class, gender, ethnic and generational differences in order to construct a homogeneous audience held together by the ideology of the nuclear family. In contrast, many forms of popular music, especially rock 'n' roll and its various mutations, have historically presented themselves as being about 'difference', emphasizing individual tastes and preferences (Frith, 2007: Chapter 12). The introduction of public broadcast television in the US and the UK, in the 1950s, coincided with the emergence of rock 'n' roll. Television helped popularize the new music and established several of its performers, most notably Elvis Presley, as youth icons. Indeed, for some fans, along with film television was their only access to 'live' performance. Television was quick to seize the commercial opportunities offered by the emergent youth culture market of the 1950s and there was a proliferation of television popular music shows.

The better known of these on US television included *American Bandstand*, one of the longest running shows in television history (1952–89), *Your Hit Parade* (1950–59) and *The Big Record* (1957–58). Britain had *Juke Box Jury* and *Top of the Pops*, both starting in the late 1950s, and *The Old Grey Whistle Test* (launched by the BBC in 1971 and aimed at more album-oriented older youth). In 1963 *Ready Steady Go! (RSG)* began showcasing new talent, who usually performed live, compared to the *Top of the Pops* staid studio lip-synchs with backing from a house orchestra. In addition to the music, such shows have acted as influential presenters of new dances, image and clothing styles. Several of these shows were subsequently marketed as sell-through videos or DVDs, documenting historically significant performers and styles (e.g. *The Best of the Old Grey Whistle Test*, BBC DVD, 2001) and showcasing contemporary acts (*Later, with Jools Holland*).

Through the 1980s and into the 1990s, a number of studies illustrated the factors at work in the emergence and nature of popular music programmes on commercial television, particularly their place within scheduling practices and the process of selection of the performers and music videos for inclusion on them. Of particular interest were the links between screen space, advertising and record sales. While it is difficult to prove a direct causal link, as with radio airplay and chart 'action' there was evidence that the television exposure had an influence on record purchases. The nature of such shows, and their tendency to play music videos that are shortened versions of the associated song, exercised considerable influence over the way in which videos were produced and their nature as audiovisual and star texts. Also significant, especially in small nations such as Australia, New Zealand and the Netherlands, was the often marginalized status of locally produced music videos that are competing for screen space compared with their imported counterparts, a form of cultural imperialism.

Television's presentation of rock music prior to the advent of music video was generally uninspiring. Performers either straightforwardly performed, even if at times in an impressively frenetic manner (as with the Who's debut effort on *RSG*) or mimed to their recordings in a pseudo-live setting. There were a few notable experiments through the 1960s and 1970s to incorporate additional visual elements (see Shore, 1985, for a full history of the development of music video in relation to television; also Austerlitz, 2007). The 1980s' success of MTV boosted televised music videos, reshaping the form and the broadcast shows that relied on music videos for their content. In the US and Canada, nearly every major city had its own televised music video show, with several nationally syndicated. MV-based programmes also became a stock part of television channel viewing schedules in the UK and western Europe, and New Zealand and Australia. These shows were significant because of their importance to advertisers, drawing a young audience whose consuming habits are not yet strongly fixed.

The increased popularity of MTV and the digital delivery of music undermined music on mainstream television. In New Zealand and Australia, which were slow to acquire cable television and more widely available satellite reception, such television shows retained the high audience ratings they achieved during the 1960s through into the 1990s, but then fell away. Many of the traditionally screened shows have now ended, including the iconic *Top of the Pops* in the UK (in 2006) and the older, chart-oriented shows, have been supplanted by music-driven reality television. Today, popular music on television is increasingly competing against other genres for scheduling space and advertising revenue, while the demographic significance and spending power of the youth audience has steadily declined since the 1990s. At the same time, web-based delivery systems for audiovisual content, notably YouTube, have proved more attractive to younger (and many older) consumers.

Reality television: from S Club 7 *to* Pop Idol

'Reality television' describes a variety of programming ranging from crime and emergency-style shows, to talk shows, docusoaps and some forms of access-style programming. Emerging in the 1980s in the US, it established itself as a central part of mainstream, popular television by the mid-1990s. In the 2000s reality television became a leading programme format, with many shows internationally franchised (e.g. *Survivor*, *Big Brother*). A hybrid genre, reality television draws on and reworks generic codes and conventions from a variety of sources, using new technology (e.g. camcorders) to convey as sense of immediacy and authenticity to viewers. Reality television has been criticized for being reliant on shock value and pandering to viewer voyeurism and the lowest common denominator, but also celebrated for its emphasis on viewer participation and its influence on producing commercial pop stars for the music industry. Popular music has provided a significant vehicle for reality television. Early series, notably *The Monkees* in the 1960s and *S Club 7 in Miami* in the late 1990s, reinforced the public profiles and commercial success of their performers.

Initial TV and 19 Management (who managed the Spice Girls) conducted a nationwide search in the UK to develop a group to star in a teen-oriented television show for BBC 1. Reflecting their name, the assembled group S Club 7 consisted of seven members whose public image was very much that of a supportive friendship group. The television show, *S Club 7 in Miami*, debuted in the UK during 1999 and went on to be screened internationally. Its success led to the show being rescreened (on BBC 2 in 2000), and to its marketing as two 'sell-through' video compilations of several episodes. A follow-up series, with S Club 7 now in Los Angeles (*LA7*), first screened in the UK on BBC 1 in early 2000 and was also sold overseas. S Club 7 appeared frequently in the teen music magazines, with several cover stories (e.g. *Smash Hits*, 5 April 2000) and on shows such as *Top of the Pops*.

Further media coverage was generated through the group's own magazine, *S Club*, and a sophisticated official website that introduced visitors to 'the s club experience' in an interactive and engaging manner. The site enabled fans to find out personal details about each member of the group, the recordings and television shows and their other activities. Fans could register to receive advance information about all of these and leave messages for the groups' members. The website consolidated S Club 7's fan base and was an early example of what has become a valuable adjunct to more traditional forms of music marketing. This fan base appeared to largely consist of young girls aged between eight and twelve, a significant 'demographic' with considerable spending power (there were some boys, too, however).

Helped by such exposure, the group's debut single 'Bring it All Back' topped the UK chart and enjoyed modest success when it was released in the US. A second single, 'S Club Party', also charted, as did the groups self-titled first album. In March 2000 a second album and the first single from it ('Reach') charted in the UK and overseas. The group enjoyed further chart success through 2001 and 2003 and made a third television series, *Hollywood 7*. In mid-2002 Paul Cattermole left the band, which continued as S Club. In 2003, after their movie *Seeing Double* and a greatest hits album (*Best*) were released, the group broke up.

S Club 7 foreshadowed later series such as the *Pop Idol*, *Popstars* and *Rock Star* series. These musical talent quests, based on audience votes but with a key role played by judging panels (especially in the initial selection of participants), have become an international phenomenon. They have created new pop and rock stars in a number of countries, although the career of some has been short lived. The popularity of such shows, their audience and the discourse of commodification and authenticity surrounding them are topics that have attracted increased attention in popular music studies.

American Idol; Pop Idol

Pop Idol first screened in the UK in 2001, then in the US (as *American Idol*). Early series of *Pop Idol* launched the careers of Will Young and Gareth Gates in the UK and Ruben Studdard in the US. The show went on to become a global success story, being produced and aired in more than 35 countries. *American Idol* has been enormously successful, especially the earlier series, with all the winners and some finalists going on to recording and touring careers. It is essentially a talent competition, with contestants initially selected (from auditions) by a panel of expert judges, followed by a series of elimination rounds, culminating in a final. Audience voting plays a major determining role in the outcome of each programme. Although primarily about musical talent, however that is defined by the judges and the viewers, the appeal of *Idol* is arguably its focus on the character development of an ever-dwindling pool of contestants, as they handle the increasing pressure.

The antecedents of *Pop Idol* lay in the high rating *Popstars* television series held in New Zealand and Australia in 1999 and 2000 respectively. The first part of this was a talent quest, auditioning singers to make up a band; the second part followed the band touring, making a record and gelling (or not) as a group. The New Zealand winners, True Bliss, attracted a good deal of media attention and had some chart success, although this was fairly short-lived. The concept and the format were then picked up in the UK and developed and screened (as *Popstars*) by London Weekend Television (LWT). After one season, it was rebranded and reshaped as *Pop Idol* by Simon Cowell and Simon Fuller, both of whom had considerable success previously as pop producers, along with Alan Boyd from Granada Television (Cowell, 2003: 97–114). The first series was aired on ITV in 2001 and demonstrated enormous audience appeal, with the consequent attractiveness of such high ratings to advertisers. The 2002 final of *Pop Idol* (UK) was watched by 15 million viewers and received some 8.7 million phone votes (although it is important to note that there was no limit on the number of votes an individual viewer could cast). Initially one of the judges in both series, Cowell's realistic and ruthless treatment of some contestants created considerable publicity. Cowell then helped create the US show *American Idol*, on which he also judged. *American Idol* enjoyed even greater success than its UK predecessor and in 2011 was in its tenth consecutive year. Although its popularity has declined since the early series, in its latest season it remained the most watched television show in the US and has been a 'cash cow' for the Fox network. According to *Billboard*, Kelly Clarkson, the winner of the first series, has been the most commercially successful of the *Idol* contestants, with a number of high-charting records.

Academic analysis of the idol phenomenon has focused on the construction of the contestants as 'ordinary', enabling closer audience identification with them;

the associated role of viewer interactivity, through the voting system; the industry tie-in; and the adaptation of the format internationally (Stratton, 2008; Zwaan and de Bruin, 2012). With the judges having a background in production or performance, the winner is usually guaranteed a recording contract, with a 'massive body of deeply invested fans' (Stahl, 2004: 212) ensuring at least initial commercial success.

Documentaries and rockumentaries

'Constructed as a genre within the field of non-fictional representation, documentary has, since its inception, been composed of multiple, frequently linked representational strands' (Beattie, 2004: 2). Popular music documentaries include concert, tour and festival films; profiles of performers, and scenes; and ambitious historical overviews. Such documentaries can be produced for either film or television as both 'one-offs' and series. The various forms of popular music documentary have served a number of economic and ideological functions. As a form of programming, they create income for their producers and those who screen them, via rights and royalties. They validate and confirm particular musical styles and historical moments in the history of popular music as somehow worthy of more 'serious' attention. While celebrating 'youth' and the mythic status of stars, they also confirm their status as 'the other' for critics of these sounds and their performers.

Concert, tour, festival and scene documentaries demonstrate a close link between the documentation of musical performance and observational modes of documentary filmmaking. Referred to in the US as 'direct cinema', and evident from the early 1960s, these documentaries have a well-established tradition (see Beattie, 2004), exemplified in the work of director D.A. Pennebaker (*Don't Look Back*, 1966; *Monterey Pop*, 1968; and *Down From the Mountain*, 2002). Direct cinema mutated into 'docusoap' and other variants of reality television, as in MTV's *The Real World* series (which frequently featured participants who were seeking musical careers), and *Meet the Osbournes*, a fly-on-the-wall depiction of the family life of aging heavy metal rocker Ozzy Osbourne.

Films of music festivals have consolidated the mythic status of events such as *Monterey Pop* (1968) and, especially, *Woodstock* (1969), with the 1970 film a major box office success. A number of other concert and concert tour films have had a similar but more limited commercial and ideological impact; for example: *The Last Waltz* (Martin Scorcese,1978), a record of The Band's final concert; *Stop Making Sense* (Jonathon Demme, 1984), featuring Talking Heads; *Hail, Hail Rock and Roll* (Taylor Hackford, 1987), featuring Chuck Berry and other seminal rock 'n' roll performers; Prince's *Sign O' The Times* (Prince,1987); and Neil Young and Crazy Horse in *Year of the Horse* (Jim Jarmusch, 1998). Such films capture particular moments in 'rock history', while at the same time validating particular musical styles and performers.

Other documentaries consolidate particular historical moments: Julian Temple's examination of the Sex Pistol's phenomenon, including the television interview that sparked off controversy (*The Filth and the Fury*, 2000); the Rolling Stones Altamont concert of 1969 (*Gimme Shelter*, Albert and David Maysles, 1970; released on DVD by Criterion in 2000); and the Beatles first tour of America (*What's Happening! The Beatles in the USA*, Albert and David Maysles, 2004). Documentaries have also been important in exposing particular scenes, sounds, and performers to a wider audience, as in *The Decline of Western Civilization, Part One* (Penelope Spheeris, 1981), on the Los Angeles punk/hardcore scene circa 1981, featuring Black Flag, the Circle Jerks, X and the Germs; its 'sequel', *The Decline of Western Civilization, Part Two: the Metal Years* (Penelope Spheeris, 1988), featuring Aerosmith, Alice Cooper, Kiss, Ozzy Osbourne, Metallica and Motörhead; and *Hype!* (Doug Pray, 1996), on the Seattle grunge scene. The success of *Buena Vista Social Club* (Wim Wenders, 1999) introduced Cuban jazz to an international audience and led to massive sales of the accompanying soundtrack album (which had initially gone largely ignored following its first release in 1996). *Genghis Blues* (Roko Belic, 2000) consolidated the appeal of world music and *Down From the Mountain* (D.A. Pennebaker, 2002) did the same for contemporary bluegrass. Documentaries have reminded us of the important role of session musicians and 'house bands', for example the Funk Brothers in *Standing in the Shadows of Motown* (Paul Justman, 2002). More frequently they celebrate major performers, as with The Who in *The Kids Are Alright* (Jeff Stein, 1979; released as a special DVD edition, 2004) and The Rolling Stones in *Shine A Light* (Martin Scorsese, 2008), a concert film of the band recorded in New York in 2006 at the end of their world A Bigger Bang Tour. As with any genre the ultimate accolade is parody, best represented by *This is Spinal Tap* (Rob Reiner, 1984).

Documentary series on the history of popular music, made for television, include the joint BBC and US co-production *Dancing in the Street* (1995; with an accompanying book, by Robert Palmer); *Walk on By* (2003) a history of songwriting; Ken Burns *Jazz* (2000); the Australian series *Long Way to the Top* (ABC, 2001); and the Martin Scorcese series, *Legacy of the Blues*, screened as part of the 'Year of the Blues' celebrations in the US in 2003. In addition to the income from their initial screenings and international licensing, such series have produced accompanying books, soundtracks and video and DVD boxed sets. Although the selection of material depends heavily on the nature and quality of what is available, they visually construct particular historical narratives, reframing the past. In the case of *Dancing in the Street*, for example, the emphasis is on 'authentic artists' rather than commercial performers: in the episode 'Hang on to Yourself', Kiss get barely a minute, while 'punk icon' Iggy Pop features throughout. In sum, as with the music press, music documentary history is situated primarily around key performers and styles, another form of canonization.

Music video

The most pervasive and significant form of musical audiovisual text is the music video, traditionally associated with the television channel MTV (established in 1981), and more recently a prominent aspect of YouTube. While MTV certainly elevated the form to a central place in popular music culture, the music video had been around in various forms since 'talkies' in the 1940s (see Shore, 1985).

Individual music video clips largely follow the conventions of the traditional 45" single: they are approximately 2–3 minutes long, and function, in the industry's own terms, as 'promotional devices', historically to encourage record sales and chart action. These clips have been the staple component in music television, especially the MTV channel; the long-form music video compilation, increasingly available on DVD; and are now widely available through YouTube. The primary focus in the study of music video (MV) has been on their nature as audiovisual texts. Various attempts to read music videos have necessarily adopted the insights and concepts of film and television studies, although these have had to be modified in the light of the different functions they often play in MVs, particularly in relation to the music. There is also some recognition, at times rather belated, of the point that MVs are not self-contained texts, but reflective of their nature as industrial and commercial products and their close association with MTV (see later).

I want to sketch some basic considerations that usefully inform specific 'textual' readings of MV and, with particular reference to the influential work of Ann Kaplan, examine the difficulties endemic in constructing a classificatory typology of music videos. Duran Duran's 'Hungry Like the Wolf' (1981), helped establish the conventions of the form. (For extended discussions of music videos as texts and examples of close readings, see Austerlitz, 2007; Vernallis, 2005.)

'Reading' music video

Two general points frequently made about MVs as individual texts are their preoccupation with visual style and, associated with this, their status as key exemplars of 'postmodern' texts. Music videos were pioneers in video expression, but their visual emphasis raises problems for their musical dimensions. As some three-quarters of sensory information comes in through the eye, the video viewer concentrates on the images, arguably at the expense of the soundtrack. This combination has been accused of fuelling performers' preoccupation with visual style, which can dominate over content. Since the 1980s MV has been a crucial marketing tool, with the music often merely part of an overall style package offered to consumers.

Cultural historian and theorist Fredric Jameson (1984) saw music videos as 'meta entertainments' that embody the postmodern condition. It is certainly clear that MVs do indeed merge commercial and artistic image production and abolish traditional boundaries between an image and its real-life referent. In this respect, their most obvious characteristic is their similarity to advertisements, making them a part of a blatantly consumerist culture. Kaplan (1987) went so far as to suggest that the MV spectator has become decentred and fragmented, unable any longer to distinguish 'fiction' from 'reality', part of postmodern culture. This conflation of MV and postmodernism is, however, difficult to sustain. While many MVs display considerable evidence of pastiche, intertextuality and eclecticism, this does not in itself make them postmodern (for an insightful discussion of this point, see Goodwin, 1993). Further, by the 2000s, the nature of MVs was arguably becoming more traditional and clichéd, as just a few hours of watching MTV then made clear.

Considering music videos as texts means applying some stock topics and questions. These are derived partly from film studies and include cinematic aspects, such as camera techniques, lighting, use of colour and editing. Different styles of video utilize different conventions; heavy metal videos, for example, make considerable use of wide-angle lens and zoom shots in keeping with their emphasis on a 'live' performance format. A major focus of MV analysis that draws on film studies is the nature of the gaze in MV – who is looking at whom, how and what do these conventions convey in terms of power relations, gender stereotypes and the social construction of self?

In more general thematic terms, there is a need to also consider:

- The mood of the video – the way in which the music, the words and the visuals combine to produce a general feeling of nostalgia, romanticism, nihilism or whatever.
- The narrative structure – the extent to which the video tells a clear time-sequenced story or is a non-linear pastiche of images, flashbacks, etc.
- The degree of realism or fantasy of the settings or environments in the video and the relationship between genres and particular physical settings, as with rap and the street.
- The standard themes evident, for example, the treatment of authority, love and sex, 'growing up' and the loss of childhood innocence, political and social consciousness.
- The importance of performance: why does this format better suit particular genres such as heavy metal?
- Different modes of sexuality – the female as mother/whore figure; androgyny and the blurring of dress codes; homoeroticism.
- The nature of MVs as a star text, centred on the role played by the central performer(s) in the video and the interelationship of this to their star persona in rock more generally.
- The music – what we hear and how it relates to what we see.

The last was often a critical absence from the early, visual-oriented, readings of MV. Andrew Goodwin goes so far as to argue that:

> a musicology of the music video image is the basis for understanding how to undertake a credible textual study. Issues relating to the sound-vision relation, the formal organization of music videos, questions of pleasure and so on, need to be related to the musical portion of the text.
>
> (Goodwin, 1993: Introduction)

In a substantial, music-based study of later music videos, Carol Vernallis (2005) sees them as utilizing visual images to represent and enhance the music, while continuing to play a commercial role as industry promotion.

These are not simply signposts to viewing individual MVs, they are also factors that can be utilized to categorize them. Although much criticized, the most thorough attempt to categorize MVs still remains that developed by Ann Kaplan, in her study *Rocking Around the Clock: Music Television, Postmodernism, and Consumer Culture* (1987). While Kaplan is primarily concerned with analyzing MTV, she also constructs an interesting typology of individual MVs. Her five categories are derived from combining a reading of rock history with theoretical tools taken from psychoanalytic and film theory, a combination that at times sits awkwardly. Her five typical video forms are: the romantic, the socially conscious, the nihilist, the classical and the postmodern. However, attempting to apply the typology to particular videos has proved difficult.

Kaplan's schema is weak partly because it mixes the bases for each category: the first three are situated in pop history – the romantic clips drawing from 1960s' soft rock; the socially conscious from 1970s' rock and the nihilist from 1980s' new wave and heavy metal music. But then the remaining two categories are based in film theory (with the classical category related to realist film texts) and the postmodern in some sort of catch-all residual category in which postmodern motifs, evident in practically all MVs, are simply more plentiful. The result is that clips placed in one category might just as easily be located in another. It is also questionable to collapse the history of pop/rock music into a series of decades, each dominated by and identified with a certain style of music. Further, the schema ignores the significance of genre and auteurship in the music industry, both of which fit uncomfortably with it. What would be a viable alternative schema? Perhaps the eclectic nature of music video makes impossible anything other than a basic distinction between performance and fictional narrative MVs? Having raised some issues surrounding the analysis of music videos, I now want to relate these to an early, now classic example. (For detailed analyses of later music videos, see Austerlitz, 2007; Vernallis, 2005.)

Duran Duran: 'Hungry Like the Wolf' (dir. Russell Mulcahy, 1981)

The career of Duran Duran provides an early example of the need to consider music videos as promotional devices as much as mini visual texts. Formed in 1978, the UK pop group achieved considerable early commercial success, with several hits in the British Top 20 in 1981, but initially failed to dent the US market. Despite intensive touring in North America and the photogenic male group's considerable exposure in the teen music press, Duran Duran's self-titled debut album on Capitol/EMI failed to yield a hit single and had only risen to no. 150 on the album charts. Exposure on MTV changed this dramatically.

The group had already attracted attention with their first video: 'Girls on Film' (1980) directed by leading video auteurs Godley and Creme. The group barely appear in the MV, which features a series of soft-core porn-style scenes, including attractive, scantily clad (nude in the uncensored version) women pillow fighting on a whipped cream-covered phallic pole! Kevin Godley acknowledges the sexism of the video, but explains:

> Look, we just did our job. We were very explicitly told by Duran Duran's management to make a very sensational, erotic piece that would be for clubs, where it would get shown uncensored, just to make people take notice and talk about it.
>
> (cited in Shore, 1985: 86)

That bands were increasingly making two versions of their videos, one for mainstream television shows and MTV and one for more adult cable outlets and clubs, demonstrates the market-driven nature of the video text and any reading of MV must take this intention into account.

In August 1981, as MTV began broadcasting in North America, EMI invested $200,000 to send Duran Duran to Sri Lanka to shoot three video clips with director Russell Mulcahy. One of them, 'Hungry Like the Wolf', became an MTV favourite. Less than two months after the two-week shoot, the clip was in high rotation on MTV and getting heavy radio airplay and this exposure helped propel the single into the Top 10 and Duran Duran's second album, *Rio*, into the upper reaches of the album charts. MTV confirmed Duran Duran as a teenage pop sensation. In 1983, in conjunction with Sony's promoting its new video 45s (which included the Duran's 'Girls On Film' – the uncensored night-club version – and 'Hungry'), along with Duran Duran's compilation, 'sell-through', video cassette, the group undertook a highly successful video tour of major clubs across North America; 'Each date on the video tour sold out, and in every city the video tour hit, Duran Duran's records sold out within days' (Shore, 1985: 93–4).

In 'Hungry like the Wolf' Singer Simon LeBon's head rises in slow motion out of a river as rain pours down. He then chases a beautiful Indian woman, who appears to be clad only in an animal skin, through a Sri Lankan tropical jungle and open air market. During the chase, he has his brow mopped by a young Indian (boy?) and overturns a bar room table. When he catches the beast/woman, they have an encounter suggestive of both sex and violence:

> Mulcahy's ravenously tracking and panning camera, insinuating erotic ambiguity, and editing wizardry (frames slide in from the left or right, double and split-screen edits on and around the beat, etc) which have been the real stars of the show all along, come into full play ... we've been dazzled seduced and abandoned.
>
> (Shore, 1985: 178)

The nature of the narrative is almost irrelevant here, serving merely to showcase LeBon and add an aura of exotic appeal and sexuality to the song.

Indeed, a satisfactory analysis of 'Hungry' as a text must acknowledge this 'focus on the star' aspect of it. Duran Duran was the pin-up band of the mid-1980s, particularly among young girls. Watching the video even now, women students focus on the physical appeal of the singer, who is variously described as 'delicious', a 'hunk' and 'sexy'. Young male viewers acknowledge that LeBon is 'conventionally handsome' and some even tentatively point to his rather androgynous appeal. The star appeal of LeBon is fed on and enhanced by the technical virtuosity of the director, already then recognized as a leading auteur of the music video form. Mulcahy is arguably the star as much as LeBon – although not, of course, to the young fans of Duran Duran in the mid-1980s.

Even purely at the level of text, 'Hungry like the Wolf' is difficult to categorize in Kaplan's terms. It has elements of the 'classical', with the male as subject and the woman as object: 'I'm on the hunt I'm after you', sings LeBon – although there is a case for reversing this distinction. Further, the video's narrative structure is a mini-drama, based loosely around LeBon's chase while his friends are being enticed by lithe beauties back in the town, a narrative that never fully realizes closure. But in Kaplan's terms, the video also has strongly 'postmodernist' features. The rapid editing creates a series of disjointed images, which disrupt linear time and leave the viewer uncertain about the sequence of the events and even if there is indeed a 'plot' to follow. Kaplan pays little attention to the music in her analysis of music video, an absence that is significant in the case of 'Hungry' (even if it is admittedly not one of the MVs she examines). The sharp rhythm and strong beat of the song, along with the single male voice, match the rapid editing and sheer physical aggression of the video. It is the music that links and 'makes sense of' the images, which would not have the same impact on their own.

The 'Hungry Like the Wolf' video also raises the issue of authorship in MVs. While it is customary to refer to MVs as being the product of the particular performer featured, and some artists take a major role in determining the nature of their MVs, 'the directors most often are responsible for the concepts, the vision, the imagery, and the editing rhythm that coalesce into a look that keeps people watching' (Shore, 1985: 97). This is still the case, particularly with 'new' performers unfamiliar with the medium. There are a number of MV directors who can be considered pioneers and auteurs in the field, including Godley and Creme, Russell Mulcahy, David Mallet, Julian Temple and Michelle Gondry. Several, most notably Mulcahy and Temple, have gone from making music videos to directing major feature films.

To explain the nature of the appeal of music videos it is necessary to go beyond their purely textual aspects and consider their function as polysemic narratives and images of viewer fantasy and desire. As with other popular culture texts, MVs present a semiotic terrain open to cultural struggles over meaning. This illustrates the general point that meanings and pleasures are not purely embedded 'in' MV texts, but are produced in the act of viewing and through their cultural location at the intersection of art and commerce.

MTV

The 24-hour, non-stop commercial cable channel 'MTV: Music Television', founded in 1981, made itself and its logo synonymous with the music video form. Originally owned by the Warner Amex Satellite Company, the channel was subsequently sold to Viacom International in 1985. Viacom, which still owns MTV and MTV 2, also has interests in broadcast and cable television, radio, the internet, book publishing and film production and distribution. By 2005 it was the third largest communications conglomerate in the world, with annual revenues of US$26.6 million.

After a slow start, with many detractors who did not think a dedicated music video channel would have an audience, MTV became enormously popular and highly profitable. The channel is credited with boosting a flagging music industry in the 1980s. Not only did it eventually capture a considerable share of the advertising directed at the youth and young adult/yuppie market, as Andrew Goodwin observes, MTV solved the perennial problem of cable television – how to generate enough revenue for new programming – by having the record companies largely pay for the 'programmes' by financing the video clips (Goodwin, 1993).

In the late 1980s MTV was reaching nearly 20 million American homes and was regularly watched by 85 per cent of 18 to 34 year olds (Kaplan, 1987). In November 1991 *MTV 10*, an hour-long celebration of MTV's tenth anniversary, was screened in prime time on the North American ABC TV network. The show asserted the cultural centrality of MTV over the networks, opening with a performance of 'Freedom 90' by George Michael: 'We won the race/Got out of the place/Went back home/Got a brand new face/For the boys on MTV.' Performers on the show included Michael Jackson, Madonna and REM and *MTV 10* was subsequently screened world wide, while the 1992 MTV Music Awards were seen in 139 countries.

By the early 1990s MTV had 28 million subscribers, and was adding one to three million new subscribers every year. MTV's success spawned a host of imitators in the US and a number of national franchises and imitations around the globe. These raised the issue of the place of local music in a context dominated by international repertoire, especially from the North American music market (Hanke, 1998). After an initial struggle to untangle cable and satellite regulations in dozens of countries, MTV Europe, launched in 1988, broke even for the first time in February 1993 and became the continent's fastest growing satellite channel. By 1993, its 24-hours-a-day MV programming was available in more than 44 million homes and it was adding subscribers at the rate of almost one million a month. Thirty per cent of its airtime was reserved for European performers and while the programme format was similar to that of its parent station, it played a substantial number of locally made videos. MTV-Asia began broadcasting in late 1991, with a signal covering more than 30 countries from Japan to the Middle East. The channel's English-language broadcasts reached more than three million households with a programme dominated by MVs by western stars, but with a 20 per cent quota of Asian performers. MTV channels continued to proliferate internationally, although a few have been short-lived (for the current situation, see the MTV web site: www.mtv.com).

The influence of MTV on the North American music industry during the 1980s – and, therefore, by association, globally – was enormous. By 1991 80 per cent of the songs on the *Billboard* Hot 100 were represented by a video and MTV became the most effective way to 'break' a new artist and to take an emerging artist into star status. Performers who received considerable exposure on MTV before they were picked up by radio include Madonna, Duran Duran, the Thompson Twins and Paula Abdul. Dave Rimmer argues that the new 'invasion' of the American charts by British groups, in the mid- to late 1980s was directly attributable to MTV (Rimmer, 1985).

Given their crucial role in determining commercial success, a key question is how particular MVs are chosen for the MTV playlist. Evidence on this point is sparse and it is clearly an area for further inquiry. Surprisingly, Kaplan's (1987) study of the channel ignores the selection issue, as do most commentators preoccupied with the videos as texts. MTV's top 20 lists are compiled from national sales data, video airplay and the channel's own research and requests, building circularity and subjectivity into the process. In his thorough study of the operation of MTV, Banks (1996: Chapter 9) looked at the gatekeeper role of the American MTV channel, the operation of its acquisitions committee and the standards, both stated and unstated, that they apply. He concluded that major companies then willingly edited videos on a regular basis to conform to MTV's standards, even coercing artists into making changes to song lyrics, while smaller, independent companies cannot usually get their videos on MTV. It would be worthwhile to know if such practices remain the case, but an update of Banks' work is lacking.

Despite the heady growth of the 1980s, the American MTV channel began the 1990s by retrenching, with MTV executives claiming that the format had lost its freshness and was becoming clichéd. The channel initiated a programme overhaul designed to lessen its reliance on videos; new shows included *Vidcoms*, combining comedy and MV, and *Unplugged*, a 30-minute Sunday series featuring live acoustic performances by bands such as Crowded House. *Unplugged* proved highly successful, particularly through associated chart-topping album releases (Eric Clapton, Mariah Carey, Nirvana). These changes were a direct response to research on viewing patterns, which indicated, not surprisingly, that people tuned in to MTV for only as long as they enjoy the clips. With MVs making up some 90 per cent of the channel's broadcast day, negative reaction to a few clips can spell problems for audience retention and the sale of advertising time. This is a situation MTV shares with 'mainstream' television and radio, which have always been in the business of delivering audiences to advertisers in a highly competitive market.

Today, while MVs are still the staple of MTV channel's programming, the channel also screens concerts, interviews and music-oriented news and gossip items, acting as a visual radio channel. Although owned by a global media giant (Viacom), 'localization' is almost a mantra for the nationally situated MTV channels, which use local VJs, play locally produced music videos and air local programming. Bill Roedy, the Chairman and CEO of MTV International provides an informative entertaining insider's account of the growth of the company, with an emphasis on how 'we took the original American MTV concept of delivering music with a creative cutting edge and adapted it to the customs and desires of almost every culture on every continent' (Roedy, 2011: 5). Rather surprisingly, given its ubiquity and continued popularity, there is an absence of current academic research into the channel.

Video games

In the past 20 years, video games, also referred to as 'electronic games', have become a pervasive part of popular media culture. They can now be played on several platforms, including Xbox 360, PS3, personal computers and the most recent mobile phones. Several of these have the capability to be linked online, enabling playing with other participants. They are no longer simply a male-dominated leisure form and have a wider and older range of consumers. In addition to the games themselves and their associated music magazines and websites, video games have 'crossed over' to feature films. Video games are an increasingly significant part of the revenue of media corporations, including the music industry, which is:

> forming closer ties with the gaming industry both in terms of direct income via licensing music for use in games and more recently as a means of extending an artist's brand equity through games designed around music performance, such as *Guitar Hero*.
>
> (Hull *et al.*, 2011: 22)

These performance games are a way for fans (and aspiring musicians) to play along with popular songs, in effect a form of home karaoke. The most successful of these has been *The Beatles Rockband* (2009); made in consultation with the surviving Beatles, it includes dozens of the group's original songs, to play on *Rockband*-style guitar, bass and drums, or to just sing along to.

There are several composers who specialize in writing music for video games. The most successful is Tommy Tallarico, whose work has appeared in over 300 video games, including the best-selling *Prince of Persia*, *Mortal Combat*, *Advent Rising* and *Tony Hawk Pro Skate*. In 2005 Tallarico hosted a multimedia show *Video Games Live*, in which an orchestra and choir performed music from popular video games, while a large screen showed excerpts from the games. The world premiere, at the Hollywood Bowl with the Los Angeles Philharmonic, attracted an audience of 11,000 and the show went on to tour internationally. In addition to licensing earlier songs for use in games soundtracks, an increasing number of 'rock' musicians are writing for video games and the British Academy of Film and Television Arts now has an awards category for video game soundtracks.

Academic studies of the composition and role of music in such video games, and the social experience of playing them, are beginning to be published (Collins, 2008) and the topic is one that is going to generate further interest.

Conclusion

The historical succession of media combining music and image tracked here have eroded the distinction between sound and pictures. Access to film, television, music video and MTV is no longer just through terrestrial, physical sites, with all of them increasingly available through the internet and practices such as streaming. You Tube has opened up access, providing an electronic portal to the whole corpus of audiovisual musical texts. In the process, it has democratized consumer choice, in terms of both the scope of the viewing and listening experiences available and the decision of when and where to engage with these.

Further reading

Film and television

Frith, S. (2007) 'Look! Hear! The Uneasy Relationship of Music and Television', *Taking Popular Music Seriously*, Aldershot: Ashgate.
Inglis, I. (2007) 'Popular Music History on Screen: the Pop/Rock Biopic', *Popular Music History*, 2,1: 77–93.
Mundy, J. (1999) *Popular Music on Screen: From the Hollywood Musical to Music Video*, Manchester: Manchester University Press.

Music video

Austerlitz, S. (2007) *Money For Nothing. A History of the Music Video from the Beatles to the White Stripes*, New York: Continuum.
Kaplan, E.A. (1987) *Rocking Around the Clock. Music Television, Postmodernism, and Consumer Culture*, New York: Methuen.
Vernallis, C. (2005) *Experiencing Music Video: Aesthetics and Cultural Context*, Columbia, OH: Columbia University Press.

MTV

Banks, J. (1996) *Monopoly Television. MTV's Quest to Control the Music*, Boulder, CO: Westview Press.
Roedy, B. (2011) *What Makes Business Rock: Building the World's Largest Global Networks*, New York: Wiley.

Reality TV; Idol

Cowell, S. (2003) *I Don't Mean To Be Rude, BUT ...* , London: Ebury Press.
Stratton, J. (2008) 'The *Idol* Audience: Judging, Interactivity and Entertainment', in P. Bloustein and S. Luckman (eds), *Sonic Energies: Music, Technology, Community, Identity*, Aldershot: Ashgate.
Zwaan, K. and de Bruin, J. (2012) *Adapting Idol: Authenticity, Identity and Performance in a Global Television Format*, Aldershot: Ashgate.

Video games

Collins, K. (ed.) (2008) *From Pac-Man to Pop Music Interactive Audio in Games and New Media*, Aldershot: Ashgate.

The essays cover a range of topics, including issues of aesthetics, economics, technology and music making. The book includes an extensive bibliography.

The Beatles Rockband (2009), Xbox 360.

Game play is easy to grasp following the tutorial included. Songs are ranked in 'level of difficulty'; you can start with their first songs played at The Cavern Club in Liverpool and work your way through to recoding Abbey Road or just choose any song to play and sing.

9 'On the Cover of *The Rolling Stone*'

The music press

The music press plays a major part in the process of selling music as an economic commodity, while at the same time investing it with cultural significance. In one of the first extended critical discussions of the music press, Simon Frith correctly argued for its central role in 'making meaning': 'the importance of the professional rock fans – the rock writers', and the music papers, whose readers 'act as the opinion leaders, the rock interpreters, the ideological gatekeepers for everyone else' (Frith, 1983: 165). Currently, the 'traditional' music press remains significant, but has been modified by the advent of online music magazines and blogs producing a democratization of music journalism.

My discussion begins with a general consideration of just what constitutes 'the music press', which I view as a diverse range of publications. Music journalism is a literary genre in which any distinction between 'rock journalism' and academic writing on popular music is frequently blurred. Music magazines include industry reference tools, musicians' magazines, record collector magazines, fanzines, 'teen glossies', 'the inkies', style bibles and the new tabloids. Although these publications have many features in common, each serves a particular place in a segmented market, in which journalism becomes collapsed into, and often indistinguishable from, music industry publicity. Despite this symbiosis, popular music critics continue to function as gatekeepers and arbiters of taste, a role examined in the concluding section of the discussion here.

The music press includes a wide range of print publications, with many now also online, along with web-based publications. General interest magazines and newspapers will also cover popular music, with regular review columns. More specifically, however, the music press refers to specialized publications: lifestyle magazines with major music coverage, music trade papers and weekly and monthly consumer magazines devoted to popular music or particular genres within it. In addition to these are privately published fanzines, usually peripheral to the market economy of commercial publishing but significant nonetheless. Although categories frequently overlap, various categories of publication can be distinguished. They include popular (auto)biographies, histories and genre studies; various forms of consumer guide, including encyclopedias and dictionaries, discographies and chart listings and compilations; and discographies, usually organized by artist, genre or historical period. The last represent an important aspect of popular music history, which they constitute as well as record, and are important texts for fans and aficionados. There are also more esoteric publications, such as rock quiz books, genealogical tables plotting the origin and shifting membership of groups and 'almanacs' dealing with the trivia and microscopic detail of stars' private lives. In one of the first bibliographies of popular music, Paul Taylor observed: 'The variety of these publications is matched by the variation in the quality of their writing, accuracy and scholarship, which means one must approach them with a degree of discrimination and care' (Taylor, 1985: 1). Almost 30 years on, this judgment still stands.

Music journalism and rock criticism

Initially, popular music journalism included a proliferation of 'quickie' publications, cashing in on the latest pop sensation. This was very much the case with the pop annuals accompanying the emergence of chart pop in the 1950s, which were largely rewritten PR (public relations) handouts. Emphasizing the pictorial aspect and providing personal information about performers rather than any extended critical commentary, these were often little more than pseudo-publicity. They reinforced the star aspect of pop consumption, feeding fans' desire for consumable images and information about their preferred performers, as did pop and rock magazines aimed at the teenage market (*Record Mirror*, UK, which began publication in 1953; and *Disc*, UK, 1958).

In the 1960s this changed with the impact of two factors: first the rise of a 'rock culture' with serious artistic intentions; second, the emergence of the 'new journalism', associated with the writing of figures such as Hunter S. Thompson and Tom Wolfe. New journalism set out to move journalism beyond simple factual reporting, by using conventions derived from fiction:

> Stylistic traits pioneered by the new journalists such as scene by scene construction, third person point of view, recording of everyday detail and the inclusion of the figure of the journalist within the text were appropriated by US and UK music critics from the end of the 1960s.
>
> (Leonard and Strachan, 2003: 254)

There was also a commitment to treating popular culture as worthy of serious analysis, an approach that has continued to be influential. The newly established *Rolling Stone* (US) magazine and a revamped *NME* in the UK exemplified this and elevated several rock critics to star status.

A major part of the historical development of music criticism was in jazz and the blues, where critics established some of the norms that later shaped the field more generally. Mark Brennan (2006a) explores the relationship between *Rolling Stone* and *Down Beat* and *Jazz*, especially the motivations for jazz publications to begin covering rock music in the late 1960s. Subsequently, other genres established their own body of work and associated key publications. Documentation and analysis of these has been particularly evident in regard to 'rock criticism', initially associated with the early periods of magazines such as *Rolling Stone* and *Creem* in the United States and *NME* in the United Kingdom and the writing of critics such as Greil Marcus, Lester Bangs, Robert Christgau and Dave Marsh in the US and Jon Savage, Dave Rimmer, Nik Cohen, Barney Hoskyns and Charles Shaar Murray in the UK. (For a thorough overview of the historical development, approaches and impact of rock criticism, see Lindbergh, *et al.*, 2005; the website Rock's Back Pages usefully brings much of this writing together.) America's most lauded rock critic, Bangs, who died in 1982, was the critic with rock star status. An early champion of the proto-punk of 1960s' garage, he is the subject of a biography (De Rogatis, 1982) and his character makes a cameo appearance in the film *Almost Famous*.

The 1980s saw a continuation of this trend, with a proliferation of articles and book-length studies of a more serious vein and intent. Angela McRobbie observed how:

> Two kinds of writing now feed into the study of youth and popular culture. These are the more conventional academic mode, and what might be called a new form of cultural journalism. Each is marked by its own history, its debates and disputes.
>
> (McRobbie, 1988: xi)

Her edited collection, *Zoot Suits and Second-Hand Dresses*, showed serious popular music journalism had changed dramatically during the 1980s, 'with interest shifting from the music itself to a more general concern with the cultural phenomena which accompany it'. This new focus was strongly evident in the new 'style bibles' of the 1980s, especially *The Face*. Some of this journalism also colonized the 'mainstream' press and the more 'serious' weekly and monthly magazines.

Alongside this developed a similar, albeit more historically situated, identifiable body of journalistic work on popular music, not only aimed at a broader readership, but also thoughtful and critically analytical of its subjects. Indicative of the commercial and ideological significance of this work is its appearance in book form as sustained, in-depth studies of genres and performers; collected reviews and essays; several encyclopedias of popular music, aimed at a broad readership; and anthologies (for example, Bangs, 1990; Hoskyns, 2003; the Da Capo series). Also significant, are a number of more thematic historical studies that imbue particular performers, their musical styles and their recordings with meaning and value, situating them as part of a critical tradition and the musical canon. For example, in *Mystery Train*, Greil Marcus uses a handful of rock artists, including Elvis Presley, Sly Stone, the Band and Randy Newman, to illuminate the 'question of the relationship between rock 'n' roll and American culture as a whole'. His concern is with 'a recognition of unities in the American imagination' (1991: Introduction).

Biography

Much music journalism has been identified with biographical studies (and autobiography), which play an important role in popular music. In relation to individuals they 'create, reinforce and also challenge the dominant representations of popular musicians' (Leonard and Strachan, 2003: 13). The biography interpolates and reflects on fandom, stardom, marketing and promotion. In spite of the proliferation of general academic writing in the past 20 years, the journalistic biography has historically been a staple of the music press and remains so; it is essential to the construction and maintenance of fandom. A number of journalists are strongly identified with the biographical form, including Dave Marsh, Barney Hoskyns, Victor Brockis and Peter Guralnick, while biographical profiles are an integral part of edited collections. Most autobiographies are written with the aid of professional music journalists, as is the case with Keith Richards (2010), who was assisted by James Fox.

Such biographies include a wide range of musical performers and vary widely in quality. There is a constant turnover of 'quickie' publications on the latest pop sensations. These remain interesting as they trace 'how star appeal has been defined at different historical moments' (Frith, 1983: 272). In some instances, such biographies seek to undermine the general perception of stars figures, highlighting the scandalous aspects of their lives; these are biographical exposés, as with Albert Goldman's studies of Elvis Presley and John Lennon. A new style of biography emerged in the UK and the US in the 1990s, the 'confessional memoir', in which fans describing their encounters with music and, at times, their own unsuccessful attempt as musicians to 'break into' the music industry, with these often represented as 'celebrations of failure' (Leonard and Strachan, 2003: 13; for example, Giles Smith, *Lost in Music*).

As with literary biography, writers of popular music biographies grapple with issues of sources, materials and objectivity; the links between the subject's life and the social context within which it occurred; and questions of musical production, creativity and authenticity. (For an insightful discussion of this process, from the author's perspective, see the introduction to Guralnick, 2002.) An instructive specific example is provided by Tom Perchard, who, with reference to several biographies of the saxophonist John Coltrane, considers 'the ways that biographical narratives are constituted from disparate source materials and the ideological agendas and political problems that attend this creative act' (2007: 119). With reference to several detailed examples, Thomas Swiss (2005) considers 'what constitutes a successful rock autobiography'. Several recent biographies exemplify the insights the form can offer into the music industry, musical creativity, and particular musical genres, sounds, and scenes, along with their 'readability' and entertainment value (Benatar, 2010; Letts, 2007; Richards, 2010; Smith, 2010).

Music magazines

We can usefully distinguish between industry-oriented, performer-oriented and consumer-oriented music magazines. The music trade papers keep industry personnel informed about mergers, takeovers and staff changes in the record and media industries and changes in copyright and regulatory legislation and policies;

advise retailers about marketing campaigns, complementing and reinforcing their sales promotions; and provide regular chart lists based on extensive sales and radio play data (the main publications are *Billboard*, *Music Business International* and *Music Week*). Musicians' magazines (e.g. *Guitar Player*) inform their readers about new music technologies and techniques, thereby making an important contribution towards musicianship and musical appropriation.

The various consumer- or fan oriented music magazines play a major part in the process of selling music as an economic commodity, while at the same time investing it with cultural significance. Popular music and culture magazines don't simply deal with music, through both their features and advertising they are also purveyors of style. At the same time, these magazines continue to fulfill their more traditional function of contributing to the construction of audiences as consumers.

The majority of popular music magazines focus on performers and their music and the relationship of consumers and fans to these. These magazines fall into a number of fairly clearly identifiable categories, based on their differing musical aesthetics or emphases, their sociocultural functions and their target audiences. 'Teen glossies' emphasize vicarious identification with performers whose music and image is aimed at the youth market (e.g. *Smash Hits*, which ended in 2006; *Melody Maker*, which ceased publication in 2000) and *New Musical Express* (the 'inkies') have historically emphasized a tradition of critical rock journalism, with their reviewers acting as the gatekeepers for that tradition; and the 'style bibles' (*The Face*) emphasize popular music as part of visual pop culture, especially fashion. Several relatively new magazines offer a combination of the inkies focus on an extensive and critical coverage of the music scene and related popular culture, packaged in a glossier product with obvious debts to the style bibles (*MOJO*, *Q*, *UNCUT*). Currently, there is a clear split between inclusive magazines, attempting to cover a broad range of musical styles, and those magazines that are genre specific.

Such magazines can be studied and compared in relation to a series of generally common features:

- Their covers: the cost, the title and the featured artists are all indicative of the magazine's scope and target audience. Further 'clues' are in the visual design (layout, graphics, typeface), the level of language and the use of promotional give a ways (e.g. *Smash Hits* key rings compared with the compilation CDs used with *MOJO* and *Uncut*).
- The general layout and design: e.g. the use or absence of colour, boxed material, sidebars, visuals and even the actual size and length of the magazine.
- Scope: the genres of music included; other media covered (the increasing reference to internet sites, X Games, video game culture); the relative importance accorded particular artists; language used; gender representation (including in the advertising).
- Reviews: length/depth tone and language used (e.g. *Rolling Stone*'s stars system; *Hot Metal*'s skull rating system). (For a helpful early analysis of the evaluative

criteria and rating systems underpinning reviews in Australia's *Rolling Stone* and *Juice*, see Evans, 1998.)

- Adverts: which products feature? The links to a target readership; e.g. teen magazines feminine hygiene ads; the proportion of the content that is adverts; and the values and associated lifestyles projected by the advertising. Often the distinction between adverts and 'real' content is blurred, with much content rewritten press copy.

- The readership involvement: letters to the editor; competitions; reader questions answered (*Q*'s 'where are they now?'); the use of their readers to survey taste and the popularity of artists and genres.

In sum, the answers to such questions provide a profile of particular music magazines, and an indication of their relationship to the wider music industry – a combination of gatekeeper and symbiotic marketing tool. While there is obvious overlap – and market competition – among these various types of music magazine, each has its own distinctive qualities. The following examples illustrate this.

NME: *the inkie tradition*

Typical of the more serious 'inkie' rock press is the *New Musical Express* (*NME*), which began publication in 1952, marketed to the new generation of teenage record buyers in the UK. As with its main competitor, *Melody Maker*, the *NME* was closely tied into the record industry. In 1952, *NME* published 'the first regular and reasonably accurate list of British record sales'; the *Melody Maker* soon followed with a similar 'hit parade' based on retailers' returns and both charts became closely tied to the industry's stocking and promotional policies (Frith, 1983: 166). Through the 1950s, the *NME* focused on the stars of popular music, with little critical perspective on the music covered. This clearly met a market demand and by 1964 the magazine was selling nearly 300,000 copies per week.

The orientation of the UK music press, including *NME*, changed with the emerging and critically self-conscious progressive rock market of the mid-1960s and the development in the US of new, specialist music magazines such as *Creem* and *Rolling Stone*, characterized by their serious treatment of rock as a cultural form. In 1972 the *NME* was reorganized, with a new team of writers recruited from Britain's underground press. After a slump in the face of a late 1960s' market assault by the now 'progressive' *Melody Maker*, by 1974 *NME* was back to 200,000 sales (Frith, 1983). Biting 'new journalist' prose for many readers became part of *NME*'s appeal – whether you agreed or not with the evaluations on offer was almost incidental.

Increasingly, the *NME* became associated with the British 'alternative' or indie music scene (see the recollections of its staff, in Gorman, 2001). To a degree, *NME*'s very hipness and cynicism in the 1980s proved its undoing, as two new groups of readers emerged in the music marketplace: ageing fans, no longer into clubbing and concerts, with an eye to nostalgia, Dire Straits, their CD collections and FM 'solid rock'/'golden oldies' radio; and younger yuppies and style-oriented professionals. Both groups of consumers were largely uninterested in the indie scene and turned instead to the lifestyle bibles and the new glossies like *Q* and (later) *MOJO*. This competition saw a decline in *NME*'s circulation, but it maintained its role as the essential chronicler of indie music.

NME remains indispensable for those wanting to keep up with this scene and invaluable for those performers and labels working within it. The magazine sticks closely to its traditional format: a tabloid-style layout, although now using better quality paper and with much greater use of colour. It continues to feature a mix of features: reviews of records and concerts, as well as film, book and video reviews; competitions and classifieds; extensive UK gig guide and tour news; and chart listings, including retrospectives of these. In addition to its print version, the magazine has a website.

Rolling Stone: *from countercultural icon to industry staple*

The American inspiration for the outburst of the rock press in the late 1960s and its reorientation, *Rolling Stone* was launched in San Francisco on 9 November 1967. Jann Wenner, its founder, wanted the publication to focus on rock music, but it was also to cover the youth culture generally. The first issue of the new fortnightly established that it was aiming at a niche between the 'inaccurate and irrelevant' trade papers and the fan magazines, which were viewed as 'an anachronism, fashioned in the mould of myth and nonsense'. *Rolling Stone* was for the artists, the industry and every person who 'believes in the magic that can set you free'; it was 'not just about music, but also about the things and attitudes that the music embraces' (cited in Frith, 1983: 169).

This rather earnest ideological mission resulted in considerable tension in the early years of *Rolling Stone*, as it attempted to fuse in-depth and sympathetic reporting of youth culture and the demands of rock promotion. In its struggling early years, *Rolling Stone* was supported by the record companies and the concern with radical and alternative politics was soon suborned by the dependence on the concerns of the music industry. In August 1973 *Rolling Stone* changed its format, becoming 'a general interest magazine, covering modern American culture, politics and art, with a special interest in music' (Frith, 1983: 171). However, it retained its now preeminent place as an opinion leader in the music business, mainly because its ageing, affluent, largely white male readership continued to represent a primary consumer group for the record industry. In addition to its print version, *Rolling Stone* now has an extensive website.

The development of 'regional editions' of *Rolling Stone*, beginning with Britain in 1969 and followed by an Australian monthly edition, along with subsequent Japanese- and German-language editions reflects the increasing internationalization of popular music and the global predominance of Anglo-American artists. In format, *Rolling Stone* retains its distinctive character through its famous cover picture feature (immortalized in the Doctor Hook single of 1972, which gained the band a cover story), but contents and presentation wise, it is similar to its newer competitors such as *Q* and the hip-hop bibles *The Source* and *VIBE*. This is hardly surprising, given that these magazines are oriented to older consumers with sufficient disposable income to allow them to purchase the music, clothes, spirits and travel opportunities that *Rolling Stone* advertises.

No Depression *and alt. country*

Along with terms such as 'roots rock' and Americana, alt. country began being used in the 1990s for performers who positioned themselves as producing 'something heartfelt and worthwhile outside the foul and cancerous dreck which typifies country music in the last 15 years' (Russell, *UNCUT*, May 2004: 98). Russell's comment typifies the discourse surrounding alt. country, with authenticity a central referent. The music evokes 'traditional', often threatened American cultures, peoples and rural landscapes and the universality of these themes is integral to its appeal. Alt. country is musically wide ranging, with many disparate artists seen as falling under its umbrella, from Gillian Welch and Lucinda Williams to Wilco, Ryan Adams and Justin Townes Earle. The loose style was picked up and marketed by record labels such as Hightown and championed and popularized by the magazine *No Depression*.

No Depression (*ND*) took its name from the Carter Family song, a classic of early country music, which was later covered by Uncle Tupelo. ND began as a peer-to-peer message board, with postings from fans of 'those groups who have followed the pioneering insurgent country band, Uncle Tupelo, by mixing indie rock aggression with country twang' (Peterson and Beal, 2001: 235). The print magazine was launched as a bi-monthly publication in 1995 and ran until 2009, when it became a web-only publication. In an extensive analysis of the magazine, Tonya Cooper documents how it became 'the seminal magazine for alt. country news and information, especially following the demise of *Country Music* magazine in 2003' (Cooper, 2012: 75). Indeed, the magazine provided another label for the emergent sub genre: 'The "No Depression" sound is the alternation or a joining of grinding punk, country rock and acoustic country; a focus on the darker side of small town life; and a heightened social/political consciousness' (Goodman, cited in Peterson and Beal, 2001: 235).

No Depression has a tagline: 'A magazine about alt. country, (whatever that is).' Remaining vague on the musical aesthetics of alt. country artists, *No Depression* instead prefers to discuss them in relation to their perceived authenticity and sincerity. Reflecting the disparate nature of alt. country music, Grant Alden and Peter Blackstock, the editors of the magazine, observed that:

> We are not biologists. It is not our purpose to identify, quantify, and codify a subgenus called alt. country, or to limit ourselves to its study … It is our purpose to write and assign articles about artists whose work is of enduring merit.
>
> (Alden and Blackstock, 2005: viii)

This indicates the way in which the magazine attempts to position itself as acting outside the music industry and to align itself with alt. country's perceived anti-commercial and anti-modernist stances (Peterson and Beal, 2001: 237). Yet at the same time *ND* played a prominent role in construct the genre's trajectory, acting as a gatekeeper, helping to define what music and performers are and (perhaps more importantly) are not, indicative of the genre. *ND* includes new artists, along with older, more established musician deemed to be indicative of alt. country: they 'do not necessarily share musical qualities, but they do share an emotional resonance, genuine sentiment and behaviour which is required of the scene' (Cooper, 2012: 77).

ND represents the 'intersection of intersection of three main factors: professionalism, perceived amateurism, and commerciality' (Cooper, 2012: 78). At one level, *ND* exhibited the standard characteristics of published magazines: a consistent format and layout; the use of a printer and international distribution; advertisements and promotional content; an editorial, and the usual mix of features, reviews and current news items. This was combined with elements of spontaneity and a DIY (do-it-yourself) attitude, exemplified in the aesthetics of its logo and typeface and the photos used throughout. As Cooper astutely observes, the logo 'usually in red or black, and all capital letters, has a heavy angular dark feeling, showing the tough, rebellious spirit of the magazine, as does the weathered, rustic feel of the typeface' (2012: 79). Performers' photos frequently lack a composed feel and are often unfocused. The online format of *ND* combines professional music journalists or writers from the print run with fans and amateur writers, 'lending it an egalitarian atmosphere, allowing readers to judge writing on its merits and opinion, rather than because of reputation or perceived authority' (Cooper, 2012: 78). This is also characteristic of other online music magazines.

Music journalism shifts online

In addition to *No Depression*, there are now a number of prominent online-only magazines on music and culture. Collectively, these exhibit a new paradigm of music journalism, characterized by a wide range of associated activities (podcasts, festivals, parties), in addition to traditional music reviews and features. Two examples are sketched here:

Resident Adviser (also referred to simply as *RA*) was founded in 2001 as a site to provide information and news coverage on the Australian dance music scene. It soon expanded to cover global electronic dance music and culture and now has offices in London and Berlin, In addition to interviews with artists, news, and reviews, the website includes event listings and ticket sales, extensive artist and record labels profiles, DJ charts and the *RA* podcast. Celebrating its tenth anniversary in 2011, *RA* held a series of high-profile dance parties in major cities around the world, involving leading DJs. The podcast, launched in 2006, has featured an exclusive weekly mix of electronic music from top DJs and producers, including Frankie Knuckles, Mark E, and Laurent Garnier.

Pitchfork: Now based in Chicago, Pitchfork Media, commonly termed simply *Pitchfork*, was established in 1995. Terming itself 'The essential guide to independent music and beyond', *Pitchfork's* focus is on indie rock. Along with extensive regular reviews, the internet publication has annual listings of album and song of the year, with many of these included in its publication *The Pitchfork 500: Our Guide to the Greatest Songs from Punk to the Present* (Plagenhoef and Schreber, 2008). An associated website, Pitchfork.tv, initiated in 2008 and now part of Pitchfork.com, presents videos and other coverage of independent music acts. *Pitchfork* is also on Twitter and Facebook. Since 2007, in conjunction with UK-based production company All Tomorrow's Parties, *Pitchfork* has held festivals featuring artists performing the content of albums in their entirety. The site has been credited with 'breaking' (helping to popularize) bands such as Arcade Fire, Clap Your Hands Say Yeah and Animal Collective, with favourable reviews and 'best of year' awards leading to further publicity and increased record sales.

To some extent, similar activities had already become part of the traditional, print-based, music magazines, but their web-based equivalents have taken them to a new level. In addition, the accessibility of these sites, along with blogs, to readers/fans wanting to post their own comments and reviews has democratized the process of music criticism. In doing so, they have followed the tradition established by fanzines.

The zines

Fanzines are often overlooked in discussions of the music press, due to their largely non-commercial nature, but play an important role in it. They are typically part of alternative publishing, which is characterized by the centrality of amateurs, readers as writers; non-mainstream channels of distribution; a non-profit orientation; and a network based on expertise from a wide base of enthusiasts. Produced by one person, or a group of friends, working from their homes, popular music fanzines are usually concentrated totally on a particular artist or group, and are characterized by a fervour bordering on the religious. This stance can be a reactionary one, preserving the memory of particular artists/styles, but is more usually progressive. Many of the original punk fanzines were characterized by a broadly leftist cultural politics, challenging their readers to take issue with the views presented by bastions of the status quo and reasserting the revolutionary potential of rock. Fanzines like *Crawdaddy* and *Bomp!* in the 1960s and *Sniffin' Glue* in the 1970s had tremendous energy, reflecting the vitality of live performances and emergent scenes.

The impact of punk rock was aided by a network of fanzines and their enthusiastic supporters. Jon Savage argues that in the early days of punk in the UK, nobody was defining 'punk' from within:

> the established writers were inevitably compromised by age and the minimal demands of objectivity required by their papers. The established media could propagandize and comment, but they could not dramatize the new movement in a way that fired people's imagination.
>
> (Savage, 1991: 200)

With photocopying cheap and accessible for the first time, the fanzines were a new medium tailor made for the values of punk, with its DIY ethic and associations of street credibility and there was an explosion of the new form. These fanzines provided a training ground for a number of music journalists (e.g. Paul Morley, Jon Savage, Lester Bangs) and, in some cases, useful media expertise for those who, taking to heart their own rhetoric of 'here's three chords, now form a band', subsequently did just that (for example Bob Geldof, the Boomtown Rats; Chrissie Hynde, the Pretenders). Fanzines producers/writers did not have to worry about deadlines, censorship or subediting and 'even the idea of authorship was at issue, as fanzines were produced anonymously or pseudonymously by people trying to avoid discovery by the dole or employers' (Savage, 1991: 279).

Fanzine readers tend to actively engage with the publication: they debate via the 'letters to the editor', contribute reviews of recordings and concerts, provide discographies and even interviews with performers. A number of studies have demonstrated the value of fanzines to producing and maintaining particular musical styles and scenes, as with Seattle in the early 1990s. In the case of progressive rock, fanzines maintain interest long after the genre had been discarded by the mainstream. Chris Atton (2009) compares how a fanzine, *The Sound Projector*, and the avantgarde-oriented *The Wire* situate their reviews within a shared paradigm of alternative music reviewing.

Despite their essentially non-commercial and often ephemeral nature, fanzines remain a significant part of popular music culture, representing a cultural space for the creation of a community of interest. The internet has provided a new medium for the international dissemination of fanzines; through their 'printing' of contemporary concert reviews and tour information, such 'e zines' have an immediacy that provides a form of virtual socialization for fans.

Gatekeepers and industry publicity

Writing in 1983, Frith saw the music papers and their writers as operating in a symbiotic relationship with the record industry, with the blurring of the boundary between rock journalism and rock publicity reflected in the continuous job mobility between them: 'record company press departments recruit from the music papers, music papers employ ex-publicists; it is not even unusual for writers to do both jobs simultaneously' (Frith, 1983: 173). The situation Frith describes has since become even more firmly consolidated. Popular music magazines have developed in tandem with consumer culture, with the variations evident among them reflecting the diversity of readers' tastes and interests. They have also become part of a general magazine culture; while they are to be found in a separate section in the magazine racks, they are competing for advertising with a proliferating range of magazines. Accordingly, the market profile (especially the socioeconomic status) of their readership must guarantee advertisers access to their target consumers. The advertising each carries firmly indicates their particular market orientation. They are providing not just an adjunct to popular music – although that dimension remains central – but a guide to lifestyle, especially leisure consumption.

The ideological role of the music press in constructing a sense of community and in maintaining a critical distance from the music companies had already become muted by the late 1980s: 'The music press has abandoned its pretensions of leading its readership or setting agendas, and contracted around the concept of "service": hard news, information, gossip, consumer guidance' (Reynolds, 1990: 27). During the 1990s the music press largely abandoned any residual post-punk sense of antagonism towards the industry, realizing that they share a common interest in maintaining consumption. This is achieved by sustaining a constant turnover of new trends, scenes and performers, while also mining music's past using the links between older consumer's nostalgia, younger listeners' interest in antecedents and the back catalogue.

They remain influential as gatekeepers of taste, arbiters of cultural history and publicists for the record industry. This influence can sometimes be spectacular, as with *Billboard* editor Timothy White's decision, on first hearing *Jagged Little Pill*, to make Alanis Morissette the focus of his 'Music to My Ears' column before the album's release; and then influencing the editors of *Spin* and *Rolling Stone* to follow suit. White's column (in the 18 May 1995 issue) was distributed with some review copies of *Jagged Little Pill*, helping set the tone for the generally positive press and magazine reviews the record received. The album was exceptional, but this coverage provided a very helpful initial boost.

Such episodes aside, there is general agreement that music critics don't exercise as much influence on consumers as, say, literary or drama critics. The more crucial intermediaries are those who control airtime (DJs and radio programmers) and access to recording technology and reproduction and marketing facilities (record companies and record producers). Nonetheless, I would argue that the critics do influence record buyers, particularly those who are looking to make the best use of limited purchasing power. Many buyers purchase (or at least acquire!) the latest releases as a matter of course, acting as confirmed followers of that artist, style or scene. But others are actively exploring the byways of fresh talent, new musical hybrids or the back catalogue.

These searches are aided by the way in which music critics don't so much operate on the basis of some general aesthetic criterion, but rather through situating new product via constant appeal to referents, attempting to contextualize the particular text under consideration:

> Canadian Angela Desveaux combines a nice mix of gentle Gillian Welch countrified flavours with a few Lucinda Williams-like rockier moments. However, unlike, say, Jenny Lewis, she ultimately falls short of her two main inspirations on her debut, *Wandering Eyes*. While Williams – and Loretta Lynn, Neko Case, and Emmylou Harris – is comfortable to wallow in the depths of despair as yet another man has used her and cast her aside, Desveraux takes a far more restrained approach, like on *Familiar Times*. And

when she does decide to take a rockier route ... it owes more to the Dixie Chicks.

(Lindsay Davis, review of *Wandering Eyes*,
Dominion Post, 9 November 2006)

In the process, popular music critics construct their own version of the traditional high–low culture split, usually around notions of artistic integrity, authenticity and the nature of commercialism. The best of such critics – and their associated magazines – have published collections of their reviews. The various editions of *The Rolling Stone Record Guide*, recent series such as the *All Music Guides*, the *Rough Guides* (to rock, reggae, hip-hop, etc.) and the *Pitchfork 500* have become bibles in their fields, establishing orthodoxies as to the relative value of various styles or genres and pantheons of artists. Record collectors and enthusiasts, and surviving specialist and second-hand record shops, inevitably have well-thumbed copies of these and similar volumes close at hand.

Yet, this body of criticism is a field in which highly idiosyncratic and disparate standards are the norm. Particular performers and their efforts will be heaped with praise by one reviewer and denigrated by another. Evaluations reflect personal preferences and matters of taste. Rarely are evaluative criteria laid bare for critical scrutiny and even where this occurs it creates as well as resolves difficulties (see McLeod, 2001). Popular music critics, and their histories, encyclopedias and consumer guides are playing a key role in defining the reference points, the highs and lows in the development of 'rock' and other styles of popular music. They imbue particular performers, genres and recordings with meaning and value, and even their internecine arguments strengthen an artist or record's claim to being part of a selective tradition. The consumers of the music themselves frequently reflect (even if only to reject) such distinctions.

This is also a strongly gendered field of writing. An example of this is the manner in which gender is marked in the press coverage of Ani DiFranco, a self-produced indie artist, who records on her own label, Righteous Babe Records. Drawing on a corpus of 100 articles on DiFranco, appearing between 1993 and 2003, in a wide range of print sources and online reports, Anna Feigenbaum shows 'how language employed in rock criticism frequently functions to devalue and marginalize women artists musicianship, influence on fans, and contribution to the rock canon' (Feigenbaum, 2005: 37). She concludes that it is necessary to move away from 'gendered binaries', to 'challenge and reconstruct the conventional language that dominates rock criticism' (2005: 54; see also Elafros, 2010).

Conclusion

There is now greater attention paid to the role of music press and music critics, placing an emphasis on the manner in which their critical discourse constructs notions of authenticity, musical merit and historical value. Music magazines play their part in the economics of popular music, encouraging readers to buy records (and posters, t-shirts, etc.), and generally immerse themselves in consumer 'pop' culture. Similarly, music critics act as a service industry to the record industry, lubricating the desire to acquire both new product and selections from the back catalogue. Music press reviews still form an important adjunct to the record company and music retail marketing of their products, while providing the record companies (and artists) with critical feedback on their releases. In the process, they also become promotional devices, providing supportive quotes for advertising and forming part of press kits sent to radio stations, websites and press outlets. Yet both press and critics also play an important ideological function. They distance popular music consumers from the fact that they are essentially purchasing an economic commodity, by stressing the product's *cultural significance*. Furthermore, this function is maintained by the important point that the music press is not, at least directly, vertically integrated into the music industry (i.e. owned by the record companies). A sense of distance is thereby maintained, while at the same time the need of the industry to constantly sell new images, styles and product is met.

Further reading

Atton, C. (2009) 'Writing About Listening: Alternative Discourses in Rock Journalism', *Popular Music*, 28, 1: 53–67.
Feigenbaum, A. (2005) '"Some Guy Designed this Room I'm Standing in": Marking Gender in Press Coverage of Ani DiFranco', *Popular Music*, 24, 1: 37–56.
Hoskyns, B. (ed.) (2003) *The Sound and the Fury: A Rock's Back Pages Reader. 40 Years of Classic Rock Journalism*, London: Bloomsbury.
Jones, S. (ed.) (2002) *Pop Music and the Press*, Philadelphia, PA: Temple University Press.
McLeod, K. (2001) '*1/2: A Critique of Rock Criticism in North America', *Popular Music*, 20, 1: 29–46.
Swiss, T. (2005) 'That's Me in the Spotlight: Rock Autobiographies', *Popular Music*, 24, 2: 287–94.

Book series

Da Capo Best Music Writing: an annual compilation, featuring guest editors, published since 2001.

Websites

www.rocksbackpages.com

An extensive archive of reviews, interviews, and features on artists; many articles are full text. Some content is freely available, fuller access is by subscription.

www.nodepression.com
www.pitchfork.com
www.residentadviser.com

10 'My Generation'

Identity and consumption: audiences, fans and social networks

This chapter, and the two that follow, consider popular music in relation to aspects of identity. Identity, rather than being fixed and static, is a process of *becoming*, which is developed out of points of similarity and difference, involving both self-description and social ascription. Popular music is an aspect of attempts to define identity at the levels of self, the local community and national identity.

Self-identity can be expressed through the use of music consumption to indicate membership of constituencies based around class, gender and ethnicity. At times, this is more loosely organized around particular scenes and sounds, as with rave culture and contemporary dance music. Self-identity can also be based on activities, such as fandom, and practices, such as record collecting. These identifications are not fixed and constraining; they produce differentially constructed *identities*, which can draw on an amalgam of factors and are subject to change. Self-identity also involves situating the self in relation to competing discourses. For example, adherence to a musical genre can be used to distance oneself from the parent culture, community and social authority.

Popular music plays a prominent role in the creation of community identity in the links between music and locality, especially in local scenes and subcultures (the subject of Chapter 12). These have remained significant, with the internet helping to consolidate links between physically removed scenes. At the national level, identity is a part of cultural policies (e.g. quotas) aimed at promoting locally produced music. National identity can be regarded as a social construct as much as a quality associated with a physical space. While such identities may be constructed or imagined, they are mobilized for particular interests and emerge partly in relation to different 'others'. Particular genres are often associated with specific national settings (as with 'Brit Pop' in the UK in the 1990s), although this, at times reductionist process, has been open to debate.

This chapter begins with an introduction to the general nature of audiences and of cultural consumption, relating these to the social construction of individual subjectivities and identities. I then consider the various modes of popular music consumption, the social categories associated with these (age, class, gender, ethnicity) and the variety of social practices through which such consumption occurs. I argue that two factors underpin the consumption of popular music: the role of music as a form of cultural capital, with recordings as media products around which cultural capital can be displayed and shaped; and as a source of audience pleasure. To emphasize these is to privilege the personal and social uses people make of music in their lives, an emphasis that falls within the now dominant paradigm of audience studies. This stresses the *active* nature of media audiences, while also recognizing that such consumption is, at the same time, shaped by social conditions.

Beyond patterns of demographic and social preferences in relation to popular music, there exists a complex pattern of modes of consumption. These include buying recorded music, viewing MTV and music videos, listening to the radio, home taping and downloading music in digital form. To these could be added the various 'secondary' levels of involvement or the social use of music texts, such as discussing music with friends and peers groups, reading the music press and decorating your bedroom walls with its posters; dancing and clubbing; and concert going. Several of these have been dealt with elsewhere in this study; here I examine how we actually access music texts in their various modes, and the associated social practices, through two examples: dance and record collecting. I conclude with the role of social network sites, which have added a new and increasingly important dimension to popular music culture and its consumption.

From the mass audience to active consumers

The study of media audiences is broadly concerned with the who, what, where, how and why of the consumption of individuals and social groups. Historically, a range of competing media studies approaches to the investigation of audiences can be identified. At the heart of theoretical debates has been the relative emphasis placed on the audience as an active determinant of cultural production and social meanings. Music is a form of communication and popular music, as its very name suggests, usually has an audience.

Social theorists critical of the emergence of industrial society in the later nineteenth and early twentieth centuries first used the term 'mass audience', alarmed at the attraction of new media for millions of people. Their fears were based on a conception of the audience as a passive, mindless mass, directly influenced by the images, messages and values of the new media such as film and radio (and, later, television). This view emphasized the audience as a manipulated market. In relation to popular music, it is a perspective evident in the writings of high culture critics and the Frankfurt School (see Shuker, 2012: 'culture' and 'mass culture' entries).

Later analyses placed progressively greater emphasis on the uses consumers (the term represents a significant change of focus) made of media: uses and gratifications, which emerged in the 1960s, largely within American media sociology; reception analysis and cultural analysis all stressed the active role of the audience, especially fans and members of youth subcultures. More recently there has been an emphasis on the domestic sphere of much media consumption and the interrelationship of the use of various media. The emerging information age is seeing a reorganization of everyday life: 'people are integrating both old and new technologies into their lives in more complex ways' and within an increasingly cluttered media environment, this means 'being an audience is even more complicated' (Ross and Nightingale, 2003: 1). Related to this is an emerging literature on music and everyday life, in a variety of settings, including the workplace and in public space (DeNora, 2000).

The opposition between passive and active views of audiences must not be overstated. What needs highlighting is the tension between musical audiences as collective social groups and, at the same time, as individual consumers. The concept of consumer sovereignty is useful here, emphasizing the operation of human agency. As an influential approach within cultural studies during the 1980s, consumer sovereignty was tied to the notion of the active audience, to produce a debated view of semiotic democracy at work. Advocates of consumer sovereignty consider that people's exercise of their 'free' choice in the marketplace is a major determinant of the nature and availability of particular cultural and (economic) commodities. While the elements of romance and imagination that have informed individual personal histories and the history of popular musical genres are frequently marginalized in the process of commodification, they remain essential to the narratives people construct to help create a sense of identity. While economic power does have a residual base in institutional structures and practices, in this case, the music industries and their drive for market stability, predictability and profit, this power is never absolute.

The sociology of music consumption

Studies of the audience(s) and consumer(s) of popular music reflect such broad shifts in the field of audience studies. Such studies have drawn on the sociology of youth, the sociology of leisure and cultural consumption to explore the role of music in the lives of 'youth' as a general social category and as a central component of the 'style' of youth subcultures and the social identity of fans. Music consumption, and cultural tastes more generally, have been closely related to age, class, gender and ethnicity, with an 'impressive and imposing literature going back almost forty years and raising some major questions of social and cultural theory' (Shepherd, 2012: 239). There has been increasing appreciation of the intersection and overlap of these social categories in the construction of social *identities*, rather than simply a singular *identity*.

The study of audiences in popular music has focused largely on 'youth'. Historically, the main consumers of contemporary (post-1950) popular music have been young people between 12 and 25. Cultural surveys since the 1970s, in North America, the UK and more widely, have all indicated youth's high levels of popular music consumption, along with a clear pattern of age and gender-based genre preferences, with these often inflected with ethnicity. Younger adolescents, particularly girls, were seen to prefer commercial pop; older adolescents expressed greater interest in more progressive forms and artists. High school (college) students tended to be more interested in alternative/indie genre tastes and less interested in the more commercial expressions of popular music. As youthful consumers get older, their tastes in music often become more open to exploring new genres and less commercial forms. This trend is particularly evident among tertiary students, reflecting the dominant forms of musical cultural capital within their peer groups.

The straightforward association of metagenres such as 'rock' and 'pop' with youth, however, needed qualifying by the 1980s. Certainly, the music was initially aimed at the youth market in the 1950s and the baby boomer bulge of the 1960s, while young people have continued to be major consumers of it and the products of the leisure industries in general. At the same time the market has increasingly catered to aging fans, who grew up with the music in the 1950s and 1960s and have continued to follow it, aging along with the surviving musical performers of the 1960s. Accordingly, attempts to locate the audience for popular music primarily among 'youth', once historically correct, no longer applied with the same force by the 1990s, with surveys undertaken by the Recording Industry Association of America showing the music-buying power of 30-somethings had risen while purchases by those under 24 have fallen: in 1993 music consumers over 30 made up 42 per cent of the American market. Throughout the 1990s, 'nostalgia rock' was prominent in popular music, with the release of 'new' Beatles material (*Live at the BBC*); the launch of the magazine *MOJO*, placing 'classic rock' history firmly at its core and with 35 per cent of its readers aged 35-plus; and successful tours by the Rolling Stones, Pink Floyd and the Eagles, among other aging performers.

These trends have continued, in part exacerbated by the decline of CD sales, especially albums, as younger listeners turned to digital downloading through services such as Napster and its successors (see Chapter 2). Today, demographics are partly responsible for the continued success of performers such as Leonard Cohen and Bob Dylan, both still touring and recording. Older consumers, in part at least, also account for the present predominance of 'classic rock' and 'classic hits' radio formats, although their tastes do not remain fixed purely at the nostalgic level. At the same time, the youth market for music remains substantial – what has changed is *how* they are getting their music. The great majority of this music is popular music, with its range of genre styles. Only a minority of students regard classical music as one of their interests, a situation that stands in sharp contrast to the continued classical music orientation of many school music syllabus prescriptions.

The various attempts to profile contemporary music consumption show a clear pattern of gender-based genre preferences. An obvious example is what has been termed 'teen pop', which is preferred by younger adolescents, particularly girls. That girls enjoy chart pop music more than boys reflects the segmented nature of the market. Performers such as Kylie Minogue in the 1980s, New Kids on the Block and the Spice Girls in the 1990s and now Miley Cyrus and Justin Bieber are oriented toward younger listeners, particularly girls, and are being marketed as such. Music and lifestyle magazines such as *Cream* (New Zealand) and *Smash Hits* are aimed at the young adolescent market. The majority of their readers are girls, who buy them partly for their pin-up posters, reflecting their frequent obsession with particular stars and what has been termed 'teenybopper' bedroom culture.

In studies of music consumption in ethnically mixed or diverse populations, black and Asian adolescents are more likely (than their white counterparts) to prefer genres such as soul, R&B, blues, reggae, hip-hop and bhangra. Such genres are carriers of ideology, creating symbols for listeners to identify with. Rap, now mainstreamed as hip-hop (see Chapter 6), has emerged as a major genre preference among black youth internationally. For instance, such differences are clear in New Zealand, a multicultural society, with almost 15 per cent of the population being descendants of the indigenous Maori people or of Pacific (Polynesian) Islander origin and the majority population descendants of the British and European immigrants ('pakeha'). Strong Maori and Polynesian support for reggae and rap music is hardly surprising, since these categories (along with the blues) have become virtually synonymous with 'black music' and black culture. For such youth, reggae does not simply describe an experience, but it politicizes it through creating symbols for listeners to identify with. Many Maori and Polynesian youth are knowledgeable about rasta and familiar with some of the metaphors in the music (Babylon, Jah, etc.). They regard reggae as relevant to the structural location of Maori and Polynesians as a major part of New Zealand's socially dispossessed working class. Rap has also established a strong following in Auckland, which has New Zealand's main concentration of Polynesians. There are several prominent local performers, specialized record labels, clubs, festivals and radio stations catering for the genre and its audience. Rap's appeal is, in part, through its links to dance and street culture, but adherents are also frequently conscious of the genre's history and the politicized work of performers such as Public Enemy and Ice-T (Henderson, 2006). In the UK, bhangra plays a similar role for young Asians in the maintenance of a distinctive cultural identity within the dominant (white) culture (Huq, 2006).

Modes of consumption

Studies of the process and nature of music consumption have used qualitative and quantitative research methodologies to examine individual practices and broader patterns. These reveal a complex set of influences on the construction of individual popular music consumption. Even younger adolescent consumers, who are often seen as relatively undiscriminating and easily swayed by the influence of market forces, see their preferences as far from straightforward, with the views of their friends paramount. Whatever their cultural background or social position, many young people's musical activities often rest on a substantial and sophisticated body of knowledge about popular music: an understanding of its different genres and an ability to hear and place sounds in terms of their histories, influences and sources. Fans, and young musicians, have no hesitation about making and justifying their judgments of musical meaning and value. Modes of consumption are complex, overlapping and reinforcing one another. They include record buying, music television and video viewing, listening to the radio, home taping (historically) and downloading from the internet. There are also various secondary levels of involvement, through the music press, dance, clubbing and concert going.

Making copies of recordings has historically been a significant aspect of people's engagement with popular music. During the 1970s and 1980s this was primarily through audio tape: home taping, a flexible and cheap way of consuming and distributing music. Aside from the convenience of ensuring access to preferred texts, selected (particularly with albums) to avoid any 'dross' or material not liked sufficiently to warrant inclusion, there was an economic aspect to such home taping, as it was, in one sense, a strategy directly tailored to recession conditions and youth unemployment. Home taping was significant as an aspect of consumption largely beyond the ability of the music industry to influence tastes and the debates around it are echoed in relation to its contemporary equivalent forms: 'burning' CDs to one's home computer and downloading digital recordings from the internet.

With the impact of the internet on consumption practices, the purchase of recorded music in its various formats from physical sites (shops) has steadily declined (see Chapter 7). The search for 'new' music, now frequently takes place through online music journalism and through accessing sites such as YouTube, iTunes and Last FM.

Music as cultural capital

Music consumption is not simply a matter of 'personal' preference. It is, in part, socially constructed, serving as a form of symbolic or cultural capital. Following Pierre Bourdieu (1984), we can see 'taste' as both conceived and maintained in social groups' efforts to differentiate and distance themselves from others and underpinning varying social status positions. Music has traditionally been a crucial dimension of this process. Writing in 1950, David Riesman astutely distinguished between two teenage audiences for popular music. First, a majority group with 'an undiscriminating taste in popular music, (who) seldom express articulate preferences' and for whom the functions of music were predominantly social. This group consumed 'mainstream', commercial music, following the stars and the hit parade. Second, Riesman identified a minority group of 'the more active listeners', who had a more rebellious attitude towards popular music, indicated by:

> an insistence on rigorous standards of judgment and taste in a relativist culture; a preference for the uncommercialized, unadvertized small bands rather than name bands; the development of a private language ... (and) a profound resentment of the commercialization of radio and musicians.
>
> (Riesman, 1950: 412)

Later studies continued to identify links between particular genres/performers and the acquisition of musical cultural capital, especially in relation to indie rock (for example, Fonarow, 2006).

Acquiring any form of popular music cultural capital involves developing a knowledge of selected musical traditions, their history and their associated performers. With this background, an individual can knowledgably discuss such details as styles, trends, record companies and the biographies of artists and even nuances such as associated record producers and session musicians. Such cultural capital does not necessarily have to be part of the dominant, generally accepted tradition, but can instead function to distance its adherents from that tradition, asserting their own oppositional stance. This is the pattern with many youth subcultures, which appropriate and innovate musical styles and forms as a basis for their identity (see Chapter 11).

Fans and fandom

Popular music fans avidly follow the music, and lives, of particular performers/ musical genres, with various degrees of enthusiasm and commitment. Fandom is the collective term for the phenomenon of fans and their behaviour: concert going, collecting recordings, putting together scrapbooks, filling bedroom walls with posters, discussing stars with other fans, both in person and online. Music industry practices help create and maintain fandom; record labels and musicians have frequently supported official fan clubs and appreciation societies. Many fan clubs (especially those associated with the Beatles and Elvis Presley) conduct international conventions, even well after the performers celebrated are dead or groups have disbanded

Writing in 1991, Lisa Lewis correctly observed that while fans are the most visible and identifiable of audiences, they 'have been overlooked or not taken seriously as research subjects by critics and scholars' and 'maligned and sensationalized by the popular press, mistrusted by the public' (Lewis, 1992: 1). Although there has been considerable study of fandom since Lewis wrote, and academic discussions emphasize a less stereotyped image, the popular view of fans has, arguably, not changed much. This reflects the traditional view of fandom, which situates it in terms of pathology and deviance, with the label 'fans' used to describe teenagers who avidly and uncritically following the latest pop sensation. These fans are often denigrated in popular music literature and, by those favouring rock styles of popular music. Their behaviour is often described as a form of pathology and the terms applied to it have clear connotations of condemnation and undesirability: 'Beatlemania', 'teenyboppers'. An early example of this was the media treatment of the 'bobby soxers', Frank Sinatra's adolescent female fans, in the 1940s. An extreme form of fandom are 'groupies' – also a largely negative term (although see the reassessment in Rhodes, 2005) – who move beyond vicarious identification and use their sexuality to get close to the stars, even if the encounter is usually a fleeting one.

Fandom is best regarded as an active process, a complex phenomenon, related to the formation of social identities, especially sexuality. Fandom offers individuals membership of a community not defined in traditional terms of status and has been regarded as the register of a subordinate system of cultural taste, typically associated with cultural forms that the dominant value system denigrates, including popular music (Fiske, 1989). Pleasure and difference are central to fandom and fans are often fiercely partisan. Hills distinguishes 'cult fandom' as a form of cultural identity, partially distinct from that of the 'fan' in general, related to the duration of the fandom concerned, especially in the absence of new or 'official' material in the originating medium or persona (Hills, 2002: Preface: x). Pop fans' commitment may last only as long as an often brief career, as with the Spice Girls, whereas the fans of performers such as Bruce Springsteen (Cavicchi, 1998) maintain their fandom over time, as did the Deadheads (see later).

Fans will collect the recordings put out by their favoured stars, but these are only one aspect of an interest that often focuses more on the image and persona of the star. A passionate identification with the star becomes a source of pleasure and empowerment. For many fans, their idols function almost as religious touchstones, helping them to get through their lives and providing emotional and even physical comfort. At the same time, fans' consumption becomes a significant part of the star system and the music industry. For example, studies of the post-punk British 'New Pop' performers of the 1980s (Culture Club, Duran Duran, Wham!, Spandau Ballet, Nick Kershaw and Howard Jones), showed how they drew on a fanatical female following, who often purchased practically anything associated with them, with their support in extreme cases bordering on the pathological. However, such 'Pop fans aren't stupid. They know what they want. And ultimately, all the media manipulation in the world isn't going to sell them something they haven't got any use for' (Rimmer, 1985: 108). This is to argue that whatever the press of 'context' – the intentions of the industry, the pop press, and musicians themselves – meaning in the music is ultimately created by the consumers.

> By participating in fandom, fans construct coherent identities for themselves. In the process, they enter a domain of cultural activity of their own making which is, potentially, a source of empowerment in struggles against oppressive ideologies and the unsatisfactory circumstance of everyday life.
>
> (Lewis, 1992: 3)

Most fans see themselves as part of a wider community, even if their own fan practices are 'private', individual activities undertaken alone. Examples of such empowerment are as diverse as heavy metallers and fans of the Bay City Rollers, the Grateful Dead (Deadheads), Bruce Springsteen and Lady Gaga's 'Little Monsters'. There is an assertion of female solidarity evident in the activities of many girl fans, for example, those of the Spice Girls in the 1990s. Similar cultural self-assertion is present in many adherents of youth subcultures knowledge of the associated music.

The Deadheads, fans of the American band the Grateful Dead, provide an example of long-term fandom. The band had been leading figures in San Francisco's psychedelic scene since the early 1960s and continued to tour and record extensively until the death of band leader Jerry Garcia in 1996. Deadheads attended large numbers of the band's concerts, often making extensive tape compilations of the various performances or purchasing bootlegs of such performances, with the band unofficially condoning such practices. The Grateful Dead's concerts functioned as secular rituals for the band's hardcore followers, who were also frequently identified with the broadly counterculture values and style of the band. This led some municipalities to ban Dead concerts, because of the 'undesirable elements' attending them (Sardiello, 1994).

Fans actively interact with texts 'to actively assert their mastery over the mass-produced texts, which provide the raw materials for their own cultural productions and the basis for their social interactions', becoming 'active participants in the construction and circulation of textual meanings' (Jenkins, 1997: 508). This process has become more evident than ever, with the rise of interactive media (email, list servers and the internet) adding a new dimension to fandom, aiding in the formation and maintenance of fan bases for performers and musical style. At the same time, digital music raises questions of the different consumption experiences and practices involved when the physical object, the 'record', lacks materiality.

Beyond possible empowerment, popular music fandom as a form of cultural activity has a number of pleasurable aspects: dance and its associated rituals of display and restraint; the anticipatory pleasure of attending a concert, as well as the concert experience itself; the pleasure of acquiring and playing new music; for some the sheer physical pleasure of handling actual physical musical artifacts (records, CDs, DVDs); and the intellectual and emotional pleasures associated with 'knowing' about particular artists and genres valued by one's peers and associates. Two of these, dance and record collecting are sketched now; each would repay further investigation.

Dance

Dance is an example of our active engagement with popular music and its wider social importance. As a social practice dance has a long history, closely associated with music, ritual, courtship and everyday pleasure. Historically, organized social dancing dates back at least to the sixteenth century and the private balls of the aristocracy, with ballroom dancing popularized in the early nineteenth century (the waltz). The title of a major documentary series on popular music, *Dancing in the Street*, reflected its emphasis on tracing an historical progression of musical genres and their associated dance styles. Dance is associated with the pleasures of physical expression rather than the intellectual, the body rather than the mind. At times, the closeness and implied sexual display of dance has aroused anxiety and led to attempts to regulate dance or at least control who is dancing with whom. Forms of dance subject to considerable social criticism include the Charleston, the jitterbug, rock 'n' roll in the 1950s, the twist in the 1960s and disco dancing in the 1970s.

Dance is central to the general experience and leisure lives of young people, and, indeed, many adults, through their attendance at and participation in school dances, parties, discos, dance classes and raves. The participants in the dance break free of their bodies in a combination of 'socialised pleasures and individualised desires', with dancing operating as 'a metaphor for an external reality which is unconstrained by the limits and expectations of gender identity and which successfully and relatively painlessly transports its subjects from a passive to a more active psychic position' (McRobbie, 1991: 194, 192, 201). Dance also acts as a marker of significant points in the daily routine, punctuating it with what Chambers (1985) labels the 'freedom of Saturday night'. These various facets of dance are well represented in feature films such as *Flashdance* (1983), *Strictly Ballroom* (1995), *Take the Lead* (2006) and TV series such as *Glee*.

Particular forms of dance are associated with specific music genres, such as line dancing in country, slam dancing and the pogo in punk, break dancing in some forms of rap and head banging and 'moshing' at concerts by heavy metal and grunge and alternative performers. Iain Chambers (1985) documented 'the rich tension of dance' in its various forms in the clubs and dance halls of English post-war urban youth culture, including the shake, the jerk, the northern soul style of athletic, acrobatic dance and the break dancing and body popping of black youth. A detailed history of American dance music though the 1970s traces the development of 'a new mode of DJing and dancing that went on to become the most distinctive cultural ritual of the decade' (Lawrence, 2003: Preface). This dance scene embraced a web of clandestine house parties and discotheques, traced back to legendary New York dance clubs the Loft and the Sanctuary. Similar dance scenes are present around subsequent locales and musical genres, notably electronic dance music.

Record collecting

Most people purchase or otherwise acquire recordings in a limited and generally unsystematic fashion; record collectors represent a more extreme version of this practice. 'Record collecting' can actually be considered shorthand for a variety of distinct but related practices (Shuker, 2010). Foremost is the collection of sound recordings, in various formats, by individuals; the dimension focused on here. Such recordings include various official releases, in a variety of formats; bootleg recordings (largely of concerts); radio broadcasts; sound with visuals – the music video or DVD; and the digital download. Individual collecting also frequently includes the collection of related literature (music books and magazines) and music memorabilia (e.g. concert tickets and programmes, tour posters). Record collecting embraces an associated literature (the music press generally, but especially the specialist collector magazines, fanzines, discographies and general guidebooks); the recording industry targeting of collectors (reissue labels; promotional releases; remixes; boxed sets); and dedicated sites of acquisition (record fairs, second-hand and specialist shops, eBay and high-profile auctions).

The popular image of contemporary record collectors is of one of an obsessive male, whose 'train spotting' passion for collecting is often a substitute for 'real' social relationships. This image can draw on some support from academic discussions of collectors and collecting. Straw shows how, for male collectors, the social role of collecting can be a significant part of masculinity, providing a point of difference and 'confirmation of a shared universe of critical judgement' (Straw,

1997b: 5). In common with other forms of collecting, record collecting can represent a public display of power and knowledge, serving as a form of cultural capital within the peer group. It can also provide a private refuge from the wider world and the immediate domestic environment: in the novel *High Fidelity*, we meet Rob Fleming, who, in times of stress, re-catalogues his album collection (Hornby, 1995: 73). In contrast to the 'high fidelity' stereotype, record collectors demonstrate a complex mix of characteristics: a love of music; obsessive-compulsive behaviour, accumulation and completism, selectivity and discrimination; and self-education and scholarship. For many collectors, record collecting is a core component of their social identity and a central part of their lives (Shuker, 2010).

The landscape of record collecting has changed dramatically in the past 30 years. The range of collectibles has increased, with promotional material and memorabilia more prominent. Record collecting has become more organized, more intense (and, at times, more expensive). The internet has added a major new dimension to collecting, adding increased opportunity but also fuelling price rises. Reflecting such developments, the record collecting press has mushroomed. The shift to online music has raised questions about the nature of collecting, especially the privileging of the album.

Digital consumption/fandom: downloading, cloud services and social network sites

Music fans once met in physical locations and settings (parties, record stores, flats) to hear, discuss and acquire music; Now, with the decline of physical retail, websites such as Spotify, iTunes, and Audioboo perform much the same function. Accessing these effectively turns your mobile device into a portable jukebox and your home computer into a stereo system with built in storage. Along with these 'cloud' services, there are now a number of online music-sharing sites, which recommend artists ('If you like X, try Y') and connect listeners with similar tastes. Last FM records the musical preferences of its listeners in detailed listening charts that can be synched to social media, enabling Twitter users and Facebook friends to 'share' their favourite musicians.

The growth of social network sites has created new modes of fandom and self-promotion for bands. Leading site MySpace began in June 1999; it enables its users to host their own profiles within its formatting protocols and the member can then post a variety of personal information that can be accessed and viewed (with possible restrictions imposed at the member's discretion) by other users of the network. Similar social network services followed, with MySpace's main competitors Facebook and Bebo the most successful. Facebook, MySpace and Bebo all require users to log on to the company's website in order to access their own and others' portfolios; this enables the services to stream advertising within the common pages that all users can see. Advertising-based media companies soon recognized the potential to move beyond traditional mass media, especially to reach younger consumers and began acquiring social network sites. This advertising potential led Fox Interactive Media, a subsidiary of News Corporation (Rupert Murdoch), to buy MySpace in July 2006.

In July 2010 Facebook announced that more than 500 million people, roughly one-third of all net users, now used it and that a user on average posted photos, links to websites, videos and news stories or created other content about 30 times each month. Mark Zuckerberg, one of its founders, was *Time* magazine's Man of the Year for 2010. The phenomenon even led to a Hollywood feature film, *The Social Network*, on the development of MySpace and the personalities and arguments around who took the credit (and the financial rewards) for this. The commercial and critical success of the film was a further indication of the impact of social networking on digital global culture.

In relation to popular music, social network sites provide an opportunity for performers to promote their music and activities, including new recordings, but also concerts and touring. Fans can get involved in this process, as well as 'meet' those interested in similar styles of music, to exchange information and debate opinions. Today, many young (and some older) fans spend up to four to five hours a day downloading, playing and listening to music and watching You-Tube and discussing music and performers as part of their Facebook and Twitter postings; all this is often while 'multitasking' (see the findings from the Pew Internet and American Life Project, summarized in Jones and Lenhart, 2004).

Conclusion

A major theoretical issue with the consumption of popular music – be it by fans, members of subcultures or 'mainstream' youth – is the problem of authenticity: the relationship between popular culture and market forces, especially the extent to which styles and tastes are synthetically produced for a deliberately stimulated mass market. As I have argued previously, we need to see culture as a reciprocal concept, an active practice that shapes and conditions economic and political processes, as well as being conditioned and shaped *by* them. The various types of consumer of popular music considered here illustrate this reciprocity, occupying a critical social space in the process whereby the music acquires cultural meaning and significance. The following chapter examines further the role of music in the construction of social identity, in relation to youth culture, subcultures and music scenes.

Further reading

Fans

Hills, M. (2002) *Fan Cultures*, London, New York: Routledge.
Lewis, L. (ed.) (1992) *The Adoring Audience: Fan Culture and the Popular Media*, London: Routledge.
Wall, T. (2006) 'Out on the Floor: The Politics of Dancing on the Northern Soul Scene', *Popular Music*, 25, 3: 431–46.

Record collecting

Dean, E. (2001) 'Desperate Man Blues', in D. Wolk and P. Guralnick (eds), *Da Capo Best Music Writing 2000*, New York: Da Capo Press. An entertaining profile of Joe Bussard, self-styled 'King of the Record Collectors'.
There is also a DVD documentary based on this: *Desperate Man Blues*, Cube Media, 2004.
Shuker, R. (2010) *Wax Trash and Vinyl Treasure: Record Collecting as a Social Practice.* Farnham, Burlington, VT: Ashgate.
Straw, W. (1997) 'Sizing Up Record Collections. Gender and Connoisseurship in Rock Music Culture', in S. Whiteley (ed.), *Sexing the Groove. Popular Music and Gender*, London: Routledge, pp. 3–16.

Social network sites

boyd, d. and Ellison, N. (2007) 'Social Network Sites: Definition, History and Scholarship', *Computer-Mediated Communication*, 13, 1, article 11. Online at: http://jcmc.indiana,edu/vol13/issue 1/boyd.ellison.html
Jennings, D. (2007) *Net, Blogs and Rock 'n' Roll: How Digital Discovery Works and What it Means for Consumers, Creators and Culture*, London, Boston, MA: Nicholas Brealey Publishing.
Mjøs, O.J. (2011) *Music, Social Media and Global Mobility: MySpace, Facebook, YouTube*, New York, London: Routledge.

11 'Sound of Our Town'

Subcultures, sounds and scenes

The preceding chapter sketched some aspects of the consumption of popular music, and its fans, in relation to identity formation. A related area of study has been the nature and significance of youth subcultures, the initial focus of this chapter. Emerging out of the earlier study of 'youth culture', subcultural analysis was prominent in popular music studies through the 1980s and 1990s. Its theoretical utility was then challenged and displaced by 'post-subcultural' theory, with greater attention being paid to musical sounds and scenes. It is now appropriate, I argue, to view particular physical locations as scenes that include subcultures, and specific sounds, with these placed within an international music and leisure market. Goth provides an example of this conflation, which has been accentuated by the impact of the internet.

From youth culture to youth subcultures

The concept of youth culture developed in the 1950s. It assumed that all teenagers shared similar leisure interests and pursuits and were involved in some form of revolt against their elders. The emergence of a distinctive youth culture was linked to the growing autonomy of youth (particularly working-class youth) because of their increased incomes. Greater spending power gave youth the means to express their own distinct values and separate ideals and large markets were developed for teenage interests, most notably music and clothes. Advertising analyst Mark Abrams, in a pamphlet aptly titled *The Teenage Consumer* (1959), estimated that in Britain there was available 'a grand total of 900 million pounds a year to be spent by teenagers at their own discretion'. In real terms, this was twice the pre-war figure. In the US, the consumer potential of the new teenagers outstripped that of any other segment of the population, as between 1946 and 1958 teenage buying potential grew to an estimated 10 billion dollars. A further explanation for the prominence of this youth or teenage culture was the dramatic growth of secondary and university education in western countries, as young people spending longer periods in educational institutions encouraged youth separateness and solidarity (Coleman, 1961).

While academic sociology now began to display considerable interest in 'youth' as a social group, it was slower to more specifically explore the relationship between music and its adolescent audience. Initially, as exemplified in the high culture perspective sketched in Chapter 10, youth were seen as a relatively passive consumer group, with 'youth culture' shaped by the burgeoning leisure industries. In the mid-1960s Hall and Whannell reflected British anxiety about the effects of the emergent teenage culture, especially in its imported American forms: 'Teenage culture is a contradictory mixture of the authentic and the manufactured: it is an area of self-expression for the young and a lush grazing ground for the commercial providers' (Hall and Whannell, 1964). Similarly, in the US, the work of Riesman (1950) and later commentators acknowledged the varied bases for American youth's musical tastes, but still saw the majority of adolescents as fodder for commercial interests.

The 1960s saw the growth of a youth counterculture, with youth protests in the universities and on the streets against the establishment and the war in Vietnam. It seemed to some that a major division in society was the so-called 'generation gap', usually believed to be between the ages of 25 and 30. Youth were now viewed as a definite social block, belonging to a generational culture that transcended class, status and occupation. Popular music, particularly emergent genres such as psychedelic or acid rock, was regarded as an age-specific means of cultural expression, uniting young people and confirming their radical potential (Reich, 1967).

By the 1970s this view of a homogeneous youth culture, offering a radical challenge to the established social order, was obviously untenable. The radicalism of the 1960s' protest movement had become defused through its commercialization, including the marketing of 'alternative rock' by the major record companies and the counterculture's continued identification with middle class rather than working-class youth. The emphasis on an age-based youth culture obscured the key fact that a major shaper of adolescents' values and attitudes was the social class background of those involved. Rather than being part of a coherent youth culture, it became clear that youth consisted of a 'mainstream' majority and minority subcultures whose distinctiveness was shaped largely by the social class and ethnic background of their members. Sociological interest now concentrated on various youth subcultures, whose members were seen to rely on leisure and style as a means of winning their own cultural space and thus represented cultural oppositional politics at the symbolic level.

Subcultures: the view from Birmingham

As indicated in Chapter 10, general consumption patterns and modes demonstrate a structural homology between the audience and various social indicators. Such homology is evident at its most extreme in youth subcultures, although in a complex rather than a simplistic and reductionist manner. As the contributors to a major edited reader demonstrate, while there is no consensus about the definition of a subculture, they can be broadly considered to be social groups organized around shared interests and practices (Gelder and Thornton, 1997: Part 2). Subcultures often distinguish themselves against others; fractions of the larger social group, they usually set themselves in opposition to their parent culture, at least at a cultural level.

Music is one of a complex of elements making up subcultural style. Its role in terms of pleasure and cultural capital is similar to that played out among more mainstream youth, but in an accentuated form. The relationship between popular music and youth subcultures was comprehensively explored in a number of influential studies during the 1970s and early 1980s. Collectively, these argued what became a frequently asserted thesis: that youth subcultures appropriate and renovate musical forms and styles as a basis for their identity and, in so doing, assert a countercultural politics. This perspective was primarily associated with writers linked to the influential Birmingham (UK) Centre for Contemporary Cultural Studies (BCCCS), whose views became more widely accepted.

For the writers associated with the BCCCS, subcultures were regarded as 'meaning systems, modes of expression or life styles developed by groups in subordinate structural positions in response to dominant meaning systems, and which reflect their attempt to solve structural contradictions rising from the wider societal context' (Brake,1985: 8). Hebdige (1979), in what is now regarded as a classic text, starts from the premise that style in subculture is 'pregnant with significance', illustrating this through a comprehensive analysis of various spectacular subcultural styles: beats and hipsters in the 1950s, teddy boys in the 1950s and 1970s, mods in the early 1960s, skinheads in the late 1960s, rastas in the 1970s, glam rockers in the early to mid-1970s and, most visible of all, punks in the mid-1970s. In his analysis, subcultures rely on leisure and style as a means of making their values visible in a society saturated by the codes and symbols of the dominant culture. The significance of subcultures for their participants is that they offer a solution, albeit at a 'magical' level, to structural dislocations through the establishment of an 'achieved identity' – the selection of certain elements of style outside those associated with the ascribed identity offered by work, home or school. The expressive elements of this style offer 'a meaningful way of life during leisure', removed from the instrumental world of work:

> Subcultures are therefore expressive forms but what they express is, in the last instance, a fundamental tension between those in power and those condemned to subordinate positions and second class lives. This tension is figuratively expressed in the form of subcultural style.
>
> (Hebdige, 1979: 132)

The majority of youth were seen to pass through life without any significant involvement in such subcultures. Associated aspects of subcultural fashion and musical tastes may be adopted, but for 'respectable' youth these are essentially divorced from subcultural lifestyles and values. Members of youth subcultures, on the other hand, utilize symbolic elements to construct an identity outside the restraints of class and education, an identity that places them squarely outside conservative mainstream society. Membership of a subculture was seen to necessarily involve membership of a class culture and could be either an extension of, or in opposition to, the parent class culture (as with the skinheads). Writers such as Hebdige were at pains not to overemphasize this class dimension and to accord due analytical weight to both gender and ethnic factors.

Youth subcultures in the 1970s and early 1980s were an international phenomenon, but with marked differences. Subcultural styles in both Britain and the US essentially developed out of their immediate social context, reworking commercial popular culture into a subcultural style that reflected and made sense of their structural social location. This process was not so clear-cut in more culturally dependent societies. In Canada, for example, the situation was confused by the nation's historical links with Britain and France and the marked contemporary influence of its close proximity to the US, a situation contributing to Canada's problem of finding a sense of national identity. Canadian youth cultures were consequently largely derivative and any potential oppositional force in them was highly muted (Brake, 1985).

For the subcultural analysts of the 1970s, homology was central to the consideration of the place of music in youth subcultures: a 'fit' between the 'focal concerns, activities, group structure and the collective self-image' of the subculture and the cultural artifacts and practices adopted by the members of the subculture. The latter were seen as 'objects in which they could see their central values held and reflected', including music (Hall and Jefferson, 1976: 56). The most developed applications of the concept of homology to the preferred music of specific subcultures are Willis's study of biker boys and hippies, *Profane Culture* (1978), and Hebdige's various case studies in his hugely influential study *Subculture: The Meaning of Style* (1979). Willis argued that there existed a 'fit' between certain styles and fashions, cultural values and group identity; for example, between the intense activism, physical prowess, love of machines and taboo on introspection of motorbike boys and their preference for 1950s' rock 'n' roll. For Hebdige, the punks best illustrated the principle:

> The subculture was nothing if not consistent. There was a homological relation between the trashy cut-up clothes and spiky hair, the pogo and the amphetamines, the spitting, the vomiting, the format of the fanzines, the insurrectionary poses and the 'soulless', frantically driven music.
>
> (Hebdige, 1979: 114–15)

The BCCCS writers' sociocultural analyses represented an original and imaginative contribution to the sociology of youth cultures, but were critiqued for their overemphasis on the symbolic 'resistance' of subcultures, which was imbued with an unwarranted political significance; the romanticizing of working-class subcultures; the neglect of ordinary or conformist youth; and a masculine emphasis, with little attention paid to the subcultural experiences of girls. And while music was regarded as a central aspect of subcultural style, its homological relation to other dimensions of style was not always easy to pin down. For example, the skinheads' preferred music changed over time, making problematic any argument for its homological role in skinhead culture. As Hebdige observed, the 'early' skinheads preference for elements of black style, including reggae and ska music, is contradictory considering their racial stance. At times, stylistic attributes were too quickly attributed to a specifically subcultural affiliation, rather than recognizing their wider adoption.

Post subcultures

A convergence between music and cultural group values continued to be evident in some contemporary youth subcultures through the 1990s, most notable in goth (see the discussion that follows), heavy metal, hip-hop and various strains of punk. However, subsequent theoretical discussions and case studies suggested that the degree of homology between subcultures and music had been overstated. Reviewing the earlier literature, Middleton concluded that subcultural analysis had drawn the connection between music and subculture much too tightly, 'flawed above all by the uncompromising drive to homology' (Middleton, 1990: 161).

Indeed the very value of the concept 'subcultures', and particularly its conflation with oppositional cultural politics, became seriously questioned (Hebdige, 1988: 8; Huq, 2006: Chapter 1; Redhead, 1990: 41–2). For many youthful consumers during the 1980s and 1990s, the old ideological divides applied to popular music had little relevance, with their tastes determined by a more complex pattern of considerations than any 'politically correct' dichotomizing of 'mainstream' and 'alternative' music or subcultural associations. This was most evident in the constituencies for indie and dance music (see Fonarow, 2006; Thornton, 1995). Newer studies began using the term 'post-subcultural' to indicate this theoretical shift (Bennett and Kahn-Harris, 2004; Muggleton and Weinzierl, 2003), with greater attention now paid to more flexible concepts such as 'tribes' and 'scene'.

Interest also turned more to the majority of youth, those who do not join or identify with subcultures, the nature of fandom and the study of local musical scenes. While the commercial orientation of the musical tastes of 'mainstream' youth are still, as with Riesman 50 years earlier, often taken as given, this consumption is seen in more active and creative terms. Further, it is by no means a homogeneous situation, as, like the earlier subcultures, the 'mainstream' is revealed as a varied audience with different tastes and allegiances informed by factors such as class, ethnicity, gender and age.

Northern soul

The cultural studies preoccupation with youth subcultures obscured the significance of subcultural affiliations held by older music fans. A case in point is the academically relatively neglected example of northern soul, a regional cult in the UK Midlands, based around ballroom/club culture and all-night dancing to 1960s' Motown and independent label (e.g. Cameo, Parkway, Verve) soul records chosen for their 'danceability' (e.g. the Exciters).

Northern soul became prominent in the early 1970s, with the Wigan Casino, a World War I dance hall, being declared by American *Billboard* to be the world's best discotheque. The subculture has maintained itself, with fanzines, continued all-nighters and record compilations; it is celebrated in feature films, musicals and compilations of recordings. Studies of northern soul challenged the preoccupation of earlier subcultural theory with music as symbol and the perceived homology between musical style and subcultural values. Northern soul produces a sense of identity and belonging based on the consumption of 'music as music', organized around a club scene and dance (Wall, 2006). Here the records have value both as commodities and as bearers of musical meaning; the exchange, buying and selling of records is an important part of the northern soul scene. Indeed, the use of 'white labels' represents a unique form of fetishization of black musical culture by white consumers (Hollows and Milestone, 1998).

Northern soul illustrates how 'contemporary youth cultures are characterized by far more complex stratifications than that suggested by the simple dichotomy of "monolithic mainstream-resistant subculture"' (Muggleton and Weinzierl, 2003: 7). Recent research in popular music has retained elements of the subculturalist approach, but moved towards a more sophisticated understanding of the activities of music audiences, drawing heavily on the concepts of sounds and scenes.

Scenes and sounds: the music of place

The intersection of music and its physical location has been a developing field of inquiry, with a number of distinct and original contribution to the critical examination of space and scale as significant aspects in the production and consumption of sound recordings. Cultural geographers have been doing research on music since the late 1960s, investigating the relationship between the social, cultural, economic and political factors in musical analysis. Traditionally, the geographical analysis of music emphasized the dynamics and consequences of the geographical distribution of recorded music around the world and how particular musical sounds have become associated with particular places. This work was largely characterized by the use of a narrow range of methods and theories and focused on only a few musical styles, notably blues, folk and country. Studies of rock and pop music, and their various genres, were notably absent from the majority of this work. In the 1990s these musical forms, and their locales, became seen as worthy of serious study and accorded greater attention by cultural geographers and popular music scholars (see Carnoy, 2003; Leyshon, Matless and Revill, 1998; Stokes, 1994).

Several areas of research into popular music and geography can be identified: (i) a concern with the spatial distribution of musical forms, activities and performers; (ii) exploration of musical home locales and their extension, using concepts such as contagion, relocation and hierarchical diffusion and the examination of the agents of and barriers to diffusion; (iii) the delimitation of areas that share certain musical traits or on the identification of the character and personality of places as gleaned from lyrics, melody, instrumentation and the general 'feel' or sensory impact of the music; (iv) pertinent themes in music, such as the image of the city. A necessary addition to these emphases is the global processes of cultural homogenization and commodification and the intersection of these with the local.

While the cohesion of their 'common' musical signatures is frequently exaggerated, such localized developments offer marketing possibilities by providing a 'brand name' with which consumers can identify. Interest in particular sounds has concentrated on the significance of locality and how music may serve as a marker of identity. Many histories of popular music refer to particular geographic locales, usually cities or regions, as being identified at a specific historical juncture with a sound. Examples include the Liverpool 'Merseybeat' sound associated with the Beatles, Gerry and the Pacemakers and the Searchers in the early 1960s; San Franciso and the psychedelic rock of the Jefferson Airplane, Moby Grape and the Grateful Dead in the later 1960s; various punk scenes since the 1970s, such as Straightedge and Washington DC. The following brief examples illustrate the interaction of history, physical location, musical style and the music industry.

Sounds: Dunedin and Manchester

A New Zealand example of this process is the emergence of the 'Dunedin sound' associated with the now internationally recognized Flying Nun label. In the late 1970s a number of bands in Dunedin, a university city of then only just over 100,000 people, established a local cult following their appearances at various pubs and university venues. National exposure and critical and commercial success followed and several bands (the Chills, the Bats, the JPS) went on to establish international reputations, largely on the 'indie' college circuit in the UK and North America. The 'Dunedin sound' and 'the Flying Nun sound' became shorthand for these bands, despite the clear differentiation among the Flying Nun label's recorded output. The sound itself, at least in its original evocation, was largely equated with a jangly guitar-driven sound, a distinctive New Zealand accent on the vocals and 'low-tech' recording and production, all serving to produce a specifically identifiable local product.

Manchester also provides an instructive example of the role of geography in forging a distinctive orientation to localized alternative music. The notion of a Manchester sound and scene was a loose label, popularized by the British music press in the early 1990s. Since the late 1970s, Manchester has been associated with several styles of indie and alternative music: in the late 1970s and early 1980s, the post-punk sound of Joy Division, which mutated into New Order; 'bedsit blues' in the mid-1980s with the Smiths and James; and the tempo and mood was revived around 1988, in the wake of 'acid house', with the arrival of the club-and-ecstasy sounds of 'Madchester', led by the Happy Mondays, the Stone Roses and Oldham's Inspiral Carpets. All three periods and styles fed off the association with Manchester: the songs often had included clear geographical references and reflected localized feelings and experiences; record covers and other promotional imagery incorporated place-related references; and a network of alternative record labels (especially Factory Records), venues and an active local press created a supportive network for the bands and their followers.

Scenes

There has been considerable exploration of the role and effectiveness of music as a means of defining community/local identity, although, as Adam Krims (2012) argues, the conflation of the two has, at times, been overstated. Situated within this work, the concept of scene has become a central trope in popular music studies, a key part of the 'spatial turn' evident in urban and cultural studies generally. To a certain extent, scene, as analytical concept of greater explanatory power, is regarded by some commentators as having displaced subcultures.

Scene can be understood as 'a specific kind of urban cultural context and practice of spatial coding' (Stahl, 2004: 76), 'describing both the geographical sites of local music practice and the economic and social networks in which participants are involved' (Kruse, 2010: 625). A basic reference point for later discussion was an essay by Straw (1992), which argued for greater attention to scene in popular music studies, defined as the formal and informal arrangement of industries, institutions, audiences and infrastructures. Also influential were Cohen's study of 'rock culture' in Liverpool (Cohen, 1991) and Shank's study of the rock 'n' roll scene in Austin, Texas (Shank, 1994). Researchers subsequently engaged with, refined and applied the concept of scene to a wide range of settings and locales. Much of this work, along with theoretical discussion of the concept of scene(s) can be found in several edited collections (Bennett and Kahn-Harris, 2004; Whiteley *et al.*, 2004). As Kruse concludes: 'Subjectivities and identities were formed, changed, and maintained within localities that were constituted by geographical boundaries, by networks of social relationships, by a sense of local history, and in opposition to other localities' (Kruse, 2010: 628).

To provide just one example from among many, locality, scene and youth culture were fruitfully brought together by Bennett in a series of ethnographic case studies. Among these, his study of urban dance music (including house, techno and jungle) in Newcastle upon Tyne, England, shows how, through their participation in club events and house parties, 'the members of this scene celebrate a shared underground sensibility that is designed to challenge the perceived oppression and anarchism of Newcastle's official night-time economy and the coercive practices of the local police force' (Bennett, 2000: 68).

In part arising from the earlier fascination with subcultures, a particular focus, especially in the US, has been on alternative music scenes. (The term 'underground' is also used for non-commercialized alternative scenes, since the performers in them are hidden from and inaccessible to people who are not 'hooked into' the scene.) Alternative music scenes fall into two basic categories: college (US tertiary institutions) or university towns or large cities that are somehow 'alternative', usually to even larger urban centres nearby (e.g. Minneapolis and Chicago). Most important American college towns had local music scenes self-consciously perceived as such in the 1980s and through the 1990s, with these linked as part of an American indie underground (see Azerrad, 2001; Kruse, 2003). The most prominent were Athens, Georgia (source of the B-52s, Love Tractor, Pylon and REM); Minneapolis (the Replacements, Husker Du, Soul Asylum, Prince), and Seattle. Sometimes a small college town and nearby large city contributed to a shared scene; as with Boston and Amherst, Massachusetts (sources of Dinosaur Jr., the Pixies, Throwing Muses and The Lemonheads), with bands moving back and forth between the two centres. Alternative scenes worldwide appear to continue to conform to this basic pattern (see Fonarow, 2006, on British indie).

While alternative music is often linked to particular local scenes, the question is why then and there? Such scenes have generally developed out of a combination of airplay on the local college radio stations, access to local live venues, advertisements and reviews in local fanzines and free papers and, especially, the existence of local independent record companies. Bertsch (1993) argues that there are fundamental links between alternative music scenes and high-tech areas, with both sharing a decentralized, do-it-yourself approach to production and with indie isolationism not far removed from the entrepreneurial spirit of capitalism, with 'every one out for himself'. Music making, equipment design and programming are undertakings one person or a small group can succeed at without much start-up capital. Seattle in the early 1990s provides an example.

Seattle

In 1992 the Seattle music scene came to international prominence, closely linked with the mainstream breakthrough of alternative music promoted by American college radio. Nirvana's second album and major-label debut *Nevermind* (Geffin, 1991) topped the *Billboard* charts; Pearl Jam and Soundgarden were major draw cards at the second Lollapalooza touring music festival in 1992 and enjoyed huge record sales. The music made by these and other bands, with many initially recording with Seattle's Sub Pop independent record label, became collectively labelled as 'grunge', although the label obscured a variety of styles (Anderson, 2007).

The Seattle scene and the grunge music with which it was associated became the most written-about phenomenon in contemporary popular music since the birth of punk. Major labels scoured Seattle for unsigned bands or internationally sought out grunge-oriented performers (for instance Australia's Silverchair). The film *Singles* (Cameron Crowe, 1992), set in the Seattle scene, was widely publicized and commercially successful. The popularization of grunge-related fashion saw spreads in *Elle* and *Vogue* touting $1000 flannel shirts from the world's most famous designers. The 'Seattle sound' became a marketing ploy for the music industry, as well as an ideological touchstone for generation X:

> Seattle defines the source of the phenomenon and organizes its often disparate expression. In writing about the Seattle scene, critics are not just chronicling a random success story. They are grappling with the notion of a geographically specific scene itself.
>
> (Bertsch, 1993)

A combination of factors explained why Seattle became prominent at that time and place: the ability of Sub Pop to feed into the majors; many good bands of similar style; the strong local alternative scene, linked to the universities of Washington and Evergreen State, (the latter a progressive, no-grades school with an alternative-oriented radio station); and the city's geographical separation from Los Angeles. Critics emphasized the perceived purity and authenticity of the Seattle scene as a point of origin, defining bands like Nirvana in opposition to the mainstream music industry. The foundations for the success of bands such as Nirvana and Soundgarden were laid throughout the 1980s by earlier alternative music scenes. What had changed was that by the early 1990s it had become easier and quicker for new alternative or indie bands to attract the attention of major labels or commercial radio, and to move to major labels and achieve some mainstream success (Azerrad, 2001).

The specific configuration and dynamics of other indie/alternative scenes have since been examined in numerous ethnographically oriented studies (see Kruse, 2003, 2010 for further discussion and examples). For example, Takasugi (2003) studied the development of underground musicians in a Honolulu (Hawaii) scene in the mid-1990s. His interest was in the values and norms shared by members of the scene and the relationship of these to the socialization and identity formation of the musicians involved: 'the resulting networks serve to sculpt and reinforce the identity of the band members within the scene' (74). This was to conceptual the scene as 'a kind of social movement' (ibid.), one in which the distinction between fans and musicians was not always clear, with both integral to the scene. O'Connor, in a study of contemporary punk scenes in four cities (Washington, DC; Austin, Texas; Toronto; Mexico City), showed that clear differences exist between such scenes, explicable in terms of the social geography of each city. For the punks involved, these scenes were identified with the active creation of infrastructure to support their bands and other forms of creative activity (O'Connor, 2002: 226). Geoff Stahl (2011) documented the manner in which the Wellington (New Zealand) indie scene was: 'Bound together as an infrastructure that supports music making in Wellington, this disparate collection of institutions, industries, venues, media outlets, events and activities cohere in such a way as to the give the Wellington indie scene its distinctive shape' (Stahl, 2011: 148).

The relationship of the local to the global is a key part of the dynamic of local music scenes, alternative or otherwise. For many participants in alternative local scenes, the perceived dualities associated with indie and major record labels are central to their commitment to the local. Here 'the celebration of the local becomes a form of fetishism, disguising the translocal capital, global management, and the transnational relations of production that enables it' (Fenster, 1995). However, the 'local' is increasingly allied with other localities, for both economic and affective reasons. Fenster notes 'the degree to which "independent" non-mainstream musics, while clearly based upon local spaces, performances and experiences, are increasingly tied together by social networks, publications, trade groups and regional and national institutions in ... locally dispersed formations' (ibid.: 83). Today, this is even more evident, with the internationalization of 'local' sounds a process encouraged and fostered economically by the major record companies and governmental cultural policies around the 'creative industries' seeking to brand 'national' music to reach a larger market in the process (see Chapter 14). Local spaces have remained important, however, through their provision of the necessary infrastructure music scenes need to survive: the rehearsal space, live venues and recording opportunities' along with the supportive networks and publicity required to make production and dissemination of the music possible.

Virtual scenes

'Today, with the widespread popularity of the internet, the nature of these local scenes has changed' (Kruse, 2010). The indie sector has flourished, with local sounds/scenes and their followers ideologically linked through internationally distributed fanzines, music press publications and the internet. With music disseminated online, people can connect easily across localities, regions, countries and continents; internet opens up more options and creates more opportunities for sharing of music and associated cultural tastes, most notably subcultural fashion. John Connell and Chris Gibson (2002) argued that the spread of the internet had increased the flow of subcultural music and information across disparate localities, in the process helping to 'de-link the notion of scene from locality' (107), enabling a sense of online 'imagined community' not tied to physical geography. Andy Bennett and Richard Peterson (2004) also noted and celebrated the emergence of such virtual scenes, comprised of mediated one-to-one communication, largely between fans:

> Fan clubs dedicated to specific artists, groups and subgenres have proliferated by using the internet to communicate with each other. Like the participants in trans local scenes, participants in virtual scenes are widely separated geographically, but unlike them … come together in a single scene making conversation via the internet.
>
> (2004: 10)

This cyber facilitation should not be overstated, with internet access not available to all and broadband width acting as a constraint when it is. It is hardly surprising that the subcultural constituencies making extensive use of the internet, notably goth and emo, consist primarily of middle-class/college youth.

Goth

Goth is an example of the historical development and continued vitality of local scenes based around a subculture. Goth is now an international phenomenon, with well-established performers and scenes, most notably in the US, Japan and Europe, especially Germany. 'Goth', or 'gothic rock', emerged as a part of post-punk alternative and 'indie' rock in the UK in the late 1970s. Its origins in cities such as Manchester in the English Midlands, and in London's suburbia, reflected a broader urban malaise and the indie scene's disenchantment with contemporary politics and culture. As such, goth was also a rejection of the utopian sentiments and commercialism of glam rock, disco and British 'New Pop' which had dominated commercial music and associated street fashion through the 1970s and into the early 1980s. At the same time, however, goth had clear debts to the visual sense and theatricality of both glam and of new romantics performers such as Adam and the Ants. Goth bands commonly adopted names with gothic and general romantic artistic connotations. Singer Siousie Sioux used the term 'gothic' to describe the orientation of her band and may even be the originator of the term.

The goth bands initiated and did much to popularize a goth 'look', especially through the image and style of charismatic and striking-looking band leaders such as Peter Murphy (Bauhaus), Ian Ashbury (Southern Death Cult), Siouxie Sioux (Siouxie and the Banshees) and Nick Cave (The Birthday Party, the Bad Seeds). Along with the music, fashion was at the heart of an emergent subcultural style and continues to be a focus (Brill, 2008; Spooner, 2006). Goths were initially characterized by their wearing of black clothes, with a taste for 'rich' fabrics such as velvet, lace and leather; the extensive use of silver jewellery; long, black-dyed hair; and the heavy use of dark eye/face makeup. To begin with, goth was primarily an English phenomenon, although it quickly developed internationally, particularly in Germany and the US.

The development of goth was underpinned by an interlinked network of clubs and other live venues, record labels and specialist music magazines and fanzines; today, these have a strong internet presence. Both the music and the associated subculture have maintained themselves in various national contexts and urban scenes, although with increasing diversity present. As with other well-established musical genres, goth has mutated into a range of subgenres, most notably dark wave, goth metal and techno goth. The goth subculture has also developed a number of distinct styles, usually linked to its musical variants (see Brill, 2008; Hodkinson, 2002; Reynolds, 2006).

As Brill documents: 'In the early 1990s the second wave of Goth shifted its impetus from Britain to Germany, which has since been the unrivalled epicentre of the scene' (Brill, 2008: 4). A network of independent record labels, magazines, clothing companies and events promoters specializing in goth had developed in Germany through the 1990s. This network included *Orkus* and *Sonic Reducer*, which established themselves as newsstand goth magazines; 'Black' summer festivals such as M'Era Lune, which routinely drew audiences of 15,000 to 20,000 people; and record labels (e.g. Trisol, Out of Line) and numerous professional bands. By the early 2000s Brill estimates that there were 70,000 to 90,000 goths in Germany, compared with roughly 15,000 in the United Kingdom (Brill, 2008: 187. In Germany, members of the goth subculture are often called *Gruftis* – in English: 'tomb creatures'). There are also significant goth music scenes and bands in Scandinavia, especially Finland (the band Nightwish); Italy (Ataraxia); Austria (L'Âme Immortelle); and Switzerland (Lacrimosa). Smaller gothic club scenes are present in cities such as Paris, Rome and Barcelona and in eastern Europe. Even countries with relatively small goth scenes have produced prominent goth bands, including Portugal (Moonspell) and the Netherlands (the gothic metal band Within Temptation), although it is noticeable that they frequently record on Germany-based record labels. In order to reach a wider audience, most European goth bands sing at least some of their recordings in English. Many of the leading goth bands and their fans congregate at the well-organized music festivals in Germany and Britain.

The continued vitality of goth is evident in these local scenes, which coalesce around the festivals, the specialist record labels and goth-oriented clubs. As part of the increased cyberspace orientation of contemporary popular music, goth bands and goth subcultures can be found on MySpace, YouTube and the internet more generally. In his study of goth scenes in Britain, Paul Hodkinson (2002) found that participants in the goth subculture were able to utilize websites that served as information nodes and clearing houses to learn about events, bands and places. A particular translocal internet effect was the transmission and discussion of style and shared subcultural values.

Conclusion

I have traced a shift from the concepts of youth culture, to subcultures, to sounds and scenes. While this is something of a progression, reflecting changing academic theoretical fashion, I would argue that aspects of each of these remain present in particular locales. Accordingly, it seems most appropriate to view particular physical locations as scenes that include subcultures and specific sounds, with these placed within an international music and leisure market. Goth is an example of the conflation of subculture and scene, historically tied to particular physical sites, with these now extended and consolidated through an online presence.

Further reading

Bennett, A. and Peterson, R.A. (eds) (2004) *Music Scenes: Local, Translocal, and Virtual*, Nashville, TN: Vanderbilt University Press.
Cohen, S. (1999) 'Scenes', in B. Horner and T. Swiss (eds), *Key Terms in Popular Music and Culture*, Malden, MA; Oxford: Blackwell, pp. 239–50.
Hebdige, D. (1979) *Subculture: The Meaning of Style*, London: Methuen.
Hodkinson, P. (2002) *Goth: Identity, Style and Subculture*, Oxford: Berg Press.
Hollows, J. and Milestone, K. (1998) 'Welcome to Dreamsville: A History and Geography of Northern Soul', in A. Leyshon, D., Matless and G. Revill (eds) *The Place of Music*, New York: Guilford Press, pp. 83–103.
Huq, R. (2006) *Beyond Subculture: Pop, Youth and Identity in a Postcolonial World*, London, New York: Routledge.
Krims, A. (2012) 'Music, Space and Place. The Geography of Music', in M. Clayton, T., Herbert and R. Middleton (eds), *The Cultural Study of Music*, New York, London: Routledge.

12 'Revolution'

Social change, conscience rock and identity politics

In the general sense of the word, 'politics' permeates popular music studies. Practically every aspect of the production and consumption of popular music involves theoretical debates about the dynamics of economic, cultural and political power and influence and the reproduction of social structures and individual subjectivity. In addition to ongoing debates over the perceived negative 'effects' and influence of popular music (considered in Chapter 13), there have always been attempts to harness the music to social and political ends and arguments around the validity of notions of music as an empowering and political force. My discussion here is on the role of popular music in fostering social change and its mobilization within social movements. I consider several examples of direct political activism and the phenomenon of 'conscience rock'. A major issue in each case is the influence of such cultural interventions and the role of music in bringing about social change. The last part of the chapter continues my earlier theme of identity and popular music, introducing the role of music in constructing identities in relation to gender (and sexuality) and, more briefly, to ethnicity and social class. While each of these 'classic' social categories is considered separately, their interrelationship needs to be kept in mind, as they frequently reinforce and interact with one another.

Music and social change

A central problem in social theory has been to explain how cultures change and to identify the forms of social activity at work in processes of social transformation. While there is considerable theoretical debate over the relative importance of social structures and human agency, a key part of social change are changes in the cognitive identity (the 'head space') of the individuals involved. Popular music has played a prominent role in articulating this process, at both the individual and collective group level. At various historical points, popular music has translated political radicalism into a more accessible idiom, identifying social problems, alienation and oppression and facilitating the sharing of a collective vision. Performers and songs contribute to forging a relationship between politics, cultural change and popular music. Popular music has frequently acted as a powerful means of raising consciousness about political causes and funds for them. At the same time, however, there is a tendency for such popular music genres, texts and their performers to be co-opted, marketed and watered down or neutralized by the music industry.

There is a lengthy historical tradition of popular music playing an overt political role, including commentary through individual songs and campaigns and interventions at several levels (see Denselow, 1990; Lynskey, 2011; Street, 2012). Internationally, the global phenomenon of Live Aid in 1985 addressed the issue of famine in Africa and the Mil Foundation and the various Concerts for Tibet (since 1995), initiated by the Beastie Boys, raised issues of repressive Chinese government policies in that country. Examples at a national level include the Campaign for Nuclear Disarmament movement in the UK in the late 1950s; civil rights and the anti-Vietnam war movement in the US in the 1960s; Rock Against Racism (RAR) in the UK in the late 1970s and early 1980s, Rock Against Bush in 2004–2006, and Live 8. I shall have more to say about several of these later.

Further, many artists have individually used their music to make political statements on a variety of issues, including racism, class, gender politics, sexuality and environmental concerns. At times 'mainstream' artists usually regarded as purely commercial and 'apolitical' also grasp the opportunity to present assertive messages, as in Destiny Child's huge hit 'Independent Women' (2001) and country star Shania Twain's 'Black Eyes Blue Tears' (1998), which alerted listeners to domestic violence.

Dorian Lynskey (2011) provides an insightful and detailed and discussion of 34 examples of individual songs, ranging, from Billy Holiday's 'Strange Fruit' in 1939, to Green Day's 'American Idiot' in 2004. These are frequently within the strong historical tradition of protest song, particularly in folk music, which has been carried on in genres such as reggae, punk and alternative music. A recent example is Bruce Springsteen's album *Wrecking Ball*, with its core argument that the current financial crisis and rising social inequality have ruined the American dream: 'We've destroyed the idea of an equal playing field. And there's a critical mass where society collapses. You can't have a society as fractionalized as that' (*The Times* in *Dominion Post*, 18 February 2012: B2). The songs on the album draw on folk melodies, welded to Springsteen's trademark big rock sound, with the lyrics echoing the early 1960s' protest songs of Bob Dylan, whom Springsteen cites as a primary influence. Springsteen compares the 2008 banking crisis in the US to theft and endorses the Occupy protest movement that sprang up in New York, London and many other cities worldwide.

The politics of rock

Rock, especially in genres such as punk/indie, is the popular music genre arguably most commonly associated with political potential. There is, however, disagreement as to the cultural significance and force of rock musicians' political statements and their role in various campaigns. For Lawrence Grossberg:

on the one hand, so much activity is attempting to explicitly articulate rock to political activism; on the other hand, this activity seems to have little impact on the rock formation, its various audiences or its relations to larger social struggles.

(Grossberg, 1992: 168)

This argument rests on a perceived 'radical disassociation' of the political content of the music of bands such as Rage Against the Machine, NOFX and Midnight Oil 'from their emotionally and affectively powerful appeals' (ibid.). It is clear that many listeners derive pleasure from such performers without either subscribing to their politics or, indeed, even being aware of them. Theodore Gracyk is also not confident of the revolutionary potential of rock music:

Rock, infused with the mythology of rebellion, would seem to attract an audience who could actually rebel and overthrow the system. We are to conclude that middle-class white teens are attracted to counterculture music ... because it openly speaks of an oppressive system that they dare not confront; the temporary release comes from the frank admission that contemporary life sucks.

(Gracyk, 1996: 158)

This is to see rock's frequent oppositional stance as diluted into symbolic consumption. By way of contrast, a variety of examples have been adduced to illustrate that many listeners *do* have their ideological horizons both confirmed and extended by association with political rock. This can also have practical benefits: for example, the Amnesty International tours of 1988 are estimated to have added some 200,000 new members to the organization in the US alone.

It has been argued that the history of such attempts to use popular music to forge mass movements will always face two problems. First, the power of popular music is transitory by nature, novelty and shock value have a short life span and routinization and disempowering follows. Second, there is the confused nature of musical power's 'collectivity':

The power of mass music certainly comes from its mobilization of an audience; a series of individual choices (to buy this record, this concert ticket) becomes the means to a shared experience and identity. The question, though, is whether this identity has any political substance.

(Frith and Street, 1992: 80)

A further dimension of this question is the tendency of many commentators to incorrectly assume that 'youth' represent some sort of 'natural left' political constituency. Furthermore, popular music is hardly the preserve of the political left and broadly progressive politics. It can be, and has been, used to support a broad range of political positions. President George Bush's inaugurations included impressive line-ups of blues and soul artists; white supremacist organizations like

the National Front in the UK and neo-Nazi groups in Germany have used punk
rock and hardcore bands to attract new recruits; and US anti-abortion activists
have co-opted 'We Shall Overcome' to maintain solidarity at sit-ins outside
abortion clinics.

I want to situate this debate in relation to three brief examples of the politics of
rock; each a particular historical moment in what is a broader history.

The 1960s: 'Give Peace a Chance'

The 1960s were a benchmark for popular music and political activism. Music
played a role in the US civil rights movement of the early 1960s, the student
protests of 1968, especially in Europe, and in the anti-Vietnam war movement
(Doggett, 2009). Musicians wrote, performed and recorded songs about these
events and their commercial success drew wider attention to the issues involved.
There are numerous examples; a few must suffice here:

* Crosby, Stills and Nash, 'Chicago', on the harsh treatment by the police of
  demonstrators at the Democratic Convention in that city in 1968.
* John Lennon, 'Give Peace a Chance' and 'Power to the People', whose
  chanted lyrics provided anthems for peace marches and rallies internationally.
* Marvin Gaye, 'What's Going On' arguably the most politically explicit no. 1
  record ever.
* The Byrds, 'Turn! Turn! Turn! (to everything there is a season)'. While this is
  not on the surface a protest song, Roger McGuin added the line 'a time of
  peace,/I swear it's not too late', to Pete Seger's bible-based song lyrics.

A number of songs spoke directly to the soldiers fighting in Vietnam, as with
the Fugs, 'Kill for Peace'; CCR's 'Run Through the Jungle' and 'Fortunate Son',
on the ability of middle-class youth to avoid the draft; the Doors, 'The Unknown
Soldier'; and Edwin Starr, 'War', which spent three weeks at no. 1 on *Billboard* in
1969. At Woodstock in 1969 Jimi Hendrix deconstructed the US national
anthem, 'The Star Spangled Banner', as a series of sirens, explosions and shrieking
feedback.

As the Vietnam War escalated, opposition to it grew. Events at Kent State
University, in Ohio in 1970, were a defining moment in the anti-war movement
in the US. The National Guard fired on student demonstrators, four were killed
and many more injured, several seriously. Responding the same night the news
was broadcast, Neil Young composed 'Ohio'. (The song is on Neil Young, *Greatest
Hits*, Reprise, 2004, CD; Young has mixed personal introspection and the political issues of the day throughout his career.) Of course, the impact of these songs
is difficult to judge and the meaning and clarity of their lyrics are at times
unclear. Yet their commercial exposure, and the widespread media and public
interest in them, suggested they certainly had an impact. As Graham Nash, who
wrote 'Chicago', later observed: 'people like us probably don't have any real
answers, but at least we brought up the questions' (*Get Up*, 2004).

Rock Against Racism (RAR)

RAR is a further example of such associations between music and politics, conducting a partially successful mass campaign to confront the racism arising in the harsh urban landscapes of inner city Britain in the 1970s. The 1950s and 1960s had seen increased immigration to England from former colonies in the Asian subcontinent and the West Indies, but the new immigrant communities were often targeted by racist organizations such as the National Front. In the three years under a Labour government between 1974 and 1977, unemployment had risen sharply, especially among youth; the National Front gained support, and racial tension increased. A later retrospective summarized the period: 'Power blackouts. Endless strikes. Police brutality. Race riots. Currency freefalls … the mood of the country was bleak and growing bleaker' (*Uncut*, February 2003).

RAR was formed against this background, following a widely reported provocative remark by Eric Clapton, during a concert, that Britain would become 'a black colony within 10 years'. RAR used demonstrations, concerts, a magazine and records to mobilize upwards of half a million people: 'black and white people, outside conventional politics, inspired by a mixture of socialism, punk rock and common humanity, got together and organized to change things' (Widgery, 1986: 8). In February 1981 *Rock Against Racism's Greatest Hits* (Virgin Records) was the first album made as a political gesture, providing a precedent for the subsequent efforts of efforts such as Band Aid. Leading groups and artists (Tom Robinson Band, the Clash) contributed to mass concerts and carnivals, and anti-National Front rallies, which served to politicize but still entertain. While the campaign failed to stop racist attacks, far less racism, it was a factor in the sharp decline of the National Front's share of the vote in the general election of 1979, following the fascist organization's surge of support in the mid-1970s.

RAR strengthened the idea that popular music could be about more than entertainment and in a sense provided the inspiration for similar campaigns in the 1980s. But as John Street notes, the RAR campaign illustrates 'the delicacy of the relationship between a cause and its music', as the reliance on the music as the source of unity and strength threw into sharp relief differences of stylistic affiliations. Political strategies were 'played out and resolved in terms of musical choices', a process which indicated 'the limitations of a politics organized around music' (Street, 1986: 78; see also his fuller discussion of the campaign in Street, 2012: Chapter 5). Similar difficulties were evident in attempts to harness rock to the cause of the striking British miners in 1984–1985 and with Red Wedge, the opposition Labour party's attempt to use rock to win the youth vote in the 1987 UK general elections. In both cases, strongly held views about the correct relationship of political principle and musical style arguably seriously limited the impact of the efforts (see Denselow, 1990; Street, 2012).

Rock Against Bush; the Dixie Chicks

During the 2004 American presidential campaign, several organizations worked to get young people to register to vote (Rock the Vote; Punk Voter). Some, including Punk Voter, were explicitly against President George Bush, who was running for another term of office. Their activities included websites (Rock the Vote was originally created through MTV in 1990); concerts and, in the case of Punk Voter, compilation albums: *Rock Against Bush*, volumes 1 and 2. The proceeds from these were used to support the concerts staged during the election year.

A number of punk bands were very active in these campaigns, including NOFX, whose singer Fat Mike (Michael Burkett) helped found Punk Voter. 'Mainstream' stars, too, were part of the presidential race. Bruce Springsteen endorsed Democratic candidate John Kerry's campaign against Bush and the star's song 'No Surrender' became its unofficial theme song. Springsteen performed it, along with 'Promised Land', at campaign rallies, referring to how 'Senator Kerry honors these ideals'. International media coverage featured images of Springsteen and Kerry, arms around one another, with press captions asking 'Who Will Be the Boss?' (*Dominion Post*, 30 October 2004) neatly linking the election outcome to the title Springsteen fans have long accorded the rock star.

The hugely successful country crossover trio, the Dixie Chicks, endorsed Rock the Vote, but became more directly involved when singer Natalie Maines confided to British fans at a London concert on 10 March 2003: 'Just so you know, we're on the good side with y'all. We do not want this war, this violence, and we're ashamed the President of the United States is from Texas' – the band's home state. Her comment was widely reported in the international media, but was often abbreviated to 'we're ashamed that the President of the United States is from Texas'. This took the words out of their original context and left out the back story to why the comment was made and ignored the Chicks' support for the American soldiers fighting in Iraq, expressed in their single 'Travelling Soldier'.

As MOJO put it, 'the Dixie Chicks went from being country darlings to being enemies of the state' (*MOJO*, October 2003: 44). Maines' remarks touched off an extreme response, with a considerable public backlash: radio stations, mainly in the American south, banned the group's new release and attempts were made to boycott their concerts. In June 2006, as the war in Iraq continued to escalate and US casualties mounted, the earlier episode and Maines' remark were reprised when the Chicks launched a new album (*Taking the Long Way*) and tour. A media marketing blitz, and numerous interviews with the group, used the 2003 episode as a starting point: did Natalie regret saying it? Was she surprised at the backlash? Of course, not only did this draw attention to Bush and American policy in Iraq, it also gave the Dixie Chicks a good deal of useful publicity: the album went to the top of the charts. After George Bush was re-elected, criticism continued of his policies and musicians remained part of this; for example, Neil Young released *Living With War* (2006), featuring lyrics condemning the president and the war in Iraq.

Conscience rock

In the 1980s questions about the viability of music in the direct service of organized political movements were addressed by a different style of cultural politics:

the 'mega-event' or what I term 'conscience rock'. This new phenomenon of political rock saw popular musician stars joining and reinforcing international concern at the grim effects of mass famine in Africa, Third World debt and taking up anti-nuclear, environmental and other international causes. The list of causes here is now a long one and includes the Concert for Bangladesh, Live Aid, Sun City, Farm Aid, Rock the Debt, the Nelson Mandela tribute concerts, several Amnesty International tours, numerous Greenpeace concerts and Music for Tibet. Such efforts are not purely political: Rock Against AIDS has raised awareness about the epidemic and funds to help combat it.

Here I want to consider Live Aid in the 1980s as an example of 'conscience rock', opening up the question of the political potential of popular music to raise consciousness and money for social interventions. Band Aid's 'Do They Know it's Christmas?' was the first of a number of singles to raise public consciousness and funds to aid famine relief in Africa and established the pattern and format for those that followed. While the very name of the effort conceded its limitations, given the scale of the problem, Band Aid proved far more successful than any of those involved had anticipated. Recorded by 37 English pop stars in London in late November 1984, the record was perfectly timed for the British Christmas market; it sold about 10 million copies and raised about £8 million (Rijven and Straw, 1989: 200; see also Denselow, 1990: 244ff.).

The record cover contrasted the well-to-do children of the west with the poverty of their Ethiopian counterparts. The back of the cover sleeve constructed and celebrated a brotherhood of rock, in contrast to the music press's usual stressing of the individual image of performers. USA (United Support of Artists) for Africa followed with 'We Are the World'. The song title neatly suggested global interdependence, while its lyrics reaffirmed nineteenth-century charity: 'Its time to lend a hand to life, so let's start giving', adding an echo of the Beatles' idealism with 'and the truth, you know, love is all we need'. The single became CBS's fastest seller ever. Together with an album, videos and the sales of posters and t-shirts, United Support of Artists grossed $50 million dollars; the bulk of this went to famine relief and longer term aid in Africa, with 10 per cent going to the hungry and homeless in the US. A number of similar regional and national Band Aid singles followed.

On 13 July 1985 Live Aid was broadcast worldwide via television, directly from Sydney, Australia, Wembley Stadium in London and the JFK stadium in Philadelphia. The performers included David Bowie, Queen, U2 and Paul McCartney in London; Eric Clapton, Duran Duran and Bob Dylan in Philadelphia. With the assistance of Concorde, Phil Collins even performed at both shows. Seven telecommunications satellites beamed the event live to an estimated one billion viewers in some 150 countries, including the Soviet Union and China. Viewers were encouraged to phone in to their national contact and pledge their contribution. The records and concerts shared an air of patriotism; the notion of each nation doing its bit for the common cause – 'donationalism' – and collectively they emphasized a sense of community and togetherness.

The Band Aid phenomenon raised a host of questions about the motives of the celebrities involved, marketing politics and the reasons for the overwhelming public response to charity rock in the mid-1980s. Much analysis was critical, finding 'the various charity projects tasteless, self-serving for those involved, symptomatic of existing geo-political relations and politically inappropriate' (Rijven and Straw, 1989: 206). There was also criticism that the line-up of artists performing at the two main Live Aid concerts consisted primarily of white stars and the majority of the recordings reflected 'the same muzak characteristics, transparant frameworks built on the conventions of pop song writing that only sell because of the Band Aid connotation' (ibid.: 203). Pragmatic rock politics, observed Will Straw, were now taking on the crasser aspects of the pop music industry.

Such criticism reflected a tendency on the part of the political left to claim the moral high ground and was rooted in a 'rock ideology' preoccupied with notions of sincerity and authenticity. This rather misses the point that Band Aid was essentially not about music and youth, but rather about using the connection between them to raise money and consciousness. The critics' preoccupation with credibility and ideological purity is accordingly misplaced. Nonetheless, the Band Aid projects showed 'a high media sensibility that feeds on itself – charity opens all doors' (ibid.). This is to acknowledge the multimedia nature of such high- profile public events, which became a feature of them in the 1990s.

Rijven concludes by critiquing Band Aid for 'a naive political attitude com-bined with a moral superiority' (ibid.: 204). This was certainly evident, although to go beyond it was expecting too much of the musicians involved. After all, how many people are aware of the international dynamics of the international econ-omy and their contribution to the Ethiopian situation? At least charity/aid is a first step, even if based initially on a simple apolitical humanitarianism. Political sophistication comes later, as Bob Geldof himself found when investigating the use of the funds the Live Aid concert generated:

> he was inevitably involved in a crash course in food aid politics, the realities of the African scene, the problems of debt, and an understanding of the strings often attached to aid offers from West or East, and the amounts Africa spends, and is encouraged to spend, on armaments.
>
> (Denselow, 1990: 246; see also Geldof, 1986)

As Will Straw puts it, 'rock's discourse on politics is primarily concerned with nudging people rather than instances of political intervention'. He makes the point, usually overlooked, that the participation of artists in the various Ethiopia records is in many ways less significant than the involvement of the music industries: 'The waiving of record label, distributor and retail profits is much more unpre-cedented and spectacular than the gathering of artists for charity purposes' (Rijven and Straw, 1989: 204, 208). Since this industry concession provided the bulk of the money to the cause, it rendered irrelevant the debates over the cred-ibility, motives and sincerity of the artists involved. The cultural significance of

Live Aid's 'We Are the World' lay in its commercial form as much as in its political focus.

Conscience rock has continued to be part of political culture, with various causes and campaigns using music and musicians to animate political participation. As John Street shows in relation to Live 8, the culmination of the campaign for debt relief through the early 2000s, 'the conjunction of music and politics is not a product of spontaneity, but of hard work and planning, of networks and various forms of capital' (Street, 2012: 74).

Music, gender and sexual politics

The term 'sex' is used to refer to biological differences between male and female, whereas gender applies to everything that is socially constructed and culturally transmitted. Masculine and feminine are characteristics of men and women respectively. The major debate in gender studies, sociobiology and sociology more generally is between those who believe that these characteristics are indicative of men's and women's biological natures (essentialists) and those who argue that masculine and feminine are ascribed roles and masculinity and femininity are cultural, shaped by socialization rather than biology (Mac an Ghaill and Haywood, 2006). For musicians and music consumers/fans, gender identity or *identities* can be seen, in part, as constructed through musical institutions, texts and practices. Accordingly, the significance of gender is evident in a number of areas of popular music studies; these can only be briefly alluded to here and warrant further investigation.

It has been forcefully argued that the dominant ideologies and discourses throughout popular music generally privilege males, while at the same time constructing a normative masculinity. The dominance of male–female binaries in popular music's analysis of gender has been challenged by studies of 'queer music', a term appropriated by gays and lesbians. There is rather less literature on male gender issues in popular music and the construction of masculinity (although see Hawkins, 2009, on the British pop dandy).

Writing in 1977, Chapple and Garofalo described a situation that has been slow to change:

> The absence of women as creators in pop music can be called sexist. Sexism is the systematic discrimination against and degradation of women, and the denial of equal power to women in human affairs. Sexism is as pervasive in rock music as in any other form of music. It pervades the structure of the music industry along with the lyrics and instrumentation of the music itself.
>
> (269)

A number of studies provide examples of the continued difficult struggle experienced by women in all phases of the music business (see Carson, Lewis and Shaw, 2004). There remains a lack of women in the male-dominated music industry; traditionally they are largely in stereotypically 'female' roles, e.g. press, office personnel. There are few women working in A&R, or as producers, managers and sound mixers; these are all spheres that are male dominated, a situation partly related to technologies as masculinist.

The history of popular music is largely constructed around male performers and male-dominated genres. While women's contribution to gospel, the blues and soul are generally recognized, there is a tendency to marginalize their place in the development of rock, metal and dance music. Compare, for example, the status accorded contemporaries Jim Morrison (heroic, romantic 'rock icon') and Janis Joplin (a 'sad figure'), despite her critical and commercial success that more than matched his in the late 1960s. Even when they are credited, their contributions are seen in stereotypical terms: divas, rock chicks (e.g. Suzi Quatro, Janis Joplin), men-pleasing angels (Doris Day), victims (Billie Holiday) or problem personalities (Judy Garland). These narratives have been challenged by popular music histories focused on women and through re-evaluations of phenomena such as girl groups and fandom. Linked to this, both traditional musicology and the popular music press have constructed a male-dominated musical canon, with this challenged by feminist scholars and music critics. A *MOJO* special issue, *ICONS* (2004), is typical of the popular construction of a gender-based canon. Of the 100 featured performers, only 14 are women; of these, Madonna is at number six, followed by Kate Bush at 29, with most women performers placed towards the bottom of the list.

In relation to audiences and consumption, girl fans and their musical tastes are often denigrated (e.g. pop's teenyboppers), while male fans are validated (especially in legitimating non-mainstream musical styles); record collecting presents itself as a highly gendered practice; and youth subcultures have been historically a male preserve, with girls generally absent, 'invisible' or socially insignificant.

The perceived masculine or feminine nature of particular genres has been vigorously debated. Pop is often seen as a genre supported by girls and younger women, while hard rock and heavy metal are regarded as primarily male-oriented genres: encoded as signifying masculinity. Even genres which, at least at the level of rhetoric, challenge gender stereotyping, such as indie and punk, demonstrate considerable sexism. Women performers predominate in a capella and gospel music and are prominent in folk and country and among singer-songwriters. These are socially constructed patterns, reflecting differential expectations and resources, including access to musical knowledge and equipment.

Mavis Bayton's discussion of 'women and the electric guitar' is a good early example of the social processes at work here (Bayton, 1997). Her Oxford study showed only between two and four per cent of instrumentalists in local bands were women and 'the reasons for women's absence are entirely social'. Gender socialization teaches girls how to be 'feminine' and not to engage in 'masculine' activities:

> Playing the flute, violin, and piano is traditionally 'feminine', playing electric guitar is 'masculine'. On TV and in magazines, young women are presented

with repeated images of men playing electric guitar; there are few female role models to inspire them.

(39)

Further, compared to boys, teenage women lack money, time, space, transport and access to equipment. Even if a girl does take up the electric guitar, they have difficulty gaining access to the informal friendship groups within rock music making, which are crucial learning environments. Guitar shops are 'male terrain' and nearly all Bayton's interviewees regarded them as alien territory. The technology associated with the electric guitar – leads, amplifiers, plug boards – is strongly categorized as 'masculine' and presents another hurdle to female performers. The association of guitar playing with masculine prowess, the 'axe' as an extension of the male body, and playing it a pseudo-masturbatory act, consolidate its status as an exclusively 'masculine' idiom. A more recent study by Monique Bourdage found that the same barriers that prevent women from succeeding in other male-dominated fields continued to apply to the electric guitar, including 'a scarcity of role models, a lack of access to education, and the masculinization of prestigious technologies'. She considers attempts to break down such barriers, including women's music festivals, rock camps for girls and riot grrrl (Bourdage, 2010).

In a classic early investigation, Sara Cohen found that in the Liverpool rock music scene she studied, women were not simply absent, but were actively excluded. All-male bands tended to preserve the music as 'their' domain, keeping the involvement of wives and girlfriends at a distance. This situation reflected the more restricted social position of women, with greater domestic commitments and less physical freedom; the lack of encouragement given to girls to learn rock instruments; and rock sexuality as predominantly masculine. Consequently, there are few women bands in rock or women instrumentalists and most women rock performers are 'packaged as traditional, stereotyped, male images of women' (Cohen, 1991: 203). In the 1990s the situation Cohen identified was challenged by the Riot Grrrl movement.

Riot Grrrl

Initially based in Washington, DC, and Olympia, Washington, in the early 1990s, Riot Grrrl quickly became the focus of considerable media attention. Through fanzines and sympathetic role models among female musicians, riot grrrls asserted the need to break down the masculine mateship of the alternative and hardcore music scenes, which marginalized girls and young women. They drew on feminism and punk DYI ideology to question conventional ideas of femininity and rejected rockist ideas of cool and mystique, challenging the view that enhanced technical virtuosity is necessary to create music. Some writers referred to them as 'punk feminists', as riot grrrls aimed to create a cultural space for young women in which they could express themselves without being subject to male scrutiny (Leonard, 2007). In the process, they played with conflicting images and stereotyped conventions; e.g. the appropriation of 'girl' and their assertive use of the term 'slut'. Musically, the performers linked to the Riot Grrrl movement (e.g. L7, Bikini Kill) sounded very like traditional hardcore and late 1970s' punk bands, but their emphasis was on the process rather than the product.

Inspired in part by Riot Grrrl, a number of prominent women-led bands emerged during the 1990s, including Hole, Veruca Salt and Echobelly. Performers associated with the 'angry women in rock' media tag of the mid-1990s, notably Alanis Morissette and Fiona Apple, selectively appropriated key concepts from the riot grrrls, with considerable commercial successs. To a degree, this represented the incorporation of Riot Grrrl and a dilution of its oppositional politics, a common historical theme in popular music. Other performers, however, remained more closely aligned to the founding philosophy, including Sleater-Keater, formed in 1995 (they broke up in June 2006), and Le Tigre, formed in 1998 by Kathleen Hanna, after she had left Bikini Kill (Marcus, 2010). Along with their predecessors, these performers have remained linked to locally based labels and continue to assert a political feminism in their work. Many contemporary local indie scenes, including Wellington, New Zealand, include bands that identify themselves with the Riot Grrrl movement.

Woman- or 'female-centred' rock bands are now more common, especially in the alternative and indie music scenes, although their members still have to negotiate the gendering of rock as masculine (Leonard, 2007) and social expectations of performers sexuality.

Sexuality

Sexuality refers to the expression of sexual identity, through sexual activity, or the projection of sexual desire and attraction. Sexuality and desire are central human emotions, or drives, that have been an essential part of the appeal of the culture/ entertainment industries, including popular music and the social processes whereby performers and their texts operate in the public arena. Popular music is a significant site for the operation of sexual politics and struggles around them.

Sexuality is central to discussions of how male and, more frequently, female performers are conceived of – socially constructed – as sex objects or symbols of desire. Here certain forms of subjectivity and identity are projected as 'normal', traditionally white, male heterosexuality. The operation of this process is a major focus in studies of music video and stardom and in relation to particular genres of music and types of performer (for example the diva, the dandy; see Hawkins, 2009). Central here are considerations of the nature of spectatorship and the (gendered) gaze, as evident in the discourse surrounding Madonna's early career (see Schwichtenberg, 1993). In the early 2000s Christina Aguilera utilized modes of sexual expression similar to those of Madonna and situated herself in the now familiar debate. On the one hand, she could be seen as presenting her body as an object for the male gaze and voyeuristic desire, through provocative poses in CD sleeve booklets (*Stripped*, 2002) and magazine covers and stories. On the other hand, she could be regarded as subverting dominant patriarchal attitudes and practices in her work, with songs following the standard heterosexual romantic narrative (woman falls in love with/desires a man), while also 'voicing compelling feminist notions of female independence, autonomy and sexual expression' (Smith, 2003), on songs such as 'Can't Hold Us Down' (on *Stripped*). Other women performers to use their careers and public/stage personas to comment on female sexuality, vulnerability and power include Polly Harvey, Tori Amos and Björk (see the discussion of each in Whiteley, 2005) – not forgetting Lady Gaga.

Sexual ambiguity is central to many forms of popular music, which has frequently subverted the dominant sexuality constructed around male–female binaries. Discussion has concentrated on exploring the relationship between sexual orientation, public personas and a performer's music. Some performers openly represent or subvert and 'play with' a range of sexualities. Others constitute themselves, at times very self-consciously, as objects of heterosexual desire or as icons for different ('deviant'?) sexualities and their constituencies. Several 1950s' male stars were 'adored objects', catering to both homosexual desire and female consumption, for example Elvis Presley and Fabian. Later performers include representations of the homoerotic (e.g. Madonna, Morrissey), androgynous (Bowie during the Ziggy period), effeminate (the Cure), asexual (Boy George), bisexual (Morrissey again; Suede) and gay and lesbian (the Village People; Freddie Mercury; k.d. lang). The application of such labels, their connotations and their relationship to actual gay communities have been at times strongly contested (Hawkins, 2002; Whiteley *et al.*, 2004).

Some genres and performers are linked to particular sexualities/communities. Disco, for example, generally celebrates the pleasure of the body and physicality and is linked to the gay community and specific club scenes. 'Hard rock', as the label suggests, was traditionally associated with overt masculinity, dominated by male performers, it has even been referred to as 'cock rock' (Frith and McRobbie, 1978). Robert Walser argues that heavy metal has historically been actively *made* as male and acts to 'reproduce and reflect patriarchal assumptions and ideologies' that underpin western society (1993: 111). He suggests that HM bands promote male bonding and legitimate male power through a combination of misogyny (in song lyrics, videos) and exscription: the creation through the music, album covers and videos of fantasy worlds without women, in which male heroes battle against monsters and superhuman villains (110). Arnett observes that even though some HM fans are women, their involvement is often through a boyfriend or due to the sexual attraction they feel toward the performers or fans; consequently they struggle 'to reconcile their enthusiasm for heavy metal with their sense of being not quite welcome in that world' (Arnett, 1996: 140). Later metal studies have taken issue with these earlier studies, arguing for a more complex process of gender negotiation within the genre (see Chapter 6). There is considerable argument over how the lyrics and the associated cultural values in 'gendered' musical genres are understood and responded to by their listeners, audiences and fans. Are the artists intended or preferred readings, embedded in their recordings and performances, acknowledged let alone assimilated into individual and social values and meanings?

In addition to gender, ethnicity and class are social categories, which have the subject of considerable attention within popular music studies. Considerations of space have necessitated a very gestural treatment here, which can be followed up through the Further Reading at the end of the chapter.

Ethnicity

The term 'race' is still widely used in popular discourse; it has historically often been considered as a biological concept, whereby humans can be classified according to a number of physical criteria. Cultural theorists now generally regard this as an untenable and ideologically motivated view, associated with *racism*. The alternative term 'ethnicity' is defined on the basis of shared cultural characteristics for a group of people, based in part on cultural self-identification, but can also include an overlay of cultural criteria onto perceived racial characteristics. There is considerable debate around both terms, which should be considered *social* categories. Ethnicity has been an important consideration in virtually all aspects of popular music studies, particularly in regard to African-American music in the US. Popular music is also involved in the social processes of 'racialization' internationally and can both cross and reinforce ethnic/racist boundaries.

The concept of 'black' music is sometimes equated with African-American music (which replaced the earlier term Afro-American) or the two terms are used interchangeably. Both concepts are linked to emotive arguments over essentialism, authenticity and the historical incorporation and marginalization of the music of black performers. The existence of black music is predicated on a notion of musical coherence and an identifiable constituency. According to Nelson George (1989: Introduction):

> black music is that which is recognized and accepted as such by its creators, performers and hearers ... encompassing the music of those who see themselves as black, and whose musics have unifying characteristics which justify their recognition as specific genres.

In such formulations, particular genres are considered 'black', most notably the blues, soul and rap. This has led to questions and debate over how this 'blackness' can be musically identified, how 'black' performers can be defined or recognized and how do we situate a song by a white composer being performed by a black artist?

In the development of popular music, it has generally been agreed that the interaction between black and white styles, genres and performers has been crucial. Black slaves shipped from Africa to the Americas brought with them their own kinds of music, which eventually mixed with the European music of white Americans to produce a fusion of styles. Early African American music had had three characteristics: a melodic line; a strong rhythmic accent; and songs that alternate improvised lines, shouts and cries with repeated choruses These were incorporated into ragtime, the blues and R&B. These characteristics aside, it has been argued that it is difficult to identify common factors that characterize black music, rejecting the idea that there is an 'essence' to black music (Tagg, 1989).

Nonetheless, some writers demonstrate that 'black music' to be a useful and important term. Brackett (1995), for example, uses 'the presence or absence of musical elements that many writers have identified with African-American musical styles, elements derived in particular from gospel music and African-American preaching', to consider the relative success of a number of songs that crossed over from *Billboard*'s R&B to the Hot 100 charts in 1965. However, it is difficult to identify common factors, an 'essence' that characterizes black music (Gilroy, 1993; Tagg, 1989). The concept of diaspora has been applied to the notion of black music to signal a community of musical expression transcending nationalism, but which avoids musical essentialism (Gilroy, 1993). More recent scholarship in relation to such issues is discussed by Ronald Radano (2012).

Class

Class is one of the fundamental types of social classification. Most contemporary discussions rely on employment categories, with class formation and identity variously related to educational attainment and life chances and to patterns of cultural consumption. It is the last that has been a significant part of popular music studies. The class nature of popular music preferences is international, with class-linked taste cultures seemingly fairly fixed over time. Bourdieu claimed 'nothing more clearly affirms one's class, nothing more infallibly classifies, than tastes in music' (1986: 18), but the relative and sometimes greater influence of gender, ethnicity, age and location as influences shaping musical tastes must also be acknowledged (see Chapter 10).

Genre studies include consideration of the class location of audiences and fans, linking this to the nature and the appeal of the genre. Wiseman-Trowse (2008), for example, extensively considers the role historically played by class in popular music in the UK, through case studies of folk music, punk and hardcore, dream pop and 'Madchester', with an emphasis on 'the ways in which representations of class in British popular music are used to articulate authenticity' (2). He considers class to be 'a mythological concept, constructed through the musical text' in order to assure the listener of the authenticity of their tastes. More specifically, Chris McDonald (2010) explores the ways in which Canadian progressive rock band Rush has been the voice of the suburban middle class: 'Rush's critique of suburban life – and its strategies for escape – reflected middle-class aspirations and anxieties, while its performances manifested the dialectic in prog rock between discipline and austerity, and the desire for spectacle and excess.'

Conclusion

The examples referred to in this chapter demonstrate the range and complexity of the role of popular music in cultural politics. For every case of a performer, genre, text or consumer constrained and regulated by gender expectations, capital, pressure groups and the state, there are counter-examples of the success-ful use of the music to raise political consciousness, finance political causes and support social movements. In terms of the identity politics of gender and sexu-ality, ethnicity and class popular music is a site of cultural struggle, with constant attempts to establish dominance, exploit cultural contradictions and negotiate dominant norms and expectations.

Further reading

Political rock

Dogget, P. (2009) *There's A Riot Going On: Revolutionaries, Rock Stars and The Rise and Fall of 60s Counter Culture*, London: Canongate.

Lynskey, D. (2011) *33 Revolutions per Minute: A History of Protest Songs from Billie Holiday to Green Day*, New York: HarperCollins.

Viewing: *Get Up, Stand Up: The Story of Pop and Politics*, a Dora Production, documentary series, 2004.

Gender and sexuality

Bourdage, M. (2010) 'A Young Girl's Dream: Examining the Barriers Facing Female Electric Guitarists', *IASPM Journal*, 1, 1: 1–15.

Carson, M., Lewis, T. and Shaw, S.M. (2004) *Girls Rock! Fifty Years of Women Making Music*, Lexington, KY: University Press of Kentucky.

Leonard, M. (2007) *Gender in the Music Industry Rock, Discourse and Girl Power*, Aldershot: Ashgate.

In addition to 'academic' studies, popular biographies and autobiographies of women performers can provide considerable insight, for example, Pat Benatar (2010) on her career as a female 'rock' artist in the 1980s.

Benatar, P. with Patsi Bale Cox (2010) *Between a Heart and a Rock Place: A Memoir*, New York: HarperCollins.

Ethnicity

Radano, R. (2012) 'Music, Race and the Fields of Public Culture', in M. Clayton, T. Herbert and R. Middleton (eds), *The Cultural Study of Music*, New York, London: Routledge.

Ramsey, G.P. (2003) *Race Music: Black Cultures from Bebop to Hip-Hop*, Berkeley, University of California Press.

Tagg, P. (1989) '"Black Music", "African-American Music", and "European Music"', *Popular Music*, 8, 3: 285–98.

Class

Wiseman-Trowse, N. (2008) *Performing Class in British Popular Music*, Basingstoke, New York: Palgrave Macmillan.

13 'Pushin' Too Hard'

Moral panics

Particular genres of popular music have sparked controversy and opposition, both on their emergence and sporadically since: rock 'n' roll in the mid-1950s, psychedelic rock in the late 1960s, disco and punk in the 1970s, heavy metal and gangsta rap in the 1980s and rave culture in the 1990s, to name only the better known examples (see Martin and Seagrave, 1988; Winfield and Davidson, 1999). Criticism has been variously on the influence of such genres on youthful values, attitudes and behaviour through the music's (perceived) sexuality and sexism, nihilism and violence, obscenity, black magic and anti-Christian nature. The political edge of popular music has been partly the result of this hostile reaction often accorded to the music and its associated causes and followers, helping to politicize the musicians and their fans.

While such episodes are a standard part of the history of popular music – music hall, jazz and other new forms of popular music were also all stigmatized in their day – rarely are their nature and cultural significance more fully teased out. I argue here that they have constituted a form of moral panic – the social concern generated by them was greatly exaggerated and the perceived threat to social harmony was by no means as ominous as many regarded it. Attempts to control and regulate popular music genres such as rock and rap are significant as part of the ongoing contestation of cultural hegemony, particularly with the emergence of the New Right.

Moral panic and regulation

The episodes dealt with here have been chosen for their value in illuminating different facets of the reaction to popular music, at particular historical moments. First, the New Zealand reaction to rock 'n' roll in the 1950s exemplifies the characteristic concerns displayed internationally towards the new form of popular music: antipathy towards it as music, the antisocial behaviour linked to concerts and rock movies and, most importantly, the associations with juvenile delinquency. Second, the issues of obscenity and free speech are examined in the light of the establishment of the PMRC and the celebrated court action against American band the Dead Kennedys in 1986–1987 and controversies surrounding the lyrics of songs by 2 Live Crew (1990) and Ice-T (1992). Third, attempts to link the Columbine massacre of 1999 to the influence of Marilyn Manson illustrate the ongoing tendency to blame 'rock' for deeper social problems. These case studies illustrate the utility of the concept of moral panic to examine how music, as a central form of popular culture, becomes invested with ideological significance.

To place such opposition to popular music in context, it is important to acknowledge that popular culture in general has historically been the target of censure, condemnation and regulation. In the 1950s, for example, psychologist Frederic Wertham's influential bestseller, *Seduction of the Innocent*, argued for a direct causal connection between comic books and juvenile delinquency. Concern over new media and the activities of their youthful consumers seems to periodically reach a peak, frequently associated with 'boundary crises', periods of ambiguity and strain in society, which lead to attempts to more clearly establish moral boundaries. In many instances, such boundary crises are forms of 'moral panic', a concept that was widely utilized in British sociology of deviance and new criminology studies of the 1970s. This writing drew on labelling theory, associated with the American sociologist Howard Becker, who argued that societies and social groups 'create deviance by making those rules whose infraction comprises deviance and by applying them to particular people, and labeling them as outsiders' (Becker, 1997: 9); that is, deviance is considered to be a social construct. The mass media are the major source for the labelling process, as they transmit and legitimate such labels, for example Cohen's 'folk devils', and contribute to the legitimation of social control. Labelling theory is evident in popular music studies of various subcultures and their perceived 'antisocial' behaviours.

The concept of moral panic was popularized by sociologist Stanley Cohen's now classic study of mods and rockers in the UK, *Folk Devils and Moral Panics*. Cohen states that a period of moral panic occurs when:

> A condition, episode, person or group of persons emerges to become defined as a threat to societal values and interests; its nature is presented in a stylised and stereotypical fashion by the mass media; the moral barricades are manned by editors, bishops, politicians and other right-thinking people; socially accredited experts pronounce their diagnoses and solutions; ways of coping are evolved or (more often) resorted to; the condition then disappears, submerges or deteriorates and becomes more visible.
>
> (Cohen, 1980: 9)

The second stage of Cohen's view of moral panic is particularly significant, involving as it does the repudiation of the 'common-sense' view that the media simply report what happens. Cohen's own case study of the 1960s' clashes between mods and rockers in the UK (the 'folk devils' of his title) showed up just such a process of the selection and presentation of news. The media coverage of the clashes simplified their causes, labelled and stigmatized the youth involved, whipped up public feeling and encouraged a retributive, deterrent approach by those in authority. (For a helpful discussion of the subsequent application of the concept of moral panic, see Critcher, 2003.)

Examining the historical relationship between youth, 'antisocial' attitudes and behaviours and popular music means considering culture as a political issue. At a deeper level, moral panics around new media are episodes in cultural politics and the continual reconstitution and contestation of cultural hegemony. Underpinning debates over popular fiction, comics, film, television, video and popular music genres and performers are a series of assumptions about popular or 'mass' culture, which is frequently seen as diametrically opposed to a 'high' culture tradition. This dichotomy is a doubtful basis for evaluating particular forms of culture. The whole notion of a 'high–low' culture distinction must be regarded as a social construct, resting on class-based value judgements. It is more appropriate to view particular cultural forms in terms of both their formal qualities and their social function for consumers, while keeping in mind the salient point that any evaluation must be in terms relevant to the group that produces and appreciates it. This is particularly the case with popular music. With these general points in mind, I now turn to examples of music and moral panics.

Rock 'n' roll: the devil's music

The music industry and the social context of the early 1950s were ready for rock 'n' roll. With fuller employment, general economic prosperity and their emergence as an important consumer group, teenagers began to demand their own music and clothes and to develop a generation-based identity. Before 1956 popular music was dominated by American sounds, epitomized by the recurrent image of the 'crooner'. The music was largely safe, solid stuff, what Nic Cohn terms 'the palais age – the golden era of the big bands, when everything was soft, warm, sentimental, when everything was make believe' (Cohn, 1970: 11). There was little here for young people to identify with, although riot-provoking performers like Johnny Ray represented prototypes for rock.

Although rock music began with rock 'n' roll in the mid-1950s, as Tosches (1984) documents, it had been evolving well prior to this and was hardly the sole creation of Elvis Presley and Alan Freed. The phrase 'rock 'n' roll' itself was popularized with its sexual connotations in the music of the 1920s and was basically 'a mixture of two traditions: Negro rhythm and blues and white romantic crooning, coloured beat and white sentiment' (Cohn 1970: 11). Negro rhythm and blues was good-time music, danceable and unpretentious. While highly popular on rhythm and blues charts and radio stations, it received little airplay on white radio stations and was frequently banned because of the sexual innuendo of 1950s' R&B songs such as Hank Ballard's 'Work With Me Annie', Billy Ward's 'Sixty Minute Man' and the Penguins' 'Baby Let Me Bang Your Box'. It is this link between sex and rock 'n' roll – the devil's music – that underpinned the moral reaction to its popularization in the 1950s.

In April 1954 Bill Haley made 'Rock Around the Clock'. The record was a hit in America, then worldwide, eventually selling 15 million copies. While it did not start rock 'n' roll, it did represent a critical symbol in the popularization of the new musical form. 'Rock Around the Clock' was featured in the MGM movie *Blackboard Jungle*, the story of a young teacher at a tough New York school. The success of the film with teenage audiences, and the popularity of Haley's song (Miller, 1999: 87–94), led to Haley's being signed to make a film of his own. *Rock Around the Clock* (1956) told how Bill Haley and his band popularized rock 'n' roll, but the thin story was really a showcase for the rock acts on the soundtrack. The film proved enormously popular internationally, but attracted controversy over its effect on audiences. In Britain, for example, local councils banned showings of the film following riots in some cinemas. According to contemporary press reports, in the Gaiety Cinema, Manchester:

> gangs of teenage youths and their girlfriends danced in the aisles, vaulted up on to the stage, and turned fire hoses on the manager when he tried to restore order. After the programme, they surged into city streets in a wild stampede, bringing traffic to a standstill in the centre of town and pounding a rock 'n' roll rhythm on buses and cars with their fists.

Haley was an unlikely hero for youth to emulate, since his image (old, balding, chubby) hardly matched the music, but others were waiting in the wings. In this brief overview, complex developments must be reduced to their key moments. The success of Haley was one, the emergence of Chuck Berry and Little Richard another. Elvis Presley's was the biggest yet:

> His big contribution was that he brought it home just how economically powerful teenagers could really be. Before Elvis, rock had been a feature of vague rebellion. Once he'd happened, it immediately became solid, self-contained, and then it spawned its own style in clothes and language and sex, a total independence in almost everything – all the things that are now taken for granted.
>
> (Cohn, 1970: 23)

Cohn is overly enthusiastic about teenagers' independence, but by the end of 1957 Elvis had grown into an annual US$20 million industry and the process of homogenization of both 'the King' and the music had begun.

The new music provoked considerable criticism, with many older musicians contemptuous of rock 'n' roll, and conservative commentators regarding it as a moral threat:

> Viewed as a social phenomenon, the current craze for rock 'n' roll material is one of the most terrifying things ever to have happened to popular music. Musically speaking, of course, the whole thing is laughable. It is a monstrous threat, both to the moral acceptance and the artistic emancipation of jazz. Let us oppose it to the end.
>
> (British jazzman, Steve Race, in Rogers, 1982: 18)

Rock 'n' roll 'down under'

Although necessarily brief, this capsule view of the early history of rock 'n' roll is apposite, since the New Zealand experience I now turn to followed developments overseas, illustrating the rapid establishment of rock as an international phenomenon. This can be seen through New Zealand's response to the film *Rock Around the Clock* and the emergence of the antipodean folk devil, the 'bodgie' (the quotes here are from contemporary press reports). The local reaction in each case contained elements of a moral panic, with youth once again being constructed as posing a social problem.

As with their overseas counterparts, by the mid-1950s New Zealand youth were more visible and more affluent. Contemporary press advertising reflected increased awareness of youth as a distinctive market, particularly for clothes and records. Dances and concerts catering for youth increased and the nationally broadcast Lever Hit Parade began in November 1955.

In late 1956 *Rock Around the Clock* arrived in New Zealand and was approved for general exhibition by the film censor, who noted that 'a somewhat compulsive rhythm pervaded the film but otherwise there was nothing unusual about it'. Anticipation of similar scenes in New Zealand to the riots accompanying screenings of the film overseas were rarely met. Despite press headlines such as 'Larrikins Take Over After Film' and 'Rock 'n' Roll Addicts in Minor Disturbance', the crowds attending screenings were, in fact, generally restrained. Indeed, there was almost an air of disappointment. The police, prepared for trouble, were present at and following some screenings, but were rarely needed. In Auckland, the country's main centre:

> in spite of a few policemen standing by, and the expectancy that had booked the cinema out, the first night's showing passed off with nothing more rowdy than some adolescent hand-clapping, some whistling and stamping, a little squealing in the rain after the show, and one charge of obstruction.

This was in spite of the cinema's provocative publicity for the film, which included a foyer display of press cuttings of the riots produced by the film overseas!

For most observers, rock 'n' roll was at worst a safety valve and a passing craze: 'It does invite one to dance with hypnotic abandon and self-display, but to listen to it is more monotonous than boogie-woogie'! As occurred overseas, there was a tendency to see rock 'n' roll as:

> not a very attractive art form for those whose tastes have made any progress towards maturity. Prime requisites appear to be that the words – or sounds – should be meaningless and repetitive, while any semblance of melody is hastily and noisily murdered.

Generally, however, the press ignored the new phenomenon, while popular music on the radio remained largely confined to the numerous Maori show bands of the day, supplemented by a bit of jazz.

New Zealand's first real rock 'n' roll hero emerged in 1957: Johnny Devlin, an 18-year-old bank clerk. Devlin was a self-conscious Presley imitator, a natural singer and showman. His first record, 'Lawdy Miss Clawdy', became the most successful local single of the 1950s. Successful tours, including a hugely successful five-month national tour during 1958, saw sell-out houses, Devlin mobbed by screaming girls and several incidents of damage to theatres and injuries to the police protecting the singer. While the tour subsequently assumed almost mythic proportions in the history of rock 'n' roll in New Zealand, there was clearly an element of media promotional hype present. Devlin, for example, wore lightly stitched clothing to facilitate the incidents where the fans 'ripped the clothes from his back'.

If both *Rock Around the Clock* and Johnny Devlin's concerts failed to measure up as local moral panics, the bodgies represented New Zealand's very own folk devils of the 1950s. Bodgies and 'widgies', their female companions, were the local equivalent of the English teddy boys, adopting similar styles:

> The males wore unusual and exaggerated haircuts. All went to extremes in the style of suits worn. The trousers were all much tighter in the legs than usual. Some favoured extreme shortness of leg exposing garishly coloured socks. Coats, when worn, were fuller in cut and much longer than is normal by conservative standards, while all favoured brightly coloured shirts, pullovers or wind-breakers, and neckerchiefs.
>
> (Manning, 1958: 9)

Although Manning makes little reference to the leisure pursuits of the group, other sources indicate that as in Britain rock 'n' roll was the musical style the bodgies most strongly identified with: Buddy Holly, Gene Vincent and Eddie Cochrane joining earlier heroes like Haley.

Manning's was an openly hostile study; it is subtitled 'A Study in Psychological Abnormality'. The New Zealand public and press largely shared his view of bodgies as juvenile delinquents who posed a social threat. The bodgie soon became a national bogey man, with alarmist newspaper reports about bodgie behaviour. During 1958 one Wellington paper reported that 'the parade of brutality' by bodgies and widgies had reached such a peak that many parents were 'fearful of allowing their children out at night'. Gender inscribed these discourses: the hysteria provoked by Devlin was a predominantly female phenomenon, which received little serious criticism; the male bodgie was a different matter: 'When they are not feeling in too violent a mood they confine their activities to pushing people off footpaths. When looking for thrills, they fight among themselves, often with knives and bicycle chains' (press reports). Bodgies became identified with hooliganism or vandalism and parliament debated the problem. Young compulsory military trainees on leave harassed and beat up bodgies, forcibly taking over bodgie milk bars in central Auckland, while incoming trainees with bodgie haircuts were initially left unshorn, resulting in harassment.

The bodgie threat was clearly an exaggerated one. In conformist New Zealand of the late 1950s, bodgies and widgies stood out. The surprising fact was not that

New Zealand had young delinquents, 'but that they are relatively such a small group' (NZ *Listener*, editorial, 18 April 1958).

Rock, free speech and the New Right

During the mid-1980s a general trend towards censorship emerged in the US, headed by well-organized and well-financed pressure groups from the 'New Right', seeking to impose censorship on musicians, filmmakers and writers whose points of view they neither agreed with nor approved of. While the 'New Right' is a complex network of political, secular and religious organizations rather than a unified grouping, it exerted considerable influence through its letter writing and petition campaigns, its television and radio programmes and the publications of its ideological think-tanks. The various New Right groups recognized that shared public concerns with social issues can be successfully mobilized to achieve and maintain political support and solidarity.

Such conservative groups have historically targeted youth subcultures, most notably punk and rock music as a threat to traditional 'family' values (Martin and Seagrave, 1988: Chapter 21). The music is perceived as embodying a range of negative influences, which need to be regulated and controlled. It is claimed that rock is:

> the single most powerful tool with which Satan communicates his evil message. MURDER MUSIC has led millions of young people into alcoholism, abortion, crime, drug addiction, incest, prostitution, sadomasochism, satanic worshipping, sexual promiscuity, suicide and much more. MURDER MUSIC has to be STOPPED NOW! The moral fiber of our country and young lives are at stake!
>
> ('Rock deprogrammer', Pastor Fletcher Brothers,
> abridged from Denselow 1990: 264)

Initially the anti-rock campaign was spearheaded by fundamentalist Christian groups, aligned with powerful right-wing pressure groups sponsored by television evangelists, such as the Reverend Jerry Falwell. While pushing for stricter censorship legislation, such groups enjoyed more success through pressure on the music producers and distributors. Tele-evangelist Jimmy Swaggart, after equating rock with 'pornography and degenerative filth which denigrates all the values we hold sacred and is destructive to youth', met with company representatives of the Wal-Mart discount chain, whose 800 outlets subsequently stopped stocking rock and teen magazines and albums by a number of bands, including Ozzy Osbourne and Mötley Crüe, because of their alleged 'satanic' and 'pornographic' content (Kennedy, 1990: 135).

The PMRC

The New Right attack on rock and free speech was boosted by the formation, in 1985, of the Parents' Music Resource Center (PMRC). Headed by a group of

'Washington wives' – most were married to Senators or Congressmen – who were also 'born-again' Christians, the PMRC dedicated itself to 'cleaning up' rock music, which it saw as potentially harmful to young people, terming it 'secondary child abuse'. One of the founding members, Tipper Gore, became involved because she had bought her eight-year-old daughter a copy of Prince's album *Purple Rain* and found that one of its songs, 'Darling Nicki', referred to masturbation ('I met her in a hotel lobby, masturbating with a magazine').

The PMRC published a *Rock Music Report*, condemning what it claimed to be the five major themes in the music: rebellion, substance abuse, sexual promiscuity and perversion, violence-nihilism and the occult. It started a highly organized letter-writing campaign and began arguing for the implementation of a ratings system for records, similar to that used in the cinema. The PMRC also sent copies of lyrics of songs it saw as objectionable to programme directors at radio and television stations, to be screened for 'offensive material' and pressed record companies to reassess the contracts of artists who featured violence, substance abuse or explicit sexuality in their recorded work or concerts.

All these measures were aimed at encouraging self-censorship in the music industry and the group's tactics met with considerable success. The high point of its efforts was the 1985 US Senate Commerce Committee hearings on the influence of music (see Denselow, 1990: Chapter 10). No legislation came out of the hearings, but the Record Industry Association of America voluntarily responded by introducing a generic 'Parents' Advisory Explicit Lyrics' label to appear on albums deemed to warrant it, a practice that became widespread during the 1990s. The next major focus for the PMRC was the Dead Kennedys' obscenity trial during 1986–1987.

Penis Landscape

In December 1985 a 13-year-old girl bought a copy of the Dead Kennedys' album *Frankenchrist* (Alternative Tentacles, 1985) from a record shop in the San Fernando Valley in California. The record contained a poster entitled 'Penis Landscape' by Swiss surrealist artist H.R. Giger, best known for his Oscar-winning work on the sets of the film *Alien*. The work was a detail from a larger painting, *Landscape #20, Where Are We Coming From?* and depicted male appendages arranged in neat rows. Jello Biafra, the Dead Kennedys' lead singer, explained that he had included the print because: 'The painting portrayed to me a vortex of exploitation and I realized that the same theme ran through the album.' The band put an 'alternative' warning sticker on the album: 'WARNING: the fold-out to this album contains a work of art by H.R. Giger that some people may find shocking, repulsive or offensive. Life can sometimes be that way.' The girl's parents saw it differently and complained to the State Attorney General's Office that it was 'pornographic'. In April 1986 police raided Jello Biafra's home and the office of Alternative Tentacles Records, the label founded by the Dead Kennedys, looking for obscene material. None was found, but in June Biafra was eventually charged with distributing harmful material to minors and the case finally went to trial in August 1987.

The Dead Kennedys had been the subject of controversy and the target of New Right censorship before. Formed in San Francisco in 1978, the band played a form of punk thrash music with politically hard-edged lyrics. Their first single 'California Über Alles' was a satirical attack on State Governor Jerry Brown, and included lines like 'Your kids will meditate in school' and 'You will jog for the master race'. Later work included 'Holiday in Cambodia' about the horrors of the Pol Pot regime and the anti-alcohol warning 'Too Drunk To Fuck', which gained chart success despite its title and the subsequent lack of radio airplay. Shunned by the mainstream record companies, while their name alone practically ensured commercial failure in the US, the Dead Kennedys' records enjoyed considerable success in the European 'indie' charts. Albums including *Bedtime for Democracy* tackled political subjects such as Reagan's foreign policy and the US censorship lobby, satirized MTV and attacked American business involvement in South Africa. While the groups punk thrash backing and Biafra's breakneck lyrics often made the lyrics almost unintelligible, this was hardly work to endear the band to the establishment.

Jello's trial in Los Angeles in 1987 was seen as a major test case for the censorship of popular music. Support from Frank Zappa and Little Steven and a series of benefit shows from European punk bands helped raise the $70,000 needed for defence costs. Biafra defended himself and was articulate in his opposition to censorship and his support for free speech. He argued that there was a danger that the US was returning to the climate of the 1950s, when anti-communist witch hunts led to the banning of an earlier political songwriter, Pete Seeger. The case ran for two weeks. The jury deadlocked (seven to five) in Jello's favour, but could make no further progress and the judge finally declared a mistrial (Kennedy, 1990: 144).

Even if it were a victory for free speech, the case had finished the Dead Kennedys. Already having internal problems, with Biafra tied up in the litigation process and prevented from performing, the group broke up in December 1986. Biafra went on to a career as a 'political performance artist', doing monologue style presentations such as 'Ollie North for President' – the PMRC remained active and moved on to new targets.

Rap

In the early 1990s rap music became the main target of the 'anti-rock, pro-censorship' lobby. The new genre had already been attacked from the left for its sexism and homophobia and was now criticized for its profanity and obscenity. A judge in Florida declared the rap group 2 Live Crew's album *As Nasty as they Want to Be* to be obscene, the first such ruling for a recorded work in US history. Following this, a record store owner was arrested when he sold the album to an undercover police officer and three members of the band were arrested for performing material from the album at a concert with an 'adults' only' rating. The band members were eventually acquitted of the obscenity charge but the conviction of the store owner was upheld.

The anti-authority political attitudes and values in some rap music also attracted the attention of the New Right. The Los Angeles rap group Niggaz Wit Attitudes (NWA) song 'Fuck tha Police' and Ice-T's song 'Cop Killer' both caused considerable controversy and calls to ban their performers' concerts and records. In the UK, in October 1990, gangsta rappers NWA released a single with a B-side 'She Swallowed It', dealing with oral sex. Many of the major department store chains and some music retailers refused to stock the record, conscious of the lack of clarity surrounding the 1959 Obscene Publications Act and fearing prosecution. In June 1991 NWA released a second album, *Efil4zaggin* (Niggaz 4 Life, backwards) in the UK, after it had already topped the American *Billboard* chart and sold nearly one million copies in its first week of release. The album contained a number of tracks featuring sexual degradation and extreme violence toward women, along with considerable swearing. The police raided the premises of Polygram, the record's UK distributor, and seized some 12,000 copies of the album and shops withdrew the album from sale. A prosecution followed, using the Obscene Publications Act's definition of an 'obscene article' as one which 'tend(s) to deprave and corrupt'. The high-profile court case revolved around free speech arguments versus claims that the record was obscene, especially in its portrayal of women. The magistrates who judged the case ruled that the album was not obscene under the terms of the act; the seized stock was returned and the album went back on sale (see Cloonan, 1996, for a detailed treatment of this episode and the associated issues).

Cop Killer

Ice-T's 'Cop Killer' (WB, 1992) is a revenge fantasy of the disempowered, in which the singer recounts getting ready to 'dust some cops off'. The warning sticker on the tape cassette version of the album *Body Count*, which includes 'Cop Killer', hardly appeased critics of the record: 'Warning: This tape contains material that may be offensive to someone out there!' It was claimed that the song glorified the murder of police and both President Bush and Vice-President Dan Quayle sided with law-enforcement groups in protesting Time-Warner's release of the record. Several US national record store chains stopped selling *Body Count* and in July 1992 Time-Warner pulled the song at Ice-T's request after police groups picketed the media conglomerate's shareholders meeting in Beverley Hills. Anxious to avoid governmental regulation, in September, Warner Music Group executives met with several of the rappers on the label, including Ice-T, and warned them to change their lyrics on some songs or find another label for their work (*Los Angeles Times*, 10 December 1992). Time-Warner's Sire Records delayed the release of Ice-T's *Home Invasion* album; the performer eventually changed labels and the album was released on Rhyme Syndicate/ Virgin in 1993.

In New Zealand, in July 1992, the Police Commissioner unsuccessfully attempted to prevent an Ice-T concert in Auckland, arguing that 'Anyone who comes to this country preaching in obscene terms the killing of police, should not be welcome here.' Several record shop owners refused to stock the album containing the song. The local music industry, student radio stations and several leading music journalists responded by defending the song as a piece of 'role play', linking it with the singer's recent performance in the film *New Jack City* and the right to free speech. Undeterred, the police took *Body Count* and the song's publishers and distributors, Warners, to the Indecent Publications Tribunal, in an effort to get it banned under New Zealand's Indecent Publications Act. This was the first time in 20 years that a sound recording had come before this censorship body and the first ever case involving popular music (previous sound recording cases before the tribunal were 'readings' from erotic novels or memoirs!). As such, it created considerable interest, not least due to the appeal of rap among the country's Polynesian and Maori youth (see Chapter 11).

The case rehearsed familiar arguments around the influence of song lyrics. The police contended that:

> given the content of the songs, it is possible that people could be corrupted by hearing the sound recording, and in the case of the song 'Cop Killer' that some individuals may be exhorted to act with violence towards the Police. The course of conduct advocated in the song 'Cop Killer' is a direct threat to law enforcement personnel generally and causes grave concern to the police.
>
> (Mr H. Woods, Senior Legal Adviser for the New Zealand Police, cited in Indecent Publications Tribunal Decision No.100/92)

Defence submissions argued that the album offered a powerful treatment of the:

> sense of disenfranchisement and hopelessness that a large segment of American youth are faced with, and the violence that is bred in such an environment. It is a social commentary that we would like to believe is far removed from our society here in New Zealand. But whether this is so or not, the album has a validity and topicality as a reflection of the disenfranchised segment of our society.
>
> (Ms Karen Soich, Warner Brothers counsel, ibid.)

After reviewing the various submissions, and listening carefully to the album, the Tribunal concluded that 'the dominant effect of the album is complex'. While 'its lyrics are repugnant to most New Zealanders, it is a much bigger step to link those lyrics to subsequent anti-social behaviour' (ibid.). It found the song 'Cop Killer' to be 'not exhortatory', saw the album as displaying 'an honest purpose' and found *Body Count* not indecent.

These moral panics around popular music can be situated against the global emergence of a New Right, embracing free market politics and a moral cultural conservatism. Lawrence Grossberg observes of this trend in the US: 'The new conservatism is, in a certain sense, a matter of public language, of what can be said, of the limits of the allowable. This has made culture into a crucial terrain on which struggles over power, and the politics of the nation, are waged' (Grossberg, 1992: 162).

As he concludes, this struggle involves a new form of regulation: 'a variety of attacks become tokens of a broader attack, not so much on the freedom of expression as on the freedom of distribution and circulation' (ibid.: 163). The earlier debates were reprised through the 1990s, in the controversy surrounding the work of performers such as Eminem, Dr Dre and Marilyn Manson.

In such a climate, the music industry moved further toward self-regulation. In 2000 white rapper Eminem's US chart-topping album, *The Marshall Mathers LP*, was heavily criticized for its homophobic and misogynist lyrics. In what has become routine industry practice, the record label (Interscope/Universal) excised entire tracks to create an alternative album that parents can buy for their children, while extensively editing the lyrics in the remaining songs to eliminate references to drugs, violence, profanity and hate (*New York Times on the Web*, 1 August 2000).

Columbine and Marilyn Manson

The massacre at Columbine High School in Littleton, Colorado, on 29 April 1999, resulted in 15 deaths and 23 injuries, some severe. The two young men responsible were students at the school and killed themselves at the end of their bloody rampage. News coverage of the shootings was intense. Speculation about its causes referred to the negative influence of violent media on youth, especially video games, neo-Nazi ideology and rock music (see the special forum in *Popular Music and Society*, 23, 3, Fall 1999). When it was revealed that the two boys who killed their classmates were Marilyn Manson fans, the band cancelled its American tour. (Ironically, at the same time, the National Rifle Association went ahead with its national meeting in Denver.) For some commentators, Marilyn Manson became the 'designated demon' for the Columbine massacre. Manson responded with an articulate statement in *Rolling Stone* ('Columbine: Whose Fault is It?', 24 June 1999: 23–4), observing that such simplistic associations missed the deeper reasons for the tragedy, which lay in youth disenchantment and alienation.

The latest in a succession of entertainers whose career is based on confrontation and shock value, Marilyn Manson (formerly Brian Warner) was accustomed to controversy. He and his band members play under aliases combining a famous woman's name with the last name of a serial killer; in Warner's case the well-known star Marilyn Monroe and Sharon Tate's murderer Charles Manson. The self-appointed 'Antichrist Superstar' (the title of the band's second album), has been termed 'one of rock's biggest personalities and smartest social commentators' (*Q*, January 2000: 118). In songs such as 'The Dope Show' and 'Beautiful People', he examined the underbelly of American life and popular culture. Their highly theatrical act, reminiscent of that of Alice Cooper, was designed to shock audiences. Along with the songs, it gained the group a cult following in the mid-1990s, mainly among the goth subculture. During 1997–1998 *Antichrist Superstar* pushed them into the commercial mainstream, while Manson hit the headlines with his proclamations against organized religion. Their third album, *Mechanical Animals* (1998), topped the charts in a number of countries, but caused outrage when Manson appeared as a naked, sexless android on the cover and in the video for the single 'The Dope Show' (D. Dalton, 'Pleased to Meet You', *MOJO*, September 1999, provides an insightful analysis of Marilyn Manson's career and persona up until that time).

Controversy over particular musical styles, their performers and fans, continues to surface sporadically, with extreme metal providing the most recent example (Kahn-Harris, 2007: Chapter 2). The debates around their influence and the associated calls for the censorship of popular music and its performers are a reminder of the force of music as symbolic politics, operating in the cultural arena.

Further reading

State censorship of music, its performers and fans, is endemic in many non-western countries, but I have not had space to include this here; see:

Freemuse documents international instances of, and campaigns against, music censorship: www.freemuse.org

Cloonan, M. (1996) *Banned! Censorship of Popular Music in Britain: 1967–92*, Aldershot: Arena.

Cloonan, M. and Garofalo, R. (eds) (2003) *Policing Pop*, Philadelphia, PA: Temple University Press.

Denselow, R. (1990) *When The Music's Over: The Story of Political Pop*, London: Faber & Faber.

Garofalo, R. (ed.) (1992) *Rockin' the Boat: Mass Music and Mass Movements*, Boston, MA: South End Press.

Street, J. (2011) *Music and Politics*, Cambridge; Malden, MA: Polity Press.

14 'We Are the World'

State music policy

Policy in relation to popular music is formulated and implemented at the levels of the international community, the nation state, regions and local government. It includes the regulation and stimulation of aspects of the production and consumption of music. At an international level there are agreements on market access and copyright provisions. At the state level policies include the regulation/deregulation of broadcasting; the use of tax breaks and content quotas; support for local copyright regulation; and, as shown in the previous chapter censorship. The local level involves venue-related regulations and the policing of public space.

State attitudes and policies towards popular culture are a significant factor in determining the formulation of such policies and the construction of meaning in popular music. At the level of attitudes, state cultural policies are indicative of the various views held about the very concept of culture itself, debates over government economic intervention in the marketplace versus the operation of the 'free market', the operation of cultural imperialism and the role of the state in fostering national cultural identity. As the Task Force Report on *The Future of the Canadian Music Industry* (1996) put it:

> Most industrialized states believe that cultural products must not be treated as commodities. The cultural exemption contained in international trade agreements reflects a recognition that it is in their diversity that the richness of human cultures is to be found and that the distinctive characteristics of each culture should be preserved.

This chapter begins with a general discussion of the state and music and cultural imperialism, globalization and music. I then consider two examples of national policy in relation to local popular music: Canada and New Zealand.

The state and music

Until relatively recently, the state has often been ignored in analyses of popular music, although there is a tradition of work on cultural policy in relation to music at both the central and local state level. Studies of local policy include Kenney's history of the evolution of Chicago jazz, which details how a mix of council regulations, licensing law, moral watchdog organizations and police practices influenced the particular genre form taken by jazz in that city (Kenney, 1993). In a similar project, Chevigney (1991) shows how successive New York City councils applied a network of zoning, fire, building and licensing regulations to discipline the venues and styles of jazz within the city. Homan (2003) demonstrated the complex relationship between city zoning, licensing and noise regulations in Sydney and the venues for rock and dance and the styles of music associated with them. Homan (2010) used a similar approach to analyzing the debates around live music in Melbourne. These contextual factors are significant in shaping local music scenes and deserve greater attention, but I concentrate here on music policy at the national level.

State cultural policies have been largely based on the idealist tradition of culture as a realm separate from, and often in opposition to, that of material production and economic activity. This means that government intervention in its various forms – subsidy, licensing arrangements, protectionism through quotas and so on – is justified by the argument that has been clearly elaborated by Nicholas Garnham:

> that culture possesses inherent values, of life enhancement or whatever, which are fundamentally opposed to and in danger of damage by commercial forces; that the need for these values is universal, uncontaminated by questions of class, gender and ethnic origin; and that the market cannot satisfy this need.
>
> (1987: 24)

A key part of this view is the concept of the individual creative artist, with the associated cultural policy problem defined as 'one of finding audiences for their work rather than vice versa' (ibid.). This ideology has been used by elites in government, administration, intellectual institutions and broadcasting to justify and represent sectional interests as general interests, thereby functioning as a form of cultural hegemony. Seeing classical music, ballet and the theatre as high culture or 'the arts' legitimizes both their largely middle-class consumption and their receipt of state subsidy. Popular culture is then constructed in opposition to this, as commercial, inauthentic and so unworthy of significant government support. Such a dichotomized high–low culture view is unsustainable, yet it nonetheless remains a widely held and still powerful ideology. A comic example was provided by civil servant Sir Humphrey Appleby, giving advice to his ministerial 'boss' in the television comedy series *Yes Minister*:

> Subsidy is for Art. It is for Culture. It is not to be given to what the people want, it is for what the people don't want but ought to have. If they really want something they will pay for it themselves. The Government's duty is to subsidize education, enlightenment and spiritual uplift, not the vulgar pastimes of ordinary people.
>
> (episode: 'The Middle Class Rip Off', BBC Television)

In the case of popular music, government attitudes have generally, but not exclusively, tended to reflect a traditional conservative view of 'culture', a high culture tradition, which is used to justify non-intervention in the 'commercial' sphere. Yet this non-intervention exists in tension with frequent governmental concern to regulate a medium that, at times, has been associated with threats to the social order: moral panics over the activities of youth subcultures, the sexuality and sexism of rock and obscenity (see Chapter 13). There have been a number of cases in which the state has played a significant role in relation to popular music through economically and culturally motivated regulation and intervention. This has usually been to defend national cultural production against the inflow of foreign media products, using trade tariffs, industry incentives and suchlike.

The past two decades have seen increased governmental (state) interest internationally in the economic possibilities inherent in the social and economic value of the arts and creative industries and popular music has been a significant part of this discourse. State and local governments have increasingly recognized the economic and social potential of popular music. By the early 1990s, as Tony Bennett and his colleagues observed, this intervention was 'becoming increasingly explicit, increasingly programmatic and institutional ... the role of government has become a crucial factor in the structural organization of rock music at the local, the national and ultimately at the global level' (Bennett, *et al.*, 1993: 9). This 'turn to policy' in part reflected a concern at the dominance of international music repertoire, along with desire to gain a larger share in this market. Popular music scholars began to pay greater attention to music policy (for example Cloonan, 2007, on the UK); they have also become more directly involved in its development, although this has at times proved an awkward undertaking (see Williamson, Cloonan and Frith, 2011).

Cultural imperialism, globalization and music

The still common preference of listeners and record buyers for foreign-originated sounds, rather than the product of their local artists and labels, is associated with the cultural imperialism thesis. Cultural imperialism developed as a concept analogous to the historical, political and economic subjugation of the developing countries by the colonizing powers in the nineteenth century, with consequent deleterious effects for the societies of the colonized. This gave rise to global relations of dominance, subordination and dependency between the affluence and power of the advanced capitalist nations, most notably the US and western Europe, and the relatively powerless underdeveloped countries. This economic and political imperialism was seen to have a cultural aspect:

> the ways in which the transmission of certain products, fashions and styles from the dominant nations to the dependent markets leads to the creation of particular patterns of demand and consumption which are underpinned by and endorse the cultural values, ideals and practices of their dominant origin.

In this manner the local cultures of developing nations become dominated and in varying degrees invaded, displaced and challenged by foreign, often western, cultures.

(O'Sullivan, *et al.*, 1983: 62; see also Hesmondhalgh, 2007)

In terms of mass media and popular culture, evidence for the cultural imperialism thesis, as it became known, was provided by the predominantly one way in which international media flow, from a few international dominant sources of media production, notably the US, to media systems in other national cultural contexts. Not only did this involve the market penetration and dominance of Anglo-American popular culture, more importantly, it established certain forms as *the* accepted ones, scarcely recognizing that there were alternatives:

One major influence of American imported media lies in the styles and patterns which most other countries in the world have adopted and copied. This influence includes the very definition of what a newspaper, or a feature film, or a television set is.

(Tunstall, 1977: Introduction)

The cultural imperialism thesis gained general currency in debates through the 1970s and 1980s about the significance of imported popular culture. Such debates were evident not only in the Third World, but in 'developed' countries such as France, Canada, Australia and New Zealand, all subject to high market penetration by American popular culture. Adherents of the thesis tended to dichotomize local culture and its imported counterpart, regarding local culture as somehow more authentic, traditional and supportive of a conception (however vaguely expressed it may be) of a distinctive national cultural identity. Set against this identity, and threatening its continual existence and vitality, was the influx of large quantities of commercial media, mainly from the US. Upholders of the cultural imperialism view generally saw the solution to this situation as some combination of restrictions on media imports and the deliberate fostering of the local cultural industries, including music.

While the cultural imperialism thesis has generally been applied to film, television and publishing, it has rarely been examined in relation to popular music. At first sight, its application here appears warranted, given that the major record companies are the dominant institutions of the music industry and local pressings of imported repertoire take the major share of national music markets. But to what extent can this situation be seen in terms of cultural invasion and the subjugation of local cultural identity? Such figures present only the bare bones of the structure of the music industry and tell us little about the complex relationship of the majors to local record companies in marginalized national contexts such as Canada and New Zealand.

Although the existence of cultural imperialism became widely accepted at both a 'common-sense' level and in leftist academia, its validity at both a descriptive level and as an explanatory analytical concept came under increasing critical scrutiny in the 1980s. The validity of the local/authentic versus imported/ commercial dichotomy is difficult to sustain with reference to specific examples, while media effects are assumed in a too one-dimensional fashion, under-estimating the mediated nature of audience reception and use of media products. The globalization of western capitalism, particularly evident in its media con-glomerates, and the increasing international nature of western popular music bring these notions into question. Furthermore, the cultural imperialism thesis is predicated on accepting the 'national' as a given, with distinctive national musical identities its logical corollary, ignoring the range of cultural and musical identities present within particular national contexts.

It is worth bearing in mind here that Anglo-American popular culture has become established as the international preferred culture of the young since the 1950s, with American rock 'n' roll an instance of the use of foreign music by a generation as a means to distance themselves from a parental 'national culture' (Laing, 1986: 338). Local products cannot be straightforwardly equated with local national cultural identity and imported product is not necessarily to be equated with the alien. Indeed, local music is often qualitatively indistinct from its overseas counterpart, although this in itself is frequently a target for criticism. And while specific national case studies demonstrate the immense influence of the transna-tional music industry on musical production and distribution globally, they just as clearly indicate that the process is rather one in which local musicians are immersed in overlapping and frequently reciprocal contexts of production, with a cross-fertilization of local and international sounds. The global and the local cannot be considered binary categories, but exist in a complex interrelationship.

More recently, reflecting the internationalization of capital – a trend particu-larly evident in its media conglomerates – the term 'globalization' has replaced cultural imperialism, As an explanatory concept, however, globalization is often used too loosely and is open to similar criticisms to cultural imperialism. Although awkward linguistically, 'glocalization' emerged as a more useful concept, empha-sizing the complex and dynamic interrelationship of local music scenes and industries and the international marketplace.

As discussed in Chapter 1, the major problem faced by record companies is the uncertainty of the music market. In the traditional (pre-internet) music industry, at best only one in eight (to ten) of the artists A&R sign and record would achieve sufficient sales to recoup the original investment and start to earn money for the artists and generate a profit for the company. This situation led major record companies to look for acts that were already partially developed and which indicate commercial potential, especially in the international market (Hesmond-halgh, 2007; Negus, 1999). This was an approach with considerable implications for local artists operating primarily at a regional or national level. Attempts at the national level to foster local popular music production are primarily inter-ventions at the level of the distribution and reception of the music. They attempt to secure greater access to the market, particularly for local products in the face of overseas music, notably from the UK and the US. Such attempts, along with the issues surrounding cultural imperialism and globalization and the status of the local can be more fully addressed through two national examples: Canada and New Zealand.

Global music, national culture: Canada

I want to look at governmental intervention in relation to Canada's popular music industry, taking the story up to 2000, when the place of the local music industry was more secure. Policy since has been largely a case of maintaining existing provisions and dealing with issues of copyright in the digital age.

The history of the Canadian music industry has been shaped largely by its relationship to the international marketplace, especially its proximity to the dominant US market for popular music. During the 1980s and into the 1990s, the Canadian music industry was dominated by the local branches of the majors. Writing in 1988, Berland observed:

> The eight largest record companies in Canada are foreign-owned; 89 per cent of the revenues from the Canadian domestic market goes to multi-nationals. Their interest in Canadian music is restricted to those recordings which are marketed across the continent. This preference also shapes current government programs for subsidizing domestic recording. All other recording remains economically, spatially, and discursively marginal.
>
> (Berland, 1988)

Economies of scale applied to production meant that indigenous product was far more costly to produce and frequently had inferior production values compared with imports (largely) from the US. With record distribution also dominated by the majors, and commercial radio frequently tied to US programme formats and broadcast sound quality, the Canadian industry and musicians had only a small market share: in 1988 the independents received approximately 11 per cent of national revenues from record sales. One consequence of this situation was that only a small percentage of music recordings bought in Canada originated there, even when it was made by Canadian artists (e.g. Bryan Adams, Celine Dion). This economic situation sat uneasily with the historical Canadian concern to encourage nationhood and a cultural identity via communications technology, while at the same time resisting the intrusion of American media and messages, concerns that pushed the state to the forefront in media and cultural policy. The two core aspects of this policy are the 'CanCon' regulations, administered by the Canadian Radio and Telecommunications Commission (CRTC) and the Sound Recording Development Program (SRDP).

The CRTC and CanCon

The CRTC was established by parliament in 1968. The Broadcasting Act requires the CRTC to ensure that each 'broadcasting undertaking ... shall make maximum use, and in no case less than predominant use, of Canadian creative and other resources in the creation and presentation of programming' (unless the specialized nature of the service makes it impracticable). The CRTC has responsibility for establishing classes of broadcasting licences, the allocation of broadcast licences, making broadcasting regulations and the holding of public hearings in respect of such matters.

In pursuit of this goal, a Canadian Content quota on AM radio was introduced in 1971 and extended to FM radio in 1976. These quotas took into account particular station airplay formats and expected a reasonably even distribution of Canadian selections throughout the day and through the broadcast week. What constitutes 'Canadian' was established by the MAPLE test, in which at least two of the following requirements must be included in a recording:

a) **M** – music is composed by a Canadian
b) **A** – artist (principal performer) is a Canadian
c) **P** – performance/production is in Canada
d) **L** – lyrics are written by a Canadian

CanCon, as the local content requirements came to be known, proved controversial, but had an undeniably positive impact on the Canadian recording industry:

> That simple regulation was a watershed. It was the expression of a protectionist policy designed to allow Canadian musicians to be heard in their own country. The overall effect of the regulations has been the creation of an active, vigorous, self-supporting, and surprisingly creative industry – one that hardly existed prior to the regulations.
>
> (Flohel, 1990: 497)

It was generally agreed that, while the current group of Canadian international stars would have 'made it' anyway, their early careers received a significant impetus from the airplay guaranteed by CanCon. Further, and perhaps more importantly, the quota allowed a 'middle' group of perfomers to make an impact – and a living – within the Canadian industry:

> there's a whole lot of middle ground Canadian artists who are fabulous acts and CanCon has helped to ensure that they get the airplay that allows them to become the stars that they have become in Canada and, in many cases, nowhere else in the world.
>
> (Doug Pringle, director of programming at Rawlco
> Communications, responsible for a number of newer radio
> stations, cited in Melhuish, 1999: 73)

The Sound Recording Development Program (SRDP)

The SRDP was created in 1986 to provide support to Canadian-owned companies for the production of Canadian audio and video music and radio programmes and to support marketing, international touring and business development. This recognized that it was necessary to assist the industry to enable it to provide the local content required under the CRTC regulations. A 1991 evaluation of the SRDP found that it had had a very positive effect on the sound recording industry, but that its resources (funding was initially $5 million) were inadequate to significantly strengthen the independent sector of the industry and, in particular, that it provided too little support to marketing and distribution. This was confirmed by a later report, which regarded the scheme has now substantially underfunded: 'A major concern for both English and French language industries is the inadequacy of the resources available to support the marketing of recordings by Canadian artists' (Task Force, 1996).

The Task Force (1996) recommended that the resources of the Sound Recording Development Program should be increased immediately to $10 million annually and sustained at that level for a period of five years, but it was not until late 1999 that government policy began to address this and a comprehensive review of the programme began. In 1999, Brian Chater, President of CIRPA (the Canadian Independent Record Producers' Association) emphasized there remained a pressing need to get 'serious structural funding' in the local industry:

> The music business has become very much like the film business; you have to have a lot of bucks to play the game, and a lot of the time it won't work anyway. Now if you don't invest three or four hundred grand on each project, nobody thinks your serious. Do five of those and you've spent a couple of million dollars. The reality with project funding is that you're always scrambling from A to B trying to pay the bills with the project money. What we want to see indies have access to is structural funding, so that you can operate a company rather than do projects.
>
> (Melhuish, 1999: 79)

The Canadian music industry as a whole was considerably stronger by the mid-1990s. Recordings now generated substantial economic activity: retail sales in Canada totalled $1.3 billion in 1997, while the royalties paid to Canadian songwriters, composers and publishers (as public performance rights) totalled $49 million in 1997, up from $34 million in 1993 (DFSP, 1999). While this overall picture was impressive, the historical dichotomy remained: Canadian firms earned about 90 per cent of their revenue from selling Canadian-content recordings, while 88 per cent of the revenues of foreign-controlled firms came from selling recordings made from imported masters. Foreign firms had five times the revenue, 18 times the profit, 10 times the long-term assets and 16 times the contributed surplus and retained earnings of Canadian-controlled firms (Task Force, 1996).

It should also be acknowledged, however, that the majors were not simply parasitic here. Brian Robertson, President of CRIA, stressed the important investment in Canadian talent by the multinationals (majors), now around

$40 million a year in Canadian Content production. 'This has escalated tremendously in the last decade, and represents a huge investment per year in Canadian music and artists and their recordings' (author interview, July 1999).

Yet in the mid-1990s, while the general picture of a marginalized local sound recording industry remained valid, there were also evident contradictions (Straw, 1996). On the one hand, there was the increased international visibility and success of Canadian artists/music within the global sound recording industry, although these artists frequently record in the US, for US-based companies; e.g. Bryan Adams, Alanis Morissette, Shania Twain. On the other hand, there was also an increased share of the local market for music of Canadian content, with commercially significant sales for several locally based performers, including Bare Naked Ladies, Our Lady Peace, Blue Rodeo and Sarah McLachlan. In 1998, Our Lady Peace's CD *Clumsy* sold over 800,000 copies in Canada, along with well over half a million copies in the US; Bare Naked Ladies had a top ten *Billboard* single ('One Week') and their album *Stunt* reached sales of three million.

At the same time the popular music market had changed dramatically, with the splintering of 'mainstream rock', once the dominant genre, into a wide range of genre styles and performers, along with the willingness of the major record companies to market/exploit these. These trends created uncertainty about the future role and status of Canada's small, locally based firms, which have traditionally nurtured and been economically dependent on new musical styles. In other words, reflecting glocalization, the relative market positions and relationship of 'majors' and 'independents' in the Canadian market had changed. The growth of foreign markets has made artist development in Canada more globally oriented. The Canadian branches of the majors and Canadian-owned independent labels such as Nettwerk Productions, Attic Music Group, True North and Marquis Classics were increasingly looking to develop artists with international appeal.

In the midst of these shifts, positive government policy toward the local music industry appeared to be more necessary than ever, a view shared by the comprehensive and influential Task Force Report, on *The Future of the Canadian Music Industry* (Task Force, 1996). The Task Force was asked to develop proposals that would ensure that the industry could maintain its central role in promoting Canada's cultural identity by providing an increasing choice of Canadian music. Objectives set for the industry were to maintain its ability to compete in Canada and abroad; to be adequately compensated for use of its copyrighted material; and to benefit from new technologies. The Task Force concluded: 'While cultural objectives should provide the basis for music industry policy, measures that strengthen the creation, performance, production, distribution and marketing of Canadian music will also generate important economic benefits' (Task Force, 1996). In early 1999, after a series of public hearings and a review of radio policy by the CRTC, the Canadian content requirement was increased to 35 per cent. This change did not indicate a 'failure' of the previous requirement, but was recognition that the local industry was now in a strong enough position to provide sufficient acceptable recordings to meet such an increase.

The Canadian case raises crucial questions about the role of music as a form of discourse actively engaged in the uniting or fragmenting of a community. Government policy presupposes that listeners consciously identify – and identify with – specifically locally produced music. However, it is misleading to automatically assume that local musicians embody and support a Canadian cultural nationalism in their work: Canada is characterized by considerable cultural diversity, with strongly developed regional music scenes and idioms. The frequent negative reaction local product provokes is an important reminder of how what counts as popular music has been identified with a particular imported form, the result of the dominance of American radio formats, music videos and production values.

New Zealand

These questions of the relationship between popular music, local cultural identity and the global nature of the music industry are also present in New Zealand, a country with a small market for recorded music, a small share for local music within the major-dominated turnover of the local phonogram market and with a relatively unimportant role for local sounds within the international music market. Historically, New Zealand's local recording companies and their products have been largely marginalized by the dominant position of the international record companies (the majors) and the sheer quantity of 'imported' material – mainly New Zealand pressings of international repertoire. Given the economic and cultural significance of recorded music, this situation has been the focus of considerable public debate and government cultural policy.

Pre-2000

The 1989–1990 debate over a compulsory quota for NZ music on the radio traversed the arguments over the importance of supporting the local music industry, the constitution of the 'local' and the relationship between airplay and commercial success (see Shuker and Pickering, 1994). When a quota was not introduced, New Zealand On Air (NZOA) was established to administer the funds collected by the broadcasting fee, with a brief that included provision for subsidizing and supporting local music. After a low period in the late 1980s (in terms of overall chart success), local artists made strong chart showings both at home and internationally during 1991–1992, greatly assisted by the introduction of NZOA's music schemes. Flying Nun, the country's main independent label, saw continued sales growth, particularly in the US. During the next few years, despite NZOA's funding of videos and CD compilations of local artists, retail sales fluctuated and chart success failed to match the peak level achieved in 1992. This was followed in the mid-1990s by the international success of OMC ('How Bizzare'), Crowded House and Neil Finn and strong local showings by artists such as Bic Runga, Shihad, Che Fu and The Feelers.

Despite such occasional successes, in 2001, the vital signs of the local recording industry remained mixed. The local scene was still insufficient to support full-time professional performers, there was still only limited radio and television exposure for local artists and initiatives to support the industry remain limited. Several explanations were offered for this: a general lack of effort on the part of the majors to sign and develop New Zealand artists; the general lack of an industry infrastructure, especially in terms of management; and the limited opportunities for radio and television airplay, especially the absence of a local content quota (as existed in Canada). New Zealand artists who stayed 'at home' remained marginal to the international music industry, since the country lacked the population base to support a music industry on the scale of neighbouring Australia. The result is a tension between the support for the purely local and the need to go offshore to follow up national success. Shihad, arguably New Zealand's premier rock band, relocated in late 1998 to Los Angeles:

> We're not turning our back on New Zealand. A lot of people are coming to the realisation that as a climate for making music New Zealand is tremendously wealthy in terms of what we have available to us and what people can produce here, but the actual platform for getting music out into the market place is absolutely shit. We're crippled in comparison to places like Australia where they have local content quotas.
>
> (Tom Larkin, drummer, Shihad, *Rip It Up*, October 1998: 14)

There are a number of established NZ independent labels, along with local branches of the majors, which still dominate the global music industry. According to industry sources, the subsidiaries of the multinational record companies have traditionally supplied approximately 90 per cent of the domestic market. While any strict division between the majors and the 'indies' is difficult to maintain, with distribution deals tying the two sectors of the industry together, there are interesting questions about the dynamics of their relationship. This is particularly the case with the operation of the majors with respect to local product.

Logically, given the economies of scale involved, the majors concentrate more on promoting their overseas artists, with their local performers treated as a lower priority. The majors also in a sense feed off local labels, treating them in the same fashion as North American professional sports franchises use their 'farm teams' to foster talent and provide local back-up as necessary. But, as in Canada, this is as much a symbiotic relationship as it is a parasitic one. The independents need the distribution and marketing support the majors can provide, particularly in overseas markets, while NZ performers who outstrip the strictly local need the majors to move up a league. This was evident with the operation of the two main New Zealand independent record labels operating in the late 1980s, Flying Nun and Pagan, and continued to be the case.

Given the marginal status of New Zealand recording industry in the international arena and the difficulties facing local artists, the initiatives taken by New Zealand On Air (NZOA) to foster New Zealand music, in operation since

July 1991, were of crucial importance. NZOA's brief is not restricted to 'popular music', but in practice this is the case, with classical music having its own sources of funding and support. NZOA is charged with ensuring that 'New Zealanders have a diverse range of broadcasting services that would not otherwise be available on a commercial basis.' A key strategy in pursuit of this goal is 'To encourage broadcasters to maintain a sustained commitment to programmes reflecting New Zealand identity and culture.' Working towards achieving this includes 'funding programming on television and radio about New Zealand and New Zealand interests, including the broadcasting of New Zealand music' (NZOA: Statement of purpose and goals).

By 2000, NZOA's popular music programme had four main schemes related to radio and television, providing the basis for its support of local music:

- **Radio hits**, which provides incentives to record companies to produce records suitable for the commercial radio playlist; and lessens the financial risk inherent in recording and releasing singles, by enabling partial recovery of recording costs.
- **The hit disc**, which assisted record companies to get airplay for new releases and made sure that 'every programme director in every NZ radio station has access to a broadcast quality copy of new singles which have commercial radio airplay potential'. The first of these, and the most important, was the *Kiwi Hit Disc*, made up of 'new New Zealand music on release or about to be released by record companies'. The *Indie Hit Disc* and the *Iwi Hit Disc* were similar schemes with more of a niche market (Iwi targets Maori radio; indie the university stations).
- **Music video**, which funded NZ music videos through subsidising production costs of selected videos.
- **New Zealand music on radio**, which involved funding specialist radio programmes promoting NZ music, for commercial radio and student radio, aimed at the youth audience.

In each of the first three schemes, the criteria for support were similar or identical. First, 'It must be New Zealand music. The priority is original New Zealand music but we accept covers as well' (Guidelines for Music Video; Radio Hits; Kiwi Hit Disc). Second, there must be a confirmed record release: 'the video must back up the release of a single or EP in NZ either by an independent or a major label' (Music Video); and 'A record company – either a major or one of the independents – must be involved in releasing the record' (Radio Hits). Priority goes to projects distributed nationally usually via one of the major record companies. Third, a key consideration is broadcast potential: 'our priority is videos which are likely to generate repeat screenings on national network television' (Music Video); 'To qualify for funding, the record must attract significant airplay on commercial radio' (Radio Hits); and 'the record must be a realistic contender for significant airplay on commercial radio' (Kiwi Hit Disc) Seven radio stations are used as barometers and the schemes use programmers from TV shows and radio as consultants to identify broadcast potential.

A mix of cultural and commercial criteria were being applied here, with an emphasis on the latter. It is important to recognize that the schemes in themselves did not guarantee exposure through local television and radio. What they did was facilitate the production of local product, including an acceptable technical quality of these videos and recordings, and make it more available to local programmers. Recognizing this, in early 1998 NZOA began employing a 'song plugger', whose role was to push (promote) the forthcoming Hit Disc to key radio station programmers. This represented a dramatic departure for NZOA, but was a necessary move given that, despite six years of effort, there appeared to have been only limited improvement in the levels of New Zealand music getting airplay on commercial radio.

Fresh initiatives

The NZOA music schemes were in effect the alternative to a local content quota. Certainly, they contributed to a gradual improvement in the proportion of local content on radio, with NZOA close to its breakthrough goal of 'double digits' (New Zealand, 10 per cent of local airplay) in 2000. Yet, even with the more forceful presentation of the products of the schemes, it remained uncertain if this goal could be achieved, thus making a quota unnecessary.

It was becoming recognized in official circles, as well as in the music industry, that the continued development of the infrastructure of the New Zealand music industry was central to generating opportunities for local musicians and for providing a launching platform for access to the international market.

In mid-2000, Helen Clark, Prime Minister and Minister of Culture and the Arts, in a Labour government elected in late 1999, announced a governmental NZ$146 million arts-recovery package, with three goals: the arts were to be nurtured for their intrinsic worth; they should help build a uniquely New Zealand national identity; and arts and culture should 'contribute to the building of strong creative industries which provide rewarding employment, opportunities for creative entrepreneurs, and good economic returns'. As part of this package, in July 2000 the funding for the NZOA music schemes was virtually doubled, from NZ$2 million to $3.78 million a year, to enable the implementation of strategies to get increased airplay for local recordings. In 2001 a New Zealand Music Industry Commission was created, with initial funding of NZ$2 million (over five years), charged simply with 'growing the industry'.

The proportion of New Zealand music played on radio had remained small through the 1990s, varying between approximately five per cent on some commercial stations and 15 to 20 per cent on student radio. This situation improved quite dramatically in 2001, when a voluntary NZ Music Code was negotiated between the Radio Broadcasters Association and the Minister of Broadcasting, and began operating in 2002. (While not mandatory, the new targets were 'strongly encouraged' with the implicit threat of non-licence renewal.) At the same time, during 2002–2003 NZOA began increasingly using 'song pluggers' to promote its releases to radio playlist programmers. Boosted by the emergence of a few high-profile local acts and several performers' international success, these initiatives contributed to a marked increase in the proportion of New Zealand artists gaining local airplay, which reached some 15 per cent in 2002. In late 2002 *Billboard*, the main industry trade magazine, featured New Zealand in its high-profile 'Spotlight' section, noting that the strength of the local music scene had set the stage for an international breakthrough (J. Ferguson, 'New Zealand Acts Aim for Global Impact', *Billboard*, 30 November 2002: 37–45).

In July 2004 a government-sponsored report *Creating Heat* (Music Industry Development Group, 2004) set out a blueprint to encourage New Zealand's music industry to increase its overseas exchange earnings (from NZ$5 million in 2003–2004) to NZ$50 million per year by 2014. This was to be facilitated by a new export model, 'NZ Out There', that would connect musicians of all genres more directly into overseas networks, a process coordinated by a reorganized New Zealand Music Industry Commission, with increased funding.

These initiatives paid off. In 2003 Hayley Westenra, Bic Runga and Scribe had the three top-selling albums for that year in the charts, the first time three 'Kiwi' acts had taken all three top spots. Westenra also had considerable commercial success in the UK, while Runga consolidated her cult status there and rapper Scribe topped the Australian charts. Launched in 2004 C4 the nationwide, free-to-air music channel, strongly committed itself to New Zealand programming, achieving solid viewer ratings. During 2005 Fat Freddy's Drop's album *Based On A True Story* spent a record 10 weeks at no. 1 in the New Zealand album charts, selling 90,000 copies (by March 2006) and winning worldwide album of 2005 at the BBC's Radio 1 Giles Peterson awards. New Zealand music accounted for a record 20.8 per cent of music played on commercial radio, meeting the Code of Practice target of 20 per cent ahead of schedule (the aim was to achieve this level in 2006). Broadcasting Minister Steve Maharey hailed this as 'a fantastic result for the music industry; it demonstrates that New Zealanders want to tune into more of their own music'. Local bands Breaks Co-op and The Feelers had the top three airplay songs for the year.

Critics of the NZOA schemes, however, pointed to their reductionist assumption of a coherent 'New Zealand' national identity (Zuberi, 2008) and the emphasis on supporting mainstream commercial artists. Tony Mitchell (Kean and Mitchell, 2011: xx) has consistently argued that state intervention is not a significant factor behind the viability and vitality of local music. However, he simplistically equates government support with direct funding and even then only includes NZOA, ignoring the contribution of the Music Commission and the significant role of the radio airplay quota. In support of his view, Mitchell cites examples of bands such as Fat Freddy's Drop and So So Modern whom he considers to have achieved local success without support from NZOA. This conveniently overlooks the success of other performers supported by the schemes; for example, in 2006–2007, nine of the ten top-selling New Zealand artists had received some form of state support (Shuker, 2008). It is worth looking further at the sole exception: Fat Freddy's Drop.

The success of Fat Freddy's Drop is frequently held up by observers, including Mitchell, as an example of the triumph of New Zealand bands through adherence to a DIY indie philosophy. The band is part of the strong Wellington independent roots/dub/reggae scene, along with groups such as Trinity Roots, the Black Seeds and Fly My Pretties. After initially debuting at no. 1 in May 2005, a chart position it held for a record ten weeks, their album *Based On a True Story* was the most successful New Zealand release of 2006 and the band won four Tui (national) music awards that year. Fat Freddy's Drop also toured Europe during 2005 and won a prestigious BBC Radio 1 Award against strong international competition. All this, it was frequently observed, was 'achieved without help from a major record label. The band had turned down offers, preferring to keep control of the music and the business' (Diaz, 2005). Neither did the group draw on support from the New Zealand On Air music schemes.

I would argue, however, that while exemplifying the indie tradition, the level of success Fat Freddy's enjoyed can't be explained simply in terms of the quality of the music itself. The indies have historically produced a body of recordings representing some of the most stylistically distinctive New Zealand music, often including elements of Maori and Polynesian music. What has now been added is the greater commercial viability and visibility of this work, reflecting a more receptive local environment. As Toby Laing (the cornet player in Fat Freddy's Drop) observed in 2006, reflecting on the band's huge success: 'It seems like a cultural renaissance or something, because people in New Zealand are so proud of their culture. All the work that bands and stuff do is great but it is actually the people supporting it that makes a difference' (cited in Smith, L. 2006). Laing is presumably referring to the fans attending the concerts and buying the records, but I would extend his 'people' to the state institutions and those working in them who have altered the local playing field.

There was also a tendency in this debate to conflate questions of identity with that of governmental support for the local music industry. As in Canada, state music policy in New Zealand has been predicated on a conception of local music as an identifiable national category, to better brand governmental support for both industry and musicians. Critics have been quick to point to the essentialism of such a conception and its perceived failure to fully recognize the variety of local music in such national contexts (Johnson, 2010; Zuberi, 2007). However, from the perspective of those making and implementing state policy, it makes sense to mobilize the notion of 'New Zealand music' (or 'Canadian music') to justify their intervention in the marketplace in the 'national' interest of upholding local culture, creating employment and income. This is also important from a marketing point of view, as a 'branded' product is more easily presentable in what is a highly competitive music market.

New wine in old bottles

In 2010 NZOA commissioned a comprehensive review of its schemes 'to determine the best way to respond to changes to the music industry and broadcasting environment' (NZOA Media Release, 22 December 2010). NZOA also asked for wider feedback on the schemes, through an online public survey. The review was conducted by former EMI music head Chris Caddick, who interviewed 100 'music and broadcast professionals' and also assessed the 655 responses from the public survey. Caddick commended NZOA's achievements in increasing air-play of 'Kiwi music', which had continued to fill 20 per cent of radio airtime, noting that radio remained people's most common source for hearing New Zealand music. His review observed that:

> While industry or artist support is not a primary goal, the stability inherent in NZ On Air's music programme has nonetheless provided strong support for the New Zealand music industry. As a consequence an industry infrastructure has been strengthened and an ever-increasing pool of new artists aspires to create music and have it heard by their fellow countrymen.
>
> (Caddick, 2010: 4)

The review also recognized that misgivings and frustration with aspects of the NZOA schemes were 'reasonably widespread throughout the industry' (5). These concerns included the focus on support for commercial radio audiences, which critics saw as 'crowding out some more cutting-edge and potentially popular music', excessive assistance to some artists; and the scheme's lack of recognition to 'modern methods of interacting with music, specifically the use of the Internet and mobile devices in discovering, consuming and sharing music'.

NZOA quickly responded to the review, making a number of changes to the schemes (these were implemented from July 2011); these included:

- Making greater use of alternative delivery sites, such as student radio, online and digital platforms, to broaden funding opportunities.
- Weighting funding support more towards emerging artists (rather than established artists).
- Placing support for music from more established artist on a more business-like footing, for example, cost sharing and income participation.
- Focusing available funding on individual tracks (including music videos) and abolishing album funding.

In announcing the changes, Jane Wrightson, the chief executive of NZOA, confirmed that the organization's 'prime focus will remain on connecting songs with the widest possible audience'.

Conclusion

The transformation of the global circulation of cultural forms is creating new lines of influence and solidarity that are not bounded by geographically defined cultures and popular music is not exempt from such processes. Accordingly, we need to be conscious of the danger of too easily dichotomizing the local and the global, recognize the dynamism and intertextuality of at least the best of contemporary popular music and avoid adopting a narrowly defined cultural nationalist position. Nevertheless, there remain important economic arguments for the support of the local. The continued development of the infrastructure of the Canadian and New Zealand music industries is central to generating opportunities for local musicians and for providing a launching platform for access to the international market.

Debates over cultural policy and popular music embrace a volatile mix of the ideological and the economic. At the ideological level, there is the maintenance of an outmoded high–low culture dichotomy, which partly serves to legitimate the general neglect of the popular, including popular music. At the same time, however, the state is also concerned to respond to the significant level of community support for local culture and the perceived necessity of defending the local against the continued and increasing dominance of international popular media. This concern is mediated by the difficulty of establishing the uniqueness of national 'sounds', be they New Zealand or Canadian.

Further reading

Local policy

Chevigny, P. (1991) *Gigs: Jazz and the Cabaret Laws in New York City*, New York: Routledge.

Homan, S. (2003) *The Mayor's A Square: Live Music and Law and Order in Sydney*, Newtown, NSW: LCP.

Kenney, W. (1993) *Chicago Jazz: A Cultural History*, 1904–30, New York: Oxford University Press.

National policy

Caddick, C. (2010) *Review of New Zealand On Air's Domestic Music Promotion and Funding Schemes* at www.nzonair.govt.nz

Cloonan, M. (2007) *Popular Music and the State in the UK Culture, Trade or Industry?*, Aldershot; Burlington, VT: Ashgate.

DFSP (1999) 'The Canadian Recording Industry', presentation prepared by DFSP, Ottawa: Department of Canadian Heritage, 5 January.

Johnson, H. (ed.) (2010) *Many Voices: Music and National Identity in Aotearoa/New Zealand*, Newcastle upon Tyne: Cambridge Scholars Publishing.

Kean, G. and Mitchell, T. (eds) (2011) *Home, Land and Sea: Situating Music in Aotearoa New Zealand*, Auckland: Pearson.

Shuker, R. (2008) 'New Zealand Popular Music, Government Policy, and Cultural Identity', *Popular Music*, 27, 2: 271–87. I consider the question of the relationship between such policies and the nature of 'the local' through the case of New Zealand's recent garage rock bands and the Polynesian-based dub-reggae performers.

Street, J. (2012) *Music and Politics*. Cambridge, Malden, MA: Polity Press.
Task Force Report (1996) *Time for Action: Report of the Task Force on the Future of the Canadian Music Industry*, Ottawa: Department of Heritage.
Williamson, J., Cloonan, M. and Frith, S. (2011) 'Having an Impact? Academics, the Music Industries and the Problem of Knowledge', *International Journal of Cultural Policy*, 15, 5: 459–74.
Zuberi, N. (2007) 'Sound Like Us: Popular Music and Cultural Nationalism in Aotearoa/New Zealand', *Perfect Beat*, 8, 3: 3–18.

Websites

Canada's Independent Record Production Association (CIRPA): www.cirpa.ca
Canadian Culture Online (funding programmes): www.canadianheritage.gc.ca/progs
Canadian Recording Industry Association (CRIA): www.cria.ca
Music Industries Association of Canada (MIAC): www.miac.net
New Zealand Music Industry Commission: www.nzmusic.org.nz
Recording Industry Association of New Zealand (RIANZ): www.rianz.org.nz

Conclusion: 'Wrap it Up'
Popular music studies and cultural meaning

I begin here with some brief comments on the 'state of the field' of popular music studies, in order to give the reader who is new to it a better sense of its development and then situate this study in relation to it.

Development and state of the field

Although the earlier work of Adorno must be acknowledged, the academic study of popular music can be traced primarily to the 1950s and the work of sociologists such as David Riesman (see Chapter 10). Subsequently, with some notable exceptions, academic analysis of popular music and its associated culture was initially slow to develop. During the 1970s and 1980s even the increasingly popular subject of media studies tended to concentrate its attention on the visual media, particularly television, and neglected popular music.

Critical early moments in the emergence of popular music as a valid academic field were the establishment of the journals *Popular Music and Society* (1971) in the US and, in the UK, *Popular Music* (1981), followed in 1981 by IASPM, the International Association for the Study of Popular Music. A small number of institutional bases for the study of popular music were also set up, such as the Institute for Popular Music Studies at Liverpool University. However, most scholars teaching popular music remained in traditional disciplinary settings or associated with the new departments of media and cultural studies and this remains very much the case. It is a situation that makes popular music studies such a vital and interesting one to be working in, but at the same time renders the field's historical ambition toward an interdisciplinary project difficult to realize.

In the 1990s there was a marked increase in publications in popular music studies, including several significant university press series and a number of canonical works (Waksman, 2010). At the same time, there was a marked increase in the number of courses either directly focusing on popular music or on it as an aspect of popular culture within media and cultural studies. The new prominence of the field reflected the recognition of popular music as a global cultural phenomenon, associated with a multibillion dollar industry and a many faceted pop-youth culture reaching out into every aspect of style. Through the 2000s the related academic literature has continued to proliferate, with new journals, substantive new publisher's series, 'weighty' readers and encyclopedias. In addition, there is important 'vernacular scholarship': I use this term as I am not comfortable with the label 'non-academic', given that I see much 'journalistic' and 'fan' writing as of *at least* a comparable standard.

This literature has taken a number of forms and approached popular music from a range of perspectives. These include musicology, sociology, history, political economy, media and cultural studies, to mention only the most obvious. These in turn display an engagement with semiotics, psychoanalysis, feminism and social and cultural theory more generally. Indeed, as this list suggests, popular music studies is not a discipline, in the coherent sense that such a term implies, but is rather a field of study. An indication of the scope of the field is given in volume one of the *Continuum Encyclopedia of Popular Music* (Shepherd, *et al.*, 2003) which devotes 100 pages to 30 entries on various approaches to it. As Gary Burns, writing in 1997, observed:

> The perfect scholar of popular music would know all the relevant literature from popular music studies itself and also from all other [related?] disciplines. Furthermore, this perfect scholar would be an expert in music theory, literary criticism, the history of popular music, the entire social and cultural milieu that surrounded the creation of the music in question, and all manner of social and cultural theory.
>
> (cited in Anderson, 2006: 285)

This tongue-in-cheek observation is obviously an unattainable ambition, but it does illustrate the daunting scope of the field. At best, it is worth adopting Steve Waksman's argument that 'there are works that any popular music scholar should know, regardless of home discipline' (Waksman, 2010: 69); and I have identified a number of what I consider to be such canonical contributions throughout this study.

A sense of shifts in the past decade can be gained from Martin Clayton, Trevor Herbert and Richard Middleton, *The Cultural Study of Music: A Critical Introduction* (2012). For this new edition, the original essays have been revised and nine new chapters added. Comparing its scope with the earlier 2003 edition demonstrates the continuing expansion of popular music scholarship and the ways in which the field has developed since the book's initial publication. Richard Middleton observes in his introduction that 'the new topics we have selected will indicate our sense of the areas that have taken on a new and increased prominence in recent years'. He identifies three of these:

- 'the materiality of musical practice, explored in relation to technologies and locations of music, cultural apparatuses within which it circulates, and the embodiment of practitioners and listeners'
- 'a sense that the social embedding of music should be considered in broader terms than has often been the case in the past, to take in such parameters as race, religion, and emotional well-being'

- 'an increased recognition of (or return to) the importance of political economy, including Marxist models – although it is fair to add that, at the same time, there is a contrasting emphasis that pushes even further than in past work against all such totalizing analytical frameworks' (2010: 10).

I am sympathetic to the aspects Middleton identifies, which can also be considered a potential agenda for future work in the field.

Understanding popular music culture

The core question I have addressed in this introductory survey is: 'how is meaning produced within popular music culture?' Cultural interpretations and understandings are embedded in musical texts and performances: records, tapes, music videos, concerts, radio airplay, internet downloads, film soundtracks and so on. Such meanings are, in one sense, the creations of those engaged in making the music in these diverse forms, but they are also the result of how the consumers of these forms interact with the music. Further, music texts and performances are cultural commodities, produced largely by an international music industry ultimately concerned with maximizing profits. Meanings, or rather, particular sets of cultural understandings, are produced by a complex set of interactions between these factors. Accordingly, the question of meaning in popular music cannot be 'read off' purely at one level, be it that of the industry, the aesthetic creators, the musical texts or the audience. It can only be satisfactorily answered by considering the nature of the production context, including state cultural policy, the texts and their creators and the consumers of the music and their spatial location. Most importantly, it is necessary to consider the interrelationship of these factors. Of course, to facilitate discussion the very organization of this text has tended to perpetuate the notation that these are indeed discrete aspects, although I have tried to stress throughout the links between them.

It is not possible to badly state a model of the interrelationship between these aspects or to claim primacy for any one of them in every case of the process whereby meaning is determined in popular music. While I regard the influence of political economy and the significance of the production context, including its technological aspects, as of central importance, its role needs to be qualified. I would argue that the commodity form that music takes and the capitalist relations of mass industrial production under which most commercial music continues to be created significantly affect the availability of particular texts and the meanings that they embody. However, such determination is never absolute: meanings are mediated, the dominant meanings of texts subverted and 'alternatives' to 'mainstream', commercial music are always present, increasingly so within the new digital environment. Accordingly, popular music must be seen as a site of symbolic struggle in the cultural sphere.

To engage with these questions is not a straightforwardly objective 'academic' exercise. My own location in pop culture, as a 'post-war baby boomer', illustrates the point that our response to popular music and the various attempts to document and analyse it, is far from a purely intellectual one. Analysis and documentation cannot be divorced from the volatile and contested area of emotions and popular memory. My own emotional ties to the music and artists of the late 1960s, to subsequent styles and performers reminiscent of these, and to the notion of popular music as a politically significant cultural force, are clear in this account.

Further reading

Anderson, T. (2006) 'For the Record: Interdisciplinarity, Cultural Studies, and the Search for Method in Popular Music Studies', in M. White and J. Schwoch (eds), *Questions of Method in Cultural Studies*, Malden, MA; Oxford: Blackwell Publishing.

Tim Anderson discusses the question of method 'by interrogating and negotiating the recorded music object as an appropriate unit of analysis' (287), while also making some observations about the development of popular music studies as a field, especially in relation to sociology and cultural studies.

Middleton, R. (2012) 'Introduction', in M. Clayton, T. Herbert and R. Middleton, *The Cultural Study of Music: A Critical Introduction*, 2nd edn, New York, London: Routledge.

Waksman, S. (2010) 'Imagining an Interdisciplinary Canon', *Journal of Popular Music Studies*, 22, 1: 68–73.

Appendix 1

Chapter song titles

[Information in this list is based on US labels and release dates.]

Introduction 'What's Going On', Marvin Gaye, Tamla, 1967. Produced by Marvin Gaye; written by Al Cleveland, Marvin Gaye and Renaldo Benson.

1 'Every 1's a Winner', Hot Chocolate, Infinity, 1978. Produced by Mickie Most; written by Errol Brown.

2 'Pump Up the Volume', M/AJR/R/S, Fourth and Broadway, 1987. Produced by Martyn Young; written by Martyn and Steve Young.

3 'I'm Just a Singer (in a Rock 'n' Roll Band)', The Moody Blues, Threshold, 1973. Produced by Tony Clarke; written by Ray Thomas.

4 'So You Want To Be a Rock 'N' Roll Star', The Byrds, Columbia, 1967. Produced by Gary Usher; written by Roger McGuinn and Chris Hillman.

5 'Message Understood', Sandy Shaw, Pye, 1965. Produced by Eve Taylor, Chris Andrews and Sandy Shaw; written by Chris Andrews.

6 'It's Still Rock 'n' Roll to Me', Billy Joel, Sony, 1977. Producer uncredited; written by Billy Joel.

7 'Shop Around', The Miracles, Motown, 1960. Produced and written by Smokey Robinson and Berry Gordy.

8 'U Got the Look', Prince, Paisley Park, 1987. Produced and written by Prince.

9 'On the Cover of *The Rolling Stone*', Dr Hook and the Medicine Show, Columbia, 1972. Produced by Ben Affkine; written by Shel Silverstein.

10 'My Generation', the Who, Decca, 1966. Produced by Shel Talmy; written by Pete Townshend.

11 'Sound of our Town', The Del Fuegos, Slash, 1985. Produced by Mitchell Froom; written by Dan Zanes.

12 'Revolution', the Beatles. Produced by George Martin; written by John Lennon and Paul McCartney.

13 'Pushin' Too Hard', The Seeds, GNP Crescendo, 1966. Producer not credited; written by Sky Saxon.

14 'We Are the World', USA for Africa, Columbia, 1985. Produced by Quincy Jones; written by Michael Jackson and Lionel Richie.

Conclusion 'Wrap it Up', Sam and Dave, Stax, 1968. Written and produced by Isaac Hayes and David Porter.

Appendix 2
Musical analysis

The main sonic elements of music are rhythm (beat), melody, harmony and, in songs, the voice. Also relevant to popular music are the related elements of riffs, hooks and lyrics. These are considered briefly here in relation to their applicability in popular music. Fuller accounts of them, and other musical terms, can be found in the glossaries and accompanying discussions in Beard and Gloag (2005), Charlton (1994), Middleton, (1990; 2000), Moore (2001), Scott, (2009) and Tagg and Clarida (2003).

Rhythm is the beat patterns underlying most forms of communication, pulses of varying lengths of time. Rhythms are often recurring or repetitive (as in a heartbeat) and follow a consistent pattern. In music, rhythm patterns generally indicate the emotional feel of different types of song, e.g. slow connotes emotional. A rhythm section is the group of musical instruments that maintain the beat pattern and the harmonic flow of a piece of music; these usually include drums, bass and guitar/keyboards. The tempo is the pace of the beat. With popular music styles that include percussion, the rhythm is best followed by listening to the drums and counting the beat aloud. The backbeat is beats two and four of a four-beat pattern, the accenting of which creates rock's basic rhythm.

Melody is an organized set of notes consisting of different pitches (high or low sounds). The melody of a song is what we would be singing if we substituted the syllable 'la' for all the regular syllables. Melody is the variation in the lead singer's voice, without accompaniment. Various melodies are present in popular music forms: the main melody (sung by the lead singer); background melodies (sung by other group members or backup singers); and bass melodies.

Harmony is the simultaneous sounding of two or more different notes at the same time, e.g. guitar chords, blocks of notes on the piano and the sounds of a chorus. The easiest place to hear harmonies is in the background melodies. Harmony varies from simple to complex and often delineates one style from another. Harmony is important in popular music because it provides the texture of the total sound; it has been prominent in genres emphasizing vocals, such as a cappella and doo-wop.

Related to rhythm and harmony are riffs and hooks. The *hook* is the melodic or rhythmic pattern that is catchy and 'hooks' or attracts the listener to want to listen to the rest of the song and, more importantly, want to hear it repeated. Hooks are central to commercially oriented popular music (see Burns, 1997). A *riff* is a short melodic or rhythmic pattern repeated over and over while changes take place in the music along with it. This 'sonic repetition' is a feature of number of 'classic' popular music records, most notably in the Rolling Stones 'Satisfaction'.

Voice: 'Popular music is primarily a "voice music". The pleasures of singing, of hearing singers, is central to it' and 'there is a strong tendency for vocals to act as a unifying focus within the song' (Middleton, 1990: 261, 264). Discussions of the role of the voice within popular music have focused on the relationship between lyrics, melodic types and the singing styles characteristic of various genres and performers. Vocal timbre is part of this: tone quality as it relates to the characteristic differences among singing voices. A key concept is the 'grain' of the voice, very broadly, its feeling, as opposed to the direct meaning of lyrics and the way in which particular styles of voice convey certain sets of emotions, often irrespective of the words they are singing.

A number of authors have discussed how the voice is used in popular music, particularly with regard to rock. Three main aspects are evident. First, attempts to distinguish between 'black' and 'white' voices, which tend to see the 'black' voice as demonstrative and communicating through a variety of vocal techniques, and the 'white' voice as more restrained and restricted. A second distinction is between 'trained' and 'untrained' voices, with the former found in a range of older popular musical styles rather than more contemporary forms. The 'untrained' voice is important in signifying authenticity in rock vocals, indicating effort, naturalness and a lack of artifice. A third approach has been to associate specific genres with vocal styles, which are linked in turn to gender.

Moore argues that such distinctions are problematic because of their essentialist assumptions: 'they emphasise only one aspect of vocal production, and attempt to read meaning into the voice's presence on the basis of that single aspect', ignoring that a multitude of factors characterizes a vocal style (1993: 42). He suggests and elaborates four such factors: the register and range that any particular voice achieves; its degree of resonance; the singer's 'heard attitude' to pitch; and the singer's heard attitude to rhythm. Moore usefully illustrates these through a discussion of the vocal styles of Bill Haley, Little Richard, Fats Domino and Elvis Presley. As Frith (1996) observes, it is the way in which singers sing, rather than *what* they sing, that is central to their appeal to listeners. Compare, for instance, the vocal styles of Elvis Presley, Björk, Margot Timmins (the Cowboy Junkies), Johnny Rotten (Sex Pistols) and Mick Jagger.

In relation to these analytical concepts that musicology draws on, as composer Michael Hannan has pointed out (personal communication), there are a wide variety of technical terms used to describe the performance, composition and production of popular music, for example groove, feel, lick, loop power chord, middle eight and shuffle. In addition, there are 'effects' such as reverb, phasing, fuzz, compression, flanging, delay, sustain, wah-wah.

For most listeners, response to popular music is 'a gut thing', at the level of the affective rather than the intellectual. While fans do intellectualize about the music, their attempts to do so are very much in terms of their physical and emotional response to it. Here students can be encouraged to interrogate the process of their listening: the foot-tapping or finger drumming response to the beat; the singing along with the chorus of well-known songs; the air guitar; the abandonment of restraint through various modes of dance. Emotional associations, the links forged between people, places, moods and particular songs means the experience of the song becomes polymorphous. Neither should the importance of the listening context be forgotten here. One of the major problems of classroom analysis of popular music is that the relatively sterile environment and the anchoring of the physical body in place are far removed from the normal contexts in which the music is consumed – the pub, the club, the concert hall and the home.

Appendix 3

The album canon

Table A3.1 The album canon

1985–1999	Album	Musician(s)	Year
1	*Revolver*	The Beatles	1966
2	*Sgt. Pepper's Lonely Hearts …*	The Beatles	1967
3	*Nevermind*	Nirvana	1991
4	*The Beatles*	The Beatles	1968
5	*Pet Sounds*	The Beach Boys	1966
6	*Abbey Road*	The Beatles	1969
7	*Dark Side Of The Moon*	Pink Floyd	1973
8	*The Velvet Underground & Nico*	The Velvet Underground	1967
9	*Blonde on Blonde*	Bob Dylan	1966
10	*OK Computer*	Radiohead	1997
11	*Astral Weeks*	Van Morrison	1968
12	*Exile On Main St.*	Rolling Stones	1972
13	*What's Going On*	Marvin Gaye	1971
14	*Never Mind The Bollocks …*	The Sex Pistols	1977
15	*Highway 61 Revisited*	Bob Dylan	1965
16	*The Joshua Tree*	U2	1987
17	*The Bends*	Radiohead	1995
18	*The Stone Roses*	The Stone Roses	1989
19	*London Calling*	The Clash	1979
20	*Blood On The Tracks*	Bob Dylan	1975
21	*Are You Experienced?*	Jimi Hendrix Experience	1967
22	*The Queen Is Dead*	The Smiths	1986
23	*Automatic For The People*	R.E.M.	1992
24	*Rumours*	Fleetwood Mac	1977
25	*Achtung, Baby*	U2	1991
26	*Ten*	Pearl Jam	1992
27	*Born To Run*	Bruce Springsteen	1975
28	*Rubber Soul*	The Beatles	1965
29	*Let It Bleed*	Rolling Stones	1969
30	*(What's The Story) Morning Glory?*	Oasis	1995

Appendix 4
Discography

This discography lists selected albums for the range of popular music metagenres identified in Chapter 5, along with a section on avant garde, lo-fi and experimental music. In an era of the digital download, it could be argued that albums do not have the commercial and critical status they have historically enjoyed, but they remain the basis for the 'best of' and canonical lists in the music press and genre studies and the successful 33 1/3 book series. (I provide references to guides to singles at the end of the discography.)

A general discussion of these metagenres and some of their constituent subgenres can be found in Shuker (2012). While the genre placement of some artists here is frequently a matter of debate, with many musicians and fans anxious to avoid such labelling, the concept of genre remains central to the production, marketing and consumption of popular music. Obviously, my selections are subjective, although I have drawn on the numerous publications that provide lists of 'recommended listening', 'best of' and the like. I have indicated some of these sources in particular entries. The range of genres and artists included here reflects the extensive breadth of 'popular music'.

The work of many 1950s' to 1980s' artists is now available on CD compilations or as CD reissues, some with additional tracks. Many key vinyl albums are also now available on 180-gram vinyl.

Blues; R&B

For further guidance to blues recordings, see Bogdanov, V., Woodstra, C., Erlewine, S. (eds) (2003) *All Music Guide to the Blues*, 3rd edn, San Franciso: Backbeat Books. This is now regularly updated on the AMG website. See also Moore, A. (ed.) (2002) *The Cambridge Companion to Blues and Gospel*, Cambridge: Cambridge University Press; Weisman, D. (2005) *Blues: The Basics*, New York and London: Routledge.

Classic blues (1920s)

Bessie Smith, *The Complete Recordings, vols. 1 & 2*, Columbia/Legacy, 1991 (includes her first major success, 'Downhearted Blues', 1923).

Delta/country blues (1920s, 1930s)

Blind Lemon Jefferson, Milestone, 1974 (compilation).
Robert Johnson, *The Complete Recordings*, Columbia, 1990 (boxed set).
Charlie Patton, *Complete Recordings 1929–1934*, JSP, 2002 (boxed set).

R&B (1930s–1950s), including jump blues

Atlantic R&B 1947–1974, Atlantic, 1991.
Ruth Brown, *Rockin' in Rhythm: The Best of Ruth Brown*, Rhino, 1996.
The History of Rhythm and Blues, Part One: The Pre-War Years, 1925–42, Proper
    Records, 2008 (boxed set).
Louis Jordan, *The Best of Louis Jordan*, MCA, 1989.
Big Joe Turner, *Big Bad and Blue*, Rhino, 1994.

Chicago (electric) blues (1950s–)

The Blues, vols. 1–6, MCA 1986–89; originally released by Chess in the mid 1960s
    as a sampler of the labels extensive blues catalogue.
Paul Butterfield Blues Band, *East–West*, Elektra, 1966.
John Lee Hooker, *The Healer*, Chameleon, 1989.
B.B. King, *Live at the Regal*, MCA, 1971.
Muddy Waters, *His Best 1947 to 1955*, Chess, Legendary Masters Series, 1997.

Contemporary blues

Greg Allman, *Low Country Blues*, Universal, 2011.
Buddy Guy, *Living Proof*, Silvertone/Jive, 2010.
Keb' Mo', *Keep It Simple*, Sony, 2004.
Omar & the Howlers, *Essential Collection*, Yellow Eye, 2012.
Bonnie Raitt, *Slipstream*, Southbound, 2012.
Irma Thomas, *After The Rain*, Rounder, 2006.
The Derek Trucks Band, *Already Free*, Legacy, 2009.

Country

See also Erlewhine, M., Bogdanov, V., Woodstra, C. and Erlewhine, S. (eds)
    (2003) *All Music Guide to Country*, 2nd edn, San Franciso: Miller Freeman;
Escott, C. (2003) *The Story of Country Music*, London: BBC.

Traditional; 'old-time' country

Carter Family, *Can The Circle Be Unbroken*, Sony Music, 2000 (originally released
    1935).
O'Brother, Where Art Thou? Soundtrack, Mercury, 2000.

Jimmie Rodgers, *A Legendary Performer*, RCA, 1965 (now on CD).
Bob Willis and His Texas Playboys, *Anthology*, Rhino, 1991 (western swing).
Various Artists, *Stars of the Grand Ole Opry 1926–1974*, RCA, 1997.

Bluegrass

The Dillards, *Wheatshaw Suite*, double CD reissue of three albums, 1965, 1968 and 1970.
Best of Bill Monroe Monroe and His Blue Grass Boys, MCA, 1975.
Alison Krause + Union Station, *New Favorite*, Rounder, 2001.

1950s–1980s

Amazing Rhythm Aces, *Stacked Deck*, ABC, 1975.
Johnny Cash, *The Sun Years*, Rhino, 1991.
Rosanna Cash, *Retrospective 1979–1989*, CBS, 1989.
Merle Haggard, *Capitol Collectors Series*, Capitol, 1990.
Emmylou Harris, *Luxury Liner*, WB 1977.
Waylon Jennings, *Dreaming My Dream*, RCA, 1976.
Willie Nelson, *Shotgun Willie*, Atlantic, 1973.
Nitty Gritty Dirt Band, *Will The Circle Be Unbroken*, EMI, 1972.
Dolly Parton, *The Essential Dolly Parton*, RCA, 1995.
Hank Williams, *40 Greatest Hits*, Polydor, 1988.

Country rock

The Byrds, *Sweetheart of the Rodeo*, Columbia/Legacy, 1968. (CD: Edsel, 1997.)
Bob Dylan, *Nashville Skyline*, Columbia, 1969.
Gram Parsons, *GP/Grievous Angel*, Reprise, 1990 (rerelease, both albums one CD).
Q Magazine Special (2004) *Johnny Cash & The Story of Country Rock* (includes the '30 country rock albums you must own').

New country; 1990s' crossover

Garth Brooks, *No Fences*, Capitol/EMI, 1989.
Dixie Chicks, *Wide Open Spaces*, Monument, 1998.
Shania Twain, *Come On Over*, Mercury Records, 1998.

Alt. country; Americana

Ryan Adams, *Gold*, Lost Highway, 2001.
The Band, *The Band*, Capitol, 1970.
The Duke and the King, *Long Live The Duke and the King*, Loose/Silver Oak, 2010.
No Depression: What it Sounds Like. Vol.1, Dualtone, 2004 (compilation).
Justin Townes Earle, *Harken River Blues*, Bloodshot, 2010.

Whiskeytown, *Strangers Almanac*, Outpost Records, 1997.
Wilco, *Yankee Hotel Foxtrot*, Nonesuch, 2002.
Lucinda Williams, *Car Wheels on a Gravel Road*, Mercury, 1998.

Contemporary country (in order of release date)

Faith Hill, *There You'll Be*, Warner Brothers, 2001.
Toby Keith, *35 Biggest Hits*, Show Dog/Ume, 2008.
Taylor Swift, *Speak Now*, Big Machine, 2010.
Tom Russell, *Mesabi*, Southbound, 2011.
Steve Earle, *I'll Never Get Out of This World Alive*, New West, 2011.
Lady Antebellum, *Own The Night*, Capitol Nashville, 2012.

EDM: electronic dance music

See also Woodstra, C. and Bogdanov, V. (eds) (2001) *All Music Guide to Electronica: The Definitive Guide to Electronic Music*, San Franciso: Backbeat Books; and the discography in Reynolds, S. (1998) *Generation Ecstasy: Into the World of Techno and Rave Culture*, Boston, MA: Little, Brown & Company.

The following is a brief selection of more influential pre-2000 releases, from what is now a huge range of subgenres. In the past decade, EDM has become part of a wide range of 'mainstream' and indie music.

Drum 'n' bass

Breakbeat Science vol. 1, Volume/Vital, 1996.
Goldie, *Timeless*, FFRR, 1995.
Roni Size, Reprazent, *New Forms*, Talkin Loud, 1998.

Techno

Kraftwerk, *Trans-Europe Express*, Kling Klang, 1997; first released in 1977.
Leftfield, *Leftism*, Hard Hands/Columbia, 1995.
The Shamen, *Boss Drum*, Epic, 1992.
Various Artists, *Techno! The New Dance Sound of Detroit*, 10 records, 1988 (includes
   Rhythim is Rhythim (Derrick May), 'Strings of Life').

Trip-hop

Massive Attack, *Blue Lines*, Virgin, 1991.

Folk

See also the discography in Cohen, R. (2006) *Folk Music. The Basics*, London: Routledge. (This is limited to compilation folk music albums that have been reissued in CD format.)

Traditional

Woody Guthrie, *The Legendary Performer*, 2000 (CD compilation; Guthrie recorded primarily in the late 1930s and 1940s).
Harry Smith, *Anthology of American Folk Music*, Folkways, 1952; reissued as a six-CD boxed set in 1997.

1960s–1970s' folk revival (US; UK)

Joan Baez, *Joan Baez*, Vanguard, 1960.
Nick Drake, *Bryter Layter*, Island, 1970.
Bob Dylan, self-titled debut, Columbia, 1962.
The Incredible String Band, *The Hangman's Beautiful Daughter*, Elektra, 1968.
John Martyn, *Solid Air*, Island, 1973.
Tom Rush, *The Circle Game*, Elektra, 1968.

Folk rock

See also the extensive discography in Unterberger, R. (2002) *Turn! Turn! Turn! The 60s Folk-rock Revolution*, San Franciso: Backbeat Books.
The Byrds, *Mr Tambourine Man*, CBS, 1965.
Bob Dylan, *Highway 61 Revisited*, 1965 (includes 'Like a Rolling Stone').
Fairport Convention, *Liege and Leaf*, Island, 1969.
Steeleye Span, *Please to See The King*, Chrysalis, 1971.
Richard and Linda Thompson, *I Want To See the Bright Lights Tonight*, Island, 2004 (CD reissue).

Contemporary folk

Devendra Banhart, *Cripple Crow*, XL Recordings, 2005.
Grizzly Bear, *Yellow House*, Warp, 2006.
Monsters of Folk, *Monsters of Folk*, Shangri-La, 2009.
Mumford and Sons, *Sigh No More*, Island, 2009.
Joan Tabor, *Ashore*, Southband, 2011.

Heavy metal

See also Berelian, E. (2005) *The Rough Guide to Heavy Metal*, London: Rough Trade Publications; Christe, I. (2004) *Sound of the Beast: the Complete Headbanging History of Heavy Metal*, New York: Harper Entertainment.

Classic (early metal)

There are arguments regarding the inclusion of bands such as Led Zeppelin here; see Chapter 6.

Black Sabbath, *Black Sabbath*, Vertigo, 1970.
Black Sabbath, *Paranoid*, Vertigo, 1970.
Deep Purple, *Deep Purple in Rock*, Harvest, 1970.
Uriah Heap, *Very 'eavy, Very 'umble*, 1970.
Led Zeppelin, *Led Zeppelin*, Atlantic, 1969.

NWOBHM (new wave of British heavy metal) (1980s)

Iron Maiden, *The Number of the Beast*, EMI, 1982.
Motorhead, *No Sleep 'Til Hammersmith*, Castle Communications, 1981 (live).
Judas Priest, *British Steel*, CBS, 1980.
Saxon, *Wheels of Steel/Strong Arm of the Law*, EMI, 1997 (double CD rerelease, originally issued in 1980).

Glam metal

The Best of Sweet, Capitol, 1993.
David Bowie, *The Rise and Fall of Ziggy Stardust*, Rykodisc, 1972.
Kiss, *Double Platinum (Greatest Hits)*, Casablanca, 1978.
New York Dolls, *Rock & Roll*, Mercury, 1994 (contains their 1973 and 1974 albums).
T Rex, *Electric Warrior*, Reprise, 1972.

Speed/thrash metal

Anthrax, *Spread The Disease*, Island, 1985.
Megadeth, *Killing is My Business ... and Business is Good*, Combat, 1985.
Metallica, *And Justice for All*, Elektra, 1988.
Slayer, *Reign in Blood*, Def Jam, 1986.

Nu-metal; rap metal

Faith No More, *The Real Thing*, London, 1989.
Korn, *Korn*, Immortal/Epic, 1994.
Limp Bizkit, *Significant Other*, Interscope, 1997.
Linkin Park, *Meteora*, Warners, 2003.
Slipknot, *Iowa*, Roadrunner, 2001.

Extreme metal

See also the discography in Harris, K. (2007), *Extreme Metal*, Oxford and New York: Berg.
Cannibal Corpse, *The Bleeding*, Metal Blade, 1994.
Carcass, *Symphonies of Sickness*, Earache, 1989.
Venom, *Black Metal*, Neat, 1982.

Contemporary metal

Bullet for My Valentine, *Fever*, Sony, 2010.
Godsmacked, *Faceless*, Universal, 2003.
Mastodon, *Leviathian*, Relapse, 2004.
Metallica, *Death Magnetic*, Warner Bros; Vertigo, 2008.
Nightwish, *Dark Passion Play*, Nuclear Blast/Roadrunner, 2007.
Wolfmother, *Wolfmother*, Modular, 2005.

Jazz

See Carr, I., Fairweather, D. and Priestly, B. (2000) *Jazz The Rough Guide*, 2nd
    edn, London: Rough Guides Ltd. As the subtitle states, this near 900-page
    encyclopedia is 'the essential companion to artists and albums'; for more recent
    releases: *Downbeat*, January 2010, *Special Collector's Edition: Best CDs of the 2000s*.
Given its huge scope, I am including only a few jazz recordings here.
Ken Burns Jazz: The Story of America's Music, (5 CD boxed set; a 20-track sampler is
    also available: *The Best of Ken Burns Jazz*), Columbia/Legacy and Verve Music
    Group joint release.
The following had a wider influence on 'mainstream' popular music in the 1960s
    and 1970s, especially rock.
Ornette Coleman, *The Shape of Jazz to Come*, Atlantic, 1959.
John Coltrane, *A Love Supreme*, Impulse, 1964.
Miles Davis, *Kind of Blue*, Columbia/Legacy, 1959.

Jazz rock fusion

Jeff Beck, *Blow By Blow*, Epic, 1975.
Miles Davis, *Bitches* Brew, Sony, 1969.
Blood, Sweat and Tears, *Greatest Hits*, CBS, 1976 (includes 'Spinning Wheel').
The Soft Machine, *Volumes 1 & 2*, Big Beat.
Weather Report, *Mysterious Traveller*, Columbia, 1974.

Pop; dance pop; disco

The term pop has been used to characterize chart and teenage audience-oriented
music, including bubblegum, dance pop, disco, power pop, new romantics/
synthpop and performers such as teen idols, the girl groups of the 1960s, their
1990s' equivalents and the ubiquitous boy bands of the modern era.

Bubblegum

Tommy James and the Shondells, *Anthology*, Rhino, 1980.
The Ultimate Bubblegum Pop Collection, Rajon, 2005 (double CD).
Very Best of the Ohio Express, Buddah, 1970.

Disco

Abba, *Abba Gold: Greatest Hits*, Polydor, 1992.
KC and the Sunshine Band, *Greatest Hits*, Rhino, 1990.
Saturday Night Fever, Original Sound Track, Polygram, 1977.
Donna Summer, *Endless Summer: Donna Summer's Greatest Hits*, Polygram, 1994.

Girl groups; girl group sound

The Best of the Crystals, ABKCO, 1992.
The Best of the Ronnettes, ABKCO, 1992.
Phil Spector, *Back to Mono (1958–1969)*, ABKO, 1991.
The Supremes, *Anthology*, Motown, 1974.

New romantics; synthpop

Adam and the Ants, *Kings of the Wild Frontier*, Epic, 1980.
At Worst … The Best of Boy George and Culture Club, Virgin, 1993.
Duran Duran, *Notorious*, Capitol, 1986.
The Human League, *Dare*, Virgin; A&M, 1981.
Ultravox, *Vienna*, Chrysalis, 1980.

Power pop

Big Star, *#1 Record/Radio City*, Stax, 1992; originally released on Ardent, 1972,
   1974.
Cheap Trick, *In Colour*, Epic, 1977
The Raspberries, *Raspberries Best*, Capitol, 1975.
Slade, *Best of Slade*, Polydor, 2000 (CD compilation).

Dance pop; teen pop (1960s–1990s)

Madonna, *The Immaculate Collection*, Sire, 1990.
Kylie Minogue, *Greatest Hits*, PWL/Mushroom, 1992.
New Kids On the Block, *Hangin' Tough*, Columbia, 1988.
The Osmonds, *Osmonds*, MGM, 1970.
The Spice Girls, *Spice*, Virgin, 1996.
Take That, *Everything Changes*, BMG, 1993.
Tiffany, *Tiffany*, MCA, 1987.
Bobby Vee, Legendary Masters Series, EMI, 1990.
The Very Best of Connie Francis, Polydor, 1963.

Post-2000 'pop' (in order of release date)

Norah Jones, *Come Away With Me*, Blue Note, 2002.
Christine Aguilera, *Stripped*, RCA, 2002.
Justin Timberlake, *Justified*, JIVE, 2002.

Scissor Sisters, *Scissor Sisters*, Polydor, 2004.
Girls Aloud, *Chemistry*, Polydor, 2005.
Gwen Steffani, *Love. Angel. Music. Baby*, Interscope, 2005.
Lady Gaga, *The Fame*, Interscope Records, 2008.
Justin Bieber, *My World 2.0*, Island, 2010.
Britney Spears, *The Singles Collection*, Jive, 2010.
One Direction, *Up All Night*, Syco, Columbia, 2011.
Goldfrapp, *The Singles*, EMI, 2012.

Hip hop; rap

See also Shapiro, P. (2004) *The Rough Guide to Hip-Hop*, 2nd edn, London: Rough
   Guides Ltd.

1980s–

Africa Bambatta and the Soulsonic Force, *Planet Rock*, Tommy Boy, 1986.
Body Count, with Ice-T, *Body Count*, Sire/Warners, 1992.
De La Soul, *Three Feet High and Rising*, Tommy Boy, 1989.
Dr Dre, *The Chronic*, Death Row, 1992.
L L Cool J, *Radio*, Def Jam, 1985.
Grandmaster Flash, *The Message*, Sugar Hill Records, 1982.
NWA, *Straight Outta Compton*, Priority, 1988 (includes 'F – Tha Police').
Public Enemy, *It Takes A Nation of Millions to Hold Us Back*, Def Jam, 1988.
Run-D.M.C, *Raising Hell*, Arista, 1986.
2 Live Crew, *As Nasty as they Wanna to Be*, Luke/Atlantic Records, 1989.

Hip-hop; rap (post-1996) (in order of release date)

The Fugees, *The Score*, Sony/Columbia, 1996.
Lauren Hill, *The Miseducation of Lauren Hill*, Ruff House/Columbia, 1998.
Destiny's Child, *Survivor*, Sony, 2000.
Eminem, *The Eminem Show*, Interscope, 2002.
Outkast, *Speaker Box/The Love Below*, LA Face/Arista, 2003.
Beyonce, *Dangerously in Love*, Sony, 2003.
Kanye West, *Late Registration*, Roc-A-Fella/Def Jam, 2005.
Gnarls Barkley, *St. Elsewhere*, Downtown, Atlantic, 2006.
Jay Z, *American Gangsta*, Roc-A-Fella, Def Jam, 2007.

Reggae; ska; two tone; dub

See also Barrow, S. and Dalton, P. (2001) *Reggae: The Rough Guide*, 2nd edn,
   London: Rough Guides Ltd.
The Harder They Come Soundtrack, Mango/Island, 1972.
Burning Spear, *Jah is Real*, Burning Music, 2008.

Bob Marley and the Wailers, *Legend*, Island, 1984 (a 'greatest hits').
Stephen Marley, *Mind Control*, Universal, Tough Gong, 2007.
Toots and the Maytals, *Funky Kingston*, Island, 1973.
Peter Tosh, *Equal Rights*, Columbia, 1977.
Tougher than Tough: The Story of Jamaican Music (four-CD boxed set; researched and compiled by Steve Barrow), Island Records, 1993.

Dub

Glen Brown and King Tubby, *Termination Dub 1973–1979*, Blood & Fire/Chant, 1996.
Joe Gibbs and Errol Thompson, *African Dub All-Mighty*, Lightning, 1975 (first in a series of compilations).
Lee Perry, *The Producer Series/Words of My Mouth*, Trojan, 1996 (compiles Perry's 1970s' work).
Various artists, *Dancehall: The Rise of Jamaican Dancehall Culture*, Soul Jazz, 2008. (double CD).
Various Artists, *5: Five Years of Hyperdub*, Hyperdub/Southbound, 2009.

Two tone

The English Beat, *I Just Can't Stop It*, IRS, 1980.
Madness, *Complete Madness*, Stiff, 1982.
The Specials, 'Ghost Town' (1981 UK no.1) (on the album *The Specials. The Singles Collection*), Chrysalis, 1991.

Rock

Most general histories of rock include extensive discographies; see also Strong, M. (2006) *The Essential Rock Discography*, Edinburgh: Canongate. This lists every track recorded by more than 1200 artists. Discographies of performers and genres of rock are a feature of the collecting press, especially the magazine *Record Collector* (UK).

Rockabilly

The Blasters, *The Blasters Collection*, Slash/WB, 1990.
The Legendary Story of Sun Records, Union Square Records, 2002 (two CDs).
Jerry Lee Lewis, *Anthology: All Killer No Filler*, Rhino, 1993.
Elvis Presley, *The Complete Sun Sessions*, RCA, 1987.
Rock This Town: Rockabilly Hits, Volumes 1 & 2, Rhino, 1991.

Rock 'n' roll (1950s)

We're Gonna Rock, We're Gonna Roll, Proper Records, London, 2005. A four-CD boxed set, tracing the origins of rock 'n' roll and its emergence in the 1950s; includes a 68-page booklet on the 118 recordings and their performers.

Chuck Berry, *The Great Twenty-Eight*, Chess, 1994.
Bill Haley and the Comets, *Shake, Rattle & Roll*, Decca, 1955.
Little Richard His Biggest Hits, 1959, Speciality, 1991.
My Blue Heaven: Best of Fats Domino, EMI, 1990.
Elvis Presley, *Elvis Golden Records*, RCA, 1984.
Various Artists, *18 Original Sun Greatest Hits*, Rhino, 1984.

Doo-wop (1945 – peaked in the late 1950s; bridged R&B and soul)

The Best of Doo Wop Up Tempo, Rhino, 1989.
Boys 2 Men, *Cooleyhighharmony*, Motown, 1991.
The Drifters Golden Hits, Atlantic, 1968.
The Four Seasons, *Anthology*, Rhino, 1988.

British beat; British R&B Mersey beat (early–mid 1960s)

The Animals, *The Best of The Animals*, MGM, 1966 (reissued on CD by ABCO).
The Beatles, *Live at the BBC* (1962–65), Apple/Capitol, 1994.
The Rolling Stones, *The Rolling Stones*, Decca, 1964.
The Searchers, *The Most of the Searchers*, EMI, 1994 (CD).
The Yardbirds, *Five Live Yardbirds*, Columbia, 1964.

Surf music; surf rock

The Beach Boys, *Best of*, Capitol/EMI, USA, 2005 (CD compilation).
Cowabunga: The Surf Box, Rhino Records/WEA, 1966 (four-CD boxed set).
Dick Dale & His Del-Tones, *King of The Surf Guitar*, Rhino, 1989.
Jan and Dean, *Surf City*, BGO Records, 2004.
Jack Johnson, *In Between Dreams*, Universal, 2005.
The Surfaris, *Wipe Out! The Best of the Surfaris*, Varese Sarabande, 1994.

Classic rock (1960s–1970s)

In addition to the albums listed here, see Thompson, D. (2008) *I Hate New Music. The Classic Rock Manifesto*, New York: Backbeat Books. Appendix: 'The Top 100 Classic Rock Songs, 1968–76'.
The Beatles, *Sgt. Pepper's Lonely Heart's Club Band*, Parlophone, 1967.
Creedence Clearwater Revival, *Creedence Gold*, Fantasy, 1972.
The Doors, *The Doors*, Elektra, 1967.
Fleetwood Mac, *Rumours*, Reprise, 1977.
Jimi Hendrix, *Are You Experienced?*, Track, 1967.
The Kinks, *Kinda Kinks*, Pye, 1965.
The Rolling Stones, *Exile on Main Street*, Virgin, 1972.
The Who, *Who's Next*, MCA, 1971.

Garage rock

The Best of The Chocolate Watch Band, Rhino, 1983.
Nuggets Volume One: The Hits, Rhino, 1984.
The Strokes, *Is This It*, RCA, 2001.
The Vines, *Highly Evolved*, Capitol Records, 2002.
The White Stripes, *Elephant*, XL Records, 2003.

Hard/heavy rock

Bad Company, *10 From 6*, Atlantic, 1986.
Deep Purple, *Smoke on the Water. The Best of Deep Purple*, EMI, 1994.
Guns 'N' Roses, *Appetite for Destruction*, Geffin, 1987.
The Who, *Live at Leeds*, MCA, 1970 (CD 1995).

Gothic rock

Bauhaus, *In the Flat Fields*, 4AD, 1980 (includes 'Bela Lugosi's Dead',
    single (1979)).
Evanescence, *Fallen*, Wind Up, 2003.
Joy Division,*Unknown Pleasures*, Factory/Virgin, 1980.
A Life Less Lived: The Gothic Box, Rhino Records, 2006 (three CDs plus a DVD).
Siouxsie and the Banshees, *Once Upon a Time: The Singles*, Geffin, 1984.
The Sisters of Mercy, *God's Own Medicine*, Elektra, 1987.

Grunge (early 1990s)

Babes in Toyland, *Fontanelle*, Reprise, 1992.
Hole, *Live Through This*, DGC, 1994.
Nirvana, *Nevermind*, Geffen (US no. 1 album) 1991).
Pearl Jam, *Ten*, Epic, 1991.
Soundgarden, *Superunknown*, A&M, 1994.

Alternative/indie rock

Since the mid-1990s, the distinction between indie rock and 'the mainstream' has
become increasingly difficult to sustain; a number of 'indie' releases are subsumed
into the contemporary, post-2000 rock list below.

Left of the Dial: Dispatches from the 80s Underground, Rhino, 2004 (four-CD
    boxed set).
Pavement, *Slanted and Enchanted*, Matador, 1992.
Pixies, *Surfa Rosa*, 4AD, 1988.
REM, *Murmer*, RS, 1983.
Smashing Pumpkins, *Gish*, Hut, 1991.
The Smiths, *The Queen is Dead*, Sire, 1986.
X, *See How We Are*, Elektra, 1987.

Progressive rock (1970s–)

Can, *Future Days*, United Artists, 1973.
Hawkwind, *In Search of Space*, One Way, 1971.
Kansas, *The Best of Kansas*, CBS, 1984.
King Crimson, *In the Court of the Crimson King*, EG, 1969 (rereleased 1989).
Yes, Fragile, *Atlantic*, 1971.

Psychedelic rock (late 1960s–)

Cave of Clear Light. The Pye and Dawn Records Underground Trip, 1967–1975, Pye, 2010.
Cream, *Disraeli Gears*, Polydor, 1967.
The Grateful Dead, *Anthem of the Sun*, Warner Brothers, 1968.
Jefferson Airplane, *Surrealistic Pillow*, RCA, 1967.
Quicksilver Messenger Service, *Happy Trails*, Capitol, 1969.
The Zombies, *Odessey and Oracle*, CBS, 1968.

'Mainstream' rock (1970s)

Aerosmith, *Rocks*, Columbia, 1976.
The Eagles, *Hotel California*, Elektra/Asylum, 1976.
Elton John, *Greatest Hits*, MCA, 1974.
Meatloaf, *Bat Out of Hell*, Cleveland International/Epic, 1977.
Queen, *A Night at the Opera*, Hollywood, 1975.
Tom Petty and the Heartbreakers, *Damn the Torpedos*, Backstreet, MCA, 1979.
Pink Floyd, *Dark Side of the Moon*, Capitol, 1973.
Bruce Springsteen, *Born to Run*, Columbia, 1975.
Rod Stewart, *Every Picture Tells a Story*, Mercury, 1971.
Steely Dan, *Aja*, MCA, 1972.

Punk rock (late 1970s, with antecedents in garage rock of the late 60s)

The Buzzcocks, *Singles Going Steady*, EMI, 1980.
The Clash, *London Calling*, Epic, 1979.
The Ramones, *Ramones*, Sire, 1976.
The Sex Pistols, *Never Mind the Bollocks*, Warner Brothers, 1977.
Patti Smith, *Horses*, Arista, 1975.
The Velvet Underground, *Velvet Underground Live*, Polygram, 1974 (includes 'White Light, White Heat', originally released in 1968).
Television, *Marquee Moon*, Elektra, 1977.

Compilations

England's Dreaming, 25 Tracks Before and After Punk, compiled by Jon Savage, Trikout, 2004.
No Thanks! The 70s Punk Rebellion, Rhino/Warner, 2003 (four-CD boxed set).

Post punk, new wave

The B-52s, *The B-52s*, Warner, 1979.

Blondie, *The Best of Blondie*, Chrysalis, 1981.

The Cars, *The Cars*, Elektra, 1978.

Elvis Costello and the Attractions, *The Best of Elvis Costello and the Attractions*, CBS, 1985.

Devo, *Q: Are We Not Men? A: We Are Devo*, Warner Bros, 1978.

Talking Heads, *More Songs about Buildings and Food*, Sire, 1978.

Rock (very broadly defined) (1980s–1990s)

Blur, *Parklife*, Capitol, 1994.

Bon Jovi, *Slippery When Wet*, Mercury, 1986.

Jeff Buckley, *Grace*, Columbia, 1994.

Dire Straits, *Brothers in Arms*, Vertigo/Warners, 1984.

Elastica, *Elastica*, Deceptive, 1995.

Michael Jackson, *Thriller*, Epic, 1982.

Alanis Morissette, *Jagged Little Pill*, Maverick, 1995.

Oasis, *(Whats The Story) Morning Glory?*, Creation, 1995.

The Pretenders, *The Pretenders*, Warner Brothers, 1980.

Prince, *Purple Rain*, Warner Bros, 1984.

The Promise Ring, *Nothing Feels Good*, 1997.

U2, *The Joshua Tree*, Island, 1987.

Weezer, *Pinkerton*, Geffen, 1996.

Z Z Top, *Eliminator*, Warner, 1983.

Contemporary rock (post-2000)

The Arctic Monkeys, *Whatever People Say I Am, That's What I'm Not*, Domino, 2006.

Black Country Communion, *Communion*, Warner Music, 2010.

Coldplay, *A Rush of Blood to the Head*, Capitol/Parlophone, 2002.

The Darkness, *Permission to Land*, Must Destroy/Atlantic, 2003.

Foo Fighters, *Greatest Hits*, RCA, 2009.

Franz Ferdinand, *Franz Ferdinand*, Sony, 2000.

P.J. Harvey, *Let England Shake*, Island, 2011.

The Killers, *Sam's Town*, Island, 2006.

Kings of Leon, *Because of the Times*, Sony/BMG, 2007.

Queens of the Stone Age, *Lullabies to Paralyze*, Interscope, 2005.

Bruce Springsteen, *Devils and Dust*, Columbia, 2005.

Bruce Springsteen, *Wrecking Ball*, Sony, 2012.

Them Crooked Vultures, *Them Crooked Vultures*, Columbia, 2010.

TV On the Radio, *Nine Types of Light*, Interscope, 2011.

White Denim, *D*, Inertia, 2011.

The White Stripes, *Icky Thump*, Third Man/XL, 2007.

Soul

'Classic' soul, including Motown

James Brown, *Live at the Apollo*, Polydor, 1963.
Ray Charles, *The Birth of Soul*, Atlantic, 1991.
Sam Cooke, *Portrait of a Legend, 1951–1964*, ABKO, 2003.
The Four Tops, *The Greatest Hits*, Motown, 1967.
Aretha Franklin, *30 Greatest Hits*, Atlantic, 1986.
Marvin Gaye, *Super Hits*, Motown, 1973.
Otis Redding, *Otis Blue*, ATCO, 1965.
Dusty Springfield, *Dusty In Memphis*, Philips, 1969.
The Temptations, *Anthology*, Motown, 1973.
Stevie Wonder, *Looking Back*, Motown, 1977.

Funk

James Brown, *Cold Sweat*, King, 1967.
Funkadelic, *One Nation under a Groove*, WB, 1978.
Michael Jackson, 'Billy Jean', on *Thriller*, Epic, 1983.
Parliament, *Mothership Connection*, Casablanca, 1976.
Prince, *1999*, WB, 1984.
Sly and the Family Stone, *Greatest Hits*, Epic, 1970.

Contemporary soul; R&B

Since the 1980s, the term R&B has largely superseded the term 'soul'; see, for example, the Grammy Awards.
Adele, *21*, XL Columbia, 2011.
Katy B, *On a Mission*, Sony, 2011.
Beyoncé, *I Am ... Sasha Fierce*, Columbia, 2008.
Chris Brown, *F.A.M.E.*, Jive, 2011.
John Legend and the Roots, *Wake Up!*, Good Music/Columbia, 2010.
Jill Scott, *The Light of the Sun*, Warner, 2011.
Joss Stone, *Mind, Body & Soul*, Relentless, 2004.

World music

As I have indicated (in Chapter 6), there are problems with the catch-all nature of this metagenre. See the discographies in the Rough Guides to world music; *Songlines*, The 50th 'Collector's Edition' issue, March 2008 (includes the '50 best top of the world albums').

A chronological listing of influential albums/artists:
King Sunny Ade, *Juju Music*, Island, Mango, 1982.
Paul Simon, *Graceland*, Warner Bros, 1986.
Ladysmith Black Mambazo, *Shaka Zulu*, Warners, 1987.

Salif Keita, *Soro*, Sterns, 1987.
Nusrat Fateh Ali Khan, *Mustt Mustt*, Real World, 1990.
Buena Vista Social Club, *Buena Vista Social Club*, World Circuit, 1997.
Baaba Maal, *Missing You*, Palm Pictures, 2001.
Ali Farka Toure, *Savane*, One World Circuit, 2006.
Tinariwen, *Imidwan*, Independiente, 2009.

The following genres are often included under the label 'world music', although they are diasporic in nature and have become prominent in 'western' contexts in recent years.

Bhangra

Apache Indian, *Make Way for the Indian*, Island, 1995.
Asia Dub Foundation, *Community Music*, FFRR, 2000.
Cornershop, *When I Was Born for the 7th Time*, Wiija Records, 1997.

Bossa nova

Bossa Nova, Verve, 2006.
Gilberto Gill, *Louvacao*, Philips, 1967.
Samba Bossa Nova, Putumayo, 2002.

Celtic

See the discography in Sawyers, J. (2000) *The Complete Guide to Celtic Music*,
    London: Arum Press.
Enya, *Watermark*, Reprise, 1988.
Horslips, *Dance Hall Sweethearts*, RCA, 1974.
The Pogues, *Rum, Sodomy & the Lash*, MCA, 1995 ('Celtic punk').
Sarah McLachlan, *Solace*, Arista, 1991.

Salsa

Reuben Blades, *Buscando America*, Elektra, 1994.
Celia Cruz, *Celia and Johny*, Voya, 1975.

Tejano

Los Lobos, *How Will the Wolf Survive*, Slash, 1984.
Sir Douglas Quintet, *Mendocino*, Acadia/Evangeline, 2002 (original release1969;
    now with bonus tracks).
Texas Tornados, *Texas Tornados*, Reprise, 1990 (won a Grammy).

Avant garde; experimental; lo-fi

See also Young, R. (ed.) (2009) *The WIRE Primers. A Guide to Modern Music*,
    London: Verso. A selection of articles from a series 'The Primer', 'conceived as

potted guides to the work and, by extension, to the lives of significant individual artists, groups or umbrella genres' (Introduction: 7).

Laurie Anderson, *Big Science*, WB, 1982 (notably the track 'O'Superman').

Beck, *One Foot in the Grave*, K Records, 1994.

Grouper, *Dragging a Dead Deer Up a Hill*, 2008.

Guided By Voices, *Bee Thousand*, Scat, 1994.

The Microphones, *The Glow. Pt. 2*, K Records, 2001.

The Mountain Goats, *The Life of the World to Come*, 4AD, 2009.

My Bloody Valentine, *Loveless*, WB, 1991.

Sonic Youth, *Daydream Nation*, DGC, 1988.

Frank Zappa and the Mothers of Invention, *Freak Out*, Verve, 1966.

Singles

For guides to singles releases, see Cresswell, T. (2007) *Rockwiz 1001 Songs: The Great Songs of All Time*, Melbourne, London: Hardie Grant Books.

Marsh, D. (1989) *The Heart of Rock and Soul: The 1001 Greatest Singles Ever Made*, New York: Plume/Penguin.

Mulholland, G. (2002) *This is Uncool: The 500 Greatest Singles Since Punk and Disco*, London: Cassell.

Plagenhoef, S. and Schreber, R. (eds) (2008) *The Pitchfork 500: Our Guide to the Greatest Songs from Punk to the Present*, New York, London: Simon & Schuster.

Bibliography

Aizlewood, J. (ed.) (1994) *Love is the Drug*, London: Penguin.

Albertazzi, D. and Cobley, P. (eds) (2010) *The Media: An Introduction*, Harlow: Longman Pearson.

Alden, G. and Blackstock, P. (2005) *The Best of No Depression: Writing About American Music*, Austin, TX: University of Texas Press.

Anderson, K. (2007) *Grunge: The End of Rock and Roll*, London: Aurum.

Anderson, T. (2006) 'For the Record: Interdisciplinarity, Cultural Studies, and the Search for Method in Popular Music Studies', in M. White and J. Schwoch (eds), *Questions of Method in Cultural Studies*, Malden, MA; Oxford: Blackwell.

Arnett, J. (1996) *Metalheads: Heavy Metal Music and Adolescent Alienation*, Boulder, CO: Westview Press.

Atton, C. (2001) '"Living in the Past?" Value Discourses in Progressive Rock Fanzines', *Popular Music*, 20, 1: 29–46.

——(2009) 'Writing About Listening: Alternative Discourses in Rock Journalism', *Popular Music*, 28, 1: 53–67.

Auslander, P. (2008) *Liveness: Performance in a Mediated Culture*, New York, London: Routledge.

Austerlitz, S. (2007) *Money For Nothing: A History of the Music Video from the Beatles to the White Stripes*, New York: Continuum.

Azerrad, M. (2001) *Our Band Could Be Your Life: Scenes from the American Indie Underground 1981–1991*, Boston, MA: Little, Brown & Company.

Bangs, L. (1990) *Psychotic Reactions and Carburetor Dung*, ed. G. Marcus, London: Minerva.

Banks, J. (1996) *Monopoly Television: MTV's Quest to Control the Music*, Boulder, CO: Westview Press.

Barfe, L. (2004) *Where Have all the Good Times Gone? The Rise and Fall of the Record Industry*, London: Atlantic Books.

Barker, C. (2002) *Making Sense of Cultural Studies: Central Problems and Critical Debates*, London: Sage.

Barker, H. and Taylor, Y. (2007) *Faking It: The Quest for Authenticity in Popular Music*, New York, London: Norton.

Barlow, W. (1989) *Looking Up At Down: The Emergence of Blues Culture*, Philadelphia, PA: Temple University Press.

Barnes, K. (1988) 'Top 40 Radio: A Fragment of the Imagination', in S. Frith (ed.), *Facing the Music*, New York: Pantheon Books.

Barrow, S. and Dalton, P. (1987) *Reggae: The Rough Guide*, London: Rough Guides.

Basu, D. and Lemelle, S. (eds) (2006) *The Vinyl Ain't Final: Hop Hop and the Globalisation of Culture*, London: Pluto Press.

Bayton, M. (1997) 'Women and the Electric Guitar', in S. Whiteley (ed.), *Sexing the Groove: Popular Music and Gender*, London, New York: Routledge.

Beadle, J. (1993) *Will Pop Eat Itself? Pop Music in the Soundbite Era*, London: Faber & Faber.

Beard, D. and Gloag, D. (2005) *Musicology: The Key Concepts*, Abingdon, New York: Routledge.

Beattie, K. (2004) *Documentary Screens: Non-Fiction Film and Television*, London: Palgrave Macmillan.

Becker, H. (1997; first published 1963) 'The Culture of a Deviant Group: The "Jazz" Musician', in K. Gelder and S. Thornton (eds), *The Subcultures Reader*, London, New York: Routledge.

Beebe, R., Fulbrook, D. and Saunders, B. (eds) (2002) *Rock Over the Edge: Transformations in Popular Music Culture*, Durham, NC; London: Duke University Press.

Benatar, P. with Patsi Bale Cox (2010) *Between a Heart and a Rock Place: A Memoir*, New York: HarperCollins.

Bennett, A. (2000) *Popular Music and Youth Culture: Music, Identity and Place*, London: Macmillan.

Bennett, A. and Kahn-Harris, K. (eds) (2004) *After Subcultures*, London: Ashgate.

Bennett, A. and Peterson, R.A. (eds) (2004) *Music Scenes: Local, Translocal, and Virtual*, Nashville, TN: Vanderbilt University Press.

Bennett, A., Shank, B. and Toynbee, J. (eds) (2006) *The Popular Music Studies Reader*, London, New York: Routledge.

Bennett, H.S. (1990) 'The Realities of Practice', in S. Frith and A. Goodwin (eds), *On Record*, New York: Pantheon Books.

Bennett, T., Frith, S., Grossberg, L., Shepherd, J. and Turner, G. (1993) *Rock and Popular Music: Politics, Policies, Institutions*, London: Routledge.

Berelian, E. (2005) *The Rough Guide to Heavy Metal*, London: Rough Guides.

Berkenstadt, J. and Cross, C. (1998) *Nevermind: Nirvana*, New York: Schirmer Books.

Berland, J. (1988) 'Locating Listening: Technological space, Popular Music, Canadian Meditations', *Cultural Studies*, 5, 3: 343–58.

Bertsch, C. (1993) 'Making Sense of Seattle', *Bad Subjects*, 5 (March/April), unpaginated.

Bishop, J. (2005) 'Building International Empires of Sound: Concentrations of Power and Property in the "Global" Music Market', *Popular Music and Society*, 28, 4: 443–72.

Bloustein, G., Peters, M. and Luckman, S. (eds) (2008) *Sonic Synergies: Music, Technology, Community, Identity*, Aldershot: Ashgate.

Borthwick, S. and Moy, R. (2004) *Popular Music Genres: An Introduction*, Edinburgh: Edinburgh University Press.

Bourdage, M. (2010) 'A Young Girl's Dream: Examining the Barriers Facing Female Electric Guitarists', *IASPM Journal*, 1,1: 1–15.

Bourdieu, P. (1984) *Distinction: A Social Critique of the Judgement of Taste*, London: Routledge & Kegan Paul.

Bowman, R. (2003) 'Session Musicians', in J. Shepherd, D. Horn, D. Laing, P. Oliver and P. Wicke (eds), *The Continuum Encyclopedia of Popular Music, Volume One: Media, Industry and Society*, London, New York: Continuum.

boyd, d. and Ellison, N. (2007) 'Social Network Sites: Definition, History and Scholarship', *Computer-Mediated Communication*, 13, 1, article 11. Online at: http://jcmc.indiana,edu/vol13/issue 1/boyd.ellison.html

Boyd, J. (2006) *White Bicycles – Making Music in the 1960s*, London: Serpent's Tail.

Brackett, D. (1995) 'The Politics and Musical Practice of Crossover', in W. Straw, S. Johnson, R. Sullivan and P. Friedlander (eds) *Popular Music: Style and Identity*, Montreal: Centre for Research on Canadian Cultural Industries and Institutions.

——(ed.) (2009) *The Pop, Rock, and Soul Reader. Histories and Debates*, 2nd edn, New York, Oxford: Oxford University Press.

Brake, M. (1985) *Comparative Youth Culture*, London: Routledge and Kegan Paul.

Brennan, M. (2006a) 'Down Beats and Rolling Stones: The American Jazz Press Decides to Cover Rock in 1967', *Popular Music History*, 1, 3: 263–84.

——(2006b) 'This Rough Guide to Critics: Musicians Discuss the Role of the Music Press', *Popular Music*, 25, 2: 221–34.

Brill, D. (2008.) *Goth Culture*, Oxford, New York: Berg.

Brown, A. (2011) 'Heavy Genealogy: Mapping the Currents, Contraflows and Conflicts of the Emergent Field of Metal Studies', *Journal for Cultural Research*, 15, 3: 1213–42.

Buckley, P. and Clark, D. (2005) *The Rough Guide to iPods, iTunes and Music Online*, London: Rough Guides.

Bull, M. (2000) *Sounding Out the City: Personal Stereos and the Management of Everyday Life*, Oxford, New York: Berg.

Burkart, P. and McCourt, T. (2006) *Digital Music Wars: Ownership and Control of the Celestial Jukebox*, Lanham, MD: Bowman & Littlefield.

Burns, G. (1997) 'Popular Music and Society and the Evolving Discipline of Popular Music Studies', *Popular Music and Society*, 21, 1: 123–31.

Butler, M. (2003) 'Taking it Seriously: Intertextuality and Authenticity in Two Covers by the Pet Shop Boys', *Popular Music*, 22, 1: 1–20.

Caddick, C. (2010) *Review of New Zealand On Air's Domestic Music Promotion and Funding Schemes*. Online at: www.nzonair.govt.nz

Callahan, M. (2010) *Poker Face: The Rise and Rise of Lady Gaga*, New York: Hyperion.

Cantin, P. (1997) *Alanis Morissette: Jagged*, London: Bloomsbury.

Cantoni, L. and Tardini, S. (2006) *Internet* (Routledge Introductions to Media and Communications), London: Routledge.

Carnoy, G. (ed.) (2003) *The Sounds of People and Places: A Geography of American Music*, Lanham, MD: Rowman & Littlefield.

Carson, M., Lewis, T. and Shaw, S.M. (2004) *Girls Rock! Fifty Years of Women Making Music*, Lexington, KY: University Press of Kentucky.

Carvicchi, D. (1998) *Tramps Like Us: Music and Meaning Among Springsteen Fans*, New York: Oxford University Press.

Castells, M. (1996) *The Rise of the Networked Society*, Malden, MA: Blackwell.

Cateforis, T. (ed.) (2007) *The Rock History Reader*, New York, London: Routledge.

——(2009) 'Sources and Storytelling: Teaching the History of Rock through its Primary Documents', *Journal of Popular Music Studies*, 21, 1: 20–58.

Cawelti, J. (1971) 'Notes Toward an Aesthetic of Popular Culture', *Journal of Popular Culture*, 5, 2 (Fall): 255–68.

Chambers, I. (1985) *Urban Rhythms: Pop Music and Popular Culture*, London: Macmillan.

Chanan, M. (1995) *Repeated Takes: A Short History of Recording and its Effects on Music*, London: Verso.

Chang, J. (2005) *Can't Stop Won't Stop: A History of the Hip-Hop Generation*, New York: Ebury Press/Random House.

Chapman, R. (1992) *Selling the Sixties: The Pirates and Pop Music Radio*, London, New York: Routledge.

Chapple, S. and Garofalo, R. (1977) *Rock 'n' Roll Is Here To Pay*, Chicago: Nelson-Hall.

Chapple, W. (1869) *Popular Music of the Olden Time*, London, Chapple & Co.

Charlton, K. (1994) *Rock Music Styles: A History*, 2nd edn, Madison, WI: Brown & Benchmark.

Chevigny, P. (1991) *Gigs: Jazz and the Cabaret Laws in New York City*, New York: Routledge.

Chignell, H. (2009) *Key Concepts in Radio Studies*, London: Sage.

Christe, I. (2004) *Sound of the Beast: The Complete Headbanging History of Heavy Metal*, New York: Harper Entertainment.

Citron, M. (1993) *Gender and the Musical Canon*, Cambridge: Cambridge University Press.

Clayton, M., Herbert T. and Middleton, R. (eds) (2003) *The Cultural Study of Music. A Critical Introduction*, New York, London: Routledge.

——(2012) *The Cultural Study of Music: A Critical Introduction*, 2nd edn, New York, London: Routledge.

Cloonan, M. (1996) *Banned! Censorship of Popular Music in Britain: 1967–92*, Aldershot: Arena.

——(2007) *Popular Music and the State in the UK Culture, Trade or Industry?*, Aldershot; Burlington, VT: Ashgate.

Cloonan, M. and Garofalo, R. (eds) (2003) *Policing Pop*, Philadelphia, PA: Temple University Press.

Cloonan, M., Williamson, J. and Frith, S. (2004) 'What is Music Worth?', *Popular Music*, 23, 2: 205 12.

Cogan, J. and Clark, W. (2003) *Temples of Sound Inside the Great Recording Studios*, San Francisco: Chronicle Books.

Cohn, N. (1970) *Awopbopaloobop Alopbamboom: Pop From the Beginning*, St Albans: Paladin, Granada.

——(1980) 'Phil Spector', in J. Miller (ed.), *The Rolling Stone Illustrated History of Rock & Roll*, New York: Random House/Rolling Stone.

——(1992) 'Phil Spector', in A. DeCurtis and J. Henke (eds), *The Rolling Stone Illustrated History of Rock 'n' Roll*, 3rd edn, New York: Random House.

Cohen, Sara (1991) *Rock Culture in Liverpool: Popular Music in the Making*, Oxford: Clarendon Press.

——(1999) 'Scenes', in B. Horner and T. Swiss (eds), *Key Terms in Popular Music and Culture*, Malden, MA; Oxford: Blackwell.

Cohen, Stanley (1980) *Folk Devils and Moral Panics*, Oxford: Robertson.

Coleman, J. (1961) *The Adolescent Society*, New York: Free Press.

Collins, K. (ed.) (2008) *From Pac-Man to Pop Music: Interactive Audio in Games and New Media*, Basingstoke: Ashgate.

Connell, J. and Gibson, C. (2002) *Sound Tracks: Popular Music, Identity and Place*, London: Routledge.

Cook, N. (2003) 'Music as Performance', in M. Clayton, T. Herbert and R. Middleton (eds), *The Cultural Study of Music. A Critical Introduction*, New York, London: Routledge.

——(n.d.) 'What is musicology?' Online at: www.rma.ac.uk/articles

Cooper, T. (2012) *'Sometimes I Live in the Country, Sometimes I Live in the Town': Discourses of Authenticity, Cultural Capital, and the Rural/Urban Dichotomy in Alternative Country Music*, MA thesis, Victoria University of Wellington.

Cope, A. (2010) *Black Sabbath and the Rise of Heavy Metal Music*, Basingstoke: Ashgate.

Corner, J. (2002) 'Sounds Real: Popular Music and Documentary', *Popular Music*, 21, 3: 357–66.

Covach, J. and Boone, G.M. (eds) (1997) *Understanding Rock. Essays in Musical Analysis*, New York: Oxford University Press.

Cowell, S. (2003) *I Don't Mean To Be Rude, BUT … ,* London: Ebury Press.

Crissell, A. (ed.) (2004) *More Than a Music Box: Radio Cultures and Communities in a Multi-Media World*, Oxford: Berghahn.

Critcher, S. (2003) *Moral Panics and the Media*, Buckingham: Open University Press.

Cross, C. (2005) *Room Full Of Mirrors: A Biography of Jimi Hendrix*, London: Spectre.

Cunningham, M. (1996) *Good Vibrations: A History of Record Production*, Chessington: Castle Communications.

Dale, P. (2008) 'It was Easy, it was Cheap, So What? Reconsidering the DIY Principle of Punk and Indie Music', *Popular Music History*, 3, 2: 171–93.

Daley, M. (1997) 'Patti Smith's "Gloria": Intertextual Play in a Rock Vocal Performance', *Popular Music*, 16,3: 235–53.

David, M. (2010) *Peer to Peer and the Criminalization of Sharing*, Los Angeles, London: Sage.

Davis, A. (1997) 'Spice Invaders!', *Record Collector*, 213 (May): 34–9.

Day, T. (2000) *A Century of Recorded Music: Listening to Musical History*, New Haven, CT; London: Yale University Press.

Dean, E. (2001) 'Desperate Man Blues', in D. Wolk and P. Guralnick (eds), *Da Capo Best Music Writing 2000*, New York: Da Capo Press.

DeNora, T. (2000) *Music in Everyday Life*, Cambridge: Cambridge University Press.

Denselow, R. (1990) *When The Music's Over: The Story of Political Pop*, London: Faber & Faber.

DeRogatis, J. (1982) *Let it Blurt: The Life and Times of Lester Bangs, America's Greatest Rock Critic*, New York: Broadway Books.

Dettmar, K. (2006) *Is Rock Dead?*, New York, London: Routledge.

Dettmar, K. and Richey, W. (eds) (1999) *Reading Rock and Roll: Authenticity Appropriation, Aesthetics*, New York: Columbia University Press.

Diaz, D. (2005) 'Tuis Flock to Fat Freddy's Drop', *Dominion Post*, 5 October.

Dickerson, J. (1998) *Women on Top: The Quiet Revolution that's Rocking the American Music Industry*, New York: Billboard Books.

Dogget, P. (2009) *There's a Riot Going On: Revolutionaries, Rock Stars and the Rise and Fall of 60s' Counter Culture*, London: Canongate.

Dougan, J. (2006) 'Objects of Desire: Canon Formation and Blues Record Collecting', *Journal of Popular Music*, 18, 1: 40–65.

Du Gay, P. and Negus, K. (1994) 'The Changing Sites of Sound: Music Retailing and the Composition of Consumers', *Media, Culture and Society*, 16, 3: 395–413.

Eisenberg, E. (1988) *The Recording Angel: Music, Records and Culture from Aristotle to Zappa*, London: Pan Books.

Elafros, A. (2010) '"No Beauty Tips or Guilt Trips": Rockgrrrl, Rock, and Representation', *Popular Music and Society*, 33, 4: 487–99.

Eliot, M. (1989) *Rockonomics: The Money Behind the Music*, New York, Toronto: Franklin Watts.

Ennis, P.H. (1992) *The Seventh Stream: The Emergence of Rock'n'Roll in American Popular Music*, Hanover, NH; London: Wesleyan University Press.

Evans, M. (1998) 'Quality Criticism – Music Reviewing in Australian Rock Magazines', *Perfect Beat*, 3, 4: 38–50.

Fabbri, R. (1999) 'Browsing Musical Spaces: Categories and the Musical Mind', conference paper. Online at: www.tagg.org

Fairchild, C. (2008) *Pop Idols and Pirates*, Aldershot: Ashgate.

Farrell, G. (1998) 'The Early Days of the Gramophone Industry in India: Historical, Social, and Musical Perspectives', in A. Leyshon, D. Matless and G. Revill (eds), *The Place of Music*, New York: Guilford Press.

Feigenbaum, A. (2005) 'Some Guy Designed this Room I'm Standing in: Marking Gender in Press Coverage of Ani DiFranco', *Popular Music*, 24, 1: 37–56.

Fenster, M. (1995) 'Two Stories: Where Exactly is the Local?', in W. Straw, S. Johnson, R. Sullivan and P. Friedlander (eds), *Popular Music – Style and Identity*, Montreal: Centre for Research on Canadian Cultural Industries and Institutions.

Finnegan, R. (1989) *The Hidden Musicians: Music Making in an English Town*, Cambridge: Cambridge University Press.

Fiske, J. (1989) *Understanding Popular Culture*, Boston, MA: Unwin Hyman.

Flanaghan, B. (1987) *Written in My Soul: Rock's Great Songwriters Talk about Creating their Music*, Chicago: Contemporary Books.

Flohel, R. (1990) 'The Canadian Music Industry: A Quick Guide', in D. Baskerville (ed.), *Music Business Handbook and Career Guide*, New York: Sherwood.

Fonarow, W. (2006) *Empire of Dirt: The Aesthetics and Rituals of British Indie Music*, Middletown, CT: Wesleyan University Press.

Forman, M. (2002) *The 'Hood Comes First: Race, Space, and Place in Rap and Hip-Hop*, Middletown, CT: Wesleyan University Press.

Forman, M. and Neal, M. (eds) (2004) *That's The Joint! The Hip-Hop Studies Reader*, New York, London: Routledge.

Fox, P. and Ching, B. (eds) (2008) *Old Roots, New Routes: The Cultural Politics of Alt. Country*, Ann Arbor, MI: University of Michigan Press.

Friedlander, P. (2006) *Rock and Roll: A Social History*, 2nd edn, Boulder, CO: Westview Press.

Frith, S. (1983) *Sound Effects: Youth, Leisure and the Politics of Rock 'n' Roll*, London: Constable, 1983.

——(1988) *Music for Pleasure: Essays in the Sociology of Pop*, Cambridge: Polity Press.

——(1993) *Music and Copyright*, Edinburgh: Edinburgh University Press.

——(1996) *Performing Rites: On the Value of Popular Music*, Cambridge, MA: Harvard University Press.

——(2000) 'The Discourse of World Music', in G. Born and D. Hesmondhalgh (eds), *Western Music and its Others: Difference, Representation, and Appropriation in Music*, Berkeley, Los Angeles: University of California Press.

——(2001) 'Pop Music', in S. Frith, W. Straw and J. Street (eds), *Cambridge Companion to Pop and Rock*, Cambridge: Cambridge University Press.

——(2007) *Taking Popular Music Seriously Selected Essays*, Aldershot: Ashgate.

——(2011) 'The Business of Live Music', *Arts Marketing*, 1, 2: Special Issue.

Frith, S. and Goodwin, A. (eds) (1990) *On Record: Rock, Pop, and the Written Word*, New York: Pantheon Books.

Frith, S. and McRobbie, A. (1990; first published 1978) 'Rock and Sexuality', in S. Frith and A. Goodwin (eds), *On Record*, New York: Pantheon Books.

Frith, S. and Street, J. (1992) 'Rock Against Racism and Red Wedge', in R. Garofalo (ed), *Rockin' The Boat: Mass Music and Mass Movements*, Boston, MA: South End Press.

Frith, S., Goodwin, A. and Grossber, L. (1993) *Sound and Vision: The Music Video Reader*, London: Routledge.

Frith, S., Straw, W. and Street, J. (eds) (2001) *Cambridge Companion to Pop and Rock*, Cambridge: Cambridge University Press.

Furgason, A. (2008) 'Afraid of Technology? Major Label Response to Advancements in Digital Technology', *Popular Music History*, 3, 2: 149–70.

Gabbard, K. (1995) *Jazz Among the Discourses*, Durham, NC; London: Duke University Press.

Garnham, N. (1997) 'Concepts of Culture: Public Policy and the Cultural Industries', *Cultural Studies*, 1, 1 (January): 2–37.

Garofalo, R. (ed.) (1992) *Rockin' the Boat: Mass Music & Mass Movements*, Boston, MA: South End Press.

——(2003) 'I Want My MP3: Who Owns Internet Music', in M. Cloonan and R. Garofalo (eds), *Policing Pop*, Philadelphia, PA: Temple University Press.

——(2011) *Rockin' Out Popular Music in the USA*, 5th edn, Neeham Heights, MA: Allyn & Bacon.

Gay, P. du, Hall, S., Jones, L., Mackay, H. and Negus, K. (1997) *Doing Cultural Studies: The Story of the Sony Walkman*, London, Thousand Oaks, CA: Sage, in association with the Open University Press.

Gebesmair, A. (2009) 'The Transnational Music Industry', in D. Scott (ed.), *The Ashgate Research Companion to Popular Musicology*, Farnham: Ashgate.

Gebesmair, A. and Smudits, A. (eds) (2001) *Global Repertoires. Popular Music Within and Beyond the Transnational Music Industry*, Burlington, VT: Ashgate.

Gelder, K. and Thornton, S. (eds) (1997) *The Subcultures Reader*, London, New York: Routledge.

Geldof, B. (1986) *Is That It?* London: Penguin Books.

George, D.R. (2010) 'Conceptualizing the Cognitive and Functional Benefits of Playing Beatles Rock Band from an Ecological Bio-psychological Perspective', *Journal of Popular Music Studies*, 22, 4: 466–81.

George, N. (1989) *The Death of Rhythm and Blues*, New York: Pantheon Books.

——(1999) *Hip Hop America*, New York: Penguin Books.

Gilroy, P. (1993) *The Black Atlantic: Modernity and Double Consciousness*, Cambridge, MA: Harvard University Press.

Glasser, R. (2010) *Music Business: The Key Concepts*, London, New York: Routledge.

Golden, A.L. (1997) *The Spice Girls*, New York: Ballantine Books.

Goodman, F. (1997) *The Mansion on the Hill: Dylan, Young, Geffen, Springsteen, and the Head-On Collision of Rock and Commerce*, New York: Time Books/Random House.

Goodwin, A. (1993) *Dancing in the Distraction Factory Music Television and Popular Culture*, Oxford, Minneapolis, MN: University of Minnesota Press.

——(1998) 'Drumming and Memory: Scholarship, Technology and Music-Making', in T. Swiss, J. Sloop and A. Herman (eds), *Mapping the Beat: Popular Music and Contemporary Theory*, Malden, MA; Oxford: Blackwell.

Gorman, P. (2001) *In Their Own Write: Adventures in the Music Press*, London: Sanctuary Publishing.

Gracyk, T. (1996) *Rhythm and Noise: An Aesthetics of Rock*, Durham, NC; London: Duke University Press.

——(2001) *I Wanna Be Me: Rock Music and the Politics of Identity*, Philadelphia, PA: Temple University Press.

Gray, J., Sandvoss, C. and Harrington, C.L. (2007) *Fandom: Identities and Communities in a Mediated World*, New York, London: New York University Press.

Gray, M. (1995) *Last Gang in Town: The Story and Myth of the Clash*, New York: Henry Holt.

Grenier, L. (1983) 'Policing French-Language Music on Canadian Radio', in T. Bennett, S. Frith, L. Grossberg, J. Shepherd and G. Turner (eds), *Rock and Popular Music*, London: Routledge.

Griffiths, D. (2002) 'Cover Versions and the Sound of Identity in Motion', in D. Hesmondhalgh, and K. Negus (eds), *Popular Music Studies*, London: Arnold.

Grigoriadis, V. (2011) 'Growing Up Gaga', in A. Ross and D. Carr (eds), *Best Music Writing 2011*, Philadelphia, PA: Perseus Books/Da Capo Press.

Grossberg, L. (1992) *We Gotta Get Out of This Place: Popular Conservatism and Postmodern Culture*, New York: Routledge.

Guilbault, J. (2001) 'World Music', in S. Frith, W. Straw and W. Street (eds), *Cambridge Companion to Pop and Rock*, Cambridge: Cambridge University Press.

Guralnick, P. (2002) *Lost Highway: Journeys and Arrivals of American Musicians*, Edinburgh: Canongate.

Hager, B. (1998) *On Her Way: The Life and Music of Shania Twain*, New York: Berkley Boulevard.

Hall, S. and Jefferson, T. (eds) (1976) *Resistance Through Rituals: Youth Subcultures in Post-war Britain*, London: Hutchinson.

Hall, S. and Whannell, P. (1964) *The Popular Arts*, London: Hutchinson.

Hamm, C. (1995) *Putting Popular Music in its Place*, Cambridge: Cambridge University Press.

Hanke, R. (1998) '"Yo Quiero Mi MTV!": Making Music Television for Latin America', in Swiss, T., Sloop, J. and Herman, A. (eds), *Mapping the Beat: Popular Music and Contemporary Theory*, Malden, MA; Oxford: Blackwell.

Hatch, D. and Millward, S. (1987) *From Blues to Rock: An Analytical History of Rock Music*, Manchester: Manchester University Press.

Hawkins, S. (2002) *Settling the Pop Score: Pop Texts and Identity Politics*, Aldershot, Burlington, VT: Ashgate.

——(2009) *The British Pop Dandy: Masculinity, Popular Music and Culture*, Aldershot, Burlington, VT: Ashgate.

Hayes, D. (2006) 'Take Those Old Records off the Shelf', *Popular Music and Society*, 29, 1: 51–68.

Haynes, J. (2010) 'In the Blood: The Racializing Tones of Music Categorization', *Cultural Sociology*, 4, 1: 81–100.

Hayward, S. (2000) *Key Concepts in Cinema Studies*, 2nd edn, London, New York: Routledge.

Headlam, D. (1997) 'Blues Transformation in the Music of Cream', in J. Covach and G.M. Boone (eds), *Understanding Rock: Essays in Musical Analysis*, New York: Oxford University Press.

Hebdige, D. (1979) *Subculture: The Meaning of Style*, London: Methuen.

——(1988) *Hiding in the Light: On Images and Things*, London: Comedia/Routledge.

Hennion, A. (2003) 'Music and Mediation: Towards a New Sociology of Music', in M. Clayton, T. Herbert and R. Middleton (eds), *The Cultural Study of Music: A Critical Introduction*, New York, London: Routledge.

Herbert, T. (1998) 'Victorian Brass Bands: Class, Taste and Space', in A. Leyshon, D. Matless and G. Revill (eds), *The Place of Music*, New York: Guilford Press.

Herman, G. (1971) *The Who*, London: November Books.

Hesmondhalgh, D. (2007) *The Cultural Industries*, 2nd edn, London: Sage.

Hesmondhalgh, D. and Negus, K. (eds) (2004) *Popular Music Studies*, London: Arnold.

Heylin, C. (1993) *From the Velvets to the Voidoids: A Pre-Punk History for a Post-Punk World*, London: Penguin.

——(1998) *Never Mind the Bollocks, Here's the Sex Pistols: The Sex Pistols*, New York: Schirmer Books.

——(2007) *Babylon's Burning: From Punk to Grunge*, New York: Viking/Penguin.

Hiatt, B. (2009) 'New York Doll', *Rolling Stone*, August, cover story: 'The Rise of Lady Gaga'.

Hill, D. (1986) *Designer Girls and Material Boys: Manufacturing the 80s' Pop Dream*, Poole: Blandford Press.

Hill, T. (1992) 'The Enemy Within: Censorship in Rock Music in the 1950s', in A. DeCurtis (ed.), *Present Tense: Rock & Roll Culture*, Durham, NC; London: Duke University Press.

Hills, M. (2002) *Fan Cultures*, London, New York: Routledge.

Hodkinson, P. (2002) *Goth: Identity, Style and Subculture*, Oxford: Berg.

——(2004) 'Translocal Connections in the Goth Scene', in A. Bennett and Richard A. Peterson (eds) (2004), *Music Scenes: Local, Translocal, and Virtual*, Nashville, TN: Vanderbilt University Press.

Hodkinson, P. and Deicke, W. (eds) (2007) *Youth Culture: Scenes, Subcultures and Tribes*, London: Routledge.

Hollows, J. and Milestone, K. (1998) 'Welcome to Dreamsville: A History and Geography of Northern Soul', in A. Leyshon, D. Matless and G. Revill (eds), *The Place of Music*, New York: Guilford Press.

Holt, F. (2007) *Genre in Popular Music*, Chicago, London: University of Chicago Press.

Homan, S. (2003) *The Mayor's A Square: Live Music and Law and Order in Sydney*, Newtown, NSW: LCP.

——(ed.) (2006) *Access All Eras: Tribute Bands and Global Pop Culture*, Maidenhead: Open University Press.

——(2010) 'Governmental as Anything: Live Music and Law and Order in Melbourne', *Perfect Beat*, 11, 2: 103–18.

Hornby, N. (1995) *High Fidelity*, London: Random House.

Horner, B. and Swiss, T. (eds) (1999) *Key Terms in Popular Music and Culture*, Oxford: Blackwell.

Hoskyns, B. (ed.) (2003) *The Sound and the Fury: A Rock's Back Pages Reader. 40 Years of Classic Rock Journalism*, London: Bloomsbury.

——(ed.) (2004) *Into The Void: Ozzy Osbourne and Black Sabbath. A Rock's Backpages Reader*, London, New York: Omnibus Press.

——(2006) *Hotel California: Singer-Songwriters and Cocaine Cowboys in the LA Canyons, 1967–1976*, London, New York: Harper Perennial.

Howard-Spink, S. (2004) 'Grey Tuesday: Online Cultural Activism and the Mash-up of Music and Politics', *First Monday*, 9, 10.

Hull, G., Hutchinson, T.W. and Glasser, R. (2011) *The Music Business and Recording Industry: Delivering Music in the 21st Century*, 3rd edn, New York: Routledge.

Hunter, S. (2004) *Hell Bent For Leather: Confessions of a Heavy Metal Addict*, London, New York: Fourth Estate.

Huq, R. (2006) *Beyond Subculture: Pop, Youth and Identity in a Postcolonial World*, London, New York: Routledge.

IFPI (2006) 'Recorded Music: Driver of a US$100 Billion Economic Sector', press release, 22 June.

Inglis, I. (2001) '"Nothing You Can See That Isn't Shown": The Album Covers of the Beatles', *Popular Music*, 20, 1: 83–98.

——(ed.) (2006) *Performance and Popular Music: History, Place and Time*, Burlington, VT: Ashgate.

——(2007) 'Popular Music History on Screen: The Pop/Rock Biopic', *Popular Music History*, 2, 1: 77–93.

——(2010) '"I Read the News Today, Oh Boy": The British Press and The Beatles', *Popular Music and Society*, 33, 4: 549–62.

Jameson, F. (1984) 'Postmodernism, or the Cultural logic of Late Capitalism', *New Left Review*, 146 (July/August): 53–93.

Jenkins, H. (1997) 'Television Fans, Poachers, Nomads', in K. Gelder and S. Thornton (eds), *The Subcultures Reader*, London, New York: Routledge.

Jennings, D. (2007) *Net, Blogs and Rock 'n' Roll: How Digital Discovery Works and What it Means for Consumers, Creators and Culture*, London, Boston, MA: Nicholas Brealey Publishing.

Johansson, O. and Bell, T.L. (eds) (2009) *Sound, Society and the Geography of Popular Music*, Farnham, Burlington, VT: Ashgate.

Johnson, B. (2000) *The Inaudible Music: Jazz, Gender and Australian Modernity*, Sydney: Currency Press.

Johnson, H. (ed.) (2010) *Many Voices: Music and National Identity in Aotearoa/New Zealand*, Newcastle upon Tyne: Cambridge Scholars Publishing.

Jones, D. (2005) *iPod, Therefore I Am: A Personal Journey Through Music*, London: Phoenix.

Jones, M.L. (2012) *The Music Industries: From Conception to Consumption*, Basingstoke: Palgrave Macmillan.

Jones, Simon (1988) *Black Culture, White Youth: The Reggae Tradition from JA to UK*, London: Macmillan.

Jones, Steve (2000) 'Music and the Internet', *Popular Music*, 19, 2: 217–30.

——(ed.) (2002) *Pop Music and the Press*, Philadelphia, PA: Temple University Press.

Jones, Steve and Lenart, A. (2004) 'Music Downlaoding and Listening: Findings from the Pew Internet and American life Project', *Popular Music*, 27, 2: 221–40.

Kahn-Harris, K. (2007) *Extreme Metal: Music and Culture on the Edge*, Oxford, New York: Berg.

Kaplan, E.A. (1987) *Rocking Around the Clock: Music Television, Postmodernism, and Consumer Culture*, New York: Methuen.

Kärjä, A.-V. (2006) 'A Prescribed Alternative Mainstream: Popular Music and Canon Formation', *Popular Music*, 25, 1 (January): 3–20.

Kassabian, A. (1999) 'Popular', in B. Horner and T. Swiss (eds), *Key Terms in Popular Music and Culture*, Oxford: Blackwell.

Kean, G. and Mitchell, T. (eds) (2011) *Home, Land and Sea: Situating Music in Aotearoa New Zealand*, Auckland: Pearson.

Keightley, K. (2001) 'Reconsidering Rock', in S. Frith, W. Straw and J. Street (eds), *Cambridge Companion to Pop and Rock*, Cambridge: Cambridge University Press.

——(2003) 'Covers', in J. Shepherd, D. Horn, D. Laing, P. Oliver and P. Wicke (eds), *The Encyclopedia of Popular Music of the World, Volume 1*, London: Cassell.

Kelly, K. and McDonnell, E. (1999) *Stars Don't Stand Still in the Sky*, London: Routledge.

Kennedy, D. (1990) 'Frankenchrist versus the State: The New Right, Rock Music and the Case of Jello Biafra', *Journal of Popular Culture*, 24, 1: 131–48.

Kennedy, R. and McNutt, R. (1999) *Little Labels – Big Sound: Small Record Companies and the Rise of American Music*, Bloomington, IN: Indiana University Press.

Kenney, W. (1993) *Chicago Jazz: A Cultural History, 1904–30*, New York: Oxford University Press.

Kernfeld, B. (2011) *Pop Song Piracy: Disobedient Music Distribution since 1929*, Chicago, London: University of Chicago Press.

Kiedis, A. with L. Sloman (2004) *Scar Tissue*, London: Time-Warner Books.

Kirschner, T. (1998) 'Studying Rock: Towards a Materialist Ethnography', in T. Swiss, J. Sloop and A. Herman (eds), *Mapping the Beat*, Malden, MA; Oxford: Blackwell.

Klein, B. (2010) *As Heard on TV: Popular Music in Advertising*, Aldershot: Ashgate.

Klosterman, C. (2002) *Fargo Rock City: A Heavy Metal Odyssey in Rural North Dakota*, London: Simon & Schuster.

Knopper, S. (2009) *Appetite for Self-Destruction: The Spectacular Crash of the Record Industry in the Digital Age*, London, New York: Simon & Schuster.

——(2011–12) 'The Music Biz Bounces Back?', *Rolling Stone*, 22 December–5 January: 13–14.

Kotarba, J. and Vannini, P. (2009) *Understanding Society Through Popular Music*, New York, London: Routledge.

Krims, A. (2000) *Rap Music and the Politics of Identity*, Cambridge: Cambridge University Press.

——(2012) 'Music, Space and Place. The Geography of Music', in M. Clayton, T. Herbert and R. Middleton (eds), *The Cultural Study of Music*, New York, London: Routledge.

Kronengold, C. (2008) 'Exchange Theories in Disco, New Wave, and Album-Oriented Rock', *Criticism*, 50, 1: 43–82.

Kruse, H. (2003) *Site and Sound: Understanding Independent Music Scenes*, New York: Peter Lang.

——(2010) 'Local Identity and Independent Music Scenes, Online and Off', *Popular Music and Society*, 35, 5: 625–39.

Laing, D. (1985) *One Chord Wonders: Power and Meaning in Punk Rock*, Milton Keynes: Open University Press.

——(1986) 'The Music Industry and the "Cultural Imperialism" Thesis', *Media, Culture & Society*, 8: 331–41.

——(1988) 'The Grain of Punk: An Analysis of the Lyrics', in A. McRobbie (ed.), *Zoot Suits and Second Hand Dresses: An Anthology of Fashion and Music*, Boston, MA: Unwin Hyman.

——(2008) 'World Music and the Global Music Industry: Flows, Corporations and Networks', *Popular Music History*, 3, 3: 213–31.

——(2012) 'Music and the Market. The Economics of Music in the Modern World', in M. Clayton, T. Herbert and R. Middleton (eds), *The Cultural Study of Music: A Critical Introduction*, 2nd edn, New York, London: Routledge.

Lawrence, T. (2003) *Love Saves the Day: A History of American Dance Music Culture, 1970–1979*, Durham, NC: Duke University Press.

Lebrun, B. (2009) *Protest Music in France: Production, Identity and Audiences*, Farnham, Burlington, VT: Ashgate.

Leiber, J. and Stoller, M. with David Ritz (2009) *Hound Dog: The Leiber and Stoller Autobiography*, New York, London: Simon & Schuster.

Leigh, S. (2009) 'Review of *Nowhere Boy*', *Popular Music History*, 4, 3: 348–50.

Lemish, D. (2003) 'Spice World: Constructing Femininity the Popular Way', *Popular Music and Society*, 26, 1: 17–29.

Lena, J. and Peterson, R. (2008) 'Classification as Culture: Types and Trajectories of Music Genres', *American Sociological Review*, 73, 5: 697–718.

Lentini, P. (2003) 'Punk's Origins: Anglo-American Syncreticism', *Journal of Intercultural Studies*, 24, 2: 153–74.

Leonard, M. (2007) *Gender in the Music Industry Rock, Discourse and Girl Power*, Aldershot: Ashgate.

Leonard, M. and Strachan, R. (2003) 'Music Journalism' and 'Music Press', in J. Shepherd, D. Horn, D. Laing, P. Oliver and P. Wicke (eds), *The Encyclopedia of Popular Music of the World, Volume 1: The Industry, Contexts and Musical Practices*, London: Cassell.

Letts, D. with David Nobakht (2007) *Culture Clash. Dread Meets Punk Rockers*, London: SAF.

Lewis, J. (2008) *Cultural Studies: The Basics*, Los Angeles, London: Sage.

Lewis, L. (ed.) (1992) *The Adoring Audience: Fan Culture and the Popular Media*, London: Routledge.

Leyshon, A., Matless, D. and Revill, G. (eds) (1998) *The Place of Music*, New York: Guilford Press.

Lindbergh, U., Goumundsson, G., Michelsen, M. and Weisethaunet, H. (2000) *Rock Criticism from the Beginning: Amusers, Bruisers and Cool-Headed Cruisers*, New York: Peter Lang.

Longhurst, B. (2007) *Popular Music and Society*, 2nd edn, Cambridge: Polity Press.

Lynskey, D. (2011) *33 Revolutions per Minute: A History of Protest Songs from Billie Holiday to Green Day*, New York: HarperCollins.

McClary, S. (1991) *Feminine Endings: Music, Gender, and Sexuality*, Minnesota, MN; Oxford: University of Minnesota Press.

McClary, S. and Walser, R. (1990) 'Start Making Sense! Musicology Wrestles with Rock', in S. Frith and A. Goodwin (eds), *On Record: Rock, Pop, and the Written Word*, New York: Pantheon Books.

McCourt, T. (2005) 'Collecting Music in the Digital Realm', *Popular Music and Society*, 28, 2 (May): 249–52.

McDonald, C. (2010) *Rush, Rock Music and the Middle Class. Dreaming in Middletown*, Bloomington, IN: Indiana University Press.

McKay, G. (2000) *Glastonbury: A Very English Festival*, London: Victor Gollancz.

McLeod, K. (2001) '*1/2: A Critique of Rock Criticism in North America', *Popular Music*, 20, 1: 29–46.

——(2005a) 'MP3s are Killing Home Taping: The Rise of Internet Distributions and its Challenge to the Major Label Music Monopoly', *Popular Music and Society*, 28, 4: 521–32.

——(2005b) 'Confessions of an Intellectual (Property): Danger Mouse, Mickey Mouse, Sonny Bono, and My Long and Winding Path as a Copyright Activist-Academic', *Popular Music and Society*, 28, 1: 79–94.

MacMillan, M. (2009) *The Uses and Abuses of History*, London: Profile Books.

McNeil, L. and McCain, G. (1996) *Please Kill Me: The Uncensored Oral History of Punk*, New York: Gove Press.

McRobbie, A. (ed.) *Zoot Suits and Second-Hand Dresses: An Anthology of Fashion and Music*, Boston, MA: Unwin Hyman.

Mac an Ghaill, M. and Haywood, C. (2006) *Gender Culture and Society: Contemporary Femininities and Masculinities*, Basingstoke: Palgrave Macmillan.

Machin, D. (2010) *Analysing Popular Music: Image, Sound, Text*, Los Angeles: Sage.

Manning, A. (1958) *The Bodgie: A Study in Psychological Abnormality*, Sydney: Angus & Robertson.

Marcus, G. (1989) *Lipstick Traces: A Secret History of the 20th Century*, London: Faber & Faber.

——(1991a) *Dead Elvis: A Chronicle of a Cultural Obsession*, New York: Penguin.

——(1991b) first published 1977) *Mystery Train*, 4th edn, New York: Penguin.

——(1992) 'Anarchy in the UK', in A. DeCurtis and J. Henke (eds), *The Rolling Stone Illustrated History of Rock and Roll*, 3rd edn, New York: Random House.

Marcus, S. (2010) *Girls to the Front: The True Story of the Riot Grrrl Revolution*, New York: Harper Perennial.

Marsh, D. (1983) *Before I Get Old: The Story of The Who*, New York: St. Martin's Press.

——(1989) *The Heart of Rock and Soul: The 1001 Greatest Singles Ever Made*, New York: Plume/ Penguin.

Marshall, P.D. (1997) *Celebrity and Power: Fame in Contemporary Culture*, Minneapolis, MN: University of Minnesota Press.

Martin, L. and Seagrave, K. (1988) *Anti-Rock: The Opposition to Rock 'n' Roll*, Hamden, CT: Archon Books.

Melhuish, M. (1999) 'The Business', *Canadian Musician*, 20th anniversary issue, 31, 2 (March/April): 67–80.

Mellers, W. (1974) *Twilight of the Gods: The Beatles in Retrospect*, New York: Viking Press.

Middleton, R. (1990) *Studying Popular Music*, Milton Keynes: Open University Press.

——(ed.) (2000) *Reading Pop: Approaches to Textual Analysis in Popular Music*, Oxford, New York: Oxford University Press.

Miles, B. (1997) *Paul McCartney: Many Years From Now*, London: Vintage.

Millard, A.J. (1995) *America on Record: A History of Recorded Sound*, Cambridge: Cambridge University Press.

——(2005) *America on Record: A History of Recorded Sound*, 2nd edn, Cambridge: Cambridge University Press.

Miller, J. (1999) *Flowers in the Dustbin: The Rise of Rock and Roll, 1947–1977*, New York: Simon & Schuster.

Mitchell, T. (ed.) (2001) *Global Noise: Rap and Hip Hop Outside the USA*, Middletown, CT: Wesleyan University Press.

Mjøs, O.J. (2011) *Music, Social Media and Global Mobility: MySpace, Facebook, YouTube*, New York, London: Routledge.

Moore, A.F. (1993) *Rock: The Primary Text – Developing a Musicology of Rock*, Buckingham: Open University Press.

——(2001) *Rock: The Primary Text – Developing a Musicology of Rock*, 2nd edn, Buckingham: Open University Press.

——(2002) 'Authenticity as Authentication', *Popular Music*, 21, 2: 225–36.

——(ed.) (2003) *Analyzing Popular Music*, Cambridge, New York: Cambridge University Press.

Moore, R. (2010) *Sells Like Teen Spirit: Music, Youth Culture and Social Crisis*, New York, London: New York University Press.

Moorefield, V. (2005) *The Producer as Composer: Shaping the Sounds of Popular Music*, Cambridge, MA: MIT Press.

Muggleton, D. and Weinzierl, R. (eds) (2003) *The Post-subcultures Reader*, Oxford, New York: Berg.

Mundy, J. (1999) *Popular Music on Screen: From the Hollywood Musical to Music Video*, Manchester: Manchester University Press.

Music Industry Development Group (2004) *Creating Heat: Tumata Kia White!*, Wellington: Government Printer.

Naughton, J. (2012) *From Gutenburg to Zuckerburg: What You Really Need to Know About the Internet*, London: Quercus.

Neal, M. (1999) *What the Music Said: Black Popular Music and Black Popular Culture*, New York, London: Routledge.

Negus, K. (1992) *Producing Pop: Culture and Conflict in the Popular Music Industry*, London: Edward Arnold.

——(1996) *Popular Music in Theory*, Cambridge: Polity Press.

——(1999) *Music Genres and Corporate Cultures*, London, New York: Routledge.

Negus, K. and Pickering, M. (2004) *Creativity, Communication and Cultural Value*, London: Sage.

Neill, K. and Shanahan, M. (2005) *The Great New Zealand Radio Experiment*, Southbank, Victoria: Thomson/Dunmore Press.

Novaro, V. and Henry, S. (2009) 'A Guide to Essential American Indie Rock, 1980–2005', *Notes*, June: 816–32.

Ochs, M. (1996) *1000 Rock Covers*, Cologne: Taschen.

O'Connor, A. (2002) 'Local-Scenes and Dangerous Crossroads: Punk and Theories of Cultural Hybridity', *Popular Music*, 21, 2: 225–36.

O'Sullivan, T., Hartely, J., Saunders, D., Montgomery, M. and Fiske, J. (1983) *Key Concepts in Communications*, London: Methuen.

Oliver, P. (ed.) (1990) *Black Popular Music in Britain*, Buckingham: Open University Press.

Parker, M. (1991) 'Reading the Charts: Making Sense of the Hit Parade', *Popular Music*, 10, 2: 205–36.

Pattie, D. (2007) *Rock Music in Performance*, Hampshire, NY: Palgrave Macmillan.

Pearson, B. and McCulloch, B. (2003), *Robert Johnson: Lost and Found*, Urbana, IL: University of Illinois Press.

Perchard, T. (2007) 'Writing Jazz Biography: Race, Research and Narrative Representation', *Popular Music History* 2, 2: 119–45.

Perry, J. (1998) *Meaty, Beaty, Big and Bouncy: The Who*, New York: Schirmer Books.

Peterson, R.A. (1997) *Creating Country: Fabricating Authenticity*, Chicago, London: University of Chicago Press.

Peterson, R.A. and Beal, B. (2001) 'Alternative Country: Origins, Music, World-view, Fans and Taste in Genre Formation', *Popular Music and Society*, 25, 1: 233–49.

Pettit, E. (2008) *Old Rare New: The Independent Record Shop*, London: Black Dog.

Pinch, T. and Bijsterveld (2003) '"Should One Applaud?" Breaches and Boundaries in the Reception of New Technology in Music', *Technology and Culture*, 44, 3: 536–59.

Plagenhoef, S. and Schreber, R. (eds) (2008) *The Pitchfork 500: Our Guide to the Greatest Songs from Punk to the Present*, New York, London: Simon & Schuster.

Plasketes, G. (guest ed.) (2005) *Popular Music and Society*, 28, 2: Special issue: Like a Version – Cover Songs in Popular Music.

Pollock, B. (2002) *Working Musicians: Defining Moments from the Road, the Studio, and the Stage*, New York: Harper Collins.

Potter, R. (1995) *Spectacular Vernaculars: Hip-Hop and the Politics of Postmodernism*, Albany, NY: SUNY Press.

Pratt, R. (1990) *Rhythm and Resistance: Explorations in the Political Use of Popular Music*, New York: Praeger.

Press, J. and Reynolds, S. (1995) *The Sex Revolts, Gender, Rebellion and Rock 'n' Roll*, London: Serpent's Tail.

Price, E.G. (2006) *Hip Hop Culture*, Santa Barbara, CA: ABC-CLIO.

Radano, R. (2012) 'Music, Race and the Fields of Public Culture', in M. Clayton, T. Herbert and R. Middleton (eds), *The Cultural Study of Music: A Critical Introduction*, New York, London: Routledge.

Ramsey, G.P. (2003) *Race Music. Black Cultures from Bebop to Hip-Hop*, Berkeley, CA; London: University of California Press.

Rautianen-Keskustalo, T. (2009) 'Pop Idol: Global Economy – Local Meanings', in D. Scott (ed.), *The Ashgate Research Companion to Popular Musicology*, Farnham: Ashgate.

Redhead, S. (1990) *The End-Of-The-Century Party: Youth and Pop Towards 2000*, Manchester: Manchester University Press.

Regev, M. (2006) 'Introduction' *Popular Music*, 25, 1: Theme (canon) issue.

Reich, C. (1967) *The Greening of America*, New York: Penguin.

Reynolds, S. (1990) 'Return of the Inkies', *New Statesman and Society*, August: 26–7.

——(2006) *Rip It Up and Start Again: Post-Punk, 1978–1984*, London: Faber & Faber.

Rhodes, L. (2005). *Electric Ladyland: Women and Rock Culture*, Philadelphia, PA: University of Pennsylvania Press.

Ribowtsky, M. (1989) *He's A Rebel*, New York: E.P. Dutton.

Richards, K. with James Fox (2010) *Life*, London:Weidenfeld & Nicolson.

Riesman, D. (1950) 'Listening to Popular Music', *American Quarterly*, 2.

Rijven, S. and Straw, W. (1989) 'Rock for Ethiopia', in S. Frith (ed.) *World Music, Politics and Social Change*, Manchester: Manchester University Press.

Rimmer, D. (1985) *Like Punk Never Happened: Culture Club and the New Pop*, London: Faber & Faber.

Roberts, K. (2009) *Key Concepts in Sociology*, Basingstoke, New York: Palgrave Macmillan.

Roedy, B. (2011) *What Makes Business Rock: Building the World's Largest Global Networks*, New York: Wiley.

Rogers, D. (1982) *Rock 'n' Roll*, London: Routledge and Kegan Paul.

Romney, J. and Wootton, A. (1995) *Celluloid Jukebox Popular Music and the Movies since the 50s*, London: BFI.

Ross, K. and Nightingale, V. (2003) *Media and Audiences*, Buckingham, Philadelphia, PA: Open University Press.

Rothenbuhler, E. (2006; first published 1985) 'Commercial Radio as Communication', A. in Bennett, B. Shank and J. Toynbee (eds), *The Popular Music Studies Reader*, London, New York: Routledge.

Sabin, R. (ed.) (1999) *Punk Rock: So What? The Cultural Legacy of Punk*, London, New York: Routledge.

Sansom, J. (2009) 'Music History', in J.P.E. Harper-Scott and J. Sansom (eds), *An Introduction to Music Studies*, Cambridge, New York: Cambridge University Press.

Sardiello, R. (1994) 'Secular Rituals in Popular Culture: A Case for Grateful Dead Concerts and Dead Head identity', in J.S. Epstein (ed.), *Adolescents and Their Music*, New York, London: Garland Publishing.

Savage, J. (1991) *England's Dreaming: Sex Pistols and Punk Rock*, London: Faber & Faber.

Schloss, J.G. (2004) *Making Beats: The Art of Sample-Based Hip-Hop*, Middletown, CT: Wesleyan University Press.

Schwichtenberg, C. (ed.) (1993) *The Madonna Connection: Representational Politics, Subcultural Identities, and Cultural Theory*, St Leonards, NSW: Allen & Unwin.

Scott, D. (ed.) (2009) *The Ashgate Research Companion to Popular Musicology*, Farnham, Burlington, VT: Ashgate.

Sernoe, J. (1998) '"Here You Come Again": Country Music's Perfomance on the Pop Singles Charts', *Popular Music and Society*, 22, 1 (Spring); 17–40.

Shank, B. (1994) *Dissonant Identities The Rock'n'Roll Scene in Austin*, Hanover, TX: Wesleyan University Press.

Shapiro, P. (2004) *The Rough Guide to Hip-Hop*, 2nd edn, London: Rough Guides.

Shaw, G. (1992) 'Brill Building Pop', in A. DeCurtis and J. Henke, J. (eds), *The Rolling Stone Illustrated History of Rock and Roll*, 3rd edn, New York: Random House.

Shaw, S. and Farren, M. (2007) *Bomp! Saving the World One Rrecord at a Time*, Los Angeles: AMMO.

Shepherd, J. (2012) 'Music and Social Categories', in M. Clayton, T. Herbert and R. Middleton (eds), *The Cultural Study of Music. A Critical Introduction*, 2nd edn, New York, London: Routledge.

Shepherd, J., Horn, D., Laing, D., Oliver, P. and Wicke, P. (eds) (2003) *Continuum Encyclopedia of Popular Music, Volume One: Media, Industry and Society; Volume Two: Performance and Production*, London, New York: Continuum.

Shore, M. (1985) *The Rolling Stone Book of Rock Video*, London: Sidgwick & Jackson.

Shuker, R. (2008) 'New Zealand Popular Music, Government Policy and Cultural Identity', *Popular Music*, 27, 2: 271–87.

——(2010) *Wax Trash and Vinyl Treasure: Record Collecting as Social Practice*, Aldershot: Ashgate.

——(2011) 'Popular Music and Revisionist History Review Essay', *Perfect Beat*, 12, 1: 91–7.

——(2012) *Popular Music: The Key Concepts*, 3rd edn, London: Routledge.

Shuker, R. and Pickering, M. (1994) 'Kiwi Rock: Popular Music and Cultural Identity in New Zealand', *Popular Music*, 13, 3: 261–78.

Shute, G. (2005) *Making Music in New Zealand*, Auckland: Random House.

Sinclair, D. (1992) *Rock on CD: The Essential Guide*, London: Kyle Cathie.

Sinnreich, A. (2010) *MashedUp: Music, Technology and the Rise of Configurable Culture*, Amherst, Boston, MA: University of Massachusetts Press.

Smith, G. (1995) *Lost in Music*, London: Picador.

Smith, Lorraine (2003) 'Christina Aguilera – Can't Hold us Down', *The F Word: Contemporary UK Feminism*. Online at www.thefword.org.uk/review

Smith, L. (2006) 'Surprising True Story of Freddy's Success', *The Wellingtonian*, 9 March.

Smith, P. (2010) *Just Kids*, London; Bloomsbury.

Solis G. (ed.) (2010) *Play it Again: Cover Songs in Popular Music*, Aldershot: Ashgate.

Spooner, C. (2006) *Contemporary Gothic*, London: Reaktion Books.

Stahl, G. (2011) 'DIY or DIT! Tales of Making Music in a Creative Capital', in G. Kean and T. Mitchell (eds), *Home, Land and Sea: Situating Music in Aotearoa New Zealand*, Auckland: Pearson.

Stahl, M. (2004) 'A Moment Like This: *American Idol* and Narratives of Meritocracy', in C. Washburne and M. Derno (eds), *Bad Music: the Music we Love to Hate*. New York: Routledge.

Starkey, G. (2010) 'Radio' in A. Albertazzi, D. and P. Cobley, *The Media: An Introduction*, 3rd edn, Harlow: Pearson.

Steffen, D. (2005) *From Edison to Marconi: The First Thirty Years of Recorded Music*, Jefferson, NC: McFarland.

Stephens, M. (1998) 'Babylon's "Natural Mystic": The North American Music Industry, the Legend of Bob Marley, and the Incorporation of Transnationalism', *Cultural Studies*, 12, 2, (April): 139–67.

Sterne, J. (2006) 'The MP3 as Cultural Artifact', *New Media & Society*, 8, 5: 825–42.

Stock, M. (2004) *The Hit Factory. The Stock Aitken Waterman Story*, London: New Holland Publishers.

Stokes, M. (ed.) (1994) *Ethnicity, Identity and Music: The Musical Construction of Place*, Oxford: Berg

Strachan, R. (2007). 'Micro-independent Record Labels in the UK: Discourse, DIY Cultural Production and the Music Industry'. *European Journal of Cultural Studies*, 10, 2: 245–65.

Strasser, R. (2010) *Music Business: The Key Concepts*, London, New York: Routledge.

Stratton, J. (2008) 'The *Idol* Audience: Judging, Interactivity and Entertainment', in G. Bloustein, M. Peters and S. Luckman (eds), *Sonic Energies: Music, Technology, Community, Identity*, Farnham: Ashgate.

Strausbaugh, J. (2001) *Rock Til You Drop:The Decline from Rebellion to Nostalgia*, New York: Verso.

Straw, W. (1992) 'Systems of Articulation, Logics of Change: Communities and Scenes in Popular Music', in C. Nelson, L. Grossberg and P. Treichler (eds), *Cultural Studies*, London, New York: Routledge.

——(1996) 'Sound Recording', in M. Dorland (ed.), *The Cultural Industries in Canada: Problems, Policies and Prospects*, Toronto: Lorimer.

——(1997a) 'Organized Disorder: The Changing Space of the Record Shop', in S. Redhead (ed.), *The Club Cultures Reader*, Oxford: Blackwell.

——(1997b) 'Sizing Up Record Collections. Gender and Connoisseurship in Rock Music Culture', in S. Whiteley (ed.), *Sexing the Groove. Popular Music and Gender*, London: Routledge.

——(1999) 'Authorship', in B. Horner and T. Swiss (eds), *Key Terms in Popular Music and Culture*, Malden, MA; Oxford: Blackwell.

——(2001) 'Dance Music', in S. Frith and J. Street (eds), *Cambridge Companion to Pop And Rock*, Cambridge: Cambridge University Press.

Street, J. (1986) *Rebel Rock: The Politics of Popular Music*, Oxford: Blackwell.

——(2012) *Music and Politics*, Cambridge; Malden, MA: Polity Press.

Strong, M. (2006) *The Essential Rock Discography*, Edinburgh: Canongate.

Suhr, C. (2012) *Social Media and Music: The Digital Field of Cultural Production*, Volume 77, ed. S. Jones, New York: Peter Lang.

Swiss, T. (2005) 'That's Me in the Spotlight: Rock Autobiographies', *Popular Music* 24, 2: 287–94.

Swiss, T., Sloop, J. and Herman, A. (eds) (1998) *Mapping the Beat: Popular Music and Contemporary Theory*, Malden, MA; Oxford: Blackwell.

Tagg, P. (1989) 'Black Music', 'African-American Music', and 'European Music', *Popular Music*, 8, 3: 285–98.

Tagg, P. and Clarida, B. (2003) *Ten Little Title Tunes: Towards a Musicology of the Mass Media*, New York, Montreal: Mass Media Musicologists' Press.

Takasugi, F. (2003) 'The Development of Underground Musicians in a Honolulu Scene, 1995–1997', *Popular Music* 26, 1: 73–94.

Task Force Report (1996) *A Time for Action: Report of the Task Force on the Future of the Canadian Music Industry*, Ottawa: Department of Heritage.

Taylor, P. (1985) *Popular Music Since 1955: A Critical Guide to the Literature*, London: G.K. Hall.

Théberge, P. (1999) 'Technology', in B. Horner and T. Swiss (eds) *Key Terms in Popular Music and Culture*, Malden MA; Oxford: Blackwell.

——(1993) 'Technology, Economy and Copyright Reform in Canada', in S. Frith (ed.) (1993), *Music and Copyright*, Edinburgh: Edinburgh University Press.

——(1997) *Any Sound You Can Imagine: Making Music/Consuming Technology*, Hanover, NH: Wesleyan University Press.

Thompson, D. (2005) *Wall of Pain: The Biography of Phil Spector*, Bodmin: Sanctuary Publishing.

——(2008) *I Hate New Music: The Classic Rock Manifesto*, New York: Backbeat Books.

Thompson, G. (2008) *Please Please Me: Sixties British Pop, Inside Out*, Oxford: Oxford University Press.

Thornton, S. (1995) *Club Cultures: Music, Media and Subcultural Capital*, London: Polity Press.

Tosches, N. (1984) *Unsung Heroes of Rock 'n' Roll*, New York: Scribners.

Toynbee, J. (2000) *Making Popular Music: Musicians, Creativity and Institutions*, London: Arnold.

Tunstall, J. (1977) *The Media are American*, London: Constable.

Vernallis, C. (2005) *Experiencing Music Video: Aesthetics and Cultural Context*, Columbia, OH: Columbia University Press.

Vogel, H.L. (1994) *Entertainment Industry Economics: A Guide to Financial Analysis*, 3rd edn, New York: Cambridge University Press.

Von Appen, R. and Doehring, A. (2006) 'Nevermind The Beatles, Here's Exile 61 and Nico: The Top 100 Records of all Time – A Canon of Pop and Rock Albums from a Sociological and an Aesthetic Perspective', *Popular Music*, 25, 1 (January): 21–40.

Waksman, S. (1996) *Instrument of Desire: The Electric Guitar and the Shaping of Musical Experience*, Cambridge, MA: Harvard University Press.

——(2009) *This Ain't the Summer of Love*, Berkeley, Los Angeles: University of California.

——(2010) 'Imagining an Interdisciplinary Canon', *Journal of Popular Music Studies*, 22, 1: 68–73.

Wald, E. (2009). *How The Beatles Destroyed Rock 'n' Roll: An Alternative History of American Popular Music*, Oxford: Oxford University Press.

Wall, T. (2006) 'Out on the Floor: The Politics of Dancing on the Northern Soul Scene', *Popular Music*, 25, 3 (October): 431–46.

Wallis, R. and Malm, K. (eds) (1992) *Media Policy and Music Activity*, London: Routledge.

Walser, R. (1993) *Running With the Devil: Power, Gender and Madness in Heavy Metal Music*, Middletown, CT: Wesleyan University Press.

Warner, T. (2003) *Pop Music – Technology and Creativity: Trevor Horn and the Digital Revolution*, Aldershot: Ashgate.

Weinstein, D. (1991) *Heavy Metal: A Cultural Sociology*, New York: Lexington.
——(2000) *Heavy Metal. The Music and Its Culture*, rev. edn, Boulder, CO: Da Capo Press.
Weisman, D. (2005) *Blues: The Basics*, New York, London: Routledge.
Wertham, F. (1955) *Seduction of the Innocent*, London: Museum Press.
White, T. (1989) *Catch A Fire: The Life of Bob Marley*, New York: Rinehart & Winston.
Whiteley, S. (ed.) (1997) *Sexing the Groove: Popular Music and Gender*, London, New York: Routledge.
——(2000) *Women and Popular Music: Sexuality, Identity and Subjectivity*, London: Routledge.
——(2005) *Too Much Too Young: Popular Music, Age and Gender*, London, New York: Routledge.
Whiteley, S., Bennett, A. and Hawkins, S. (eds) (2004) *Music, Space and Place: Popular Music and Cultural Identify*, Aldershot, Burlington: Ashgate.
Widgery, D. (1986) *Beating Time: Riot 'n' Race 'n' Rock 'n' Roll*, London: Chatto & Windus.
Williams, R. (1983) *Keywords*, London: Fontana.
Williamson, J., Cloonan, M. and Frith, S. (2011) 'Having an Impact? Academics, the Music Industries and the Problem of Knowledge', *International Journal of Cultural Policy*, 15, 5: 459–74.
Winfield, B. and Davidson, S. (eds) (1999) *Bleep! Censoring Rock and Rap Music*, Westport, CT: Greenwood Press.
The Wire (2005), 'The singer not the song', 261: 44–51.
Wiseman-Trowse, N. (2008) *Performing Class in British Popular Music*, Basingstoke, New York: Palgrave Macmillan.
Wynette, T. with J. Drew (1980) *Stand By Your Man: An Autobiography*, London: Hutchinson.
Zak III, A.J. (2001) *The Poetics of Rock: Cutting Tracks, Making Records*, Berkeley: University of California Press.
Zollo, P. (1997) *Songwriters on Songwriting*, New York: Da Capo Press.
Zuberi, N. (2007) 'Sound Like Us: Popular Music and Cultural Nationalism in Aotearoa/New Zealand', *Perfect Beat*, 8, 3: 3–18.
Zwaan, K, and de Bruin, J. (2012) *Adapting Idol: Authenticity, Identity and Performance in a Global Television Format*, Aldershot: Ashgate.

Index